THE

FIRST AFGHAN WAR

AND ITS CAUSES

THE

FIRST AFGHAN WAR

AND ITS CAUSES

BY THE LETE MAJOR-GENERAL

HENRY MARION DURAND, K.C.S.I., C.B.

GYAN

Published by

Gyan Publishing House
5, Ansari Road
Daryaganj, New Delhi-110002
Phone: 011-47034999, 9811692060
E-mail: books@gyanbooks.com

Distribution Network
gyanbooks.com
India, USA, Canada, UK, Australia

ISBN: 978-93-6208-964-9 (PB)
First Published, 1879

2nd Impression 2024

Printed at: Gyan Press, Delhi.

THE FIRST AFGHAN WAR AND ITS CAUSES

Author: HENRY MARION DURAND

THE
FIRST AFGHAN WAR

THE CABUL GATE OF GHUZNEE

FROM A SKETCH MADE ON THE SPOT BY SIR HENRY DURAND

THE

FIRST AFGHAN WAR

AND ITS CAUSES

BY THE LATE MAJOR-GENERAL

SIR HENRY MARION DURAND, K.C.S.I., C.B.

OF THE ROYAL ENGINEERS

WITH FRONTISPIECE

LONDON

LONGMANS, GREEN, AND CO.

1879

INTRODUCTION.

More than thirty years ago my father, then Captain Durand, of the Bengal Engineers, being at home on leave, began to write this history of the Cabul War. He had some special qualifications for the task, for he had served through Keane's campaign, had personally known most of the men whose actions he was to chronicle, and afterwards, as private secretary to Lord Ellenborough, had enjoyed unusual opportunities of obtaining correct and full information upon many important matters connected with the subject of his work.

It was never completed; for in 1848, convinced that an outbreak in the Punjab was imminent, he threw up his furlough and returned to India—just in time to take a part in the battles of the second Sikh War. For two or three years after the close of the campaign his duties afforded him a certain amount of leisure; but the life of an Indian official is at best ill suited to the prosecution of a literary task requiring such close and constant application as the one he had undertaken, and I believe he never resumed it. A portion of the manuscript was converted into a long review article, which is repeatedly quoted by Sir John Kaye, and has had a marked effect upon the historian's treatment of some parts of his subject. The rest was left untouched, and the narrative breaks off abruptly with the arrival of Lord Ellenborough in India. It is, therefore, a fragment, and in parts a rough one.

Nevertheless, fragmentary though it be, I have ventured to bring it to light. Now that war has again been declared against the Ameer of Cabul, and that the defiles of the Khybur have once more reverberated the roar of British guns, I think the story of our victories and reverses in Afghanistan, told by one who bore a part in the former, and early recognised the errors of policy which led to the latter, cannot be altogether devoid of interest. I have not attempted to elaborate or complete the narrative. Such an attempt could only have had the effect of detracting from any value it may now possess; and the manuscript goes to press almost as I found it. In one or two places, however, I have permitted myself to deviate from the original text. With some hesitation—for truth is truth, and I would not willingly garble my father's work—but in deference to the opinion of others, and with the desire of sparing pain, I have suppressed the statement of certain circumstances which, though indubitable and not wholly devoid of historical interest, were not, perhaps, necessary to the completeness of the story. And I have slightly altered that portion of the manuscript which tells of the storm of Ghuznee. A writer is necessarily at a disadvantage in describing an exploit in which he was one of the chief actors, and I found it difficult to supplement the text satisfactorily by means of notes. The alterations are, however, slight, and there is not a sentence of my own in the account. The whole is taken from papers in my father's handwriting, and I have kept his words.

It is, probably, needless for me to point out that a work like this, written thirty years ago, and left in the rough, affords neither an exposition of my father's views with regard to our policy in Central Asia, nor a fair specimen of his literary powers. For the opinions of men and measures which the book puts forward I offer no apology. They differ considerably in some respects from the ideas now generally entertained, and they are often as strongly expressed as they were strongly held. But, however strongly held and expressed, they were not hastily formed; and, right or wrong, they are the result of careful and conscientious thought.

For those who knew the writer personally, or who are acquainted with the course of events in India during the last forty years, it would not, perhaps, be necessary to add anything more. But the career of an Indian official is as a rule little known in England, and rapidly forgotten by Englishmen, even in India;

and as this book may fall into the hands of some who are wholly ignorant of the writer's claims to a hearing, I add a brief account of his life. I cannot, of course, pretend that the account is an impartial one, but I have done my best to make it truthful and accurate.

Henry Marion Durand was born on November 6, 1812. The son of a soldier, he early manifested an inclination for a military career; and after a brief education at Leicester and Putney, where one of his schoolfellows was his future chief (Lord Canning), he entered the East India Company's College, at Addiscombe. Here his success was marked. He passed out of Addiscombe on June 7, 1828, 'with more prizes than he could find hands to carry from the table,'[1] and five days later received his commission as Second Lieutenant in the Corps of Bengal Engineers. It was, I believe, a rule of the Company that no cadet should be admitted to the service before the age of sixteen, but the rule was set aside in his favour.

In October of the following year, after having passed with special credit through the course prescribed for Engineer officers, he set sail for India. The voyage was not altogether uneventful; for the 'Lady Holland,' after running some risk from pirates, was wrecked upon Dassan Island, and my father, exerting himself to save the lives and property of others, lost everything he possessed. It was not until the end of May 1829 that he reached Calcutta.

In the vessel which brought him from the Cape he had met Alexander Duff, the first missionary from the Kirk of Scotland, and afterwards one of his staunchest friends. The two had much in common. It was said of my father after his death, by one who wrote in no friendly spirit, that he 'looked at everything through the pure crystal of Christianity;' and the remark was as true of him when he landed in India as it was thirty years later. Even in those days his conduct was controlled by a firm belief in the truth of the Bible, and to the end of his life that belief never wavered. No record of his life, however brief, would be other than thoroughly false if it failed to bring pro-

[1] Seven out of eight, and the sword for good conduct.

minently forward the fact that a steadfast faith in the teaching of Christ, free from the slightest admixture of cant or bigotry, was the very foundation of his character. Humbly and fearlessly serving one Master, and relying upon a strength not his own, he strove to do his duty unflinchingly from beginning to end; and, passing through many trials, he closed an upright, uncompromising life by a death which was strangely calm and peaceful.

When he arrived in India the country was in a condition of profound tranquillity. The stormy Administration of Lord Amherst had come to an end; and Lord William Bentinck, secure from foreign aggression, and harbouring no dreams of conquest, had entered upon a policy of unsparing retrenchment. The army was being rapidly reduced, and everything seemed to presage a long peace. But then, as ever, the most promising field for a man of soldierly aspirations was the line of our North-Western Frontier; for though our statesmen troubled themselves but little about the countries west of the Indus, the old 'Lion of Lahore' lay within four marches of the Sutlej, with a large and eager army; and other elements of danger were not wanting.

Immediately after his arrival, therefore, my father applied for employment in the North-West Provinces. He obtained it without difficulty; and after a year spent in acquainting himself with the work of the Building Department, and in surveying sites for European troops in the Himalayas, he was appointed, by special request, an assistant to Major Colvin, the Superintendent of Canals. His fellow-assistants were all picked men. It would not be easy to find three more distinguished names in the ranks of Indian Engineers than Proby Cautley, William Baker, and Robert Napier.

For the next five years, during which time large works were executed and the system of canal irrigation was much developed, my father was employed upon the canals west of the Jumna. The nature of his duties afforded him, during the hot weather, ample opportunities for study; and as he was from the first an untiring reader—'a strange mixture of the soldier and the student,' to use the words of one of his earliest friends—those opportunities were not wasted. At the same time his work threw him into constant contact with the people, and under peculiarly favourable circumstances. Regarding a Canal officer as their benefactor, one who had nothing to do with trying or taxing them, they behaved towards him with an openness which natives of India rarely show to a European; and he always felt that he had gained more insight into the customs and character of the agricultural classes during this time than at any subsequent period of his career. Knowledge brought with it a kindly feeling which it never lost.

In 1834, hearing that a detachment of officers was about to be sent to Persia, to organise and drill the native army, he applied for the service; and his chief supported the application, adding that if Government wanted another officer of the same stamp they would find him in Henry Lawrence, of the Artillery. Fortunately, perhaps, though to my father's great vexation at the time, the application was unsuccessful.

Meanwhile the little party of Engineers had directed their attention to another field. The heads of the irrigation canals were drawn from the Jumna, where that river debouches from the outer ranges of the Himalaya, and it became a favourite amusement with the Canal officers to make excursions into the hills. It was in the course of one of these excursions that a clue was obtained to the discovery of the Sewalik fossils, which startled the scientific world, and contributed so materially to the development of the study of palæontology. The value of the discovery is attested by Dr. Murchison, in his palæontological memoirs of Falconer. By it, he says, 'a sub-tropical mammalian fossil fauna was brought to light unexampled for richness and extent in any other region then known.' Following up their subject, the young officers sent to the Journal of the Asiatic Society of Bengal, then under the management of James Prinsep, a series of articles descriptive of the most interesting specimens brought to light; and when my father left the canals three years later, the names of Cautley, Baker, and himself were well known to English men of science.

I have dwelt upon this part of my father's early life because the taste for geology and its kindred studies which he first acquired among the Sewalik fossils always remained with him. His journals are full of geological jottings ; and wherever he was employed, from Burmah to Afghanistan, he seems to have found time for the prosecution of his favourite subject.

In 1838, after some time spent in examining and reporting upon the Nujjufghur Marsh and a large tract of country to the south of Delhi, which it was proposed to drain, his connection with the canals finally closed. The Surveyor-General of India, Colonel Everest, had previously applied for his services ; and he was now nominated for the duty of drawing up reports on the condition and progress of the Trigonometrical Survey. This duty, however, he never took up. Lord Auckland and his distinguished secretary, Thomason, had been struck with the detailed knowledge of the people and their tenures which my father had acquired during his work on the canals ; and at the close of the hot weather he was offered, and accepted, the appointment of Secretary to the Revenue Board of the North-West Provinces. This appointment, a singular one for a young military officer, he was about to enter upon, when the assembly of a force for war in Afghanistan turned his thoughts in a different direction. Though fully sensible of the distinction conferred upon him, he was not of a temper to resign, for any inducement that could be offered, the chance of active service ; and at once throwing up his secretaryship, he applied for employment with the army in the field. The application was granted, and he was attached to the Army of the Indus, as one of two Engineer officers charged, in addition to their other professional duties, with the work of the Topographical Department, surveys of fortresses, and the like. Upon their labours were based in a great measure all subsequent maps of Afghanistan, for the old maps were very incorrect.

Having assisted in the preparation of the Engineer Park at Delhi, and the bridging of the Indus, my father accompanied Sir Willoughby Cotton's division to Quetta, and was with Sir John Keane's force in the advance to Candahar. From Candahar, after bearing part in Sale's expedition to Girishk, he marched with the main body upon Cabul. When Keane arrived before Ghuznee, the provisions of the force so nearly exhausted that capture of the fortress by a *coup de main* could alone save the expedition from calamitous failure, he was offered by the Chief Engineer, Thomson, the command of the party which was to blow in the Cabul Gate. The offer was a tempting one, for the command of the party was a certain opening to distinction; and to be specially selected for the duty by Thomson, as fine a soldier as ever stepped, was in itself no small honour. Nevertheless it was declined. Knowing that Captain Peat, of the Bombay Engineers, an excellent officer, and his senior, expected the command, my father requested that it might be offered to him, asking only to be entrusted with the duty of heading the explosion party, placing the powder, and firing the train.[1] How he performed that duty I need not tell here. Hardly able to walk, from the effects of severe illness, he had, while reconnoitring in the course of the day preceding the attack, narrowly escaped death at the hands of the Afghan skirmishers, and it was with extreme difficulty that he bore up until the work was done. Immediately after the storm he was forced to take to his bed.

After the arrival of the British force at Cabul my father was appointed Engineer to the Shah; and in this capacity he did his best to oppose the fatal error of abandoning the Bala Hissar. Fortunately for himself, perhaps, he found that this lucrative appointment debarred him from active service, and he soon resigned it. His successor, Sturt, fell in the fatal retreat of Elphinstone's division. Returning to India with Sir John Keane, he had the opportunity of becoming to some extent acquainted with the Punjab and the condition of the Sikh army shortly after the death of Runjeet Sing—an acquaintance which was of use to him a few years later.

When the maps, plans, and reports connected with the campaign in Afghanistan had been completed, my father went to England on furlough. His religious convictions growing stronger year by year, had led him at this time to contemplate resigning his career in India in favour of the Church. But after

[1] Sir Colin Campbell's comment upon this unselfish act when, years afterwards, he ascertained the truth of the story, was a very characteristic one: 'By God, Durand, I wouldn't have done that for my own father!'

much self-examination and consulting of friends he found he was 'unfit for so serious a charge as entering the ministry,' and the idea was eventually abandoned. Shortly afterwards he was introduced to Lord Ellenborough, then about to assume the government of India, and was asked to draw up a military memoir on the Punjab. The paper was shown by Lord Ellenborough to the Duke of Wellington, and elicited from the latter a warm expression of approval. At the same time my father received, and after some hesitation accepted, the offer of an appointment on Lord Ellenborough's Staff as aide-de-camp. Before the new Governor-General reached Calcutta the appointment was exchanged for that of private secretary.

In this position my father remained throughout Lord Ellenborough's Indian administration, refusing in succession several high political posts. He was greatly tempted by the offer of the Agency on the North-West Frontier, at that time perhaps the most responsible appointment in the Governor-General's gift; but he feared that by accepting it he might compromise the reputation of a chief for whose character and abilities he had early cause to entertain a high respect, and he decided to decline the honour. Lord Ellenborough appreciated the motives which influenced him in this decision, and a warm personal friendship sprang up between the Governor-General and his secretary, which was never interrupted. The careers of both were very nearly cut short at the same time on the field of Maharajpore, where Lord Ellenborough's coolness and courage under the close fire of the Mahratta guns won him the admiration of many brave men.[1]

Upon Lord Ellenborough's recall by the Court of Directors my father was appointed by Lord Hardinge Commissioner on the Tenasserim coast. Until this time his success had been

[1] Lord Ellenborough has been blamed for thrusting himself into a false position at Maharajpore. As a fact he followed the directions of the commander-in-chief, and it was only by an unforeseen change of disposition on the part of the enemy that he found himself in front of their batteries. Once in the thick of the action, his spirit was roused—and, as my father afterwards said, he 'thoroughly enjoyed it.' But he retired to a less dangerous position when it was pointed out to him that he was unduly exposing himself.

rapid and uninterrupted. For the next thirteen years he was destined to experience incessant trouble and disappointment; to meet with censure and supersession for honestly doing his duty; to face a storm of calumny and vituperation; and to find himself, after seven-and-twenty years of varied military and political service, a nearly ruined man.

Without writing at considerable length it would be impossible to enter into the story of his administration in Tenasserim, and of his recall by Sir Herbert Maddock. So long as Lord Hardinge remained in Calcutta all went well, and he earned the special commendation of the Indian Government. But directly Lord Hardinge had departed for the North-West Provinces, leaving Maddock in Calcutta, as Deputy-Governor of Bengal and President in Council, the aspect of affairs changed. From circumstances which this is not the proper place to detail, Maddock's relations with my father had been far from cordial. Freed from Lord Hardinge's control, he lost no time in openly manifesting his ill-will; and the Governor-General being fully occupied with the course of events in the North, he ventured, after a series of proceedings of which it is difficult for me to speak with patience, to remove my father from his appointment. That the removal was wholly unmerited was afterwards shown to the satisfaction of the highest authorities; but the story is a long one, and I cannot follow it here.

On hearing of his recall my father appealed, as was natural, to the Governor-General. This Maddock refused to permit, on the ground that the appeal from his decision as Deputy-Governor of Bengal lay to the President in Council; that is, to himself and one other member, the commander-in-chief and the military member being absent. It is needless to comment on the propriety of this dictum, whatever doubt there may be as to its legality. At the same time that he thus officially refused my father the right of appeal to the Governor-General, Maddock, as afterwards appeared, was privately canvassing Lord Hardinge's concurrence. He failed to obtain it; for the Governor-General, though he did not interfere with the President's action, declined, to use his own words, being made registering clerk to Maddock's orders, and immediately offered my father the post of Chief Engineer in the Punjab. While war was going on my father had placed his services at the disposal of Government for employment in the field, and had been censured for so doing by the Deputy-Governor. But now that war was over the offer was refused, and he returned to England to seek justice from the Court of Directors.

During this time he was fiercely assailed by the Bengal press, misled as to the facts of the case, and roused to indignation by his stern treatment of an unprincipled member of the fraternity in Moulmein. 'The Jeffreys of India,' as he was called, found, however, an able defender in Alexander Duff; and the warm expressions of sympathy which he received at parting, from every class of the community he had been declared unfit to rule, did much to console him for the injustice and calumny he had gone through. Foremost among those who deplored his loss were the little band of American missionaries, headed by Judson, whose work in Burmah my father had aided by every means in his power.

His appeal to the Directors was too late. The legality of the decisions which had led to his removal was strongly affirmed by counsel in England; but the Court had meanwhile sanctioned the Deputy-Governor's order. The President of the Board of Control, however, assured him that on his return to India he should be employed exactly as he had been before, and that he should be no sufferer in any respect from what had passed. With this assurance he was forced to be content.

It was at this time that he began to write his account of the Cabul War. I have already described how the work was interrupted by his return to duty in 1848. Although the peace in the Punjab was, by those who should have known best, confidently represented as solid and lasting, he was persuaded that an outbreak was certain; and his predictions were verified with curious rapidity, for on arriving at the Sandheads he found awaiting him orders to join the army at once—the outbreak had already occurred. Hastening up to the frontier, he arrived in time to witness the sanguinary battle of Chillianwalla. The morning after that battle he did all that his position allowed him to bring about an immediate advance; and it was, I believe, afterwards admitted by the Sikhs themselves that if an advance had been made the complete defeat of the Khalsa army, shaken and demoralised by the conflict of the previous day, would have been almost inevitable. But we had lost fearfully, and it was not then understood how severely the Sikhs had been tried by the fight. The opportunity was, therefore, allowed to go by, and long weeks of weary inaction followed before the final victory of Gujerat. Through that decisive battle my father was with Colin Campbell's division.

After the close of the campaign, the Tenasserim commissionership and several suitable appointments in the newly annexed province of the Punjab being vacant, my father confidently expected that the assurance given to him by the President of the Board of Control would be fulfilled. He was disappointed; for the Governor-General, Lord Dalhousie, knowing nothing of him, and surrounded by men avowedly hostile to his interests, set his claims aside; and after a short stay at Gwalior, as an assistant for the affairs of Sindia, he was relegated to the subordinate political agency of Bhopal. There, with a brief interval of absence, he remained until the close of 1853.

Sir Charles Napier, no mean judge of a soldier, to some degree compensated him for the slur by an offer which surprised and gratified him more than he could say—the command of the sappers and miners. But, war being over, my father, smarting under a sense of wrong, and determined to obtain from the Governor-General a clear recognition of the injustice inflicted upon him, refused the offer. The refusal was unfortunate, for a man of Lord Dalhousie's imperious nature was little likely to grant promotion which was demanded as a right, not asked as a favour; and my father lost a promising opening for distinction in his own branch of the service.

This period of his life was a trying one. Time after time he saw political posts of importance, any one of which he could have had for the asking ten years before, given away to his juniors, while he remained unnoticed in his obscure charge. And year after year he strove without success to obtain the military rank which was unquestionably his due. By an oversight on the part of Lord Ellenborough his name had been omitted from the list of recommendations for brevet rank after the fight at Maharajpore; and though Lord Ellenborough deeply regretted the mistake, and afterwards did his best to repair it, the ground lost was never recovered. The satisfaction of his claim was deferred from year to year; and finally, after it had been supported by Lord Ellenborough, by Sir Charles Napier, by Lord Gough, and even by Lord Dalhousie, the Court of Directors declined to recommend it, on the ground that the grant of the promotion would bring him over the heads of too many officers who had now risen above him—thus, as one of his supporters observed, making the very magnitude of the original injustice the excuse for not repairing it. The decision was one which almost irremediably ruined his prospect of advancement in his profession—a profession which was the pride and passion of his life.

But if this period of his career was one of disappointment and dejection, it was not altogether wasted. The confidence and goodwill with which he inspired the ruler of the Bhopal State have borne good fruit. Throughout the Mutiny there was no stauncher friend to the British cause than that brave and cool-headed woman; and the traditions she left behind her have not been forgotten. Moreover, the leisure which he enjoyed enabled my father to use his pen to some purpose. The 'Calcutta Review' was then in its prime; and, though he always rated his power of writing very low, some of the essays which he contributed to the 'Review' at this time attracted considerable notice both in India and at home. Besides articles on the wars in Cabul, Burmah, and the Punjab, he wrote a series of papers showing up the abuses of the system upon which India was then governed, and advocating reforms which the Mutiny has since forced us to adopt. These papers excited no small annoyance in Leadenhall Street, for the existence of the Court of Directors was at this time threatened, and use was made of my father's essays by reformers at home to deal some heavy blows.

In December 1853, despairing of redress at the hands of Lord Dalhousie, and finding his health seriously impaired, my father threw up his charge at Sehore and returned to Europe, where he remained for nearly two years, endeavouring to find some employment which might spare him the necessity of continuing his career in a country now become hateful to him. He failed to do so; and towards the close of 1855 he sailed again for India. His first appointment was not a promising one. No political or military position being offered him, he was forced to fall back upon a subordinate charge in the Department of Public Works; and for more than a year he was employed as Superintending Engineer of the Presidency Circle. He felt this keenly; but the experience was of use to him in after life, and during the latter part of this time he was enabled to do some good outside the limits of his nominal duties. Lord Canning had not been slow to recognise the fact that in the superseded and neglected Engineer officer he had found a man whose views on questions of policy and war were worth considering; and before long my father's opinion came to be frequently asked, and not infrequently taken, by the Governor-General. Twice in particular, during 1856, he was, I believe, mainly instrumental in dissuading Lord Canning from projected military operations which must have had a disastrous effect upon our position in India. I refer to the proposals to occupy Quetta, and to attack Persia overland through Afghanistan. In combating these proposals he dwelt strongly upon the danger of denuding India of British troops; and it is unnecessary to point out how terribly we should have regretted the mistake if, at the outbreak of the Mutiny, a considerable part of our then scanty European garrison had been hundreds of miles from our own provinces. As he had expected, Persia was rapidly and easily coerced by our operations in the Gulf, and our troops were set free in time for the crisis of 1857.

In the beginning of that year Lord Canning offered my father the charge of the Central India Agency, about to be temporarily vacated by Sir Robert Hamilton, and the offer was accepted. He took charge of his new appointment in April, and retained it until the middle of December, throughout the most critical period of the Mutiny.

The tract of country comprised in the Central India Agency was a point of special importance during this time. Through it ran the direct road from Bombay to Agra, by which troops from Bombay could be brought into operation against the North of India, and by which also telegraphic communication between Calcutta and the Madras and Bombay Presidencies could alone be effected, for there was then no direct telegraphic line from Madras to Calcutta. The maintenance of this line of communication was, therefore, invaluable. Nor was it less important to maintain intact the line of the Nerbudda river, which, roughly speaking, formed the southern frontier of the Agency, for the Nerbudda was the one barrier between the mutinous Bengal troops and the doubtful armies of Madras and Bombay. To hold Central India, and if this failed at least the Nerbudda line, was to localise the revolt, by preventing its spread over the Southern Presidencies. For the attainment of these objects my father had most insufficient means. His European force consisted of a single battery of foot artillery, which contained a source of weakness in the shape of native drivers, and was moreover forced to remain stationary to check the native troops at Mhow. The one chance lay in the fact that the bulk of the armed forces in the Central India Agency were troops belonging to the several State contingents; and he hoped that by carefully isolating these troops and playing them off against the regulars, it might be possible to maintain his position.

For six weeks after the outbreak at Delhi he succeeded in doing so. But, contrary to his wishes and orders, the contingent troops to the north were allowed to come into contact with the mutinous sepoys. Their fidelity gave way, and gradually the circle of insurrection closed southward upon Indore. On July 1 the crisis came. News had been received in the bazaar that the late reports of the capture of Delhi by the British were untrue; and it now leaked out that the advance of a small column of Bombay troops, ordered up to secure Central India, had been arrested. This turned the scale. Holkar's troops rose and attacked the Residency; the force collected for its defence, with the exception of fourteen artillerymen and five Sikh troopers, refused to fight; four hundred of them joined the insurgents; and after a two hours' cannonade, seeing that they were being surrounded by overwhelming numbers, and that all hope of successful resistance was at an end, the little garrison determined to withdraw. The retreat was effected in good order. Slowly and deliberately, at the rate the gun-bullocks would walk, the force moved off under the fire of the enemy's guns—the ladies and children being mounted on the gun-waggons, and the loyal but panic-stricken troops covering the rear. The mutineers soon gave up the pursuit and turned to the more congenial task of plundering the treasury.

The line of retreat chosen was that on Mhow, where the European battery was stationed, and upon which the Bombay column had been ordered to advance; but the contingent troops refused to follow, and it became necessary to strike off towards Bhopal territory, which, after a harassing march, was safely reached. Here the party was hospitably received; and after a day's stay in Sehore my father struck southward across the Nerbudda, to bring up the Bombay column. Having arrested the retirement of the Madras troops holding the Nerbudda, which suicidal measure had been ordered during the first burst of alarm caused by the news of the Indore outbreak, he joined and pressed up Woodburn's force, and by August 1 the line of the Nerbudda was once more secure.

During the rains the little column remained in enforced idleness at Mhow, but directly the state of the country permitted it moved into the field. The whole force at my father's disposal consisted of 600 Europeans and 1,200 natives. At Indore, fourteen miles north of Mhow, were Holkar's troops—1,400 horse, five battalions of infantry, and thirty guns. Beyond these, at Gwalior, Sindia's large contingent had broken out. To the north-west several thousand Mewatees and Velayutees, stubborn fighting men, had collected at Mundesore, and threatened to overrun all Western Malwa. To the north-east the prospect was even worse. It seemed only too probable that the Nana's forces, broken by Havelock about Cawnpore, might strike southward, and, gathering to themselves the Banda and Gwalior mutineers, pour down in one overwhelming mass upon Central India, where there was nothing to stay their advance but the small column at Mhow. Meanwhile, immediately to the eastward, a body of Velayutees menaced Nimar, while immediately to the westward a force of Afghans and other mercenaries rose and occupied the strong fort of Dhar.

The plan of operations adopted to meet this combination of difficulties was as follows: In order to avoid street-fighting, and the risk of driving the insurgents northwards into a junction with those at Mundesore, it was resolved to disregard the former for a time, and, leaving Indore on the right, march upon Mundesore by way of Dhar. After dispersing the Mundesore army the column could swing round on Indore, where it would probably find a disheartened enemy, or if necessary strike across the main road above Indore and hound back the Nana to the north-east. The plan proved completely successful. Dhar fell after a ten days' siege; the Mundesore army was shattered and dispersed after some very severe fighting. Neemuch was relieved; and when the little column arrived at Indore the mutinous regiments quietly laid down their arms. These operations cleared the way for Sir Hugh Rose's brilliant campaign in Central India.

The day after the Indore troops had been disarmed my father handed over charge of the Agency to Sir Robert Hamilton, who had now arrived on the scene. Lord Canning's opinion of my father's administration in Central India was afterwards expressed in the following words: 'Colonel Durand's conduct was marked by great foresight and the soundest judgment, as well in military as in civil matters. He had many points to guard, and the force at his disposal was almost hopelessly small; but by a judicious use of it, and by the closest personal supervision of its movements, Colonel Durand saved our interests in Central India until support could arrive.'

I have not space to enter here into a notice of the controversy which has arisen upon this portion of my father's career. Shortly after his return from Indore his action was attacked by Sir Robert Hamilton, and sedulously misrepresented by a portion of the Indian press; and years afterwards Sir Robert Hamilton's intimate personal friend, Sir John Kaye, followed up the attack in his 'History of the Sepoy War.' But Colonel Malleson, who has re-written this part of Kaye's work, has taken an entirely different view, and there is hardly room for further misrepresentation in the matter.

After handing over charge of the Central India Agency my father went down to Bombay, and thence to Calcutta, where he remained for a short time unemployed. At the end of April 1858 he was placed by Lord Canning upon special duty in connection with the reorganisation of the Indian army, and for some months he was hard at work collecting and noting upon the opinions of the principal military and civil officers regarding the measures to be pursued. The work was one of difficulty and importance, for the Mutiny had broken up the Bengal army, and had shown the utter insufficiency of our European garrison. It had become, in fact, necessary to remodel altogether the military system on which the maintenance of our Indian empire depends. The conclusions arrived at by my father as the result of his inquiries were accepted by Lord Canning; and in September 1858, a Royal Commission having been appointed to investigate the question, he was sent to England, to lay before the Secretary of State the views of the Governor-General. Those views were in the main his own; for Lord Canning's memorandum on the subject, which was laid before the Commission, was closely in accord with one submitted by him shortly before. In particular both felt strongly the necessity for the formation of a local European army, and on this point my father dwelt strenuously in his evidence before the Commission. He considered the measure the only one which could be relied upon to prevent the Home Government in time of pressure from hastily denuding India of British troops, and thus perilling the safety of the empire. The native regular army he wished to see greatly reduced, and an irregular force raised in lieu of a portion of the old regular regiments.

In the following January my father was appointed to a seat in the Council of India, and in this position he remained for rather more than two years. They were to him a period of continual striving against hopeless odds. Firmly persuaded that the measures adopted in regard to Indian reorganisation were unwise and unjust, he never ceased to exert himself to the utmost in support of Lord Canning's views, and in defence of the rights of the Indian armies. The influences on the other side were, however, too strong, and his exertions resulted chiefly in injury to his own prospects. The armies were amalgamated; the staff corps was brought into being; and most of the minor measures he opposed in council were carried against him.

In May 1861 he received a letter from Lord Canning offering him the Foreign Secretaryship in Calcutta, and pressing him to accept it. This appointment Lord Canning had wished to give him in 1859; but circumstances then rendered it impossible, and the Governor-General had been forced to make other arrangements. When offered, the post was at first refused—my father had many reasons for preferring to remain in England. The care of a large family, his own weariness of an Indian exile, and the feeling that his services had met with scant appreciation, all combined to dissuade him from returning. His first decision was, however, reversed. Pressed by others to go out for the good of the service, and feeling that he owed much to Lord Canning, he withdrew his refusal, and on July 4 started for India. It was, I think, characteristic of him that he was strongly influenced in this matter by the desire of making room in council for Outram, who was about to risk his life by taking up his appointment in Calcutta.

My father's selection was at first viewed with some disfavour by the Civil Service, for the Foreign Secretaryship was much coveted, and Lord Canning had been guilty of a somewhat startling innovation in giving it to an officer of Engineers. Yet I believe I am safe in saying that when it was vacated, after four years' tenure, there was no dispute as to its having been ably filled. Strongly opposed to the sweeping annexations of Lord Dalhousie, which had unsettled the minds of our Indian feudatories and sown fear and distrust broadcast; as strongly averse from the retrograde non-interference views of Cornwallis and Bentinck;[1] and alive to the responsibilities which had been devolved upon us as the supreme power in India, my father was well suited for

[1] He often said—and it was an opinion shared by many thinking natives—that the surest way of extinguishing native States was to abstain from all interference in their affairs. I see that a late writer in the 'Quarterly Review' quotes a remark to the same effect made by the well-known Minister, Sir Madava Rao: 'If left to themselves they will wipe themselves out.'

carrying out the wise and conciliatory policy of Lord Canning—a policy which he had some share in forming. With the ignorant pseudo-tenderness which made a certain class of political officers treat native States in India as foreign powers, and foster the obsolete pretensions of the chiefs at the expense of their subjects, he had, indeed, no sympathy. He always felt for the peasant as much as for the prince. But native rulers who ruled well had no truer friend, and they knew it. His views on this important branch of Indian policy were expressed by himself in an essay contributed to the 'Calcutta Review' in 1865, and I cannot, I think, do better than quote it here. After commenting upon the inapplicability of international law to the relations between the Supreme Government and the native States, and the folly of fostering notions of independence which could not fail to prove destructive to the States themselves, he wrote:—

'These remarks are made in no other than the most friendly feeling to native States, and from the conviction that the course most conservative of their permanent interests is that which prevents their rulers from entertaining chimerical notions of their footing with respect to the Supreme Government. A just apprehension of their real position will show them the wisdom of avoiding opposition to the onward start which India is at length making under British rule, and the expediency of identifying themselves and their States with the progress now effecting around them.

'By thus making common cause with the British Government in its beneficent exertions, their own abiding interests will be far better fostered than by the indulgence of empty pretensions. The English Government neither wishes to curtail their honours or their possessions. The only thing which can now be fatal to them is gross misrule, and its consequent isolation from the policy of the Government of India, namely, the rapid improvement of India and its races. The days of the annexation policy are passed, and nothing but gross and obstinate dereliction from the obligations and duties of their position can henceforward endanger them; but they must honourably discharge the trust devolved upon them. If the days of annexation are gone, so too are the days of gross cruelty and tyranny; for British supremacy can neither tolerate nor cloak such abuse of administrative powers under the ægis of its protection.'

The views here expressed were in perfect accord with those of Lord Canning; and Lord Canning's rule in India, closed all too soon, marked the starting-point of a new era in our Indian feudatory policy. It is true that others before Lord Canning had held much the same views; but it was not until his time that the British Government formally and finally accepted them, and sealed its acceptance by entering into engagements from which for the future there can be no withdrawal.[1]

In the summer of 1865 my father's connection with the Foreign Office ceased, by his appointment to a seat as military member of the Viceroy's council. Lord Canning had wished to appoint him to this post some years before in place of Outram. But his views on army questions were not such as to gain him favour at home, and the place fell to his old friend Napier, who who had also been named by Lord Canning. It is possible that this may have deprived him of what he afterwards was anxious to obtain, the command in Abyssinia. To the end of his life he never lost his enthusiasm for his profession, and his strongest desire was to command an army in the field. He never succeeded in doing so; but he never grudged others the success denied to himself. 'Napier,' he used to say, 'has *le feu sacré*, —there is no truer soldier alive.'

In the beginning of the year he had entertained some slight hopes of succeeding to the Lieutenant-Governorship of the Punjab, which post Lord Elgin had, I believe, intended for

[1] My father's clear comprehension and acceptance of Lord Canning's views was not, I think, his only qualification for the post Lord Canning had given him. His knowledge of Indian history was remarkably deep and accurate; and his attainments as a linguist were considerable. Natives have often remarked to me upon the fluency and correctness with which he spoke Hindustani; and he was at home both in Persian and Arabic.

Putting aside the languages most immediately useful to him in the Indian Foreign Office, he knew French, German, and Italian as few Englishmen know them, and he always retained his love for classical authors, particularly the Greek poets. I remember, when he was last at home, in 1868, being surprised, and humbled, by his familiarity with Greek poetry, and the perfect ease with which he read it. He also knew something of Hebrew, Burmese, and Spanish.

him. Sir John Lawrence, however, preferred a man after his own choice, and Sir Donald Macleod was chosen. Though to some extent disappointed he was not surprised. His views differed so widely from those of the Governor-General on many important points that he had hardly expected any other result, and he entered upon his new duties with none the less zeal. I cannot notice at any length the matters which filled the last five years of his life. His varied experience and fearless, uncompromising character rendered his voice a weighty one in council, and that upon matters apart from his special charge. The work of the Foreign and Military Departments was, of course, that with which he was most familiar; but he could hold his own on other questions, as some of his ablest colleagues have testified. As regards our policy in Central Asia, the measures of Lord Lawrence had his general support. What his opinion might have been upon the later phases of our relations with the trans-Indus powers I cannot, of course, say. Circumstances have so greatly changed since his death, that much of the reasoning upon which he founded his conclusions is no longer applicable. But while there was a good prospect of maintaining a strong and friendly power in Afghanistan he deprecated any advance beyond our frontier. In 1856 he had opposed the occupation of Quetta as a counterpoise to Persian aggression on Herat. Ten years later he opposed it. He thought it easy to conceive circumstances which might combine to necessitate the partial or entire occupation of Afghanistan. Invasion from the westward was one contingency; and a variety of others might, he thought, be quoted as possible inducements to an advance beyond the Indus frontier. But under the circumstances as they then stood he saw no necessity for such a step.

'I know,' he wrote, 'that we could again seize Afghanistan, if it were advisable or necessary, and that, with our Indus frontier complete in its communications, parallel and perpendicular, no power on earth could shake us out of that country. I know, too, that with the Afghans friendly and cordial we could, without the actual seizure of the country for ourselves, organise its defence in a most destructive manner against hostile invasion. But neither alternative is at present imposed upon us as of the smallest necessity.'

My father's period of duty as a member of the Viceroy's council closed early in 1870. Lord Mayo had from the beginning of his rule in India been impressed with the idea that the organisation of our political relations with the feudatory States was not all that it might be; and in 1870 his views took shape in a project for the amalgamation under one head of the two great Agencies of Central India and Rajputana. He proposed to appoint an Agent-in-Chief, who was to have charge of all the States comprised within the limits of the two Agencies, besides the administration of the outlying British district of Ajmere. The Agent would, he thought, require 'rarer qualities than those which would enable a man to be a successful Governor or Lieutenant-Governor,' and in my father he believed that he had found those qualities. 'Of all men in India,' he wrote, 'the most likely to exercise influence of a powerful and at the same time persuasive character is Sir Henry Durand. He has great experience of the best mode of dealing with these men; he knows most of them personally; he has a thorough knowledge of the history of modern Indian diplomacy, and a fine appreciation of that mixture of firmness and kindness which is so essential. . . . . . Sir Henry Durand is greatly esteemed and somewhat feared. He is a thoroughly honest and most upright man—very laborious, and possesses great and wide experience. I have had the misfortune to differ with him on several occasions, especially on barrack expenditure and other matters of smaller importance; but nevertheless I have always done so with regret, for his views are always well stated, and dictated by honest purpose. I think his great forte is political work, and he possesses the qualities which enable him to govern and direct men by personal influence, which are much more rare than administrative or judicial talent.'

Accordingly the proposed appointment was offered to my father. The offer is an instructive comment upon the opinions of Sir John Kaye and others who have stigmatised him as wanting in sympathy and a bad political officer. It was declined. He objected both to the principle of the scheme and to accepting the post himself. Nothing, he said, would induce him to stay in India except the Lieutenant-Governorship of the Punjab or a military command. The former was thereupon offered to him, Lord Mayo remarking, however, that he considered the Agency the higher appointment of the two—'the greatest prize in the service'—and that he regretted having to carry out his intentions without my father's assistance. He never did so. Whether the objections which my father brought against the scheme dissuaded him, or a fitting man could not, in his opinion, be found, the amalgamation of the Agencies was not carried into effect.

On June 1, 1870, my father was sworn in as Lieutenant-Governor of the Punjab.[1] He had been much pleased at the manner in which his appointment was received. Lord Mayo had announced his name at a farewell dinner to Sir Donald Macleod, adding that his hearers would find their new Governor 'firm and fearless, honest and brave;' and the speech had been cut short by a sudden storm of cheering, the purport of which was not to be mistaken. 'Well,' Lord Mayo afterwards remarked, in surprise at the applause his words had called forth, 'men often say what they don't mean, but they don't cheer like that if they don't mean it.' And he telegraphed to my father that the reception of his name had been 'enthusiastic.' That reception was only an index of the general feeling; and the few months my father had to live were cheered by the knowledge that his selection for the most important post in India had been approved without a dissentient voice. What, perhaps, pleased him most of all was the fact that he received from no one more warm and hearty congratulations than from his old opponents of the Civil Service.

His tenure of the Lieutenant-Governorship was short. The congratulatory letters of his friends in England had hardly ceased to pour in upon him before his place was vacant. After a visit to Cashmere he started, in the beginning of the cold weather, for a tour round the North-West Frontier; and by the

[1] Three years before he had been given the Star of India, and he had been recommended for the K.C.B. after the Mutiny by Lord Canning.

close of the year he had arrived at Tonk. On the evening of December 31, as it was growing dusk, the elephant on which he was seated was taken up into a low, covered gateway through which there was not room to pass. The mahout, seeing that he could not go on, tried to back the animal, but it took fright and started forward; the howdah struck against the beams overhead, and my father was thrown out. A man of great size, he fell heavily, and the injury to his spine was fatal. He lingered for a day, and at first it was thought that he might survive the shock. Towards evening of January 1 the doctors saw that this was impossible, and he was told that he could not live through the night. He met the announcement with perfect calmness. 'What a little thing!' he said. 'It will be a warning.' His first thought was for his work; and, calling for an officer of the Punjab Secretariat, he gave orders that a telegram should he despatched at once to inform the Government of India. Then he sent for those of his children who were with him in camp; and after explaining to them where they would find all important papers, and entrusting them with some messages for others, he spoke a few words of farewell. He told them he was dying; that his life had been a hard and bitter one; and that the only thing which had borne him through it was the love and fear of God. He begged them, as his last advice, to look to Christ in all things, to do justice, and to love the right. A few hours later he passed quietly away.

It would be useless for me to attempt to describe my father's character. All men seem small to me compared with him. But I may, perhaps, without impropriety quote what was written of him not long ago by one who learnt to know him during the last five years of his life :—

'None who knew him well can speak otherwise than with deep love of him. The combination of extreme strength and tenderness were to me his chief charm. His manner to those who were in any way objects of pity was the very beauty of gentleness; yet he was a man of iron—his will, like his frame, were cast in an heroic mould. Of course a man so open to sympathy might without much difficulty be imposed upon —I daresay he sometimes was—but he must have been a dangerous man to trifle with. To those who deserved his confidence he was without reserve. His long experience, his wide reading, his culture, his natural cheeriness and fun, made him, to younger men especially, a delightful companion. Finally, as in most really great men, there was nothing of the unapproachable "swell" about him. He would talk to a shoeblack as he talked to His Excellency in Council; only I think he would have been most courteous to the shoeblack. He had strongly the fascinating *camaraderie* of the soldier. If he had enemies, a man of his strong views and his contempt for what he thought selfish or unjust was sure to have them. He spoke sometimes, too, in public with a warmth which seemed to justify the complaint of those who characterised him as "bitter." Warmth was of the essence of his character. But I have often been struck by the manner in which he weighed his words, and spoke as if protesting to himself when in private conversation he disparaged any of those about him in public life. I am amazed, looking back, to remember how often I heard him criticised, and how rarely I heard him criticise others.'

H. M. DURAND.

December 11, 1878.

PREFACE

BY

THE LATE SIR HENRY DURAND.

THE events which the following work endeavours to bring before the reader in their connection did not fail, as they severally occurred, to strike the public mind with humiliation and grief, or with joy and exultation. They partially aroused England to a sense of the greatness of the trust conferred upon her by Divine Providence, and forcibly called her attention to the vast Empire won by the genius and courage of a few great men; repeatedly perilled by the weak and rash; and the preservation of which may at any hour depend on the individual to whom for the time its destinies have been entrusted. A consideration of events after the excitement of defeat or victory has been allayed, and when the retrospect can be calmly made, may want freshness of novelty in its incidents, but can scarcely fail to prove instructive. With truth for his object, and the honour and real interests of his country at heart, the writer feels that he discharges a duty to some able and to many brave men in placing before their countrymen an impartial review of their deeds. For his own opinions he offers no apology but the ancient one—

'Justum est bellum, Samnites, quibus necessarium, et pia arma, quibus nulla nisi in armis relinquitur spes.'

CONTENTS.

CHAPTER I.

1826–1835.

CHAPTER II.

1799–1837.

CHAPTER III.

1834—APRIL 1838.

CHAPTER IV.

NOVEMBER 1837—SEPTEMBER 1838.

CHAPTER V.

JUNE—OCTOBER 1838.

CHAPTER VI.

SEPTEMBER—NOVEMBER 1838.

CHAPTER VII.

OCTOBER 1838—FEBRUARY 1839.

CHAPTER VIII.

FEBRUARY—APRIL 1839.

CHAPTER IX.

APRIL—JUNE 1839.

CHAPTER X.

JUNE—AUGUST 1839.

CHAPTER XI.

AUGUST—OCTOBER 1839.

CHAPTER XII.

OCTOBER—NOVEMBER 1839.

CHAPTER XIII.

NOVEMBER 1839.

CHAPTER XIV.

WINTER OF 1839–40.

CHAPTER XV.

JUNE 1839—FEBRUARY 1840.

CHAPTER XXII.

DECEMBER 1840–AUGUST 1841.

CHAPTER XXIII.

SEPTEMBER–OCTOBER 1841.

CHAPTER XXIV.

OCTOBER–NOVEMBER 1841.

CHAPTER XXV.

NOVEMBER 1841–JANUARY 1842.

CHAPTER XXVI.

NOVEMBER 1841–FEBRUARY 1842.

CHAPTER XXVII.

NOVEMBER 1841—FEBRUARY 1842.

CHAPTER XXVIII.

NOVEMBER 1841—FEBRUARY 1842.

CHAPTER XXIX.

FEBRUARY—MARCH 1842.

THE

FIRST AFGHAN WAR.

CHAPTER I.

1826–1835.

ADMINISTRATION OF LORD WILLIAM BENTINCK—RELATIONS BETWEEN THE BRITISH GOVERNMENT AND THE FRONTIER POWERS AT THE CLOSE OF HIS RULE.

AFTER the conclusion of the Burmese War, and the capture of Bhurtpore in 1826, British India enjoyed a state of tranquillity but partially disturbed by the military operations in Coorg, and the petty warfare in the Cole country. Under the pacific and economical administration of Lord William Bentinck, the public revenue was well husbanded; and at the close of his rule that nobleman left a full treasury, the sources of revenue in a healthy and improving condition, the public credit of the Government high, and its name and power generally respected. The native States in close relation with the Anglo-Indian Government felt confidence in the honesty and moderation of the man who had wielded great power with a scrupulous regard to existing treaties; to the rights both of dependent and of independent States; and to the system of non-interference carried by his administration to an unprecedented extent. A rule, on the whole, thus wise and just was, though not free from errors, rewarded with the blessings of prosperity and peace; and in 1835 nothing threatened to disturb their continuance.

A concise review of the political relations existing between the Supreme Government of India and the chief frontier powers at the period that Lord William Bentinck's sway ceased is necessary in order to form a clear understanding of the measures subsequently taken, and a just apprehension of their nature and influence.

Burmah, occupied with its own internal dissensions, and still smarting under the humiliation of our hasty Treaty of Yandaboo, was, though hostile in feeling, powerless for offensive measures. This was proved by the Court of Ava failing to attempt the recovery of the ceded territory on the coast of Tenasserim, when an excellent opportunity was afforded by the rebellion at Tavoy and the panic flight from Mergui. The Burmese on that occasion evinced no alacrity for the renewal of hostilities; the insurrection of 1829 was speedily quelled; and in 1835 all was tranquil in that quarter.

The Government of Nepaul, torn by the struggles of contending factions, isolated in position, and sensible of its inability alone to cope with the British power, courted its favour. Recent events had not allayed the politic jealousy of the Ameers of Scinde. They had permitted Burnes's mission to explore the Indus; they had also entered into treaties opening, under restrictions, the navigation of that river to the enterprise of British trade; and had thus complied with all reasonable demands; but the unprovoked invasion of their territory by Shah Shooja, our pensioner; his occupation of Shikarpore; and the defeat they sustained at his hands on January 9, 1834; were not events calculated to render the relations of the Ameers with the British Government more cordial than was their wont. There was, however, nothing to apprehend from so weak and divided a State.

The Khan of Bhawulpore maintained a cordial alliance with the British. With everything to fear from Runjeet Singh of Lahore, and much to dread from the Ameers of Scinde, his safety lay in the goodwill of the Anglo-Indian Government, the only counterpoise to his comparatively powerful and unscrupulous neighbours.

The Punjab, under its wily ruler Runjeet Singh, merited attention. He had gradually established his authority over the Sikh chiefs, and, controlling to his own purposes the military propensities of the race, had formed a large standing army. Well equipped, and provided with a numerous artillery, animated by success, and under the sole command of a man who had known how to inspire it with confidence, such a force was not lightly to be despised. It would have followed him had he led it against the British provinces, but his natural shrewdness, aided by the sound advice of the leading French officers in his service, warned him of the danger attending too early a measurement of strength with the Anglo-Indian army. Satisfied of the pacific policy of the Governor-General, Runjeet Singh directed Sikh energy and thirst of conquest to the extension of empire where such could be effected with less chance of discomfiture. To the successful issue of such operations, and to the consolidation of his power, a friendly alliance with the British Government was essential; and in 1835 the only event which threatened to disturb the North-Western Frontier was the contingency of the death of the ruler of the Punjab. Partaking of all the vices of his race, and having full scope for their indulgence, a sudden termination to a career of constant dissipation was not an improbable event. Such an occurrence might be anticipated, first, to lead to internal commotion rather than to external aggression; and thus time would be afforded for preparing to meet the exigencies of the period. In the meanwhile all was tranquil and promised so to remain.

Thus on the west, from north to south, there was a peaceful border. The ruler of the Punjab, the chief of Bhawulpore, and the Ameers of Scinde, actuated either by their interests or their fears, were severally anxious for the maintenance of peace, and a good understanding with the British Power. To the latter the continuance of this state of affairs, though not as essential to its existence, was of very great importance. Hitherto, sometimes with and sometimes without equitable cause, but always with the pretext of necessity, war had been the normal state of our growing power; it was the inevitable consequence of the first territorial acquisition on the mainland of India, and of the resulting contact of the mind, commercial energy, courage, and ambition, of the English race with masses having no common bond of nationality or religion, under the sway of arbitrary rulers with complex views and interests, and therefore utterly wanting in unity of purpose and action. The sword once drawn in such a contest could not permanently be sheathed, until one of two events had come to pass: the native princes and people must either sweep from the land its invaders, or submit to their supremacy. In the inscrutable Will of the great Ruler of the universe, the latter was to be the consummation of a long series of independent, and therefore mis-timed struggles, on the part of the Hindoo and Moslem princes and people of India. That supremacy was now fully established, and generally acknowledged; and every consideration of policy, humanity, and religion pointed out the hour as propitious to the concentration of the energies of the Anglo-Indian Government on the advancement of the moral and physical welfare of the millions in that vast empire entrusted to its care.

In this spirit were the measures pursued by Lord William Bentinck. Secure on all frontiers, he was enabled to reduce the army to the strength sufficient for the maintenance of internal order and external respect, but unequal to foreign aggression for the extension of territory. In compliance with the wishes of the Home Government, a few officers were sent to Persia to aid in forming Persian troops; but such a mission was not in accordance with the opinions of the Governor-General, who, content with the North-West frontier then existing, and entertaining no apprehensions of danger from the countries to the west of the Indus, viewed with calm indifference their state of weakness and division.

The desert, separating the British Provinces from the river Indus, formed a good frontier to the south of Ferozepore on the Sutlej. North of that place, and throughout the petty Sikh States under British protection, the frontier was more practicable, and Runjeet Singh with a large force at Lahore was within four marches of the fords of the Sutlej. A post of observation was therefore maintained at Loodianah; but the main strength in Northern India was kept on the lines of the Ganges and Jumna, the troops being cantoned in considerable force at Cawnpore, Meerut, and Kurnaul, and in minor strength at Allahabad, Agra, and Delhi, the latter place being the most advanced magazine of the army. Other posts occupied by the troops need not here be detailed, but it may be observed that by reducing the number of small detached posts and concentrating the regular troops, the military occupation of the country was improved without injury to its general internal security.

Lord William Bentinck quitted India, leaving it in a profound peace which nothing threatened to disturb; and which held out the promise of the concomitant blessings of economy in the public expenditure, improvement in the condition of the people, and of the rise of institutions which, linking the prosperity and advancement of the millions of India with the British rule, should enable the latter to strike root in the affections as well as in the fears of its subject races. The contemplation of the origin of a war which effectually blasted these dawning hopes, and delayed indefinitely their fulfilment, will prepare the reader for a consideration of the military operations, which, though on a distant theatre, are devoid of instruction neither to those who have to bare their swords at their country's bidding, nor to the men whom she may invest with the fearful power of unfurling in her name upon those distant shores the British ensign for war.

CHAPTER II.

1799–1837.

DESIGNS OF NAPOLEON IN THE EAST—EARLY RELATIONS BETWEEN PERSIA AND THE EUROPEAN POWERS—THREATENED INVASION OF INDIA BY SHAH ZEMAN OF CABUL—SHAH SHOOJA AT LOODIANAH—HIS RELATIONS WITH THE BRITISH AGENT, WADE—HIS TREATY WITH RUNJEET SINGH AND EXPEDITION TO CANDAHAR IN 1834—DIFFICULTIES OF DOST MAHOMED—CAPTURE OF PESHAWUR BY THE SIKHS—CONNECTION BETWEEN THE AFGHAN CHIEFS AND PERSIA—GROWTH OF RUSSIAN INFLUENCE AT TEHERAN—CONTEMPLATED ATTACK UPON HERAT BY THE SHAH OF PERSIA.

THE review of our connection with Persia need not, for present purposes, be carried back to a more remote period than that in which the intrigues and daring energy of Napoleon, extending their activity to a theatre flattering alike to his imagination and ambition, were in India met and baffled by the vigour and wisdom of a Wellesley. The occupation of Egypt by Napoleon; the alliance which Tippoo, a bitter foe to the British, eagerly made with the French; the spreading influence of the latter amongst the leading Mahratta powers; the threatened invasion of India by Shah Zeman of Cabul, who, urged on by the implacable enmity of Tippoo, advanced to Lahore, bent on rendering the Mahometan power supreme in the north of India whilst his ally should strive for the same cause in the south and centre;

the existence of French settlements in India and its seas; the loose scattered power of the British in the east; all concurred in forcing extreme vigilance upon the man, who, aided indeed by the genius of a Wellington and the courage of a Lake, found that he had a fierce struggle not alone for empire but for existence to maintain. He proved equal to the difficulties which beset him. Seringapatam was taken and Tippoo slain in its defence; French intrigue, checked in all and foiled in some, waned amongst the native States; and Shah Zeman, recalled from Lahore to the defence of his own dominions, invaded by Persia, saved Herat, but lost the opportunity of achieving an enterprise the prospect of which was hailed with delight by the Moslem population of India.

Although the year 1799 had been further rendered remarkable by the failure of Napoleon before Acre and his inglorious retreat from under its walls, and by his desertion of the army in Egypt, yet that army remained, and the policy of France with respect to the East, when Napoleon should be in a position to influence her councils, was uncertain. The Marquis of Wellesley therefore determined to cultivate the alliance of Persia, which he had already led to render valuable aid in the interruption caused to the Afghan scheme of Indian conquest by the Shah's attack on Herat. In 1800 Malcolm was at the Court of Persia, and in 1801, the year in which an Anglo-Indian force under Baird was thrown into Egypt by the able ruler of India, treaties political and commercial were signed between the British and Persian Governments.

But the compulsory evacuation of Egypt in 1801 by the French army, the subsequent growth and consolidation of our power in India by the victories of a Wellington and a Lake, and the struggle of the allied nations of Europe, foremost amongst whom were England and Russia, against Napoleon, combined to preclude attention being paid to the affairs of Persia, which, in contact with Russia, and failing to obtain aid from England, sought in 1805 assistance from France. In May 1807 a treaty was concluded, and Napoleon entrusted the establishment of French interests and influence to General Gardanne as his ambassador, sending at the same time French officers to discipline the Persian troops.

The sudden reconciliation of the Emperors of France and Russia at Tilsit in 1807, accompanied by the secret treaty there entered into for the invasion of India, gave importance to General Gardanne's mission, and alarmed the British Government. The sufferings of the French army in Egypt had not effaced the impression made by its first success, and British statesmen, inexperienced in war, and always apt to measure the difficulties of moving armies by the smooth surface of a map, might be pardoned for fearing that what Napoleon as General of the Republic had dared to contemplate, he might as Emperor of France, in friendly alliance with Persia and aided by Russia, carry into execution. Sir Harford Jones was therefore despatched to Persia in 1808, and succeeded in re-establishing British influence, concluding the preliminary treaty of March 12, 1809.

British officers were now employed in training Persian

troops, and although their services were never needed to repel French battalions, they were appreciated by the Russian troops in future contests with the armies of the Shah.

The fears of the British Government did not last long. The invasion of Russia by Napoleon and the destruction of his army not only removed all apprehension on account of the designs upon India entertained by the French Emperor, but was a practical lesson to Europe that enterprises of distant conquest by large armies demand the combination of great skill with vast means. British statesmen, engrossed by the war in the Peninsula and on the Continent, again in cordial alliance with Russia, and freed from their once vivid apprehensions for India, viewed, if not with entire indifference, at least with sobered jealousy, the encroachments of Russia on Persia. The latter, unable to cope with her powerful antagonist, now pressed England for the fulfilment of the engagements incurred in 1809, but it was not until Russia was wringing from Persia, by the treaty of 1813, the cession of her acquisitions south of the Caucasus and the undisputed command of the Caspian, that the British Government was moved to aid the Shah. Persia was as an ally weak, costly, and proverbially uncertain, yet she had some claim to consideration; and therefore the definitive treaty of 1814, defensive in its stipulations, was concluded upon the basis of the preliminary treaty of 1809. England thus bound herself, in case any European nation invaded Persia, to afford aid to the Shah either by sending a force from India, or by the payment of an annual subsidy fixed at 200,000 tomaums. The treaty evinced some jealousy of the possibility of India being invaded from the westward, and it remained the basis of such connection with Persia as the British Government henceforth considered it expedient to maintain.

That connection was not very intimate. It would be here needless to follow the series of operations which engaged Persia on her northern frontier subsequently to 1814, and which led, after the war of 1826 and the treaty of Toorkmantchai, signed in February 1828, to the predominance of Russian influence in her councils. The Shah found England, no longer under alarm for her Eastern Empire, but a cold ally; and, embarrassed by the liquidation of the indemnity due to Russia, was glad to compound with England for the sum of 200,000 tomaums, at which price the Shah, in March 1828, annulled the 3rd and 4th articles of the definitive treaty, and thus liberated England from an obligation she had, while it existed, been slow to fulfil. A weak and wretched Government, with disordered finances, and, through all the vices of Eastern despotism, grown impotent, would have squandered as much gold as England might give, but could never have been raised from misrule, sloth, and corruption, to the exercise of wisdom, economy, and energy. A golden wand has not the magic power of regenerating a disorganised kingdom such as that of Persia; and it was evident that the check upon Russian designs of extended empire, when such should become dangerous, was not to be found in subsidising the Court of Teheran.

Before resuming the subject of our subsequent relations with Persia, it will be advisable concisely to trace the series of events which brought the rulers of Afghanistan into communication with a power they had in general found cause to fear and to oppose rather than to court.

The threat of an Afghan invasion of Hindustan had on two occasions, in the youth of our power, created alarm, and caused regiments to be added to the strength of the Indian army. Wellesley, by the advance of the Shah of Persia on Herat, found, on the first occasion, occupation for Shah Zeman's scimitars in another field; and although subsequently this enterprising ruler again contemplated an invasion of the rich plains of India, yet the internal dissensions of his ill-compacted State, and foreign aggression from the westward, once more recalled him from his favourite project. The revolutions which ensued in Afghanistan, the growth of the Sikh State, and the consolidation of the British Empire, removed for the future all dread of Afghan irruption.

It is unnecessary here to follow the revolutions of the Cabul State through their chequered current until 1809, when the French alliance with Persia led us to conclude a treaty with the State of Cabul, of which Shah Shooja was at the time king. Equally needless would it be to follow the maze of adventures and misfortunes which ended in Shah Shooja's deliverance, through the energy and skill of his consort, from the close durance in which he had been kept by Runjeet Singh. He found an asylum under the protection of the British Government, in 1816, at Loodianah. His vain attempt to recover his throne in 1819 does not immediately connect itself with our present subject; but his want of success on that occasion, and the reverses and sufferings he had previously undergone, in no degree quenched his desire to rule, and the tedium of his residence at Loodianah was relieved by scheming for remounting his lost throne.

His position at our frontier post was a favourable one for the indulgence of such intrigues. Safe under British protection, he there enjoyed frequent communication with Lahore and Cabul, and could without difficulty maintain a correspondence with his real or pretended adherents. At the same time he had the opportunity, which he did not permit to escape him, of ingratiating himself with the British agent, Captain C. M. Wade. Bland in speech and in manner, and not inexperienced in men, he saw the importance of gaining this functionary, and did so—a feat not difficult even with less art and leisure than Shah Shooja enjoyed.

Towards the close of 1831 the schemes of Shah Shooja began to assume form, and he made advances to Runjeet Singh which were favourably listened to by that ruler, who in reply penned propositions the most important of which were assented to by Shah Shooja, and subsequently formed the basis of a treaty. Wade had been won to the Shah's interest by flattering deference and attention, and by the skill with which the ex-monarch had gradually during their long intercourse engaged Wade in his confidence. Provided no alarm were given to the Governor-General's policy of non-interference, and this the British agent could easily avoid, no difficulty was apprehended in that quarter.

The great obstacle to be surmounted was the want of funds. Shah Shooja tried his new friend and former jailor; but Runjeet Singh, hopelessly avaricious and exacting, was found impracticable. The bankers of the chief cities in Hindustan and the Punjab were too conversant with Afghan faith and promises to risk capital on such an adventure; and at last there appeared no hope unless the Shah could induce the British to interfere in his behalf. Bold in assertion, he had succeeded in convincing the British agent that his influence and popularity was unbounded amongst the Afghan tribes. Toorkistan was equally devoted.

'The people of Scinde, Beloochistan, and Seistan to the confines of the Ocean,' wrote the Shah, 'are well inclined towards me. They wear the symbol of submission, and their country is mine.' He took care likewise to dwell on the schemes of conquest and the military operations of the Persians under Abbas Meerza in Khorassan. The pith of the application lay, however, in few words: 'Try, if it be possible, by the mediation of my friends' (i.e. the British), 'to find a banker ready to make a loan.' However cautiously put forward by Wade, with an allusion to the news from Khorassan, such a request was not of a nature to meet with attention from Lord William Bentinck, who enjoined the strictest non-interference. But most unfortunately he attached sufficient importance to the information from Khorassan to direct that a person should be deputed to Candahar as a mere reporter of passing events. This, though nothing in aid of Shah Shooja's empty military chest, was a point gained, and encouraged him to proceed in his intrigues. He was now sure, through Wade, of a safe emissary in the person of the accredited newswriter of the British Government. Accordingly, communications with Herat, Afghanistan, and Scinde thickened ; and Wade, blinded by his sympathies and predilections for Shah Shooja, reported in September 1832 that the Ameers of Scinde wrote in terms of great devotion to the Shah's interests, inviting him to prosecute his intentions, and enter their territories on the conditions that he should relinquish all claim to the sovereignty of Scinde and Shikarpore, should confer it as a bequest on its then rulers, their heirs, and successors, and should not remain at Shikarpore, his intended base of operations, more than ten days.

With reference to the pretensions of the Cabul throne to the sovereignty of Scinde, these terms of great devotion were neither flattering nor palatable to Shah Shooja, who, in addressing the Governor-General, was careful to adopt other grounds for recommending his contemplated enterprise and seeking pecuniary aid : 'As Abbas Meerza is come to Herat, if I can procure assistance from the British Government I will proceed to that place, and the country from Khorassan to the Oosbecks, and to the boundary of the sea, will fall into my hands and become friendly to the British.' The reply to such gasconade was, that the British Government religiously abstained from intermeddling with the affairs of its neighbours when this could be avoided—that Shah Shooja was master of his own actions, but that to afford him assistance for the purpose he contemplated would be inconsistent with that neutrality which on such occasions is the rule of guidance adopted by the British Government.

The reply was, so far as it went, correct; but it was an error not to have accompanied it with advice against re-fomenting civil war in a country which had now for seventeen years disowned Shah Shooja's rule. Such advice the British Government was entitled to offer to the man who had long found an asylum under its protection and lived upon its bounty, and who could not therefore have objected to a remonstrance having for its object the maintenance of general tranquillity. Lord William Bentinck was bent on economy, and if the Shah succeeded, his pension of nearly 5,000*l.* a year would revert to the coffers of the State; and the prospective embarrassment of his rapidly increasing family would be shifted upon his reconquered country. But this view of affairs was narrow and circumscribed, the view of a mind not sufficiently alive to the high duty of the ruler of such an empire as India. That duty is not limited to bald non-interference. We owe to the East those offices of humanity which engage every sovereign to cultivate peace not alone within the borders of his own territory, but also, in so far as his influence extends, within those of neighbour nations. Firm advice from the Governor-General of India, coupled with a refusal to make an advance of pension to Shah Shooja, would certainly have preserved Scinde from unwarrantable invasion, and Afghanistan from civil war and the loss of Peshawur. It would have tended to calm the apprehensions of the Ameers of Scinde, and would have checked the disposition of Dost Mahomed and the chiefs of Candahar to look for an alliance with Persia.

The Governor-General committed a grave error, one not to be measured by the smallness of the sum, in granting an advance of pension to Shah Shooja when about to start on his expedition. Such an act could not fail in the East of being construed into a material aid and effectual countenance of the Shah's designs. It encouraged him, and incensed his opponents against the British Government, which, with professions of peace and goodwill on its lips, appeared to furnish means for the war and permit the levy of troops within its territory, a system of non-interference on the part of a very powerful government not at all comprehensible to the Afghan rulers.

Runjeet Singh, well aware of the community of feeling between Wade and the Shah, deemed the vaunted neutrality of the British Government of doubtful complexion. It seemed expedient, therefore, whilst negotiating with Shah Shooja the treaty of March 12, 1833, which might not be altogether palatable to the Governor-General, to pretend suspicion of the man he had once so deeply injured, and to address the Governor-General for the purpose of eliciting a clear explanation of his views with regard to the Shah's expedition. Assured by Lord William Bentinck that the British Government had no concern in it, the Sikh felt himself at liberty securely to watch the progress of the adventure, and to turn it, if successful, as much as possible to his own advantage.

Shah Shooja failed in his endeavours to realise

money upon his jewels; but, furnished with an advance of pension, he was enabled to quit the neighbourhood of Loodianah on February 17, 1833. His march lay along the left bank of the Indus, through the territory of Bhawulpore, the ruler of which gave him a cold reception and very trifling aid. The Ameers of Scinde were not prepared at that season to offer any resistance to the Shah's progress; and he was permitted to pass the Indus, and to occupy Shikarpore without opposition. Once in possession of that place, he had not only a base for his future operations, but also, what was still more necessary, the opportunity of levying contributions. Runjeet Singh, seeing so fortunate a commencement, now considered it advisable to ratify the treaty of March 12, which act had been delayed until success on the part of the Shah should render it expedient.

When the season for military operations returned, the Ameers pressed the Shah to leave Shikarpore, from which place he had already wrung a considerable sum of money, besides seizing the crops. The supply thus obtained was insufficient for his exigencies, and for the protracted operations he contemplated. He was therefore bent on exacting a heavy subsidy from the Ameers. But the Scindian rulers, as adverse to the subsidy as anxious to be rid of Shah Shooja, collected their forces, and determined to try the issue of a battle. Fortune once more smiled on the Shah, giving him on January 18, 1834, a victory which enabled him to dictate terms of peace to the Ameers, and to replenish his military chest. Animated by this success, Shah Shooja hastened his preparations, and in the middle of February was on his advance towards Candahar.

Dost Mahomed laboured under disadvantages so great that nothing but skill and daring promptitude could have extricated him. His brothers, the chiefs of Candahar and Peshawur, were combining for his overthrow; and the latter were intriguing with the Sikhs, whom they ultimately invited to cross the Attock. Many of his chiefs were in communication with Shah Shooja, the newswriter of the British Government, in constant correspondence with Wade, having become a partisan of Shah Shooja, and the channel for the letters of those well affected to him. The expedition of the Shah was regarded throughout the country as countenanced and supported by the British Government, and those well disposed to Dost Mahomed were discouraged by a report apparently so well founded. The Cabul ruler could with much difficulty, chiefly by means unfavourable to his popularity, raise a small amount of money with which to prepare for the coming storm. He collected together as many men as he could hope to maintain, and for a time remained inactive, watching the progress of the intrigues of his enemies. He had three to contend against—the Sikhs, Shah Shooja, and his brothers of Peshawur and Candahar. Leagued together for his ruin, his brothers were urging him, towards the close of 1833, to march to Candahar to assist in opposing Shah Shooja. The Shah had not then advanced from Shikarpore, and Dost Mahomed, aware that the object sought was to afford the chiefs of Peshawur an opportunity of moving upon Cabul, if he could be induced to leave the place, and that Shah Shooja could not march up the Bolan Pass for some time to come, resolved to strike first where the most necessary. Accordingly, having dismissed the Candahar chief with the assurance that he was about to hasten to his assistance, he caused his troops to encamp a short distance from Cabul on the road to Candahar, but snow setting in as usual at that time of the year, he recalled the troops on the plea of the severity of the season. His intentions were, however, soon apparent by his march on December 31 from Cabul towards Jellalabad. His advance was rapid, and the second day after he appeared under the walls of Jellalabad he stormed the place, carrying it by a breach effected by a mine in one of the towers. Its chief being in league with those of Peshawur and Candahar, the establishment of Dost Mahomed's power at Jellalabad was a severe blow to the machinations of his brothers, and strengthened his own position. It now became a question whether, pushing on to Peshawur, which would at once have fallen into his hands, he should from thence contest the approach of the Sikhs, or whether he should retrace his steps to Cabul, and, marching to Candahar, oppose Shah Shooja. Aware of his own inability to cope with the large, regular, and well-organised force of Runjeet Singh below the passes, and calculating that the Sikh ruler's caution would make him slow to risk his columns in the defiles between Peshawur and Jellalabad, Dost Mahomed determined on a rapid march to Candahar to measure his strength with a foe more immediately endangering his power amongst his chiefs and subjects, and against whom, if once permitted to gain secure footing on the highlands of Afghanistan, the Cabul chief could not hope to excite a fanatic opposition, such as he had a sure prospect of kindling against the Sikhs, whatever might be their first successes. Shah Shooja once disposed of, reliance could be placed on the religious and national feelings of the Afghans for the popularity of a crusade against the hated unbelievers.

In the meantime Runjeet Singh's troops on the Attock were in readiness; and as soon as the intrigues with the chiefs of Peshawur were ripe, and it was thought that the advance of Shah Shooja had made itself felt, the Sikh commander, Hari Singh, moved forward. He crossed the Attock without difficulty or conflict, seized Peshawur on May 6, and drove the Afghans to the mouth of the Khybur Pass. Peshawur, thus obtained without loss, was speedily reinforced by Runjeet Singh, who hastened to render his new conquest secure.

The Candahar chiefs, unable to offer serious resistance to the advance of Shah Shooja, retired to Candahar, and the place was invested and attacked, but Dost Mahomed appeared in time to save it. Shah Shooja, as soon as he was apprised of the near approach of the Cabul chief, moved out of the strong position he occupied at old Candahar into a weaker; allowed, without an attempt to prevent it, the junction of the Cabul and Candahar leaders; and then offered battle to their combined forces; making at the same time every arrangement for flight from the action he was thus bringing on. The safety of Dost Mahomed depended upon his being able immediately to close in fight with his antagonist; for he was sensible of the growing disaffection of the chiefs and troops, and that the intrigues of the Shah had proved successful in undermining his authority. He showed no hesitation, therefore, in accepting the proffered battle; but attacked with his uncertain troops, keeping in reserve under his own command a small body of men upon whom he could depend. The Afghans on neither side evinced much appetite for the fight, and a loose skirmish rather than a battle ensued. The small body of disciplined Hindustanee men in the Shah's service, about a couple of battalions, under a half-caste of the name of Campbell, would, if supported, have won the Shah a victory, for they drove everything before them. But Shah Shooja, gifted with no kingly courage, had fled the fight; his Afghans, mistrusting their leader, had abstained from committing themselves deeply in the action, and were not slack to follow his example; and the Hindustanees, deserted by their friends and overwhelmed by numbers, found it useless any longer to maintain a combat alike objectless and disproportioned. Dost Mahomed, master of the field without bringing his reserve into action, treated the wounded Campbell well, and entertained him in his own service. The artillery, camp equipage, stores and records of the Shah fell into the hands of the Cabul chief, who did not seem to consider his pusillanimous opponent worth capture or pursuit. The correspondence of the Shah revealed the web of intrigues in which many of Dost Mahomed's kindred and chiefs were implicated, and the full extent of the dangers by which he had been surrounded, foremost amongst which was the disaffection of the Kuzzilbash leaders, whose conduct, with that of their horse, had been of a very doubtful complexion in the late engagement. He found also a copy of the Shah's treaty with Runjeet Singh, and numerous letters with the seal of the British agent, Wade, addressed to persons whose assistance might prove useful to Shah Shooja, and who were exhorted to render such aid as an acceptable service to the British Government. The Cabul ruler, whether he believed the letters to be genuine or not, could not but see in them a sure proof of how universal was the impression that the Shah's expedition had the countenance of the British Government.

This defeat of the Shah on July 2, 1834, disheartened for a time even Wade, who held it 'perhaps fatal to every hope of his restoration,' and contemplated for a while supporting Dost Mahomed Khan. The latter returned from Candahar to Cabul, where, inviting the aid of the faithful in a crusade against the Sikhs at Peshawur, and extorting from Hindoos and others all the money they could be compelled to yield, he prepared for his march to Jellalabad. At the end of February 1835 he quitted Cabul, and on reaching Jellalabad assembled his forces. From thence he marched to the Khybur, cleared it of Sikh posts, and took up a position in the plain of Peshawur. Runjeet Singh had now, however, 25,000 men for the defence of his new acquisition, and Dost Mahomed found himself forced to retire out of the plains and to withdraw from before his powerful enemy.

As a natural consequence of the combined invasions of Shah Shooja and Runjeet Singh, carried into execution with the cognisance, if not the secret approval, of the British, Dost Mahomed and the chiefs of Candahar were driven to seek the alliance of Persia. Upon the throne of that country the candidate nominated by Russia had lately been seated, and the influence of the Czar was paramount at the Court of Teheran. We have now traced the causes which led to an understanding between the rulers of Persia and Afghanistan. It is time to return to the consideration of our own relations with the former power, and to mark the course of action pursued by us until the outbreak of the Cabul war.

Early in 1834 the Russian Government expressed its anxiety for a good understanding with England respecting the affairs of Persia. It was urged that the interests of the two European Courts were very similar, and that there was a prospect of civil discord arising upon the death of the Shah unless the order of succession to the throne were determined in favour of some one candidate by the joint influence of Russia and England. The British Government, concurring in support of the hereditary prince, whose pretensions had already received the countenance of the Russian envoy at the Court of Teheran, issued corresponding instructions to the British representative ; and upon receiving information from Russia that the Shah of Persia had decided on nominating the hereditary prince his successor to the throne, Lord Palmerston signified the gratification of the British Government at finding that Russia and England were acting with regard to the affairs of Persia in the same spirit, and were equally animated by a sincere desire to maintain, not only the internal tranquillity, but also the independence and integrity of the kingdom. The Shah died shortly after the settlement of the succession, and the prince nominated by Russia and approved by England ascended the throne of Persia. He soon manifested a thirst for conquest, and certain provocation offered to him by the ruler of Herat led him to contemplate the invasion of that principality. He was encouraged in this resolve by the submissive tone in which the chiefs of Cabul and Candahar had sought his alliance; and before long the Shah's designs began to give umbrage to the British envoy, Ellis. The latter ascertained that these ambitious schemes were fostered by the Russian envoy, who pressed the Shah to lose no time in undertaking the projected expedition, advancing as a reason for the immediate urgency of the measure the desire of the British Government to see the Afghan monarchy restored, a desire evidenced by the late attempt of Shah Shooja. Nor did the agents of Dost Mahomed and the Candahar chiefs fail to dwell on the facts that Shah Shooja had started from his asylum in British India to attempt the recovery of the throne of Cabul, and had been aided by the co-operation of the close allies of the Anglo-Indian Government, the Sikhs.

The British envoy, however desirous of counteracting Russian influence, laboured under peculiar difficulties; for not only had the Shah a just cause of war with Herat, but he also had the right to demand, in virtue of the ninth article of the treaty with England, that the latter should not interfere in the hostilities contemplated. The article in question stipulated that, 'If war should be declared between the Afghans and Persians, the English Government shall not interfere with either party, unless their mediation to effect a peace shall be solicited by both parties.' The obligations of good faith were therefore clear and imperative; and their full force was felt by Ellis, who stated them with precision in a memorandum to his Government, dated January 15, 1836. He wrote:—

'The Shah of Persia lays claim to the sovereignty of Afghanistan, as far as Ghuznee, and is fully determined to attempt the conquest of Herat in the spring. Unfortunately the conduct of Kamran Meerza in violating the engagements entered into with his Royal Highness the late Abbas Meerza, and in permitting his Vizeer, Yar Mahomed Khan, to occupy part of Seistan, has given the Shah a full justification for commencing hostilities. The success of the Shah in the undertaking is anxiously wished for by Russia; and their minister here does not fail to press it on to early execution. The motive cannot be mistaken. Herat, once annexed to Persia, may become, according to the Commercial Treaty, the residence of a Russian consular agent, who would from thence push his researches and communications, avowed and secret, throughout Afghanistan. Indeed, in the present state of the relations between Persia and Russia, it cannot be denied that the progress of the former in Afghanistan is tantamount to the advancement of the latter, and ought to receive every opposition from the British Government that the obligations of public faith will permit; but while the Russian Government is free to assist Persia in the assertion of her sovereign pretensions in Afghanistan, Great Britain is precluded, by the ninth article of the existing treaty, from interfering between the Persians and Afghans, unless called upon to do so by both parties; and therefore, as long as this treaty remains in force, the British Government must submit to the approach of Russian influence, through the instrumentality of Persian conquests, to the very frontier of our Indian Empire.'

One opening offered itself to Ellis—to obtain the assent of the Shah to the mediation of England between Herat and Persia; but the latter was too wary to yield compliance. Nevertheless, under an impression of the great danger to the tranquillity of our Eastern Empire which would result from the extension of the Persian monarchy in Afghanistan, Ellis continued throughout 1836 repeatedly to remonstrate against the expedition to Herat. He had no success, for the very earnestness and anxiety displayed by him confirmed in the Shah's mind the accuracy of the statements of the Russian envoy, and gave weight to the latter's suggestions. Even had the damage he apprehended for India been as real and imminent as it was remote and imaginary, the course pursued by the British envoy would have been ill-calculated to secure his object; and, viewed with reference to the undoubted right of the Shah to demand redress by force of arms, such pertinacity was specially impolitic. Ellis had, however, brought himself to regard Persia, under Russian influence, 'as no longer an outwork for the defence of India, but as the first parallel from whence the attack may be commenced or threatened;' and the British Ministry, either adopting or affecting to adopt these views, impressed upon McNeill, his successor at the Court of Persia, the necessity for continuing to pursue the same line of policy as had been followed by, and had failed under, Ellis. Further, a serious reference was made to the Russian Government through the British ambassador at St. Petersburg to ascertain whether it was under instructions from that Court that its envoy in Persia was exciting the Shah to military expeditions against neighbouring States. The Russian Government disavowed responsibility for the conduct of its agent, and doubted the accuracy of McNeill's information; but, whatever the commands of the Czar may have been, Simonich deemed it advantageous to the interests of the Russian frontier authorities and their measures that the Shah with his force should be removed to as great a distance as possible. He therefore advised and pressed on the expedition to Herat. The Shah, well inclined to demand redress from the Herat ruler, and jealous of the re-establishment of a consolidated Afghan power, was nevertheless not blind to the real motives of the Russian envoy; and having to check the plundering Turcomans, who had lately insulted his frontiers by their raids, he marched to Asterabad and threatened Khiva. But the expedition resulted in an inglorious failure; and its issue supplied an additional incentive for an advance into Afghanistan. The co-operation of the Cabul and Candahar chiefs seemed to promise success in an attack upon Herat, and the achievement recommended itself to the Shah as one which would wipe away the disgrace he had suffered, reflect honour upon his arms, and augment his reputation and strength amongst his own subjects. England in the hour of Persia's need had shrunk from the fulfilment of the defensive treaty, and had taken advantage of the necessities of the Shah in 1828 to absolve herself from engagements which, no danger threatening her Eastern possessions, were regarded as embarrassing. More was to be expected from her fears than from her goodwill; and the Shah might be pardoned if, reasoning from experience, he anticipated the possibility of turning to good account her eager apprehensions on the subject of Herat, and eliciting from a cold but rich ally that which the Court of Teheran always needed and coveted —gold.

Lord Auckland, then Governor-General of India, quickly adopted the tone of alarm with which the British envoy in Russia spoke of the predominance of Russian influence and the military operations contemplated by the Shah against Herat. In the early part of 1837 the Government of India reiterated its injunctions to the envoy, urging him to dissuade the Shah from the prosecution of his ambitious enterprise, upon the ground that the Governor-General 'must view with umbrage and displeasure schemes of interference and conquest on our western frontier.' The advance from the figurative opinion of the British envoy in April

1836, who thought Persia a Russian first parallel of attack against India, to the assumption in April 1837 of Herat as our western frontier, marks the rapid progress of diplomatic alarm and rashness. Such unwarrantable pretensions could produce no favourable effect on the Shah of Persia, who, with right on his side, and regardless alike of the advice, remonstrance, and proffered mediation of England, marched towards Herat on July 23, 1837.

CHAPTER III.

1834–APRIL 1838.

RETURN OF SHAH SHOOJA TO LOODIANAH—WADE'S EXERTIONS IN HIS FAVOUR—MASSON'S CORRESPONDENCE WITH WADE—BURNES'S MISSION TO CABUL—DOST MAHOMED'S ATTACK ON JUMROOD, AND PARTIAL SUCCESS AGAINST THE SIKHS—MISSION OF VICOVICH TO CABUL—FAILURE OF BURNES'S NEGOTIATION.

THE British rule in India would be more beneficial were it not accompanied by such rapid changes of men, policy, and system, that all confidence in the permanence of its measures has been destroyed. The evil is great; and not less baneful in the internal administration, of which it forms to the native community the characteristic feature, than in the external relations of our Government with foreign States. It has been shown that Lord William Bentinck carried even to excess the principle of non-interference, and left India in profound peace. Passing over the short interregnum which elapsed before Lord Auckland became Governor-General, the departure from the principle of non-interference and the headlong plunge into a line of policy directly opposed to it, which have rendered this nobleman's career in India for ever remarkable, must here be traced. It was one of those sudden transitions from one policy to another for which the British rule is noted, and it exemplified by its fruits the evils of the system.

After the defeat of Shah Shooja, and his return to Loodianah, he succeeded in softening Wade, who ill brooked the issue of the expedition, which had proved so contrary to his anticipations and prophecies. Wade was in correspondence with Masson, an antiquarian, long resident in the countries west of the Indus. Calm, unassuming, and sensible, Masson had won the respect of chiefs and people, who honoured the truthful simplicity of the man's character, and long had him in favourable remembrance. From this source accurate information was obtained of the events passing at Cabul throughout 1836 and the greater part of 1837. Masson's letters were forwarded to Wade, who, transmitted the information thus derived to Lord Auckland, accompanied by his own observations and deductions, always with a favourable leaning to Shah Shooja. The Governor-General evincing a lively jealousy with respect to the state of the countries to the west of the Indus, and no ordinary apprehension of Russia and Persia, the advocacy of Shah Shooja, steadily persevered in by Wade, gradually produced its intended effect. Nor was this, his object, interrupted by the arrival of Burnes to the west of the Attock. It is true that Masson had thenceforward to communicate with Burnes instead of Wade. But the correspondence, having to pass through Wade's hands, was always forwarded to the Governor-General with his opinions and surmises; and, there being no inconsiderable jealousy between the two men, Wade was ever inclined to frustrate rather than to adopt Burnes's views, which were favourable to Dost Mahomed.

If the Indian Government was unfortunate in the strong bias of its agent at Loodianah, it was still more so in the choice of Burnes for a mission to which importance was attached. A man of inordinate ambition but of average ability and shallow acquirements, sanguine in temperament and wanting in self-control, Burnes was not possessed of the qualifications essential to success. Lord Auckland and his advisers were misled by the reputation which Burnes's amusing but most inaccurate book of travels had obtained for its author, and thought to reward merit and secure popularity by selecting him for the duty. His mission was styled a commercial one to the countries bordering on the Indus, and comprised a variety of objects. Government itself, having no clear conception of what was attainable, gave vague, rambling directions, necessarily leaving much to the discretion of a mind the constitution and calibre of which needed the most definite instructions for its safe guidance. Burnes, aware of the apprehensions entertained by both the Home and Indian Governments respecting the Persian schemes of conquest, saw with eager aspirations that his commercial mission was in fact quickly assuming the functions of a political mission; and, his imagination being already inflamed by McNeill's despatches before he reached Cabul, he entered that city on September 20, 1837, quixotically prepared to find, and to combat, giants of Russian influence and Persian intrigues.

Dost Mahomed having failed, after his victory over

Shah Shooja at Candahar, to expel the Sikhs from Peshawur, was occupied in 1836 with the intrigues of his relatives and their partisans, emboldened as these were by the Ameer's want of success in his crusade, and by the position at Peshawur of his brother, Sultan Mahomed Khan, whom Runjeet Singh had found it convenient to re-establish there with a certain degree of power. The Sikh governor of Peshawur, Hari Singh, determined to command the mouth of the Khybur, occupied Jumrood, a small fort in the plain near the entrance of that pass. Dost Mahomed felt it important to reassure the tribes of the Khybur, and to check the measures adopted by the Sikhs for their intimidation. He therefore, in the early part of 1837, despatched a force, under his son Akbar Khan, to occupy the defiles. The Afghans, meeting with no opposition in the pass, advanced to Jumrood, and with their artillery commenced to batter its walls. The Sikh governor, moving out from Peshawur to the relief of his advanced post, attacked the Afghans, and, capturing fourteen of their guns, drove the besiegers from under the walls of Jumrood, and pursued them sharply into the broken ground at the entrance of the pass. Here, however, the Sikhs, who had in the ardour of pursuit become disordered, were met by a large body of horse, which was moving forward to share in the fight. Around them rallied many fugitives, and the whole coming briskly upon the Sikhs, who expected nothing less than such a vigorous renewal of the fight, pushed them back in confusion. The Sikh governor, Hari Singh, was mortally wounded in this affair, and his troops were for a time disheartened by the loss of a gallant leader; but being shortly reinforced, they compelled the Afghans to withdraw from the plains and to retire into and through the Khybur Pass. The tribes which held the defiles were nevertheless encouraged by the success of the Afghan arms at Jumrood, a success of course much exaggerated, but which enabled Dost Mahomed to effect the object he had in view, to curb Sikh aggression, to give heart to the Khybur tribes, and to increase his own reputation and strength at Cabul.

Burnes, when on his road to Cabul, had with characteristic indiscretion written letters to the Ameer Dost Mahomed, and to his son Akbar Khan, remonstrating against the renewal of hostilities with the Sikhs. Dost Mahomed did not comprehend the object of a purely commercial mission, and such an introductory step was ill-calculated to counteract his belief that Burnes's mission meant something more. The belief was of the nature of a hope, for he had not been elated by his partial success at Jumrood; and, understanding well his exact position both with regard to the Sikhs and to his own countrymen, he was well disposed to seize any opportunity of strengthening himself by an alliance with the powerful British Government. He had already sought the countenance of that Government in 1835, and had continued his exertions in 1836. He had now seen that the bare intimation of the wishes of the Governor-General was sufficient to curb Runjeet Singh's ambitious designs against Scinde. By a word the British Government had thwarted the eager cravings of the Sikh ruler for the acquisition of the treasures of

Hyderabad, and for a sea-board to the Sikh kingdom, objects within his grasp. It might with equal ease mediate in his own favour and strengthen his position by checking Sikh schemes of aggression to the westward of the Indus. He hailed, therefore, with a pleasure perhaps rather increased than damped by Burnes's mistimed remonstrance, the arrival of an agent of the Government from whose influence he had everything to hope, and the dread of whose support to Shah Shooja and the Sikhs had driven him and his brothers to court the alliance of Persia, a power upon whose friendship no reliance could be placed.

Meanwhile the loss of the Sikh governor and the sacrifices which the possession of Peshawur entailed, had not been without their effect on the mind of Runjeet Singh. To hold his late acquisition it was necessary to maintain a large body of troops to the west of the Attock. This force, averse to the particular service on which it was detached, far removed from his own control, and for a considerable portion of the year having its communications with Lahore completely cut off, was a source of constant anxiety to the Sikh ruler. It was often turbulent; its position was a dangerous one; and its cost was necessarily very great. These considerations had disposed Runjeet Singh, could he do so with honour, to assent to any arrangement which might relieve him of his troublesome conquest, without compromising his own position or strengthening his inveterate foes the Afghans. Could his sovereign rights be insured to him, and the subordinate government of Peshawur conferred upon some trustworthy person, able and willing to hold the country for the Sikhs, this object would be attained. In Dost Mahomed's hostile brother, Sultan Mahomed Khan, Runjeet Singh had precisely the man he required ; and accordingly, with a shrewd eye for his own real interests, he showed every disposition to carry the arrangement into effect at a word from the British Government. That word was not spoken, for the British Government, having curbed Runjeet Singh with regard to Scinde, pretended delicacy as to further dictation, being in reality far from sorry that occupation for a large portion of his force was found at a distance from the British frontier. Moreover, influenced by Wade's prejudices, the Governor-General was unwilling to do anything which could strengthen the Barukzye family, so hostile to Shah Shooja, and represented by Wade, who kept the Shah's cause steadily in view, as devoid of power and influence in Afghanistan, a country torn to pieces by their incessant discord.

Lord Auckland was, in fact, at this time wholly undecided what line of action to pursue in regard to the western powers. The Home Government had taken up the tone of alarm which McNeill fostered, and this had been hastily responded to by the Governor-General. Before, however, committing himself further, either by forming connections with the remote countries beyond the Indus, or by any other overt measure, he hesitated, and, having no sound general principle of policy for his guidance, but being afloat on a sea of conjecture, allowed the shaping of his future course to depend in great measure on the success of Burnes's mission.

Swayed by the vague apprehensions of a remote danger entertained by others rather than himself, Lord Auckland felt the difficulty of encountering the Russo-Persic phantoms; and, having no fixed views of his own, was wholly unable to furnish Burnes with definite instructions. Nominally commercial, the mission was in fact one of political discovery, and its real object was to sound the state of affairs in the countries to which it was deputed.

Burnes's ambition was, however, of too hot a flame for the cautious fulfilment of this duty; it would not admit of such mere pioneering in politics; and it impelled him to create importance for his mission and himself. Sanguine and credulous, never pausing to weigh events or information, and not gifted with a comprehensive mind, he was easily carried away by the alarm which McNeill and the Home Government rang; to chime in with it was to raise his *ambassade* to consideration; and he needed not the epistolary encouragement of a chairman of the Court of Directors, breathing war from his seat in Leadenhall Street, to render him an apt instrument for kindling the fears of others by his own, and for urging rash measures upon his Government.

If Wade's prejudices were enlisted in behalf of Shah Shooja, Burnes's were no less strong in favour of Dost Mahomed, whose acquaintance he had first formed when travelling in 1832. He based his hopes for counteracting Russian influence in Afghanistan, not upon the resuscitation of Afghan monarchy under Shah Shooja, but upon winning Dost Mahomed to British views and interests by strengthening his position at Cabul and affording him British countenance.

Wade and Burnes were, therefore, opposed to each other on all points but one, and that unfortunately was concurrence in the danger to be apprehended from the extension of Persian empire to the eastward, and from the associated advance of Russian power and intrigue in her train.

Dost Mahomed, a man whose shrewd sense and natural ability had been developed by constant collision with character of every hue and intrigue of every form, quickly fathomed the British envoy. He was disappointed to find Burnes unprovided with definite instructions; but as the goodwill and pliancy of the envoy were at once apparent, the Ameer, working upon these, entertained the hope, if Burnes had influence with his own Government, of drawing considerable advantage from the mission. Burnes's want of reserve early laid open to Dost Mahomed the importance attached to the Persian advance on Herat, and the consideration with which this event invested Afghanistan; and Dost Mahomed, conscious of the credulity of the agent, nourished hopes of being able through him to act upon the fears of the Anglo-Indian Government. He experienced no difficulty in moulding Burnes to his purpose. The commercial agent proved only too willing an instrument, and was easily induced to forward propositions to the Governor-General, principal amongst which was, without any previous attempt to ascertain Runjeet Singh's wishes, the cession of Peshawur to the Ameer, on the condition that one of his sons should reside as a hostage at Lahore. The chiefs of Candahar being at this time in correspondence with Persia, Dost Mahomed, to prove his sincerity, wrote at Burnes's request to dissuade them from the prosecution of the connection. Correspondence ensued, which ended in an inconsiderate offer from Burnes of three lachs of rupees to enable the Candahar chiefs to make head against Persia.

These negotiations were carried on with so little diplomatic caution that Runjeet Singh became aware of the nature of the communications from Cabul, and himself addressed a warning letter to Burnes, indicating Sultan Mahomed Khan as a faithful servant of the Maharaja, and Dost Mahomed as a person for whom he could entertain no feeling of confidence. This communication from Runjeet Singh was made in the same spirit in which he had, prior to Burnes's arrival in Afghanistan, consulted Wade regarding the terms of peace he should tender to Dost Mahomed. The answer of the Government had been that, if Runjeet Singh desired it, Burnes should be instructed to convey from him any reasonable proposition to the ruler of Cabul. But Wade, through whom the reply was made, hostile to any measure which could strengthen the Cabul chief, had found no difficulty in alarming Runjeet Singh, and in effectually deterring him from the endeavour to effect a reconciliation with Dost Mahomed. So anxious, however, was the Lahore ruler to be rid of Peshawur, that he was now again willing to have entered into arrangements for peace, provided that by the cession of that place to Sultan Mahomed Khan he could have avoided materially strengthening the Cabul chief, whom he had been taught to regard with jealous dread.

Burnes's conduct at Cabul was no less wanting in decorum, which in a Mussulman country is seldom departed from, than in diplomatic caution and reserve. His behaviour in this respect, coupled with his undignified bearing, speedily lost him the respect of the chiefs and people. Nor was their respect increased by Burnes's attitude upon the arrival of the Russian Cossack officer Vicovich, said to be the bearer of a letter from the Emperor of Russia—an event which cast the British agent into a state of ludicrous excitement and despondency. The Candahar chiefs, as well as Dost Mahomed and his advisers, were almost as much astonished and perplexed as the British agent by the apparition of Vicovich at Candahar and Cabul. At both places the credentials of the Russian were the subject of controversy and doubt, and at Cabul they were submitted to Burnes. Burnes at once pronounced them genuine, though entirely inexperienced in the official forms of Russian correspondence, and ignorant of everything which could have qualified him to express an opinion.[1]

[1] In the writer's private journal I find the following entry, under date January 31, 1839:—

'We called on Mr. Masson. He gave us a very amusing account of Burnes's rencontre with Captain Vicovich at Cabul. This Russian officer reached Cabul "with a pair of black kid gloves, a French translation of Burnes's travels, and a long Persian epistle, well powdered with gold leaf, purporting to be from the Emperor of Russia." The Afghans, of whom Mr. Masson speaks highly, laughed at this *soi-disant* envoy, and discredited him *in toto*. Had Burnes had the sense to laugh too, all would have gone well; but he took the thing seriously, lost head, and was himself the person who induced the Afghans to consider Captain Vicovich in the light of an accredited envoy.'

Leech, a young officer of Engineers, not deficient in talent, but inexperienced and wanting discretion, was now deputed by the envoy to Candahar. The object of his mission was vague: to watch events, gain information, and promote British influence. Leech, unfortunately, was not more decorous in his conduct at Candahar than his superior at Cabul. Being a younger man it was less surprising, but it was equally injurious; for it lost him the respect which even a subordinate representative of the Anglo-Indian Government should make it his study to obtain by the exercise of those qualities which seldom fail to command it.

It has been before observed that Burnes's despatches, passing through Wade's hands, were transmitted to their destination accompanied by the biassed comments of Shah Shooja's staunch advocate. This gave the latter the advantage of opposing, either by argument or by flat contradiction of facts, the views and opinions of Burnes, who on the contrary had no opportunity of retorting. Uncontradicted as Wade's communications were, they could not fail of having an effect unfavourable to Dost Mahomed's interests, for they were received at a time when repeated intimations that the chiefs of Cabul and Candahar were seeking alliance with Persia had indisposed the Indian Government, ignorant of the real nature of these advances, from placing confidence in the Barukzye family. The siege of Herat by the Shah of Persia, the correspondence of Russian authorities with Candahar, and the arrival of Vicovich at Cabul, still further disinclined the Governor-General from strengthening Dost Mahomed and consolidating his power—a measure which might give umbrage to Runjeet Singh, whose alliance assumed additional importance in proportion as the alarm of the Indian Government waxed greater. Wade, invalidating Burnes's opinions by plausible arguments and contradicting his facts by bold assertion, arrayed McNeill and Masson against him, and urged that 'Runjeet Singh would be brought with difficulty to acknowledge the elevation of Dost Mahomed Khan to the sovereignty of the Afghans, while, should the consolidation of that people become a measure of indispensable necessity to the establishment of security on the frontier of the Indus, the election of Shah Shooja, would only be in fulfilment of the compact which was formerly made with him, and would exact no new concessions.'

The suggestion was made at a right conjuncture; and the seed thus sown produced as its first-fruit a despatch from the Governor-General which disapproved of the propositions stipulating the cession of Peshawur to Dost Mahomed, and ordered that the offer of three lachs of rupees to the Candahar chief should be rescinded. The despatch was accompanied by a letter to Dost Mahomed, urging him to effect a reconciliation with Runjeet Singh; to relinquish the idea of recovering Peshawur, as a hope which could not be realised; to repose confidence in the good offices of the Indian Government; and not to seek connection with other powers without the approbation of the Governor-General, on pain of the discontinuance of that favourable influence for the exertion of which Government claimed the merit of having induced Runjeet Singh to cease from his schemes of conquest in Afghanistan, and also on pain of the withdrawal of the mission.

Dost Mahomed was not only disappointed at the result of Burnes's sanguine expectations, but hurt and displeased by the tone of Lord Auckland's letter. The Ameer well knew the progress of Runjeet Singh's arms to the westward had only been checked by the dread which the Sikhs entertained of the Khybur defiles, and their ruler's mistrust of his own power to subdue the Afghans. He regarded, therefore, as an insulting presumption of his ignorance the weight ascribed to British intervention. Aware of the treaty framed, with the cognisance of the British Government, between Shah Shooja and Runjeet Singh, on which the latter professed to hold Peshawur, he could only esteem the threat of an interruption of good offices as practically pointing to a direct or indirect sanction to the renewal of such operations as had been in 1834 frustrated by his own energy and the pusillanimous timidity of Shah Shooja at Candahar. He had no confidence either in Persia or Russia. The designs of the former he dreaded; of the latter, except in name, he was ignorant; and the presence of her agent, Vicovich, though Burnes had pronounced his credentials genuine, the Ameer himself held of small moment. But seeing that great importance was attached to the fact by the British agent, and that the Governor-General, alarmed by events at Herat, was seeking to establish British influence in Afghanistan, Dost Mahomed determined not to further this policy by entering into obligations which would isolate him from foreign connections, unless indeed some more palpable equivalent were in return made to him than general expressions of goodwill.

The conduct of the mission, official and private, had sunk it into contempt, and the irascible vanity of Burnes — wounded by the proceedings of his own Government, by the countenance now given to Vicovich at Cabul, and by the neglect shown to himself—impelled him to a line of conduct hasty and injudicious, and which, wanting in truth, composure, and dignity, exasperated the Ameer. Negotiation, after some fruitless attempts for its renewal by the wiser part of Dost Mahomed's advisers, was broken off, and, finally, on April 26, 1838, Burnes quitted Cabul.

Thus terminated a mission which, entrusted to wiser and better men, might have had very different results. In the absence of definite instructions, much was left to the discretion of its leader; and therefore the entire failure of a futile commercial mission, metamorphosed into a political mission of discovery and vague negotiation, must not altogether be attributed to the instrument selected. At the root lay the original error of a vacillating Government, having no clear settled line of policy or principle for its guidance, and therefore unable to furnish its agents with that which was a desideratum to itself. In pronouncing judgment upon Burnes's unfortunate negotiations, the fact must be borne in mind that he was deputed at a time when Lord Auckland professed to adopt a line of policy entirely the reverse of that which he ultimately pursued. On April 10, 1837, the Governor-General wrote 'that the circumstance of the British Government having resolved decidedly to discourage the prosecution by the ex-King, Shah Shooja-ool-Moolk, so long as he may remain under our protection, of further schemes of hostility against the chiefs now in power in Cabul and Candahar,' might be found on the part of Burnes a means useful in the establishment of British influence. The enunciation of such a resolution could not, in the absence of detailed instructions, but serve as a key to the views of the Government in the course they wished pursued in Afghanistan; and a more judicious and cautious diplomatist than Burnes, left entirely to his own discretion, might, acting upon the assumption of a moderate degree of stability in the decisions of a Governor-General, have partially compromised himself before he could learn how short a time sufficed for an entire change of opinions, views, and policy.

CHAPTER IV.

NOVEMBER 1837–SEPTEMBER 1838.

SIEGE OF HERAT BY THE PERSIANS—POTTINGER—MCNEILL'S NEGOTIATIONS WITH THE SHAH—HIS VIEWS REGARDING PERSIAN DESIGNS UPON AFGHANISTAN—VALUE OF HERAT TO PERSIA.

HAVING briefly traced the conduct and failure of a mission from which Lord Auckland anticipated, in April 1837, no further result than 'the collection of accurate information, the extension of commercial intercourse, and the conciliation of friendly sentiments,' the progress of events which were contemporaneously taking place in Khorassan must now be followed. The Shah of Persia, having mustered his army, which was estimated at 10,000 infantry, 2,000 cavalry, and thirty guns, marched to the frontier, and besieged Ghorian, a fortress about forty miles from Herat. The place was treacherously surrendered to the Shah on November 15, 1837, after a siege of ten days; and he then advanced to and commenced the siege of Herat.

The Russian envoy evinced great joy at the capture of Ghorian; but he remained at Teheran, not wishing by his presence in the Shah's camp to appear to take a more active part in the military operations which his Government pretended to discountenance. The British envoy abstained from accompanying the Shah, in order to mark the disapprobation with which the advance of the army was viewed by his own Government. Both envoys, however, had subordinates in attendance on the besieging army to watch the progress of events and to further the views and interests of their respective Governments.

An officer of the Bombay army, Lieutenant Pottinger, having obtained permission to be absent from his military duties for the space of a year, had, from a spirit of curiosity and enterprise, been travelling in the countries to the west of the Indus. Leaving Cabul in July 1837, he found his way in disguise to Herat. He had been there a short time when the news of the Persian advance reached him. The conditions of his leave of absence made Pottinger desirous to avoid being shut up in a besieged place; but he found it impossible to do so, partly in consequence of severe sickness, and partly on account of the disturbed state of the neighbouring country. Moreover, the Herat authorities desired to retain a British officer in the city, thinking to derive advantage from his presence, as a token of the countenance of the British Government. Once in communication with McNeill, however, Pottinger was soon at ease with regard to breach of military rules: and his love of enterprise, no longer running counter to the sense of duty, found accidentally a promising field.

The medium of communication between the two British officers was a horseman whom McNeill despatched with the Herat envoy, when the latter, having failed in his mission, was dismissed by the Shah of Persia. This messenger was stopped by the Russian agent, Borowski, when passing through the Shah's advancing army, and Pottinger's letter was for a time taken from him. It was not read, but it created much suspicion, exasperated the Shah, and enabled the Russian mission to assert the presence of a British officer, bearing no accredited political functions, among the besieged.

The Shah, on his arrival before Herat, did not feel himself strong enough to invest the place effectually. Three of its five gates were kept open by the besieged, who drove out their cattle daily to graze, and maintained an uninterrupted intercourse with the surrounding country. The siege, conducted with little skill and small energy, made slow progress; whilst the Heratees, confident in their own courage and defences, showed little respect for their adversaries. They made nightly sorties, inflicting loss upon the working parties and guards, and capturing guns, which they capsized into their own ditch. Occasionally their attacks were extended to the foraging parties of the enemy, which suffered considerably from the alertness of the Afghans. The Persians, however, showed themselves capable of enduring hardship and privations; and the season proving a mild one, the Shah, though he lost many of his irregulars by desertion, was enabled to hold on in his dilatory siege operations. But his supply of ammunition, originally insufficient, was quickly expended; and additional supplies arriving slowly, at considerable intervals of time, and never in large quantity, the firing was renewed after long periods of rest, during which the Afghans had abundance of time to repair whatever damage an ill-directed fire of short duration might have caused to their defences. The system thus pursued by the Persians, of expending in a day or two their store of shot, and then having to wait a month before they could again open their guns upon the place, was quaintly spoken of by Pottinger as doing just enough mischief to point out where repairs were requisite. The mining operations were not better managed; indeed, they were so conducted as to render doubtful the wish of the besiegers that they should be effective. Certain it is that the battalion of Russian deserters which formed part of the Shah's army did not appear much in earnest at their attack, but contented themselves with proving to the Afghans, whenever a sortie from the place attempted to assault their posts, that this could not be done with impunity. A considerable number of the men were Poles, who, though not of a temper to suffer disgrace by hasty turning from Afghan scimitars, yet had no very goodwill for the cause in which they were engaged, and seemed, so far as consistent with their fidelity as mercenaries in the pay of Persia, to be but little indisposed towards the Heratees. Perhaps the fact that the price of provisions in the besieged place was one-fourth that of provisions in the camp, conveys in fewest words a correct idea of the real character of this siege, in which the besieging army required strong escorts for its foraging parties and for its convoys of stores and ammunition, and yet repeatedly had the mortification of losing its caravans, and of having its foraging parties driven in with loss.

Owing to the protracted nature of the siege and the exhaustion of the surrounding country, the supplies of food for the Persian army became very precarious, and rendered it hopeless to think of gaining the fortress by a blockade, which would have brought more suffering on the besiegers than even their patient endurance could be relied upon to sustain. At the same time the gallantry and confidence of the defenders held out no promise of an easy capture, should the endeavour be made to storm works, in which no breach had been effected. Affairs were in this state, after the siege had continued for four months, when McNeill received an intimation from Leech at Candahar, which led him to conclude that the Governor-General of India had written, directing him to attempt to withdraw the Shah from Herat by treaty or otherwise; the preservation of the integrity of that place being considered of vital importance. In consequence of the receipt of this intelligence from Leech, McNeill determined, without awaiting Lord Auckland's instructions, to proceed to the Shah's camp, and to endeavour by every means in his power to induce the Shah to come to terms with the ruler of Herat. Colonel Stoddart, the subordinate placed in the Shah's camp by McNeill, first received Leech's communication; with singular indiscretion he at once divulged it to the Shah; and by this premature step put the Shah and the Russian agents on their guard. Lord Palmerston being made acquainted with the intentions of the British envoy, wrote on May 21, 1838, in approval of the step. He authorised McNeill to state explicitly to the Shah that the British Government looked upon his enterprise as undertaken in a spirit of hostility towards British India, and incompatible with the spirit and intention of the treaty with Persia; and that consequently perseverance in the Shah's military operations against Herat would cause Great Britain to consider friendly relations at an end, and to take steps for the security of the possessions of the British Crown.

McNeill, upon his arrival in the camp, was coldly received, for the Shah had endeavoured to stop him at Ghorian, urging that his presence at Herat could not fail to encourage the besieged. The British envoy found that the tardy and frequently interrupted siege operations had been diversified by repeated attempts at negotiation, which, as the Shah was not inclined to moderate his pretensions or demands, had always failed. In another quarter Persian intrigue seemed successful; for McNeill, in constant correspondence with Burnes and Leech, heard from the former of the progress of Vicovich at Cabul, and from the latter of a treaty between the chiefs of Candahar and the Shah of Persia, the draft of which had been accepted by the chiefs. If McNeill's despatches had in 1837 unduly disturbed Burnes's excitable mind, Burnes's letters now exerted a corresponding effect upon McNeill, and seem to have cast him into a fever of apprehension for the consequences of the fall of Herat—an event which from the state of affairs he could not but perceive to be improbable, and which he so reported both to Lord Palmerston and Lord Auckland at the self-same time that he dwelt on the imminent peril with which India was threatened by the siege, and informed the Shah that if the attempt were not abandoned, the British Government would be obliged in self-defence to remove the Persian army by force. Some of Burnes's private communications were intercepted by the Shah. The importance attached to the siege of Herat by the Indian Government and its functionaries, and the failure of the British missions at Cabul and Candahar, were thus divulged in all the colouring of Burnes's heated fancy, and acted as a spur to the Shah's perseverance in the enterprise on which he had embarked.

Both Lord Palmerston and Lord Auckland approved the views of McNeill. Lord Palmerston, on July 27, 1838, instructed the British envoy to state to the Shah that as he had thought fit to enter upon a course of proceeding wholly at variance with the spirit and intent of the treaty with Great Britain, the latter felt herself at liberty to adopt, without reference to that treaty, such measures as a due regard for her own interests, and the security of her dominions, might suggest. Lord Auckland, receiving about the same time the news of the failure of Burnes's mission at Cabul, and of McNeill's ungracious reception in the camp before Herat, prepared to carry McNeill's threats into effect; and the Bombay Government was ordered to make a demonstration in the Persian Gulf by the despatch of troops and cruisers to the Island of Karrak, whilst the Governor-General at the same time turned his attention to the re-establishment, by force, of British influence in Afghanistan.

The British envoy having allayed the animosity which his unwelcome arrival had produced, commenced after a few days to urge measures which might lead to an accommodation. On April 19 he entered the besieged town, with the consent of the Shah, for the purpose of mediating a treaty, and was engaged during that night in settling with the Herat minister the draft of an agreement, which, conceding more than was reasonable, and all that the Shah demanded, preserved the independence of Herat. McNeill had not, however, left the town on the morning of the 20th, when he heard of the arrival of the Russian envoy in the Shah's camp. That functionary had hastened to follow the British envoy, and arrived in time to frustrate his negotiations when apparently on the eve of a favourable termination. Thenceforward the Shah, instead of evincing any inclination to accept the terms he had last dictated, renewed his demand for the acknowledgment of his sovereignty, and, aided by the advice of Count Simonich and the exertions of the officers of the envoy's suite, prosecuted the siege with renewed vigour and more skill. The Russian furnished money to the Shah, and enabled the latter to encourage his dispirited troops by the payment of a portion of their dues and by the prospect, under more soldierly management, of a speedy conclusion to their labours and dangers. On the other hand, the Heratees were nothing daunted by the failure of the negotiations. Making a sortie in force they took, and kept for two days, a Persian trench; swept into the town a hundred horses of the enemy; and, by sending out of the place about two thousand persons not needed for the defence, diminished the consumption of food and the risk of a successful blockade. Whatever hopes the Shah of Persia may have entertained from the arrival of emissaries announcing that aid was about to be despatched from Candahar, and that no apprehensions need be had of a hostile movement from Cabul, the Heratees knew better both the power and circumstances of the Barukzai chiefs than to care for such reports; and whilst the Persians were flattering themselves with rumours of division and discord amongst the besieged, the latter, sallying out sword in hand, dashed boldly into the enemy's trenches, stormed his batteries, and succeeded in carrying off a couple of guns.

The Shah, thus insulted, was forced to wait the arrival of ammunition. In the meantime he occupied himself in constructing additional batteries, under the direction of Russian officers, and in amusing the British envoy with a show of readiness to comply with the demands of England. He professed himself willing to conclude a treaty with Herat, provided he were enabled to relinquish his enterprise with honour, by means of an explicit threat of hostility on the part of the British Government. The Shah had no intention of acting as he promised, and the request was an instance of Eastern finesse, having no other object but to gain time and to draw any advantage which by accident might accrue from the re-opening of discussion and diplomatic notes. McNeill's threat, conveyed in the terms subsequently authorised by Lord Palmerston's instructions, produced, therefore, on the part of the Shah, instead of a treaty with Herat, a long paper containing a series of complaints and accusations against the British Government, and maintaining the right of Persia to inflict punishment on the Heratees for their acts of rapine and plunder against Persian subjects. A quantity of diplomatic notes were hereupon exchanged; but the British envoy, weary of his hopeless undertaking, and sensible that his further stay was fruitless and derogatory to the dignity of his Government, at length quitted the Persian camp on June 7, 1838, completely foiled in his endeavours to induce the Shah to discontinue his military operations.

The crops now ripening, provisions became more abundant in the Shah's camp, and reinforcements from Tabreez and Azarbijan began to reach him in small numbers both of horse and foot. But the Heratees, neither dispirited nor failing in their alertness, continued to harass the besiegers; and the Hazarah and Jemsheedee tribes, taking the opportunity which Persian negligence offered them, swept from the plains into their own hills a number of horses, mules, and attendants, belonging to the Persian camp.

The Shah, through Burnes's despatches to McNeill, was thoroughly conversant with the state of British influence in Afghanistan. Encouraged by the alarm displayed, and by the importance which the Indian Government and its agents attached to Herat, he scarcely needed the urgent advice of Count Simonich to fortify him in his resolution; and the supplies of ammunition having at length reached in some quantity, and the batteries erected under Russian supervision being completed, the Persian artillery reopened its fire. After six days of continuous battering, a grand assault, planned and arranged by the Russian envoy, was made on June 23. It failed of success. The Persian troops were at one time in possession of the rampart, and were in the act of bringing up gabions to form a lodgment and secure the standing they had gained in the body of the place; but by one of those strange events with which war is chequered, and which mock the calculations of far more skilful leaders than those who directed the Persian assault, this temporary advantage was suddenly thrown away. A body of Afghans, driven by the Persian attack from another part of the defences, came rushing in their flight along the Shirazee, or lower line of work, which skirted the main rampart; and the Persians, engaged in forming their lodgment on the upper line of works, stricken with panic at what appeared the charge of their foes to cut off their retreat, deserted their lodgment and fled hastily from the position they had won. The assault was ultimately repulsed with heavy loss, although the endeavours of the besiegers were, if not very gallant, yet repeated. Many officers of rank were killed and wounded, amongst the former Major-General Borowski, of the Russian service; and the Shah, dispirited by the failure of an attack for the success of which the greatest exertions had been made, now relinquished the hope of capturing the place, and turned his attention to withdrawing his troops, artillery, and stores from a position which would have been by no means satisfactory had the Heratees pursued with the same degree of energy and courage as they had shown in defending their town.

The strength of the place, the resolution of the

besiegers, the skill of the Russian military advisers, and the gallantry of the besieged, were severally subjects of much exaggeration. The siege was, from first to last, thoroughly ill-conducted; and the defence, in reality not better managed, owed its *éclat* to Persian ignorance, timidity, and supineness. Pottinger's advice was seldom asked, and still more seldom taken, by the defenders, who viewed his presence as a political rather than a military advantage; and no one spoke more impartially or plainly of the conduct of both besiegers and besieged than did Pottinger himself.[1]

In fact, any advantage which may be supposed to have resulted from the presence of Pottinger at Herat, was more than counterbalanced by the exasperation which it provoked in the Shah against the British envoy, and by the justification it afforded for the active aid rendered to the besiegers by Count Simonich and the Russian officers of his staff. But if the presence of Pottinger was of questionable utility, there can be

[1] The British envoy's accounts of the siege are perplexing. The Shah's army is stated when mustered to have been about 10,000 infantry, 2,000 cavalry, and thirty guns (September 28, 1837). Subsequently, that is after the siege had continued three months, it is stated at 40,000 men and eighty guns (February 23, 1838). At this time Persian casualties are estimated to have been thirty men daily, which in three months would amount to 2,700 men, exclusive of desertions, and if, as afterwards mentioned (April 11, 1838), the loss continued to average from ten to twenty men daily, taking the mean of McNeill's number, for the daily loss, the ten months' siege would appear to have cost the Shah about 6,000 men. It admits of little doubt that had the Persian army been 40,000 strong the place would have been better invested and the relative positions of besiegers and besieged far different from what they were; but the Shah could not have fed and kept together that number of men. The first estimate of the strength of the besieging force appears on every ground the most accurate, and the loss sustained may with safety be reduced to about one sixth.

no doubt that McNeill's arrival in the camp before Herat was of essential dis-service to the cause espoused by the British Government; for the step rendered the presence of Count Simonich in camp not only defensible but necessary, and enabled him, at a most important period of the siege, to encourage its energetic prosecution, and to advise and ultimately arrange an assault which only failed of success through an unforeseen accident—one of those accidents beyond the control of man, by which, in derision of his best efforts, the results of war are often determined. The Shah was never in earnest in his negotiations with the Heratees, whether such were mediated by NcNeill or by others. They merely served as a diversion to both parties during the intervals when the besiegers were awaiting ammunition and stores, and afforded the opportunity to renew intrigues in camp and city from which either side hoped to derive advantage. Gross indignity to the British envoy, complete failure of his object, increased energy in the siege operations, and enhanced danger to the besieged, were the fruits of McNeill's visit to Herat, which was a measure both unnecessary and injudicious.

As the British envoy's opinions relative to the treaty were not only approved but acted upon both by the British and the Indian Governments, the soundness of these views merits examination. They were based on the assumptions that Afghanistan was at the time our frontier; that the capture of Herat by Persia involved imminent peril to the security and internal tranquillity of our Indian Empire; and that Persia, in prosecuting the siege of that place had, acting in concert with Russia, entered upon a course of proceeding, avowedly unfriendly, if not absolutely hostile, to British interests and at variance with the spirit and intent of the definitive treaty.

If the assumptions be conceded that Afghanistan was our frontier, and that the integrity of Herat was of vital importance to the British power in India—the fall of that place to the Shah being equivalent to its becoming a Russian parallel of attack against India—few casuists would deny that England was justified in taking measures of active defence without reference to the prohibition contained in the ninth article of the treaty; for the spirit and purpose of that treaty, as prescribed in the first article, was in direct opposition to the line of policy pursued by Persia, acting, under the foregoing supposition, in subordination to the control and influence of Russia. The prohibition contained in the ninth article, and the promise by England to observe it, were evidently relative to a state of affairs in which Persia was understood to hold an entirely different position from that which, under Russian dictation and supremacy, the present argument supposes her to have held, when she claimed the validity of the specification which precluded England from interfering in wars between the Afghans and Persians. The independence of Persia from foreign European control was undoubtedly a tacit consideration which not only originated the general object of the treaty as specified in the first article, but also the promise made in the ninth article; and the fulfilment of the main purpose of the treaty as well as of the minor promise were already conditional on the preservation by Persia of her independence. That condition lost, England could no longer be bound by an engagement founded on its existence.

Afghanistan, however, so far from being our frontier, was not even in contact with British India; but was separated from our possessions by the countries on the Indus, namely, the Punjab, Bhawulpore, and Scinde, and by the tract of desert which, comprising Bikaneer, Jessulmeer, and Jodhpore, was in itself alone no bad frontier, and far removed from the highlands of Afghanistan.

The exaggerated fears of Russian power and intrigue entertained by Ellis, McNeill, Burnes, and Wade, the flame of which was communicated by them to the British and Indian Governments, invested Herat with a fictitious importance wholly incommensurate with the strength of the place and its position in regard to Candahar and the Indus. To speak of the integrity of the place as of vital importance to British India was a hyperbole so insulting to common sense as scarcely to need refutation, and which ignorance of the countries west of the Indus, and inexperience of military operations in the East, could alone palliate. An excursive imagination might deem it of possible importance at some remote future, but it required the hallucinations of chimerical alarm to render it an object of vital solicitude.

Although Russian influence might predominate at Teheran, Persia could not with propriety be regarded by England as so completely under the guidance and protection of the Czar as absolutely to alter the state of affairs and the conditions under which the engagement to fulfil the terms of the ninth article was incurred. Since 1828, when England freed herself from the embarrassment of the third and fourth articles of the treaty, Russian influence at the Court of Teheran had on the whole increased, but not to that degree that Persia was to be regarded as having annulled all alliances with England or any other foreign power which hinged on her existence as an independent State. She had been humbled, but not conquered by Russia, and therefore she had a right to expect that the faith of treaties should be observed with her, and that England should not, upon groundless assumptions, conclude herself authorised to act in contravention of the clear and precise terms of an article to which she had on two several occasions promised to adhere. The punishment of Herat for its infractions of a convention with Persia could not legitimately be construed into a hostile breach of the definitive treaty. It might be unpalatable to England, but the latter had solemnly consented to neutrality in case of war arising between the Persians and Afghans; and she was bound, without cavil or chicanery, to observe scrupulous non-interference even at the hazard of a less remote danger than was the possible capture of Herat. It is a national misfortune when the interpretation of treaties becomes dependent on the vague apprehensions of statesmen, to whom it costs but a figure of speech to advance their frontier ten or twelve degrees of longitude, in order there to seek and combat a chimerical danger and to involve the intermediate countries in a long series of desolating wars. No dispassionate judgment can approve the morbid sensitiveness of a policy which in its endeavours to ward off a hypothetical and remote peril can coldly overlook the mass of immediate suffering, evil, and injustice which its measures must produce.

Almost simultaneously with the final assault on Herat was the occupation of the Island of Karrak by the British troops despatched from Bombay. McNeill having received intimation of this event, and also the instructions of Lord Palmerston for his guidance, despatched Colonel Stoddart to the Shah with a written message founded on the communication of the British minister, and explicitly stating that perseverance in the siege would interrupt the friendly relations between Persia and Great Britain and cause the latter to take such steps as she might think best calculated to provide for the security of the possessions of the British Crown. This was accompanied by an announcement of the occupation of Karrak and a demand for reparation on account of insults to the British mission. The message found the Shah disheartened by his late failure and already engaged in making preparations for breaking up the siege and retreating within his own frontiers. The demonstration in the Persian Gulf was much exaggerated by public rumours, and was a source of uneasiness to the Shah, rendering his return to Teheran doubly advisable. He therefore acceded to such of the requests of the British envoy as were in unison with his predetermined retirement from Herat; and all things being arranged for the rapid retreat of the Persian army, the camp broke up on September 9, and returned by rapid marches, unharassed by the enemy, within the frontiers of Persia, leaving garrisons, however, in Ghorian, Furrah, Subzar, and Khoorookh. When it is considered that the Shah calculated upon occupying sixty days on his return to Teheran, and that it was held by military men that if the distance were completed in seventy-five days the troops would have marched very well, a definite conception of the real value to Persia of Herat as a possession may be obtained. The army, when advancing on Herat, had, however, taken a longer time ; the Shah quitted Teheran on July 23, and only reached Ghorian in the beginning of November, being upwards of three months *en route*. Fortresses so much in advance of the main territories and strength of a country as are Ghorian and Herat, with respect to Persia, add neither to the offensive nor defensive powers of a State, but compromise a certain portion of its strength in men and means by isolating them at a vast distance from support in the midst of a hostile country.

CHAPTER V.

JUNE—OCTOBER, 1838.

LORD AUCKLAND RESOLVES TO RESTORE SHAH SHOOJA—THE TRIPARTITE TREATY — MACNAGHTEN APPOINTED ENVOY — RECEPTION OF THE TREATY BY THE AMEERS OF SCINDE—ORGANISATION OF A FORCE FOR THE INVASION OF AFGHANISTAN—PROCLAMATION OF OCTOBER 1, 1838.

SIMULTANEOUSLY with the despatch of instructions for the demonstration in the Persian Gulf by the occupation of the Island of Karrak, Lord Auckland, contemplating the subversion of the authority of the Candahar and Cabul chiefs, and the re-establishment in Afghanistan of some power friendly to British influence, had resolved upon entering into negotiations with Runjeet Singh for this purpose.

With great reason the Governor-General was at this time averse from engaging the Anglo-Indian army in support of such a policy; and his inclinations leaned to casting on Runjeet Singh and the Sikh army the enterprise of conquering Cabul, and of thus raising a friendly barrier to Russo-Persian influence and territorial acquisition. Wade's suggestions and insinuations presented Shah Shooja as more available for the furtherance of the Governor-General's views; and pointed to the treaty of 1833 between the ex-king and Runjeet

Singh as a precedent which admitted of being converted into a pretext for the renewal of analogous measures in subservience to British interests. Undecided as to the course to be pursued, Lord Auckland sent Mr. Macnaghten in May 1838 on a mission to Lahore, to discuss and arrange with the Sikh ruler the manner in which, with his consent, the desired measure could be best effected. Macnaghten was accustomed to give weight to Wade's views, and finding on consultation with Burnes and Masson that both disapproved of the attempt to establish a Sikh government as supreme in Afghanistan, while Masson coincided with Wade in preferring Shah Shooja as an instrument for overturning Dost Mahomed and his brothers, the latter expedient was deemed the best, and was finally adopted by the Governor-General. At first, however, there was on Lord Auckland's part no intention of plunging the Indian Government into the expenses and hazards of a trans-Indus war; cold, cautious, and reflecting, but infirm of purpose, it was by gradual steps that he unfortunately suffered the alarms, real or pretended, of others, and their importunities, ultimately to prevail over his own judgment. The plan first contemplated was that Shah Shooja, aided by British officers and funds, and by the hearty co-operation of Runjeet Singh, should achieve the recovery of his throne without the appearance of British bayonets in his train; but Burnes, who had been summoned by Macnaghten to Lahore, was resolute in urging as a necessity that English troops must accompany the Shah, and argued that if only a regiment or two were sent, their presence would be a source of great strength and security, and insure success. This opinion was adopted, but Sir H. Fane, the Commander-in-Chief of the army, objected, upon military grounds, to risking so small a detachment of troops upon a distant and hazardous expedition; the more particularly as the enterprise had, as an object co-ordinate with the establishment of Shah Shooja, the relief of Herat, or its recapture from the Persian army, according as circumstances might demand. Under the supposition that the presence of British troops was essential, the arguments by which Fane deprecated the impolicy of risking disgrace to the British arms and colours, by isolating a small body of men amongst open foes and very doubtful friends in distant countries, were unexceptionable; and Lord Auckland, unable with good grace or consistency to forego the line of policy upon which he had already embarked, and eagerly pressed by those around him to persevere, determined to assemble and move a British army into Afghanistan in support of his views and measures.

The operations ultimately resolved upon were in accordance with the counsels which had been pertinaciously, though for long cautiously, pressed upon the Government by Wade. Not only was the treaty of 1833 between Runjeet Singh and Shah Shooja made the basis of the tripartite treaty now entered into by those potentates and the Anglo-Indian Government, but the same system of invading Afghanistan by double line of operations, the one by Peshawur on Cabul, and the other by Shikarpore on Candahar, was adopted. Wade had thus the satisfaction of seeing his schemes in favour of Shah Shooja in the end completely triumphant, and there only remained to fill up the measure of his success that the carrying into execution his own plans should be entrusted to him as envoy with the Shah. In this, however, he was disappointed, as also his rival Burnes, for as Fane was to command the army, Mr. Macnaghten's proposal of himself for envoy met with the acceptance of the Governor-General, who felt that if the superior political functions were to be separated from the military command, a person of higher rank and official situation than either Captain Wade or Captain Burnes must, out of courtesy, be placed in control of the Commander-in-Chief, Sir Henry Fane. The selection was unhappy, for Macnaghten, long accustomed to irresponsible office, inexperienced in men, and ignorant of the country and people of Afghanistan, was, though an erudite Arabic scholar, neither practised in the field of Asiatic intrigue nor a man of action. His ambition was, however, great, and the expedition, holding out the promise of distinction and honours, had met with his strenuous advocacy.

The tripartite treaty negotiated by Macnaghten, and concluded on June 26, 1838, was remarkable, amongst other of its stipulations, for the consideration shown to our allies the Ameers of Scinde. The Anglo-Indian Government had previously formed engagements with these princes as independent rulers of the countries in their possession. In 1834 when Shah Shooja invaded their territories, Lord W. Bentinck, although he failed to discountenance the expedition, which it lay in his power to stop by a word of remonstrance, was yet careful to observe and to enjoin a strict neutrality; and instructed the British agents on the Sutlej and Indus to do their utmost to remove the impression, should it anywhere exist, that the British Government was connected with the plans of Shah Shooja or otherwise than entirely indifferent to his movements. The fourth article of the treaty entered into between Runjeet Singh and the Shah had implied by its terms the cognisance of the Anglo-Indian Government, and rendered its agent, Wade, the elected mediator in respect to Scinde. It ran as follows:—'Regarding Shikarpore and the territory of Scinde lying on the right bank of the Indus, the Shah agrees to abide by whatever may be settled as right and proper, in conformity with the happy relations of friendship subsisting between the British Government and the Maharajah through Captain Wade.' This unauthorised use of the name of the British Government having been pointed out, the necessary precautions were taken to prevent the clause creating misapprehension or alarm, and to deny any participation in the treaty on the side of the Governor-General of India. Subsequently, in 1836, when Runjeet Singh captured Roghan, the chief town of the Mazarees, a tribe on the right bank of the Indus, and nominally dependent upon the Ameers; carried by assault a fort in the neighbourhood of Shikarpore, garrisoned by their troops; and, collecting forces, had made all necessary preparations for a regular campaign against them; Lord Auckland, deeming the opportunity favourable for establishing British influence in Scinde upon a solid basis, interposed to deter the Sikh ruler from advancing against Shikarpore, and from any hostile intentions which he entertained 'towards the territories of the Ameers of Scinde.' The Commander-in-Chief in Bengal was warned of the possibility of hostilities with the Sikh ruler, and the Bombay Government was directed to have troops in readiness to move into Scinde, on the requisition of the resident, Pottinger, should armed interference become necessary, from the Ameer accepting the offered protection of the British Government against Runjeet Singh's threatened invasion. Runjeet Singh chafed at the curb put upon his schemes of aggrandisement and extension of territory, but wisely yielded to the friendly remonstrance, and withdrew his troops from the frontier, being on every account desirous not to afford the British power an excuse for placing a military cantonment in Scinde. The Ameers were equally unwilling to admit armed intervention or the residence of a British agent at their court, but were ready to accede to the proposal, that an officer on the part of the British Government should reside at Shikarpore, and be the medium of communication between the Governments of Hyderabad and Lahore. Negotiations, however, continued throughout 1837, and in April 1838 a treaty was concluded with some, not all, of the Ameers of Scinde, by which it was agreed that an accredited British minister should reside at the court of Hyderabad. After such a termination to this series of negotiations the Ameers were naturally surprised to receive, in September 1838, from the British resident, as a first-fruit of his office, the following communication of the wishes and intentions of Lord Auckland :

'Their Highnesses have, of course, long heard of the unsettled state of Khorassan and Afghanistan; and, in the opinion of the Governor-General, a crisis has now arrived in those countries which imperiously demands the interference of the British Government, both with regard to the settlement and well-being of the countries in question, and also for the tranquillity and security of Hindustan and the States adjoining it.

'His Lordship is further of opinion that it is now necessary that the real friends of the British Government should unequivocally stand forward to evince their friendly feelings by assisting in the measures which the Governor-General may consider requisite to frustrate and render null the combination which the governments to the westward of India are known to have formed, with the object of disturbing and injuring the possessions of the British Government, and with them those of its allies and tributaries.

'A treaty was made about five years ago between his Majesty Shah Shooja-ool-Moolk and the Maharajah Runjeet Singh, consisting of fourteen articles. In the fourth article of that treaty it was written:—

'"Regarding Shikarpore and the territory of Scinde lying on the right bank of the Indus, the Shah will agree to abide by whatever may be settled as right and proper, in conformity with the happy relations of friendship subsisting between the British Government and the Maharajah, through Captain Wade."

'The said treaty was not, for certain reasons, acted on at the time it was first written, but at present it has been resolved to bring it into execution; and the

Governor-General of India has agreed to become a party to it, with the addition of four articles. One of these articles provides for Maharajah Runjeet Singh receiving annually two lacs of rupees from the Shah, in consideration of which his Highness is always to keep 5,000 Mussulman troops ready at Peshawur for the king's service when required. Another article stipulates that when Shah Shooja-ool-Moolk shall have established his authority over Cabul, &c., his Majesty is not to make any demands upon or to molest Kamran Shah of Herat. A third article provides for the Shah entering into no negotiations or treaties with any foreign powers without the knowledge and consent of the British and Lahore governments. And the fourth article is to the following effect :—

'"Shah Shooja-ool-Moolk agrees to relinquish for himself, his heirs and successors, all claims of supremacy and arrears of tribute over the country now held by the Ameers of Scinde, which will continue to belong to the Ameers and their successors in perpetuity, on condition of the payment to him by the Ameers of such a sum as may be determined under the mediation of the British Government; 15,00,000 of rupees of such payment being made over by him to Maharajah Runjeet Singh. On these payments being completed, article 6 of the treaty of March 12, 1833, will be considered cancelled, and the customary interchange of letters and suitable presents between the Maharajah and the Ameers of Scinde shall be maintained as heretofore."

'For the purpose of giving full and perfect effect to the said treaty, Shah Shooja-ool-Moolk has been furnished by the British Government with money, arms, and other necessary means for raising and equipping an army, which is to march, under his Majesty's personal command, by the route of Bhawulpore and Shikarpore into Afghanistan; whilst another army, belonging to Maharajah Runjeet Singh, is to march with the king's eldest son from Peshawur by the direct road to Cabul. With the object of supporting, in case it should be requisite to do so, the king's own army, a British force is also to take the same route by Shikarpore, and both these armies may be expected to reach the Indus about the beginning of the month of Sheval (December 19), and to cross at Bukkur, or in that neighbourhood. They will thence move by the route of Shikarpore on Candahar; and the Governor-General of India relies on the friendship and goodwill of the Government of Scinde to render every assistance, by ordering boats to be collected for crossing the river, and camels and grain to be also furnished as far as may be required. The hire and price of all boats, camels, grain, &c., will be punctually paid agreeably to the custom of the British Government in friendly countries.

'The Governor-General confidently trusts that the Ameers of Scinde will see the magnitude of the benefit which they will derive by being secured, by the payment of a moderate sum of money, from all future claims, either as to the tribute payable to the monarchs of Cabul or the undoubted pretensions of the latter to Shikarpore. His Lordship also believes and thinks that their Highnesses, as sincere friends and near neighbours, will be happy and ready to take this opportunity of meeting the views and assisting in the great objects of the British Government, from which the Ameers have already derived such essential relief and advantage by its mediation with Maharajah Runjeet Singh, and which has not, in the arrangements now in progress forgotten or overlooked their interests and well-being, as is clearly demonstrated by the article of the treaty above quoted.'

It was no wonder that this communication furnished matter of amazement to the Ameers. Participation in the treaty formerly concluded between Runjeet Singh and Shah Shooja, when the latter took Shikarpore, had at the time been expressly repudiated by Lord William Bentinck. It was now spoken of by the British Government as the basis for the stipulations of the new tripartite treaty. The very article which had called forth remonstrance against the unauthorised use of the name of the British Government was now specifically quoted, followed by the announcement that though the treaty which contained it had not, for certain reasons, been acted upon at the time it was first written, it was now to be brought into execution. And this announcement was made by the self-same Governor-General who, at the close of 1836, deeming Shikarpore a territorial possession of the Ameers, had interposed to prevent the Sikh ruler from invading it. Forgetful of this admission and voluntary assertion of the Ameers' rights, Lord Auckland now revived the pretensions, which he termed undoubted, of Shah Shooja to Shikarpore, and to a claim for tribute, making these the pretext for the formal demand of a heavy and undefined subsidy, of which Runjeet Singh's share alone was to amount to fifteen lacs of rupees.

The Ameers, having in their hands Korans in which the Shah had granted them receipts in full for all demands duly signed and sealed, were naturally slow to perceive the magnitude of the benefit thus imposed upon them; they regarded the whole measure as one of shameless extortion; and undoubtedly on but few, if any, occasions has the British Government lent its name to the sanction of a more iniquitous demand.

Pottinger was sensible of the character of the duty which was thrown upon him. He thus wrote on August 27, 1838: 'Had our present connection existed some years, and our resident thereby had time, by constant kindly intercourse with the chiefs and people, to have removed the strong and universal impression that exists throughout Scinde as to our grasping policy, the case might have been widely different; but I enter upon my new duties without anything to offer, and with a proposal that will not only strengthen the above impressions (for many besides the Scindees will believe, at the outset, that we are making a mere use of the Shah's name), but revive a claim to tribute which has been long esteemed obsolete.'

Pottinger had, however, enabled the Anglo-Indian Government to class the Ameers amongst those who were in communication with Persia, for he had forwarded to the Governor-General the copy of a letter from the Ameers of Hyderabad to the Shah. Although this letter contained nothing but the usual flowery compliments of Eastern potentates, and was made so little a matter of importance or secresy that its contents and composition had been openly discussed, yet it suited the purpose of the British Government to amplify its contents into a tender of allegiance. The Ameers were thus implicated amongst those entertaining designs hostile to British interests, and colour was given to the harsh and unjustifiable terms thrust upon them by our power for compulsory acceptance. Nay, further, the letter in question being translated into an act of hostility and bad faith committed toward the British Government, the transfer of the share of the government of Scinde from the guilty parties to more faithful members of the family was held by Lord Auckland to be clearly justified, and was urged upon Pottinger. He was not, however, in a position, had he wished, to adopt hastily the suggestion, and the unpalatable demands which were to be pressed on the Ameers had led him to apply to the Bombay Government to hold troops in readiness to move into Scinde upon his requisition.

All scruples at first entertained by the Government had now been swept away, and, military operations on a great scale being contemplated, it was deemed essential to success that a British force of not less than 5,000 men should be sent by the Bombay Government with the least practicable delay for the occupation of Shikarpore, or such other parts of Scinde as might be deemed most eligible for facilitating our operations beyond the Indus, and for giving full effect to the provisions of the tripartite treaty. This resolution was notified to the resident with the following remark from the Governor-General: 'He deems it hardly necessary to remind you that in the important crisis at which we are arrived, we cannot permit our enemies to occupy the seat of power; the interests at stake are too great to admit of hesitation in our proceedings, and not only they who have shown a disposition to favour our adversaries, but they who display an unwillingness to aid us in the just and necessary undertaking in which we are engaged, must be displaced, and give way to others on whose friendship and co-operation we may be able implicitly to rely.'

The resident was deterred from acting on these repeated instructions to displace the obnoxious Ameers from all share in the government of the country by considerations of expediency. Power was in their hands, and a premature disclosure of so rigorous a measure would at once have caused the Ameers effectually to paralyse all arrangements for the collection of supplies. Grain, camels, boats, and money were wanted for the armies about to concentrate in Scinde, and the resident felt, in spite of his urgent instructions to the contrary, that to raise a civil war in the country would not facilitate the obtaining of these necessaries.

The Hyderabad Ameers ill-brooked the communication of the tripartite treaty, and, far from evincing alacrity to aid Shah Shooja's invasion of their territory and treasury, wrote to inform him that he would be opposed. With the British resident they temporised; but he clearly saw that after the receipt of the terms of the tripartite treaty no dependence could be placed on the Ameers of Hyderabad as allies, and that all professions of friendship and willingness to aid were lip-deep. The feeling amongst their retainers was violent, and

Pottinger, returning from a visit, was openly insulted by the populace, and stones were flung at him and his companions.

Affairs in Scinde were in this state when Pottinger, on October 18, 1838, called upon the Government of Bombay to despatch the force of 5,000 men which had been prepared to embark for service in Scinde.

Prior to this—that is, by October 15—information which could be relied upon had been received in Scinde of the breaking-up of the siege of Herat and of the retreat of the Persian army from before its walls. Intimation of the event had also reached Lahore from Peshawur about the same time, and was immediately communicated to the Governor-General.

In the meanwhile, on September 10, Lord Auckland had issued directions for the formation of an army, destined for operations in Afghanistan; and on October 1 he had published a proclamation assigning the causes and reasons which led the Anglo-Indian Government to resolve upon the restoration of Shah Shooja to the throne from which he had been driven nearly thirty years before. There being no just ground of quarrel with Dost Mahomed Khan, the declaration spoke of the measures taken by the Cabul ruler in 1837, to repel Sikh aggression at the mouth of the Khybur, as a sudden and unprovoked attack upon the troops of our ancient ally Maharajah Runjeet Singh; and alleged this circumstance as the cause for giving to Burnes's purely commercial mission political functions; the avowed object of that step being to mediate just and reasonable terms between the Sikh and Afghan rulers, and to avert the calamity of war. Dost Mahomed was accused of urging unreasonable pretensions, which had precluded the attempt to mediate; of avowing schemes of aggrandisement and ambition injurious to the security and peace of the frontiers of India; of adherence, together with his brothers of Candahar, to the Persian policy; and of consequently compelling Burnes's mission to leave Cabul without success.

The attack upon Herat was designated a most unjustifiable and cruel aggression; and intrigues were said to be actively prosecuted throughout Afghanistan for the purpose of extending Persian influence and authority to the banks of, and even beyond, the Indus. Further, it was said, the envoy in Persia had been compelled by a refusal of his just demands, and by a systematic course of disrespect, to quit the court of the Shah, and had officially communicated, under the express order of Her Majesty's Government, the necessity under which Great Britain was placed to regard the advance of the Persian arms against Herat as an act of hostility towards herself.

The preceding combination of events, denominated a crisis of affairs, was stated, after serious and mature deliberation, to have satisfied the Governor-General that pressing necessity, as well as every consideration of policy and justice, warranted the British Government in espousing the cause of Shah Shooja, who when in power had cordially acceded to measures of united resistance to external enmity, and whose popularity throughout Afghanistan was contrasted with the disunion and unpopularity of Dost Mahomed Khan and his brothers. The latter were represented as ill-fitted under any circumstances to be useful allies to the British Government, and to aid us in our just and necessary measures of national defence. Allusion was made to the tripartite treaty and its conditions, by which the independence of the Ameers of Scinde and the integrity of Herat were guaranteed. And hopes were expressed that, from the measures completed or in progress, the general freedom and security of commerce would be promoted; that the name and just influence of the British Government would gain their proper footing among the nations of Central Asia; that tranquillity would be established upon the most important frontier of India, and that a lasting barrier would be raised against hostile intrigue and encroachment.

This proclamation, in which the words 'justice' and 'necessity,' and the terms 'frontier,' 'security of the possessions of the British Crown,' and 'national defence,' were applied in a manner for which there is fortunately no precedent in the English language, concluded as follows:—'His Majesty, Shah Shooja-ool-Moolk, will enter Afghanistan surrounded by his own troops, and will be supported against foreign interference and factious opposition by a British army. The Governor-General confidently hopes that the Shah will be speedily replaced on his throne by his own subjects and adherents; and when once he shall be secured in power, and the independence and integrity of Afghanistan established, the British army will be withdrawn.'

How that British army performed its duty; how the multifarious hopes of the Government were realised; how the integrity of Afghanistan was re-established; and how the pledge of the withdrawal of the British troops was fulfilled, will hereafter be related.

CHAPTER VI.

SEPTEMBER—NOVEMBER 1838.

ASSEMBLY OF THE BENGAL TROOPS AT FEROZEPORE—DEBARKATION OF THE BOMBAY DIVISION ON THE COAST OF SCINDE—PLAN OF THE CAMPAIGN—RESIGNATION OF SIR HENRY FANE—ASSUMPTION OF COMMAND BY SIR JOHN KEANE.

A HEAVY rainy season, which continued to a late period in the year, was not favourable to the march of troops in part brought from distant cantonments; but previous warning having been given, the orders for the rendezvous of the army at Kurnaul, issued on September 13, 1838, by the Commander-in-Chief in India, Sir Henry Fane, found the corps prepared for motion, and by November 28 he had assembled at Ferozepore, under his own personal command, a carefully-selected force of 14,000 men of all arms. The Shah's contingent, under British officers chosen by Sir Henry Fane, was also at Ferozepore. Five months only had elapsed since the commencement of its organisation, and as the service was not popular, and the recruiting necessarily hurried, the general appearance of the men was not very soldierly, nor was their discipline in a forward state. Under good officers, however, it was rapidly improving. In strength the Shah's contingent amounted to 6,000 men of all arms, natives of the British provinces of India, and equipped from the British magazines. The whole available force was therefore at this point 20,000 men.

Simultaneous with the rendezvous of the Bengal troops at Ferozepore was the debarkation on the coast of Scinde of the Bombay division, amounting to 5,000 men of all arms, under the command of Sir John Keane. They laboured under all the disadvantages of troops landing from ship-board on no friendly coast, necessarily without the means of movement and ignorant of the country in which they had to act; but they enjoyed, in consequence of their short sea-voyage and the necessity it entailed of economising room, comparative freedom from the host of camp followers which was the embarrassment of the Bengal divisions.

The British army, consisting altogether of 25,000 men, was thus in two bodies, separated from each other by the whole length of the course of the Sutlej and Indus, that is by a distance of 780 miles; the main body at Ferozepore movable, but that on the sea-board of Scinde, paralysed for a time by the want of camels or other beasts of burden, immovable.

The main objects for which this army had been assembled were the invasion of Afghanistan in order to establish Shah Shooja; and the succour or recapture of Herat, if the place should have fallen to the Persians. The ancillary objects were the exaction of a heavy subsidy from the Ameers, and the occupation of a part of Scinde by a British force in support of the invasion of Afghanistan. Vast political importance was attached to what was termed the integrity of Herat. To raise the siege, or to retake the fortress, was the paramount consideration to which all others were made subordinate. Time, therefore, was of great moment, for the defence had been obstinate, and it was hoped that the town might hold out until succoured by the British advance. Should this hope not be realised, it was still of the utmost importance to attack the Persians before they should have had time to fresh munition the fortress, and to recover from the fatigues and exhaustion of a long siege.

The periodical rains may be said as a general rule to prescribe the season for the commencement of military operations in India. The winter, during which the highlands of Afghanistan are long covered with snow, may be said likewise as a general rule to prescribe the favourable time for military operations above the passes. With reference to the distance of the point of rendezvous, Ferozepore, from the various cantonments of the Bengal troops, and the period at which the rainy season terminated, the army could not judiciously have been earlier put into motion than it was. Assembled at Ferozepore in the end of November it had before it the best season of the year for military operations in the plains of Scinde and the Punjab, whether it moved in a north-west direction upon Attock, in a westerly course straight upon Dera Ismael Khan, or in a south-west direction upon Bukkur and Shikarpore.

The last of the three was the line selected. When the plan of the campaign was formed—that is, before the retreat of the Persians had become known—the principal object in view was the early succour of Herat, and for the attainment of this object the south-west route was undoubtedly the most favourable. Advancing by Dera Ismael Khan, the army would certainly have had a shorter road into the interior of the Afghan country. Ascending by the Gomul Pass, not then known, however, and leaving Ghuznee to its right, it might have struck off by the Ab Istadat and so reached Candahar. But this route, though short, would nevertheless have involved greater delay than the more circuitous one by the south, for snow lies longer on the high ground at the head of the Gomul Pass and in the neighbourhood of Ghuznee, and the country consequently is longer impracticable for the movement of troops. The same objection applied to the northerly route by Attock upon Cabul; and, moreover, the route from Cabul to Herat is long and difficult for an invading army. The route by Shikarpore on Candahar, therefore, though circuitous and demanding more abundant means of transport, commissariat stores, provisions, and troops, was yet the best adapted to the end in view—an early appearance before Herat; and it was on this ground that the Commander-in-Chief assented to the advance of the Bengal column by a line of operations which entailed so great a development of means. The Commander-in-Chief had, however, little to say to the plan of the campaign, or indeed to anything but to the details regarding the constitution of the force, which necessarily in a great measure devolved upon him. The arrangements for the supply of the army, which it did not rest with him to initiate, were, contrary to his wishes, deferred till too late a period, and then thrown into the hands of the various political functionaries. The latter, not acting in systematic communication with each other and the commissariat department of the army, exerted themselves zealously but independently, and sometimes in competition with the commissariat officers, thus enhancing the cost of supplies to the Government.

The plan of the campaign originated in the political negotiations which have been detailed, and was formed without advertence to purely military considerations. Taking the treaty between Runjeet Singh and Shah Shooja, and the Shah's campaign in 1834, as a basis, the plan was at first confined to an exact imitation of that series of operations. Burnes urgently pressed for the presence of a regiment or two with the Shah; Sir Henry Fane would accede to no small detachment; then came the news of the failure of McNeill's negotiations before Herat, and his withdrawal from the Persian camp; and lastly was superadded the unwillingness of the Ameers to admit the obsolete claims of Shah Shooja, to have their treasury plundered for his benefit and to see their country invaded without even a plausible pretext. These various circumstances modified the strength and constitution of the force to be employed, but they never affected the original plan of operations. The Governor-General, anxious for the cordial co-operation of Runjeet Singh, shrank from exciting his apprehensions by a proposal to march across his territories. It was felt that such a proposal could not fail to be disagreeable to the wary Sikh, who had indeed willingly permitted the Shah's son Timoor to advance through the Punjab direct upon Cabul, engaging also to support him with a Sikh contingent of 6,000 men, and to maintain a force in observation at Peshawur, but who could not so easily have been brought to accede to the passage of a large British army.

The plan of the campaign thus, a close imitation of the former unsuccessful enterprise of Shah Shooja, presented no feature of originality, except the prominent part taken by the British Government in operations eminently characterised by an absolute disregard of all sound military principles.

Of the 14,000 regular troops brought together at Ferozepore, the chief part had been drawn from the cantonments of Meerut, Kurnaul, and Delhi, though some of the battalions had marched to the rendezvous from the still more distant cantonments of Agra, Lucknow, and Cawnpore, and even from Allahabad and Benares. Meerut and Kurnaul thus weakened were not correspondingly reinforced by the moving up of troops to replace those withdrawn, so that although the different military cantonments were not left wholly unprovided, yet Cawnpore was the only station held in force, and was distant from Meerut about 260 miles. Admitting, however, that on an emergency the troops occupying Kurnaul, Meerut, Delhi, and even Muttra and Agra, could by a concentric movement have been with tolerable rapidity brought together, still the reserve thus assembled must have been about 250 miles from

Ferozepore. The plan of the campaign was therefore as follows :—20,000 men, of whom 6,000 were raw troops, were to start from Ferozepore and effect a junction with a force of 5,000 men separated from them by a distance of 780 miles of march. The latter, being landed on the coast of Scinde without means of motion and without a depôt of provisions, were entirely at the mercy of the Ameers of Scinde, known to be hostile to the military occupation of their country, and having the power to cut off all supplies whether of food or of beasts of burden.

In moving to effect this junction, only the preliminary step to far more extended operations, Fane was to have no reserve nearer than the scattered cantonments on the Jumna and Ganges with which to watch the Sikh forces and insure Sikh fidelity. In maintaining his communications with Ferozepore he must therefore always feel that these were at the mercy of a large well-appointed Sikh army at Lahore, which was only four marches from the Sutlej, whilst his unconcentrated reserve was 250 miles from the same point. In short, he was to leave in his rear, and virtually in possession of his communications, a large army which might act against us at any moment that the will of an Eastern despot, or his death, should render the measure agreeable to Sikh politics, notoriously jealous of the establishment of British power on the west of the Punjab.

If the forbearance of the Ameers, or their intimidation, permitted the pacific march of the two bodies, whose first duty was to enforce the levy of a heavy subsidy and the cession, nominally for a time, of

Bukkur and Shikarpore, with such other points as might be deemed essential, the British commander was to leave the injured and plundered rulers of Scinde and their untried Belooch strength in his rear, and in possession of his communications, in order to advance against Afghanistan.

That country was known to be rough and difficult, and it was supposed to be inhabited by warlike tribes, proud of their independence, bigoted in their faith, and unlikely to endure a king forced on them by British bayonets. Moreover, the resources of Afghanistan were poor, and the provisioning of an invading Indian army, with its swarm of followers and cattle, was a problem of doubtful solution. To form depôts of provisions in advance was impossible; no large towns or rich districts lay on the route. To depend on caravans of food from the rear, even if food could be provided, involved heavy escorts; for passes such as the Bolan and the Khojuk, infested with plunder-loving tribes knowing every step of their recesses, were not to be passed with impunity by rich unguarded convoys; and it was fair to calculate that the chiefs of Candahar would raise all the opposition in their power. Between Sukkur and Candahar 404 miles were to be traversed, through a country offering strong points; and to ensure the maintenance of free communication with the rear, a matter essential to the safety of the army, the whole of this line of operations must be protected by a chain of posts.

Arrived in Candahar, the British commander would have, altogether, some 850 miles of communication through Scinde with Ferozepore; and before moving onwards to Herat, 370 miles further, it would be necessary for him to leave a strong detachment with Shah Shooja to oppose Dost Mahomed, in case the latter should advance from Cabul.

Thus, after leaving his original base, Ferozepore, at the mercy of a powerful but doubtful ally, Runjeet Singh; and what may be termed his new base, Upper Scinde, but too much at the mercy of the injured Ameers; it is evident that Fane could have brought to Herat but a small force with which to repulse the Persian army or to besiege and storm the fortress.

Throughout this long series of operations, extending over 1,200 miles of country, a single serious check was almost inevitable ruin, and nearly tantamount to destruction. The British commander could look for no support, no reinforcements; for his reserves, whether the troops on the Ganges and Jumna or those in the Bombay Presidency be regarded as such, were at least 1,400 miles to his rear, and the intervening powers were sure to be disaffected in case of reverse. Everything in the expedition was matter of the utmost uncertainty, even to the feeding of the troops, for Afghanistan merited the character given to Spain by the Fourth Henry of France: Invade with a large force, and you are destroyed by starvation; invade with a small one, and you are overwhelmed by a hostile people. And as if to superadd ridicule to the dangers of the enterprise, which was avowedly undertaken to relieve or recapture a fortress famed for its strength, and possibly defended by a large Persian artillery and

Russian engineers, the complement of battering-guns taken with the force was four eighteen-pounders.

In a few words, the plan of the campaign violated in a glaring manner all usual military precautions. Although in Eastern wars the leaders of our armies have dared much, counting boldly on the inferiority of discipline and organisation in the armies opposed to them, yet never before, during the history of the British power in India, had so wild, ill-considered, and adventurous a scheme of far-distant aggression been entertained.

The official intimation of the retreat of the Persians from before Herat modified to some extent the scheme of operations. Fane, naturally haughty, had brooked with impatience the crude military ideas of men who, ignorant of the very rudiments of war, had been entrusted by the Governor-General with arrangements for which they were incompetent. Yet, confident in his own powers, and in the force he had brought together, the very hazard of the enterprise had until now possessed a charm for his soldier ambition. When, however, the safety of Herat reduced the approaching operations in Afghanistan to the raising of a puppet king under the pupilage of Macnaghten, his pride revolted at a position so humiliating for the Commander-in-Chief of the Indian armies, and he relinquished the command of the expedition. On November 30 it was notified that, under the altered circumstances consequent on the retreat of the Persians, the command of the detachment of the Bengal army was to be assumed by Major-General Sir Willoughby Cotton, and that the second division of infantry, under General Duncan, was to stand fast at Ferozepore, also occupying Loodianah.

A small corps of observation was thus formed; but it was far too small to be of real utility as a check upon the Sikh army, 40,000 strong, and it reduced the force destined for Afghanistan by 4,500 men.

The troops, indifferent to the reduction of numbers, heard with regret that Fane would not lead them, for his many soldierly qualities had gained their respect, and they were temporarily handed over to the command of a man for whom they had none. Their future leader, Sir John Keane, was unknown to them, save that by common report he possessed courage. His qualities for command had had no trial except at New Orleans. There, unfortunately for his country, he was superseded when on the point of attacking an enemy at the time unprepared and incapable of offering effectual resistance. For his successor's delays and the failure of the attack, which was not made until the proper moment had long past, he was not responsible.

After the halt of the second division, the force for the operations on the Indus and in Afghanistan amounted to 20,500 men of all arms, of whom 6,000 were but half-trained; so that Keane could only calculate on 14,500 disciplined troops with which to effect the various objects of the Government. Subsequently, as will be hereafter noted, a reserve of 3,000 men was landed at Kurrachee, but this was not until February 3, 1839. Of the 14,500 disciplined troops, 5,000 only were with Keane at Vikkur, and 9,500 men were at Ferozepore about to commence their march.

No position could well have been more disagreeable for a commander. Unable for want of transport to move from the ground he occupied, without supplies, and with the strength of Scinde, whatever that might be, interposed between himself and the Bengal troops 780 miles distant from him, Keane had but a remote prospect of effecting a junction between his two divisions and bringing actually under his own hand the army of which he was nominally in command.

CHAPTER VII.

OCTOBER 1838–FEBRUARY 1839.

STATE OF AFFAIRS IN SCINDE—BURNES'S NEGOTIATIONS WITH MEER ROOSTUM—DIFFICULT POSITION OF THE BRITISH RESIDENT POTTINGER—ADVANCE OF KEANE FROM VIKKUR—CESSION OF BUKKUR—MARCH OF THE BENGAL TROOPS TO CO-OPERATE WITH KEANE—CONCLUSION OF NEGOTIATIONS WITH THE AMEERS OF HYDERABAD.

THE first information conveyed to Keane after his landing, that on the morning of the 29th a shot had been fired from the Ameers' artillery park over the resident's tent, was an instructive commentary upon Pottinger's intimation that the troops were to land with the concurrence of the Scinde Government, and that the officer in command was to consider himself in a friendly country. Coupled with the facts that no boats, grain, or camels had been collected; that orders had been issued for the assembly of the Belooch army and its rendezvous at Hyderabad; that the Ameers had endeavoured to intimidate the owners of camels and the boatmen from engaging themselves with the British force; and that attempts had been made to induce the Ameer of Khyrpore to join the Hyderabad Ameers in open war against the invaders; the insult offered to the resident opened Keane's eyes to the real state of affairs. He was still more enlightened when Pottinger joined his camp on December 9, and apprised him of the course of preceding negotiations.

The treachery of the Ameers had been, in the eyes of the Governor-General, fully established by their having written 'a slavish ureeza to the Shah of Persia,' by their having treated with honour a self-styled Persian prince to whom this complimentary letter was entrusted; by their communication to Shah Shooja, which was designated insulting; and by their announcement that they would oppose the Shah's advance. On such alleged grounds, Lord Auckland had determined to establish a British subsidiary force in Scinde at the earliest practicable moment, and being of opinion that such a measure was 'just and necessary on the principle of a regard for our future security,' he directed that the reception of a subsidiary force should be made a *sine quâ non* in any new engagement with the Ameers. As a spur to the negotiations, use was to be made of the overtures which the British Government had received from a descendant of the old Kalora dynasty, then residing at Bikaneer, whose pretensions might, the resident was informed, be favourably regarded by the British Government, should no member of the reigning family be found disposed to accede to the arrangements deemed 'absolutely indispensable to the safety and tranquillity of our Indian possessions.' These negotiations were, however, not to be pressed until the presence of British troops in Scinde should give support to the authority of the resident.

Meanwhile, by a strange neglect of experience as to the character and diplomatic conduct of Burnes, the Governor-General had again selected him for the exercise of discretion on vague and indefinite instructions; and he was, unfortunately for Pottinger, in Upper Scinde. Baulked at Cabul, and sore at Macnaghten's selection for the post of envoy, he had been in some measure soothed by the charge of a mission to Kelat. Had his orders been consistent with his avowed office, no immediate inconvenience might have ensued from his again being invested with political functions; but this was not the case. The most important part of his instructions consisted of a reference to the temporary cession of Bukkur, and Lord Auckland's readiness to enter into a new treaty with Meer Roostum which should guarantee the independence of Khyrpore and assure its ruler of the protection of the British Government against all external enemies. This treaty, indeed, was to be dependent on contingent events at Hyderabad—for it was palpable that transactions at Khyrpore were of secondary importance. But such a provision was not likely to suffice for the guidance of Burnes. Prior to actively entering upon the duties of his new field, his ambition had received no slight stimulus by the honour of knighthood, and, as before this he was ill able to brook the secondary place assigned to him, he was now still less inclined to take a subordinate part in affairs. The news of the retreat of the Persian army from before Herat having arrived, Burnes found, in the middle of October, that the Khyrpore Ameer was complimentary and full of professions of friendship for the British Government. Meer Roostum was not uninfluenced by the hope that the retreat of the Persians, removing the main cause of the contemplated operations in Afghanistan, might preserve

Northern Scinde from the passage and occupation of British troops. Burnes disabused the Ameer of any such hopes, which were rather entertained than expressed, and spoke in such a manner as to call forth the observation 'that it was very evident the jungles of Scinde would soon be on fire if our wishes were not met.' Meer Roostum and his advisers felt themselves differently circumstanced from the Ameers of Hyderabad, and whatever their secret repugnance to the advance of Shah Shooja, the facility with which either the Sikh ruler or the Bengal force from Ferozepore, or both together, could assail Northern Scinde rendered it essential to self-preservation that all ebullitions of feeling should be smothered in the presence of a man so hasty and unsafe as the envoy of Kelat, whose conduct in Cabul was well known in Scinde, and who was regarded as a torch of discord. Meer Roostum was therefore very complimentary to Burnes, and guarded in his overt communications with the Ameers of Hyderabad, to whom he wrote: 'Captain Burnes arrived at Khyrpore on October 18. In the first meeting I have only welcomed him, and learnt from his expressions that both he and Colonel Pottinger have been appointed by the Governor-General of India to manage the affairs of Scinde. You know that the English possess India and many other extensive countries; notwithstanding the Sikhs are so aspiring, still they lean towards the English with extreme friendship, harmony, and mutual concord, as if they were of one party. In such a case it is but foresight to make friendship with them, and advisable to act according to Colonel Pottinger's inclination, that he may not be offended, for he is ambassador and guest.' Thus, under the form of advice to Noor Mahomed Khan and his relatives, Meer Roostum, without compromising himself, conveyed to them, with the cognisance of Burnes, the real reason of the temporising policy of Khyrpore. In his secret communications, Meer Roostum avowed himself ready to be guided by Noor Mahomed Khan.

Burnes, deceived by what he deemed a sincere instance of friendship and devotion, was still further won by the show of confidence with which Meer Roostum treated him in making him acquainted with the contents of a letter received from Hyderabad. In this letter Noor Mahomed wrote: 'I have written to you frequently since by messengers, and once by a camel rider, and requested you to come to Sehwan. Colonel Pottinger is here, and we have not settled with him till we hear from you. Let me hear immediately what Captain Burnes is doing. Why have you not sent your son and acted with me? Your answer will decide all. I am ready for peace and for war, so be quick.' Heedless of foregone negotiations and engagements, Burnes had already forwarded an ill-considered draft of a treaty to Pottinger for his approval. He now hastened to convert into pledges the hopes held out by himself in discussing the draft treaty, and wrote to his Government: 'With such adherence, I feel quite at a loss to know how we can either ask money, or any favour of this family. I have never doubted their sincere disposition to cling to us, but in their weak state I did not expect such firmness in the day of trial.'

Pottinger was not carried away by Burnes's enthusiastic admiration of the conduct of Meer Roostum, whose agents at Hyderabad had been less wary and guarded than the more sagacious minister of the Ameer, and had with considerable *naïveté* inquired from the resident 'what could induce the Governor-General to revive the obsolete question of the Scinde tribute to the kings of Cabul.' The question had been accompanied with the remark, 'It is a joke talking of it as a demand of the king; you have given him bread for the last five and twenty years, and any strength he has now, or may hereafter have, proceeds from you, so that the demand is literally yours.' And the resident had been at the same time given to understand that Meer Roostum was averse to the temporary cession of Bukkur and its occupation by the British troops.

Pottinger therefore objected to the draft treaty, which was a mere repetition of that already in full force, with the two additions of fixing a British resident at Khyrpore and taking that principality under British protection. The first of these stipulations was wholly unnecessary, as by existing treaties the resident was competent either to reside at Khyrpore himself or depute a subordinate. The second was a great and free boon, which might prove embarrassing to the Government, and was conferred without any sacrifice whatever on the part of the Khyrpore Ameer.

Pottinger stated the terms on which he was prepared to form a separate treaty with Meer Roostum —but he added that it was unnecessary to point out that the period for forming and carrying into effect such an arrangement had not then (October 29) arrived.

Unhappily, on the same day on which Pottinger issued his instructions to Burnes, curbing the precipitate eagerness of the envoy of Kelat, the Governor-General wrote his; and the latter were far more consonant to Burnes's views and wishes. The time being, in his lordship's opinion, arrived when a separate treaty guaranteeing the independence of Khyrpore might with all propriety be tendered, Burnes was empowered to enter into a negotiation with Meer Roostum. With reference, however, to the state of affairs at Hyderabad, which rendered it advisable that Pottinger should press no demands on the Ameers until, backed by the Bombay force, he could do so with effect, Burnes was enjoined the utmost secrecy in the communications he was authorised to make to the Khyrpore chiefs regarding the guaranteed independence of their territory. Thus it so happened that on the self-same day Pottinger, on the spot, and responsible for the state of political relations with Scinde, issued one set of instructions to a person acting in a subordinate political capacity, whilst the Governor-General, distant from the scene of negotiations, not only issued instructions of a diametrically contrary nature, but by simultaneously empowering a subordinate functionary to act in independence of his principal, suddenly introduced an element of disorder and confusion which might have proved seriously detrimental to the views of Government.

Hitherto it had been the policy of the Governor-General to acknowledge and support the paramount position of Noor Mahomed as the head of the confederacy of the Ameers; but the defection of Meer Roostum from the cause of his family, and the want of unanimity among the Hyderabad Ameers themselves, now suggested to the Governor-General that a sub-division of authority might be productive of advantage. The resident was accordingly further instructed that a separate treaty might be formed with each Ameer on the terms proposed to the Ameer of Khyrpore. The latter, in consideration of the temporary cession of the fort of Bukkur, was to be exempt from the payment of subsidy; but this privilege was not to be extended to other members of the family, whose possessions were to be guaranteed to them on the condition of their agreeing to pay such quota of a fair and reasonable subsidy as might be deemed proper to require from them.

Keane, at the same time that he was apprised of the instructions which the resident had received, learnt that the latter indulged no hope of carrying Lord Auckland's commands into effect. Pottinger felt himself bound to inform the Governor-General that the announcement of the intention to station even a company of Sepoys in Scinde would be the signal for a coalition against the British and their plans; that no single Ameer had expressed a heart-felt sentiment in admission of the justice and necessity of the cause in which the British Government had embarked; and that not one of them, nor the whole collectively, would willingly give 10,000 rupees to see the Governor-General's measures perfected. Moreover, the guarantee of their territories individually, without the payment of one farthing, but coupled with the stipulation that a force was to be maintained in Scinde at the expense of the Indian Government, was a proposal which would be rejected; and with which compliance could only be obtained by coercion.

The facility with which the Governor-General persisted in flattering himself that the preliminary arrangements in Scinde could be concluded, and the instructions based on this assumption, evidently arose from a misapprehension of the real state of affairs; and before Keane could think of the ulterior operations in Afghanistan, it behoved him to extricate himself from the awkward position into which he had been thrust, and which any premature discovery of Lord Auckland's intentions towards the Ameers of Hyderabad could not fail of rendering much more embarrassing, and probably dangerous. Pottinger felt this, and that he must hazard no demand which he was not prepared by force to exact, not only out of regard to the success of such demand, but also with respect to the peculiarly helpless condition of the troops at Vikkur. Camels came in slowly in spite of all exertions, and the Bengal troops were too distant to make themselves felt in Scinde. Keane and Pottinger were therefore equally desirous that no event should precipitate measures with the Ameers, whom both felt to be at the moment under very advantageous circumstances, if they either knew or were accidentally excited, to seize them. Matters were in this state in the middle of December, when Burnes, who had never rested until he induced the

Governor-General to grant him independent powers, acting without reference to the state of affairs in Lower Scinde, took a step marked with more than his customary indiscretion, and calculated to bring on the very difficulties which Keane was anxious to avoid, and which Pottinger by patient temporising was staving off.

The injunctions of Government to Burnes regarding secrecy had arrived too late. His negotiations at Khyrpore had transpired, and had inflamed the suspicion of Noor Mahomed and his relatives. Their altered tone towards the resident, and the measures they adopted to assemble the Belooch force, evinced that they had a clear appreciation of the policy which those negotiations foreboded, and that they guessed the motive of Pottinger's studied procrastination in deferring all questions of importance for the decision of Macnaghten. Pottinger was therefore anxious that no further disclosures of the ultimate intentions of the Indian Government should be inconsiderately made, and on December 3 he wrote to Burnes inquiring whether the latter deemed it advisable that the demands to be brought before the Ameers of Hyderabad should be delayed until there were means in Northern Scinde to protect the grain depôts which Burnes was collecting for the army. Pottinger knew that, by the time the Bengal column approached Scinde, Keane's force would be in a condition to move; and every consideration of policy and military precaution rendered the suggestion a wise one. Burnes, who received it on December 9, instead of paying attention to advice so wholesome, and offered in a manner the most unpresuming, resolved at once to carry into effect the commands of the Governor-General, and to tender the specified terms to the chiefs of Upper Scinde, demanding a written pledge that he was not answerable for any evils that might immediately flow from their acceptance, and that the Khyrpore Government was to become answerable that no harm befell the grain depôts. In tendering the terms for acceptance they were contrasted with what was to befall Hyderabad, and Burnes notified his intention of withdrawing from Scinde if they should be refused.

The reasons assigned for this ill-timed determination were the instructions of the Governor-General to Pottinger suggesting the sub-division of authority by the formation of separate treaties; and the allegation that there was no chance for the next two months of the grain depôts being better protected than they then were. That allegation was incorrect, for there was every prospect that the advance of the Bengal division and the Shah's force would be in Northern Scinde by the middle of January. And it might have occurred to Burnes that Pottinger was the best judge of the proper time for carrying into effect instructions specially entrusted to his discretion.

Pottinger, receiving on the one hand instructions from a Government which was either unable or unwilling to apprehend the real state of affairs, and, on the other hand, having to negotiate with a Government thoroughly hostile in feeling, but balancing between the evils of open war with vastly superior powers and a dishonourable compact, tantamount to the relinquishment of its independence, had by his cautious bearing avoided the errors into which his own Government were pressing him to plunge, and had restrained the Ameers of Hyderabad from an appeal to the pride and courage of the Belooch tribes. Burnes's indiscretion endangered all, and promised to increase tenfold the difficulties with which he had long been patiently struggling. Apprehensive of the possible consequences of such ill-judged haste, he wrote to Burnes pointing out that the pledge he had required was futile; that the ill-advised and premature disclosure of the Governor-General's plan would, if it did not cause the Ameers to commence hostilities, enable them to make preparations for resistance; that by looking only to his own object of settling the petty question of Khyrpore he jeopardised the safety of the officers at Hyderabad and Tatta; and that the Ameers might at once cripple Keane's force by inducing the camel-drivers to desert with their camels. The letter concluded with the observation that if Burnes could not carry out his measures at Khyrpore without interfering with the affairs of Lower Scinde, in however slight a degree, it was his duty to have waited until he ascertained Pottinger's sentiments.

This reproof was merited; but what had been done could not be recalled, and Keane found that he must be prepared to contend not only against the difficulties arising from the peculiar situation of his force, but also against those which might arise from the unconcerted action of independent political functionaries.

Burnes, elate with the independent powers he had received, and with the measures he had pursued, wrote on December 17 to announce the latter to Cotton, as also the probability of hostilities with Hyderabad, and pressed for the rapid advance of the troops upon Scinde.

If Burnes gloried to Cotton in having thus done his utmost to provoke the wrath of the Ameers, Keane by no means partook of his satisfaction. Finding that the Belooch army was assembling in his front, that hostilities might at any moment commence, and that in that case he must look to the security of his base and depôts at Vikkur, and the maintenance of the communications of the army with the sea-board, from whence alone it was in the first instance sure of supplies, he hastened to make use of the six remaining weeks of fine weather on which he could depend, and pressed for the immediate despatch of the reserve force from Bombay with four months' provision. Pottinger had on December 15 written to the Governor-General, deprecating the despatch of the reserve on the grounds of the smallness of the force ordered; but in communication with Keane he now altered his views, and on December 20 applied to Bombay for the despatch of this additional force to Kurrachee with all possible expedition, truly remarking that even if the Ameers allowed Keane's force to pass quietly through the country, Scinde could not be left on its then footing in rear of the army, and that Burnes had already apprised the Ameers of the Governor-General's intentions with regard to the maintenance of a subsidiary force. It was a fortunate circumstance that this call for reinforcement was made and unhesitatingly complied with.

It was now imperative that as little leisure should

be afforded to the Hyderabad Ameers for hostile preparations as circumstances permitted; but Keane was still hampered by the want of baggage cattle, and but for the cordial aid of the Rao of Cutch, and the exertions of a private native merchant at Kurrachee, he would have been still longer forced to stand still at Vikkur. The want of camels was far from being the only need, for a great difficulty was the want of money and the impossibility of raising it. Pottinger had above twenty-five lacs of bullion, and yet could not raise 1,000 rupees for the use of the force. In spite of wants and difficulties, however, Keane, anxious to make a forward movement, advanced on December 24 with one half of his division, the remainder following two days after. On the 28th he reached Tatta, a position on the Indus which insured his communications with Kurrachee, the point of debarkation for the reserve he expected, and was at the same time not so far from Vikkur but that his line of operations by the river was well covered. His heavy stores, ammunition and the like, having to be moved by water, it was imperative that he should jealously secure his river communications. Having gained unopposed the position of Tatta, he could there await, if advisable, the nearer approach of the Bengal force, and the debarkation of the reserve, watch the proceedings of the Ameers, and more easily than at Vikkur obtain supplies from the surrounding country.

Pottinger had at first intended not to bring forward the terms to be offered to the Hyderabad Ameers until the arrival of the Bombay force before Hyderabad should enable him to dictate, and if necessary enforce his demands; but the Government, anxious that the expedition into Afghanistan should not be deferred to another season in consequence of military operations in Scinde, now notified its willingness to moderate its requisitions both as to territory and treasure, and urged Pottinger to a speedy and if possible amicable termination of negotiations. The resident knew that the advance of the Bengal troops had crossed the Indus on the 10th and 11th at Gote Amil, and reached Sukkur on the 12th; that Shah Shooja had, with his contingent, commenced the passage of the river on the 11th, seven miles above Roree, and marched to Shikarpore; and that the head-quarters, marching with the cavalry brigade of the Bengal force, was not above ten or twelve days in rear of the Shah, and might therefore be expected about the time that the treaty would be presented and discussed. The proximity of the force could not fail to have effect; and it was not unreasonable to hope that the Ameers, who had refrained from active hostilities against Keane when such could with the greatest advantage have been entered upon, would now feel that they had lost their opportunity. Pressed by Government, therefore, and aware that the terms he had to offer had long ceased to be a secret, Pottinger resolved not to await, as originally intended, the arrival of the army at Hyderabad, and on January 18 he despatched a draft treaty for the acceptance of the Ameers.

Keane advanced from Tatta on January 23 by the road on the right bank of the Indus, and on the 25th reached Jurrukh, a place two marches from Hyderabad, where he was forced to halt to allow the ammunition and provisions coming by water to close up to him. While at Jurrukh he learnt that the Ameers had rejected the proffered treaty; that the Belooch were in strength at Hyderabad; and that hostilities appeared inevitable. He thereupon wrote to Fane stating his position, and his intention of crossing the Indus where he best could; and called for the march of a part of the Bengal force down the left bank of the Indus to co-operate with the Bombay troops in a movement on Hyderabad.

Fane had, however, anticipated the call, for having received a letter from Keane of January 15 announcing that Pottinger was about to despatch the treaty on the acceptance of which the question of war or peace depended, he had at once advised Cotton to push forward a part of his force. Advice from Fane was a command, and Cotton prepared to execute the movement as soon as his rear should close up. Orders for the march of 5,600 men of all arms, were accordingly issued on the 27th, but the departure of the troops was delayed until the cession of Bukkur and its occupation by a British garrison should be completed.

On January 26, Meer Roostum and his brothers waited on Fane, and received from his hands the separate treaty ratified by the Governor-General on January 10, 1839, by which the Khyrpore Ameer entered into subordinate alliance with the Anglo-Indian Government; the latter, in return, binding itself not to covet one jot of his country, and to protect the principality and territory of Khyrpore.

Meer Roostum was exempted from the payment of tribute to the Shah or subsidy to the British Government, but by a separate article the occupation of Bukkur during war was ceded. This fort, occupying a rocky island in the Indus where the river takes a sudden turn to break through a limestone ridge, was a place of no real strength except from the circumstance of its insular position. In Scinde, however, its reputation was great, and as it commanded the most eligible, because the narrowest, point for the bridging of the mighty stream, its occupation was a matter of some temporary importance. In the East the surrender of a fortress is always felt a disgrace; and the cession of Bukkur, to which an exaggerated idea of strength and importance had long been attached, was a source of sorrow to the aged Ameer of Khyrpore, who felt humiliated by so open and manifest a token that his independence was at an end. There were doubts, therefore, whether quiet possession would be yielded, and the march of the Bengal troops towards Hyderabad was delayed until the fort should have been secured. Notwithstanding Fane's anxiety to save time, the 27th and 28th were passed before Burnes succeeded in obtaining the formal surrender of the keys; for the news of the rejection of the treaty by the Ameers of Hyderabad threw the Khyrpore Ameers into doubt, and made them hesitate on taking so decided a step as that of the cession of Bukkur. If hostilities ensued, and fortune smiled on the Belooch arms, the surrender of the fortress would seriously compromise the Ameers of Khyrpore with their brethren. They shrank, therefore, from incurring the odium of a measure which, unpopular under any circumstances, might prove to have been traitorously impolitic. But, having put off the delivery of the keys as long as appeared compatible with safety, the Khyrpore Ameers at length yielded, and, intimidated by the presence of a force with which they felt themselves wholly unequal to cope, made over the keys to Burnes on January 29, 1839. The matter having been settled, a wing of the 35th N.I. and the flank companies of the 16th N.I. were embarked in boats, and pushed across to the island of Bukkur. To the last, doubts were entertained whether the fort would be quietly given up; and Cotton's want of arrangement on this occasion was well calculated to encourage opposition. The garrison was, however, seen to embark on board boats and quit the fort before the troops were half across the noble breadth of water which lay between the British camp and the rock of Bukkur; and when they reached the island and scrambled on shore the place was at once surrendered. In mockery of respect to Meer Roostum's sovereign rights his flag was displayed on the ramparts, and a guard of Beloochees permitted to attend it; but our colours were also uncased upon the walls, and the Sepoys, who shouted to see the ensign of British power float domineeringly over the magnificent river at their feet, knew well that where once planted in the East that emblem of dominion was seldom known to be struck.

On the morning of the 30th the troops destined to co-operate with the Bombay division moved southwards under Cotton, marching by the direct road on the left bank of the Indus upon Hyderabad. A detachment of the Shah's contingent advanced from Shikarpore upon Larkhana almost simultaneously with Cotton. Fane had thus put in motion for Keane's support a larger force than Keane had under his own hand; for on the left bank Cotton was at the head of 5,600 men, whilst the parallel column on the right bank of the river under Simpson was of about half that strength.

Meanwhile, however, negotiations had been reopened by the Ameers of Hyderabad, and Keane remained at Jurrukh awaiting their result. Aware of the orders issued on the 27th for the advance of the Bengal division, and that Bukkur, ceded by treaty, would without doubt be in the hands of the British, the Ameers awoke to the fact that they were about to plunge single-handed into a contest with upwards of 21,000 men in Scinde, 15,000 of whom were good troops provided with excellent artillery. They, therefore, sent a vakeel to Pottinger to reopen negotiations, and to intimate a desire to accept the terms of the proffered treaty after a satisfactory explanation of two of its articles should have been afforded. The golden opportunity for attacking Keane's isolated, ill-provisioned, and unmovable force had been lost; time had been given to equip and move; and the position of the Ameers was now far different from what it had been two months before. From 15,000 to 20,000 Belooch troops were concentrated at Hyderabad; but, however brave individually, they lacked the discipline for which the Anglo-Indian army is renowned, and they felt themselves vastly inferior in cavalry and artillery, potent arms in a plain-country like Scinde. It was no longer a question whether 15,000 or 20,000 Beloochees could overwhelm Keane and his paralysed force at Vikkur, but whether they could maintain a contest with superior numbers, discipline, and equipment; for to the 21,000 men in Scinde was to be added the Bombay reserve, with the strength of which the Ameers were necessarily ignorant, but which they knew would prove a considerable accession of force. The advantage derivable from their concentrated position, and the isolated condition of the columns moving against them, was rather apparent than real. To cross such a river as the Indus with the view of attacking Keane was a delicate operation in front of an alert enemy, who might contest the passage; and a defeat on the right bank exposed the capital and its treasure as an easy prey to Cotton. To march against the latter was more feasible; but a considerable force must be left to occupy Hyderabad, watch Keane, and oppose his passage of the river, should he, as was probable, attempt to cross. Their force thus divided, they would have attacked Cotton without any great superiority of numbers, and with a great inferiority in serviceable artillery and good cavalry. Having committed the grave errors of losing two months without an endeavour to harm Keane when in a critical position, and of affording time for the assembly in Scinde of 21,000 fighting men, the Ameers of Hyderabad now wisely resolved not to risk their power and country by an ill-timed appeal to arms.

Pottinger received their deputation, but feeling that every day strengthened his position, and that he was in a condition to dictate terms, he added to those already preferred the old demand of the payment of tribute to Shah Shooja, limiting the amount to twenty-one lacs of rupees.

Keane, uncertain of the effect of the diplomatic notes and measures, contemplated, in case of the rejection of the treaty and the renewed requisition, crossing the Indus in face of the Belooch army, and opposite to the capital, depending upon the fire of his artillery and the steadiness of his troops to enable him to effect the passage.

The transport of infantry and cavalry in flat square-headed unmanageable boats across a river of swift stream, and averaging a thousand yards of breadth, would have been tedious, and, in front of a numerous enemy, extremely hazardous; for Keane would have found that the fire of his artillery, whatever its precision, would have afforded weak support to the boats full of troops, swept down by the stream, and landing where and how they best could, on banks covered with thick wood. Fane, a more able soldier than Keane, and alive to the hazard of such an operation, was not free from anxiety for the result. Contemplating the possibility of serious hostilities, and of a siege of Hyderabad, he instructed his engineers to be prepared, if ordered, to break up the nearly completed bridge at Bukkur, and embarking battering-guns, ammunition, engineer park, artillery, and sappers and miners, to drop down the river with all speed to the neighbourhood of Hyderabad,

Keane, however, was spared the fulfilment of his bold enterprise; for on February 1, the intimidated Ameers of Hyderabad announced to Pottinger their readiness to accede to the terms of the proffered treaty, and to the now superadded, though once relinquished, exaction of tribute to Shah Shooja. In consequence of this favourable turn of negotiations, orders were despatched to Cotton to halt the Bengal column. This reached him on the 7th; and on February 9 he received further instructions, directing him to countermarch his force on Roree; for Keane, having on the 3rd marched from Jurrukh, and reached Kotree, opposite to Hyderabad, on the following day, had there been informed of the arrival of the reserve on February 2, at Kurrachee.

In consequence of shots fired from the Kurrachee fort, the 'Wellesley' had battered down its southern face. As the Ameers had notified their acceptance of the treaty, there was now little doubt of their submission, and of the final settlement of affairs without recourse to arms, but Pottinger, on receipt of the news, intimated to the Ameers that a shake of their lip would bring upon Hyderabad the same fate that the 'Wellesley' had inflicted on Kurrachee. The threat was unnecessary, for the Ameers, sensible that the time for opposing the British was passed, had determined to succumb; and, on February 7, began to pay the first instalment of the tribute money, completing the delivery of ten lacs of rupees by the evening of the 9th.

The treaty having been signed by the Ameers, Keane now issued orders for the march of the Bombay column upon Shikarpore; upon which place, by the route of Roree, Cotton with the Bengal column was also in full march on the 10th.

Thus was concluded the overthrow of the independence of rulers, our allies by treaty, whom we professed to befriend and to secure, at the time that we sanctioned and instigated an obsolete demand for tribute preferred against them by a puppet king of our own raising; and unscrupulously subjugated their country, on the plea that it was an integral part of Hindustan, and that its occupation was essential for the defence of our frontier and the peace and security of India.

If want of truth characterised the reasons put forth for the invasion of the friendly territory of Scinde, want of common acquaintance with the rudiments of war marked the course pursued in effecting it. The measure was as imbecile in conception as it was iniquitous in principle.

To argue in its favour from its fortuitous success, is to overlook the most palpable of errors. The first step in the scheme of operations was to jeopardise a British force of 5,000 excellent troops, landing them, without means of movement or subsistence, in a country where the very fact of their appearance in so helpless a condition might have been the signal for a harassing system of hostilities which, without compromising the Belooch, would not improbably have worn out and destroyed the invaders. No one could calculate on the injured princes proving so weak and vacillating, so blind to the opportunity thrust upon them, that they should fail to strike in defence of their country and rights, when a mere handful of men was thrown on their shores, helpless from want of cattle and provisions, and distant more than 700 miles from any armed aid.

All camels and camel-drivers, boats and boatmen, were, as well as provision, within the grasp of the Ameers, and but for an extreme solicitude to avoid rupture with the powerful British Government, every motive which could actuate brave men pointed out that it was better to fight for independence, and timely to resent invasion, than to wait until plans should be matured, and scattered forces concentrated on their coveted territory, in order to constrain them to accept terms alike a dishonour to those who proffered and to those who were to receive them.

The discreet conduct of Pottinger, neither to be driven into injudicious measures by the miscalculating haste and eagerness of his own Government, nor to be disturbed from a patient and firm bearing by angry negotiations with incensed princes, gained time when most essential, and, by preventing the outbreak of hostilities at an early stage, enabled the presence of 21,000 men in Scinde subsequently to exact submission to the humiliating conditions which he was aware nothing but force could induce the Ameers to entertain. The instructions of the Government, suggestive of almost everything most ill-timed, even to the kindling of a civil war; and the want of consideration and sagacity in Burnes; would, but for Pottinger's forbearing policy, have brought on a conflict with the Ameers, and delayed the invasion of Afghanistan until Scinde should be conquered, an operation which might have taken time to complete.

The simultaneous launch upon Scinde of the envoys Macnaghten, Burnes, and Pottinger, and the commanders Keane, Fane, and Cotton, all to a certain extent independent authorities, having very partial intercommunication or general understanding with each other, was another remarkable feature in these preliminary transactions. Fortunately Pottinger had discretion, Fane decision and a commanding temper, and Keane courage and confidence; otherwise affairs might have been very seriously compromised by the jarrings of triplicate envoys, and triplicate commanders, and the want of concert amongst the isolated columns of the latter.

CHAPTER VIII.

FEBRUARY–APRIL 1839.

BRIDGING OF THE INDUS—ADVANCE OF THE BENGAL DIVISION INTO BELOOCHISTAN—THE BOLAN PASS—ADVANCE OF THE BOMBAY DIVISION—FAILURE OF FORAGE AND SUPPLIES—KEANE'S ARRIVAL AT QUETTA.

THE reserve force being in possession of Kurrachee, and the Ameers having accepted the treaty and completed the payment of the first instalment of tribute, Keane felt himself at liberty to enter upon that which was entitled 'the grand object of reinstating Shah Shooja on the throne of Afghanistan.' As late as February 6, Macnaghten, in entire ignorance of the state of affairs at Hyderabad and of the intentions of Pottinger and Keane, was in anxiety in consequence of the delay in settling Scinde, which appeared to threaten the loss of a whole season, a period in which, he observed, 'it is impossible to say what may happen to prevent the success of our grand enterprise.' Under these apprehensions he urged that if the state of affairs were such that Sir John Keane required the co-operation of the Bengal column, the subjugation of Scinde and the invasion of Afghanistan might, notwithstanding, be simultaneously carried on; the Shah's contingent being strengthened by a brigade of the regular army, a regiment of native cavalry, and a sufficient proportion of field and battering-guns, and thus enabled to undertake without delay the advance upon Candahar, the disposal of Dost Mahomed, and the despatch of a detachment to Herat. This suggestion reached Hyderabad after the Ameers had submitted, and Keane was already in motion up the left bank of the Indus, purposing to reach Shikarpore about the 4th or 5th of March. His troops were still much straitened by the want of camels, and there was the greatest uncertainty as to obtaining supplies on the route selected; nevertheless he determined to push on, trusting to fortune in the absence of those pre-arrangements which the exercise of foresight might have insured.

Cotton was simultaneously in motion, returning by the same route on which he had advanced down the left bank of the Indus. Upon his arrival at Roree, he found that on February 9 the artillery park, consisting of seventy ordnance carriages and 212 bullock carts, had passed over to the right bank, and that on the 13th the heavy guns had been crossed over on platformed rafts of boats coupled together, the embarkation and disembarkation of the eighteen-pounders having been facilitated by pier-heads constructed on each bank of the river. There was nothing, therefore, to retard the immediate passage of the troops, who crossed over by brigades on successive days, accompanied by their baggage, and were by the 18th all on the right bank of the Indus, having effected the passage without accident.

The construction of a bridge of boats is not difficult where no opposition is offered, where boats, material, and practised men are abundant, and where the stream is moderate. The breadth of the river, provided means are ample, makes little difference. But in this instance, boats were scarce ; the platform timbers of the bridge had in part to be floated from Ferozepore to Sukkur, and there to be sawn up ; the supply, thus brought with much labour from a great distance, was insufficient; and there was nothing to be had on the spot but the khugoor palms, which when felled and split were used in lieu of timbers. Rope had to be manufactured, and anchors had to be made; for the Indus at Bukkur is narrowed to a total breadth of 500 yards, and the main body of its waters flowing between Bukkur and Roree through a channel of 367 yards in breadth, it rushes over its rocky bed with an impetuous current; the use of heavy anchors is therefore imperative. With Sappers untrained to such operations, and with a few Scindian boatmen whose language was not understood, these difficulties had to be overcome and the work constructed. It was several times in jeopardy, and once was nearly swept away by a sudden rise in the river; it was further constantly endangered by the action of boughs and trees caught by the cables and swayed by the swift stream with an incessant vibratory motion that wore quickly through the cables and gave them the appearance of having been cut with a sharp instrument. Much vigilance and exertion was therefore required, both to complete and then to maintain the structure. It proved of great service to the army, enabling about 38,000 troops and camp-followers, 30,000 camels, the field artillery of the force, the ordnance carriages of the park, and the long train of bullock-carts, to effect the passage of this noble river rapidly, easily, and safely. The chief engineer, Thomson, was justly praised for opening the campaign by a successful work of such utility and magnitude; for, to have bridged the Indus was a fact at once impressive and emblematic of the power and resources of the army which thus surmounted a mighty obstacle.

Fane saw the force pass to the right bank and then took leave of the army, the command of which had devolved upon Keane. His farewell was read with feelings of regret. Of a commanding presence, which accorded with a character strict, stern, and decided, he had acquired the confidence of men and officers; and though he was untried in Indian warfare, the troops augured well of his qualities for the conduct of an expedition which without him was likely to want a master spirit.

Fane's farewell to the troops praised them for their discipline, and for their conciliatory behaviour towards the inhabitants of the countries through which they had passed. He did them but justice; for 9,500 fighting-men, accompanied by upwards of 28,000 camp-followers, and 30,000 camels, had performed a march of altogether 600 miles, not only without an act of atrocity, but without a serious complaint of plunder or ill-usage—a fact alike creditable to the excellent discipline of the troops, and to that which has great influence independently of discipline, the orderly and considerate disposition natural to the Bengal Sepoy, who, himself in general from the agricultural classes, has always sympathy with the cultivator.

Six hundred miles of march performed in seventy days had, however, already taken effect on the baggage-cattle of the troops; the camels were beginning to suffer, and a proportion to be disabled; and the horses of the cavalry and artillery were also deteriorated in condition, the march from Roree towards Hyderabad and back again to Roreé having proved very trying, especially to the horses in harness. These effects were not attributable only to the distance traversed. The want of forage had been a frequently recurring evil; the camels were very generally overloaded, and they were in such quantities that the food in the neighbourhood of a halting-place generally sufficed only for those of the leading camp, and the baggage-cattle of every succeeding camp had to stray further in search of grazing ground. In proportion as they gradually fell off in strength, in consequence of constant work under heavy loads, they took a longer time to accomplish a march, and had, therefore, less time for rest and grazing; and this, coupled with often having far to wander for food, was speedily destructive of their efficiency; add to which that in Scinde the camels fed chiefly upon the tamarisk, a plant which proved injurious to those which had been accustomed to the various kinds of mimosa and thorny shrubs, which form the usual food of the camel in Hindustan. In two important branches of efficiency, namely camels and horses, the Bengal force under Cotton when it reached Sukkur had therefore suffered.

By February 20, with the exception of the 35th Regiment N.I., left to garrison Bukkur, the whole force was assembled at Shikarpore, where, including the Shah's contingent, 15,500 men of all arms awaited with eagerness the order to advance. Keane was aware that time was of great importance, and he must have known that the above force, fully equipped and ready for movement, would be at Shikarpore on or about the 20th, by which time the Bombay division could not be further north than Sehwan, and therefore at a far greater distance from the mouth of the Bolan Pass than Cotton's division. Keane ought, therefore, to have hastened to place himself at the head of the main mass of his army, regarding the Bombay troops as the rearward of his advancing columns, and entrusting them to Willshire. Once in communication with the envoy and Shah Shooja, he would have been better able to judge how the advance should be made and what arrangements were to be adopted for maintaining the communications of the army with the new base of its operations, Shikarpore. This obvious course never appears to have occurred to him, for he remained long watching the slow progress of the Bombay division.

Macnaghten, pressed by his Government to expedite the advance into Afghanistan, and brooking impatiently the delay in Scinde, was desirous of pushing forward as soon as Cotton should arrive ; and it happened that the information which he received on the evening of the

20th, afforded him grounds for urging the necessity of an immediate advance of the force.

It was already known that Shah Kamran had ordered Pottinger and Stoddart to quit Herat. The former of these officers had granted bills upon the credit of the British Government to large amounts; the exigencies of the siege had at first been the reason for such advances, but they had been continued when the Persian army retreated from before Herat, in order to preserve the wretched inhabitants from starvation. Moreover, the king and his chiefs had to be supported by an allowance; the ordinary sources of revenue having failed, some of them, such as the traffic in slaves, being repugnant to the newly existing connection with the representatives of the British Government. Notwithstanding the liberality of Pottinger however, Kamran and his Wazeer, Yar Mahomed, could not abstain from exactions and from a line of conduct towards the Heratees which, though doubtless in unison with their own ideas of power and its legitimate exercise, were made the subject of objection and remonstrance on the part of the British officers. Pottinger and Stoddart became, therefore, obnoxious to Shah Kamran and his minister, and the ill feeling was increased by a delay on the part of the Indian Government in honouring the bills which Pottinger, without authority to warrant such payments, had granted. Discussions ensued, ending in no dignified conduct on the part either of the Wazeer or of Pottinger, and the British officers were ordered to leave the Herat territory. Stoddart did so, and proceeded to Bokhara, but Kamran and his minister, becoming alarmed at the length to which matters had proceeded, now requested Pottinger to defer his departure. He complied with the request, but was shortly again subjected to insult, and a rough altercation followed between Pottinger and the Wazeer which left little prospect that a good understanding with the Herat ruler could be maintained.

In the meantime the Persians still held Ghorian, and McNeill continued to write in a tone of alarm to Burnes, and to dwell on the intentions of the Shah to renew operations against Herat. Burnes added fuel to the flame which McNeill's despatches were calculated to excite, by reporting that Vicovich was accompanying the Candahar chiefs and forces to Herat with the view of capturing the place.

Such communications kept alive solicitude for the integrity of Herat; and on February 20 Macnaghten received the further intimation that the Bolan Pass was about to be occupied in force and the passage of the army there contested. The receipt of this information produced a consultation between Macnaghten, Burnes, and Cotton, at which it was hastily decided to advance at once into the Bolan Pass, without a prior reference to Keane, in order to secure that entrance into Afghanistan. The next day Cotton issued corresponding orders to the force, the advanced portion of which, consisting of the engineers and sappers, strengthened by a detachment of infantry and native cavalry, was to march on February 22.

The Shah and the contingent had been at Shikarpore upwards of a month when the forward movement was determined, and the interval might have been employed to great advantage in ascertaining the supply of water and forage available for the advancing force throughout the ten marches which lay between Shikarpore and the mouth of the Bolan Pass. A very ordinary degree of foresight thus exercised would have saved the cattle of the army much needless distress, and greatly diminished the loss which ensued. Grain might have been sent on from Shikarpore, forage collected from the surrounding country upon the line of route, and precautions taken as to water. Time, men, and means were ample for the execution of such obvious and essential measures; but the army soon learnt that it might abound in envoys and major-generals, yet grievously suffer from a lack of foresight.

The distance between Shikarpore and Dadur is 171 miles, ninety-six of which are over a comparatively desert country, in which the villages are far asunder, water scarce and bad, and forage even of the poorest description very difficult to procure. Thirty-nine miles from Shikarpore this inhospitable tract first presents itself; and for a space of twenty-six miles the Pāt, as it is termed, offers neither blade of grass, bush, nor water, but an even surface of arid, friable, saline soil, crispy under foot like hoar frost, and glistening by moonlight in a manner not dissimilar. This boundary between Scinde and Cutch Gundava being passed, the country is not so absolutely sterile; but it is still comparatively a desert. Later in the year than the troops were to cross, that is from April to August, the passage of the plains of Gundava is an undertaking of peril, for the burning heat of the sun and the pestilential exhalations of the soil are often fatal to the man who dares them. The end of February was a favourable season for crossing the Pāt and the barren country beyond it; and had the antecedent month's leisure of the cavalry of the contingent been devoted to collecting, upon the line to be traversed, one or more depôts of grain, and supplies of forage at every halting-place, the march to Dadur might have been effected with small loss and inconvenience, and the cattle would have been in better heart for the difficulties and privations which awaited their onward progress. Instead of sweeping the surrounding country of the only fodder procurable, namely, straw or stalk of the jowar and bajra grains, which is always carefully stored by the villagers as provender for their cattle, the troops were marched into this tract of country as if upwards of 3,000 horses and 30,000 camels were in the possession of miraculous powers of abstinence.

At Shikarpore it had become known that the Bombay division and its commissariat must depend upon the aid of the commissariat of the Bengal division to furnish both camels and provision. This unforeseen demand did not diminish the difficulties of the single department upon which the onus of supplying an additional and a distant division was thrown; and having regard to the fact that no preparations had been made in advance, no depôts of grain or fodder established, and that it was impossible to calculate upon any supplies but such as the force carried with it or brought up from the rear, the exercise of common prudence was imperative. Fifteen thousand fighting men, accompanied by

Shah Shooja and his court, were to move on one line to Dadur; and upwards of 5,000 men by another on the same point; from thence both bodies were to advance on the same route upon Candahar. The division which landed with Keane ran little chance of being much encumbered by followers, but the 15,000 men at Shikarpore, with a march of 380 miles before them through a difficult and miserably poor country, from which little or no aid in supplies could be expected, might well have spared a part of its mass of non-combatants. Taking the most moderate estimate, there were not less than 80,000 men at Shikarpore, only 15,000 of whom were combatants, dependent on the commissariat for food. The army was proceeding into a sterile mountainous country equipped exactly in the same manner as if for service in the plains of India; whereas every consideration pointed out the expediency and necessity of adapting the number of mouths to be fed, and the equipage of the force, to the entirely different climate and country in which it was to act. No attempt was, however, made to limit the numbers of an embarrassing rabble, nor to diminish the lumbering baggage of the force. Common sense demanded that resources should be husbanded, and needless mouths be left where they could be fed without incurring risk to the expedition from the consumption of rations sure to be required for the fighting men. The display of foresight and of common sense at the opening of this campaign were, however, on a par.

The troops which were to lead marched on February 22. They were followed by the cavalry on the

23rd, and by the brigades of infantry on successive days; Shah Shooja and the contingent, strengthened by a brigade of regular troops, bringing up the rear. A battalion of infantry and a regiment of cavalry from the contingent were left at Shikarpore.

The leading body crossed the Pāt on the night of the 24th, reaching Bushor on the morning of the 25th; but finding the supply of water bad and insufficient, the engineer camp moved on to Meerpore on the 26th, accomplishing fifty-seven miles in forty-eight hours.

The cavalry, though marching by half-regiments, was much distressed in the advance from Shikarpore to Bushor by want of water and forage, and the possibility of a retrograde movement in consequence of the dearth of these necessary supplies was contemplated; but the officer sent forward to learn what promise the country held out was directed to return with the opinion of the engineer, Thomson, that at all hazards the cavalry should come on, as a retrograde movement at that time would be the ruin of the expedition. Thomson also intimated that he, with his small body of troops, would march on, whatever the course pursued by the cavalry. Thus early, however, did the want of timely and feasible arrangement for a moment endanger the conduct of operations.

By March 10, Cotton's force was assembled at Dadur. The horses had suffered severely from want of forage. from deficiency and badness of water, and from obtaining a partial supply of green wheat or barley, which proved most destructive to their condition and efficiency. The camels, rapidly disabled by want of food, by the heat of the weather, and by the fatigue of long marches and heavy loads, were dying fast; and the Beloochees had learnt from several successful sweeps, in which they carried off considerable booty, that a golden harvest awaited them when the columns and the baggage should once be engaged in threading the mountain passes. These losses in the open plains were very discreditable to the vigilance of the force, but it seemed the opinion that no effective measures to secure the line of march should be taken for fear of exciting the hostility of the Belooch tribes; and Burnes, when informed that in consequence of an attack upon a hospital waggon, and the wounding of some sick, orders had been issued to the leading detachment that the parties covering the line of march were at liberty to act against marauders, complained to Cotton against instructions which he characterised as 'bloodthirsty and calculated to bring on a blood feud.'

No supplies had been obtained between Shikarpore and Dadur, and great difficulty was already experienced in bringing them up from the rear, a difficulty not diminished by the necessary diversion of camels for the aid and supply of the Bombay division. On March 8 it had been found advisable to place the camp-followers on half-rations; yet no steps were taken at Dadur, before plunging into the defiles of a barren mountain country, to send back part of the non-combatants and to reduce the baggage. Cotton contented himself with directing that a better road than that between Bagh and Dadur should be made through the Bolan Pass, replying, when informed of the nature of the defile and the degree of clearance which could be effected, that 'the stones might be broken!'

The army was now to surmount a pass of much celebrity, but before entering upon this portion of its labours, rest was essential to the jaded cattle, and for commissariat arrangements. Accordingly a halt of five days was made at Dadur, but a detachment of cavalry and infantry under a good soldier, Cureton, was at once sent on to form the advance of the force, escort Burnes proceeding to Kelat, and cover the engineers, who moved into the Pass on March 11, with the view of rendering it practicable for the troops. The main body remained at Dadur until the 16th.

The ascent from the plains of the Indus to the highlands of Afghanistan is not effected by one sudden rise, but is spread over a considerable extent of country, throughout which parallel ranges of mountains form a series of steps from the burning plains to the elevated plateau. Where the streams draining these chains break through them, the most practicable passes are formed, and amongst them the Bolan is one of the least difficult. Its course is winding; where it lies along or slants across the valley between two ranges, the pass is wide and spacious; but where a break through a range is to be traversed, the defile narrows, and is close, jagged, and overhung by the precipices of the cleft chain. Water is abundant, fodder scarce, the road stony, and trying to the feet of camels and horses, but particularly so to those of bullocks, which wear to the quick from constant attrition in shingle and sharp gravel. The pass is fifty-nine miles in length.

Of this the first twenty-one miles present a very gradual ascent, though parts of the road are rough and bad, and not more than about 300 feet of elevation are gained; in the next nine miles the rise is more rapid, being about 600 feet; whilst in the next eight and a half miles a rise of 900 feet is surmounted; but the most trying part is that from Ab-i-goon to Sir-i-Kujour, where in nine and a half miles a rise of 1,950 feet has to be won by a fatiguing march in a great measure over boulders and rough ground. The last ten miles are not so distressing for cattle, although a rise of nearly 1,300 feet is made before the Dusht-i-bedowlut ('the profitless plain') greets the eye with a southernwood-covered expanse, bounded in the distance by snow-capped ranges of mountains.

From March 16th to 23rd the force under Cotton was threading the Bolan, unopposed in front except by the nature of the road, but losing many camels from fatigue, and some from the petty attacks of marauders. Much baggage was sacrificed, which was no disadvantage to the force, though it necessarily whetted the appetite of the Belooch for plunder; but the fall of many commissariat camels was a grievous matter for the troops, as each camel that carried flour bore a day's food for 160 Sepoys, and the loss of other stores and supplies, though less valuable, was far from unimportant. Encouraged by success, the marauders harassed the rear brigade, which, however, found no difficulty in making good its way, the opposition being slight; but an officer was badly wounded in the course of the desultory skirmishing. The 37th Regiment N.I. was left to secure the head of the Bolan, three of its companies having been left at Dadur to hold the *débouché* of the pass until the Shah and the troops escorting him should enter it.

Cotton reached Quetta on March 26, and as Keane's orders prohibiting a further advance were positive, he determined there to await the arrival of his chief with the Bombay troops.

The latter quitted Larkhana on March 12, but Keane, mortified at Cotton's advance, instead of marching, as was his original intention, to Shikarpore, struck off to his left and reached Gundava on the 21st, hoping to find the pass from thence to Kelat practicable, and to reach the highlands of Afghanistan and Quetta almost as soon as Cotton. Ten days were, however, spent in a halt opposite the mouth of the pass, the only result of the delay being a reconnaissance and a final decision not to attempt an advance on Kelat.

On the 31st the march was resumed, and on April 5 the Bombay force was at Dadur; Keane, however, having given up the hope of advancing on Kelat, had at length deemed it time to push ahead of the Bombay division, and had joined Shah Shooja's camp on March 26, within a march of the mouth of the Bolan Pass.

Cotton, as already stated, had reached Quetta on the same day; but apprehensions on the score of food beginning to be felt, Burnes on the 25th had started for Kelat, with the view of inducing Mehrab Khan, its ruler, to furnish supplies, and to pay his respects to Shah Shooja when that monarch should arrive. The Khan's promises to have depôts of grain collected both at Dadur and Quetta had proved fallacious, and there were other symptoms that the presence of an invading army was agreeable neither to him nor to his subjects. Burnes, however, having waited until the force reached Quetta, thought that, backed by the vicinity of such strength, he could induce or intimidate the Belooch into more energetic measures for provisioning the army.

At the same time Cotton despatched his Adjutant-General, Craigie, to acquaint Keane with the dilemma in which his peremptory orders forbidding a further advance placed the Bengal division, whose store of food was running so short that Cotton was overwhelmed with apprehension, and had already taken a most discouraging view of affairs.

The camp-followers had been on half-rations since March 8, notwithstanding which reduction in the daily consumption of food, the Bengal force found itself on the 27th with only about ten days' supply in camp. Candahar was 147 miles from Quetta, and before reaching the former place the Khojuk range of mountains must be passed. The value of the Khan of Kelat's promises was manifest, Quetta being disfurnished of grain; and the hope of obtaining supplies further in advance and nearer the enemy was evidently still more doubtful than that of finding them at Quetta. Whatever the course, therefore, which might ultimately be pursued by Keane, it became imperative to stave off absolute famine by economising to the uttermost the supply of food which remained. Nevertheless, Cotton, with a certainty that a few days of indecision was tantamount to the miserable ruin of his gallant troops, still hesitated from a fear of arousing discontent. He proposed, it is true, that the Sepoys should, in lieu of a pound of flour, receive half a pound of flesh, mutton being procurable; and as two pounds of flour is their full ration, there would thus have resulted a doubling of the period for which the stock in camp would be calculated to last. But the Sepoys, with the exception of the sappers and miners, refused the offer, as contrary to their habits and feelings; and Cotton shrank from any further action, either by advancing in contravention of Keane's orders or by ordering a necessary reduction of rations. Under these circumstances it seemed a question whether he would not close his temporarily independent command with no other decision on this all-important matter than that of leaving Keane, when too late to remedy Cotton's error, to meet as he best could gaunt famine in his camp.

The chief engineer, however, having learned the exhausted state of the commissariat, saw the necessity for instant decision, and urged the immediate adoption of the only measure which could fend off disaster, assuring Cotton that he would be responsible for the men under his command receiving the order for half rations without a murmur. Thus encouraged, and having subsequently ascertained from other officers commanding regiments that they concurred in the opinion that no danger need be apprehended from an order evidently imperatively necessary, Cotton at last issued his instructions for placing the fighting-men on half and the camp-followers on quarter rations, granting at the same time money compensation for the deduction. As foretold, the order was received without a murmur by the troops. It fell with great severity on the crowd of wretched camp-followers, who, unable to obtain sufficient sustenance in camp, sought it in the neighbouring villages, running the risk of being plundered and murdered whilst on such food-hunting wanderings; and in this manner many perished.

There was no grain for the cavalry horses; and the commissariat failing to procure forage of any description, the officers commanding corps were empowered to make their own arrangements—a liberty which, as it could fill no granaries and conjure up no stores of forage, effected no improvement in the condition of the cavalry. The grain-crops then rising were the only resource, necessarily a very partial one, and, moreover, affording but little nourishment. Officers, anxious for their chargers, paid the most exorbitant sums for dry lucerne and chopped straw.

The inhabitants of the surrounding villages, pressed to supply all they possessed in the form of food, were at first, though alarmed by the craving eagerness with which the search and requisition for provisions was carried on, in part reconciled to such proceedings by the readiness with which the most extravagant prices were paid for the necessaries of life; but at last they became exasperated at the prospect of everything being eaten up by the halting multitude of troops, camp-followers, and cattle; and finding the opportunity favourable for plunder, they deserted their villages, and sought to indemnify themselves for any losses which the presence of the force entailed by carrying off camels, and by stripping and murdering the camp-followers, who, though wanting food, were constantly found to have a good deal of money on their persons.

Matters continued in this state from March 27 until April 6, the force for eleven days idly consuming supplies, camp-followers starving, or seeking food at the peril of their lives, and the horses of the cavalry and artillery rapidly losing the little strength which was left them, when at last Keane came into camp and assumed the command of the army, thanking Cotton for the able and judicious manner in which he had conducted the long march of the Bengal troops, and for having arrived in Afghanistan in a highly creditable order.

CHAPTER IX.

APRIL–JUNE 1839.

BURNES'S NEGOTIATIONS WITH THE KHAN OF KELAT—ADVANCE OF THE FORCE — CHARACTER OF THE COUNTRY BETWEEN QUETTA AND CANDAHAR—ARRIVAL AT CANDAHAR—CONDITION OF THE TROOPS—EXPEDITION TO GIRISHK—ADVANCE UPON CABUL—POSITION OF DOST MAHOMED.

FANE had early taken the precaution to warn the commissariat department that failure on the part of the political officers would not be held a valid excuse in the event of a deficiency of supplies for the army being felt in the course of military operations. Burnes, entrusted with the formation of depôts of grain and stores in Upper Scinde, had failed to accomplish this object; and Macnaghten passed a month in inactivity at Shikarpore, during which time he had the opportunity of partly remedying Burnes's failure by the establishment of depôts of grain and forage on the route to the mouth of the Bolan Pass. The army very early had occasion to think of Fane's prophetic warning.

Macnaghten's impatience for an advance, urged on by his Government and by Burnes, and acceptable to Cotton, thrust the troops onwards without any sufficient reason, and before such arrangements as were feasible and necessary with respect to water and supplies could be made. The Shah's contingent, strengthened by a few regular troops, had been pronounced on February 6 sufficient for the march on Candahar and Herat; a far smaller detachment could, therefore, have marched to, and if thought desirable through, the pass, and secured right of way for the columns, which could subsequently have followed when commissariat arrangements for the combined Bengal and Bombay forces had been effected.

After the submission of the Ameers, Keane's presence was essential at Shikarpore, where he could have controlled operations. He had seen Fane and learnt from him the qualities of the various officers, envoys, and generals, and being responsible to his country for the safety, welfare, and success of a considerable force about to launch on a hazardous expedition, he ought not to have left the direction of events one moment longer than avoidable in the hands of men whose rule of action seemed to be neglect of all that foresight and prudence demanded; and who, whatever their abilities in other respects, proved from the first that commanding an army was not their vocation, and that they wanted the military ability which it is the fashion to despise, but which on trial few men are found to possess, whether soldiers by profession or civil envoys vested with the control of operations. Keane's contemplated movement of the Bombay column up the Gundava Pass would have been a good one, had his force been properly provided with camels and food, and had he properly reconnoitred the pass; but neither was the case, and he turned from a defile which was practicable because he thought it the reverse, having intended to attempt it without the necessary equipment of provisions and baggage-cattle for his troops. Though it was a difficult, because a very fatiguing, pass to ascend, had he succeeded in his object the Bombay division would have had the advantage of a line on which forage had not been consumed; both the Bengal and Bombay columns might have been on the highlands of Afghanistan about the same time; and being a shorter period in threading the passes they would have offered less opportunity for the Belooch to assemble, watch column after column, and attack and plunder as circumstances favoured. The Khan of Kelat, moreover, would have been in direct communication with the Commander-in-Chief, and Burnes might have been spared the exercise of a diplomatic wisdom which promised to furnish Mehrab Khan with a lac and a half of rupees likely to be used, if he were not well-disposed, in raising and paying the tribes. The conception, therefore, was good, had means corresponded and proper arrangements been made.

Keane's peremptory orders to Cotton to halt at Quetta without advertence to the condition of the Bengal column were most ill-judged. For eleven days he kept a body of fighting men on half rations, and a mass of camp-followers on quarter rations, uselessly consuming their scanty supply, which even with such severe husbandry was barely enough to enable them to reach Candahar; and, when about to enter a hostile country having the character of furnishing formidable horsemen, he gave the finishing blow to the greater part of his own cavalry by thus confining them to a spot which was soon bald of forage. To have instructed Cotton to continue advancing by easy marches, without pressing his jaded cattle, husbanding provisions and forage to the uttermost, and keeping his troops as well together as circumstances admitted, would have been the safest and the wisest course, that least destructive of the efficiency of the cavalry arm of the force, and calculated to give the earliest relief to starving followers and half-fed soldiers, whilst at the same time affording the rear brigades the required opportunity of closing up.

Keane risked much by the order which bound Cotton to Quetta, and gained nothing but exemption from the fatigue of the few forced marches which would have sufficed to have early placed him with the advance. In fact, he had perilled the success of the expedition, as was proved by the perusal of despatches found in the Bolan Pass, and opened by Colonel Dennie. The retreat, by forced marches, of the Bengal and Bombay columns had been the subject of consideration.

Weary of a halt, the tedium of which was only diversified by rumours of a petty, futile, and discreditable diplomacy; by the success of marauders, who plundered and murdered with comparative impunity; and by the contemplation of the wretchedness and misery of the starving followers; the army hailed with pleasure the arrival of Keane, well assured that the circumstances under which he assumed command were such that an immediate forward movement was the only course open to him, unless, as from his known courage was altogether improbable, he preferred the ignominy of a disastrous retreat. The troops were confident that the adoption of the latter alternative was not to be expected from a brave man, and he lost no time in justifying their expectations.

Inquiry soon satisfied Keane that the prospect of obtaining provisions from Kelat could not for a moment be entertained. Burnes had, it was true, concluded a treaty with the Khan of Kelat, by which the latter bound himself to supply grain and camels for the force, and to pay a visit of homage to Shah Shooja, receiving in return the guarantee of the sovereignty of Beloochistan, the disposal of its revenue, and the promise of a subsidy to the amount of a lac and a half of rupees. As an earnest of the generosity and friendly intentions of the British authorities acting in the name of the Shah, Burnes had, moreover, paid down to Mehrab Khan 20,000 rupees, and he calculated on thus inducing the Kelat ruler to proceed to Quetta without delay and there to pay homage. But Burnes's temperament and conduct marred every diplomatic transaction in which he engaged, and whilst in Upper Scinde he had indisposed the Khan of Kelat towards himself. Upon a report hastily made, and credulously received, which charged Mehrab Khan with confiscating grain collected in Cutchee for the army, Burnes wrote a menacing and imperious letter to the Khan, and further induced Shah Shooja basely to threaten his benefactor, who had received him when a helpless fugitive, had afforded him a safe asylum from his pursuers, and had secured his unmolested escape to the plains of the Indus. Mehrab Khan was reminded that Shah Nawaz Khan, a rival claimant of the Kelat throne, was in Shah Shooja's camp. This ingratitude, and Burnes's insulting letter, had early sown distrust.

The Khan was, however, very desirous of a good understanding with the British Government; for it had curbed Scinde, and was about to bit the mouths of the Candaharees, and in so doing it effected what was most desirable for his own safety and independence. He had nothing to apprehend from an alliance with a Government powerful but distant, and devoid of any motive for coveting a territory so little worth as that of Kelat, while he had much to fear from the Ameers of Scinde and the chiefs of Candahar. Open hostility towards the British power was certain and inevitable destruction. Considerations of future policy and present safety, therefore, alike counselled him to accept the very favourable treaty proffered to him. But to place himself in the hands of Shah Shooja, after the threat he had received, was a step repugnant to Belooch caution, and the Khan's suspicion was not allayed by Burnes's eagerness to purchase his march to Quetta with the gratuitous donation of 20,000 rupees. Burnes's hasty departure from Kelat, after deputing the notorious Mohun Lal to escort the Khan to the Shah's presence, left the doubtful and wavering chief to the full play of his own fears and the evil suggestions of plotting foes in his councils.

Whether alarmed by the intimation that treachery was contemplated, or anxious to communicate the nature of the arrangements made at Kelat, Burnes had unfortunately quitted the place without the Khan; and, being attacked by plunderers on the road, he was the first, on reaching Quetta, to protest against the treaty he had concluded, assuming, without inquiry and against all probability, that the attack on his baggage had been made by order of Mehrab Khan. The latter was consequently still more averse to submitting himself to Shah Shooja, having no confidence in the good faith of the Shah or in the discriminating justice of his advisers, and being naturally disinclined to compromise personal safety by placing himself at the mercy of the disreputable natives by whom the envoy and minister Macnaghten was led in his attempts to effect strokes of policy.

That which most concerned Keane was the evident failure of the endeavour to draw supplies of grain from Kelat. The treaty, whether repudiated or not by the person who had dictated it, signified little provided grain had been found, purchased, and brought into camp. Even if it had been ascertained that any store existed at Kelat, the circumstances of Keane's position would have warranted an armed requisition for supplies. But though a commissariat officer had accompanied the diplomatist, and had offered prices so extravagantly high that the avarice of dealers would have been amply satiated, not only was there a want of success in effecting purchases, but no knowledge was obtained of the existence of stores of grain. Keane therefore gave up at once any further thought of obtaining the much-needed aid of supplies from Kelat and its environs, and issued instructions for the immediate advance of the force; directing Nott, who chafed at being left in the rear, to command at Quetta with two regiments of native infantry and a rissalah of Shah Shooja's horse under his orders.

The country which the army had to traverse before reaching Candahar may be divided into two distinct tracts, separated from each other by the Khojuk range of mountains. The first, comprising the whole extent of country between the crest of the Bolan Pass and the Khojuk chain, may be regarded, notwithstanding the gradual descent indicated by the course of its streams in a westerly direction, as an elevated plateau of about fifty miles in breadth, having the Bolan mountains for its retaining wall towards the plains of the Indus, and the declivities of the Khojuk range for its revetment towards the plain of Candahar. This tract, the highlands of Beloochistan, is intersected by subordinate chains of hills and a few inconsiderable streams, so that its surface is a chequered series of southernwood-covered plains, bounded by barren, snow-capped mountains. The population, consisting chiefly of the Belooch, but partly of Afghan tribes, is wild, poor, and scanty; the villages are few, and the towns inconsiderable in magnitude and strength; the produce of the cultivated soil is moderate, and not exceeding the wants of the inhabitants, who, finding abundant pasture for their sheep in the grasses and aromatic plants of their broad plains, regard their flocks as a material portion of their food and wealth. Although the tamarisk is found at the river which drains the Pisheen Valley, the tract of country under consideration presents no great difference in its vegetable productions, whether cultivated or wild; the gradual descent from Quetta to the base of the eastern slope of the Khojuk, producing no other effect than somewhat earlier crops in the lower districts. The wild flowers on plain and mountain are in spring and summer numerous and beautiful, and the flora of this region may be more correctly compared with that of the Levant than with the customary forms which decorate an Eastern soil.

The Khojuk chain, which separates the foregoing plateau from the lower plain on which Candahar is situated, is a mountain range of no marked outline, in consequence of the rounded features assumed by the slate formation which in general occupies the most elevated part of the range. The ascent from the side of Quetta is comparatively easy and gentle, until near the summit; the descent, however, on the Candahar side is more bluff-like and difficult, the underlying sandstone presenting precipitous slopes, and the drop to the plain beneath being accordingly not only greater than on the Quetta side, but also more sheer and abrupt.

After descending to the lower level, there is a marked difference in the climate, the Candahar plain being in level two thousand feet beneath the Quetta plateau. The heat even in the month of April is great,[1] and the crops are earlier than on the highlands of Kelat. The villages are, however, few, and the tract may be characterised as interspersed with low ranges of hills, chiefly of limestone capping plutonic rocks, and thus offering to the traveller a series of stony unproductive plains, bounded by barren mountains of jagged,

[1] 98° and upwards in tents, according to the writer's private journal, in April 1839.

precipitous, and frequently singular forms. The plains are, however, in reality, long glacis-slopes to the bases of the ranges of hills and mountains which hem them in; the effect of such even, gradual, and unbroken slopes in a pure clear atmosphere on the apparent distance of objects is most deceptive, and often the weary and exhausted soldier, whose eye had been formed by the experience and perspective of the denser air of the heated plains of India, or of the moist clime of England, was disappointed by finding that the apparent was far different from the real distance of the encampment towards which he was marching. The streams are few, and water scarce; but the inhabitants have an ingenious method of bringing it to the surface for purposes of irrigation; the system is a result of the configuration of the plains above described, and consists in the excavation of underground galleries, which, by being carried nearly horizontally from the point at which a good spring of water is struck high up on the glacis-slope, gradually bring it to the surface at a lower level. Having no means of ventilating galleries in the course of excavation, the Candaharees necessarily effect this object by sinking frequent shafts or wells at short distances apart, by means of which the execution of the subterranean galleries is much facilitated, the proper direction secured, and the water-level carried on correctly; the wells gradually diminishing in depth as they approach the point where the gallery or *kariz* discontinues and delivers the water upon the surface to be irrigated.

From the foregoing general description it will have

been understood that the country to be traversed by the army between Quetta and Candahar was difficult, presenting many natural obstacles and strong positions, and throughout deficient in the prime necessaries for the subsistence of an army—wood, water, forage, and provisions. Rivers in a mountainous country are usually deep of channel and precipitous of bank. The ravines, which drain the glacis-slopes at the base of the hills, falling into rivers of deep bed, are themselves deep, and numerous. Mountain passes, where of formidable elevation, must be surmounted by roads which have to be cut; and this labour is succeeded, first, by that of dragging guns, ammunition-waggons, and bullock-carts up the steep way, and then by the scarce minor exertion of carefully running or lowering them down the reverse slopes. Where mountain passes need no carving of new roadways, they are rough, stony, narrow, and difficult of ascent or descent, and call for constant labour on the part of the troops. An ancient army had its *impedimenta*, but these were playthings in comparison with the ordnance train of a modern army; and the toil which it inflicts, whenever difficulties are to be overcome, on the not degenerate soldier of the nineteenth century must be witnessed to be comprehended. When this toil is superadded to half-rations and the customary want of water in such positions, the patient endurance of the modern soldier in honourless labour merits praise as high as that bestowed upon the iron soldiery of Rome, and such praise was, on this occasion of the passage of the Khojuk, fairly won by the first European regiment of the

Bengal army to whom Keane was mainly indebted for the successful manner in which the obstacle was surmounted.

On April 7 the army marched from Quetta, and on the 11th the engineers, having pushed on into the pass, were engaged in preparing a practicable road over the Khojuk for the wheeled carriages and baggage-cattle of the force; on the morning of the 13th the work was completed, and the sapper camp crossed over to the western side of the range.

The Candahar chiefs had thrown forward small bodies of horse to observe the passes of this mountain chain, and to watch and report the advance of the British troops. The vedettes of one of these parties occupied the crest of the ridge, and nearly succeeded on the morning of the 11th in cutting off a captain of engineers and a brigadier of cavalry, who had somewhat carelessly ridden up the pass; but catching sight of the head of the column of the sappers and miners, the Afghan vedettes, who had been pressing their horses in pursuit boldly down the steep spurs of the mountain, suddenly drew up, and, saluting the two officers with a few long shots, quietly withdrew to the crest of the ridge and watched the progress of the advancing column. Seeing the men ground their knapsacks and in two bodies rapidly ascend the separate gorges by which the crest could be reached, the Afghan horsemen leisurely descended the Candahar side of the mountain, and when the sappers had reached the summit, the enemy were seen drawn up out of musket-shot at the base of the steep descent. After observing for a while the crest from which they had withdrawn, and which was now for the first time glancing with British bayonets, the small body turned their horses' heads towards the plain, and marched off in the direction of Candahar. This was the first and only show of military alertness which the Candahar chiefs displayed in the course of the campaign, and therefore merits notice for its insignificance.

There was, however, no lack of activity amongst the marauding tribes who infest these hills: they carried off camels, plundered baggage, and murdered camp-followers, whenever such feats could be performed with impunity. Fortunately they were neither bold nor skilful, otherwise the loss sustained would have been far greater; and it was evident that they were impelled simply by the love of booty, and that, as they were acting without concert in small independent parties, the army had to contend with no organised scheme of guerilla warfare. The existence of the force depended wholly upon its camels, and the fact was so obvious that the rapid destruction of these would undoubtedly have formed the main object, because the most practicable and effective, had the wild Belooch and Afghan tribes been summoned into the field to exterminate their invaders. Every march offered repeated opportunities in which a few resolute men, keeping the above fact steadily in view, could, with little or no risk to themselves, have shot down the baggage-cattle in hundreds. There was no necessity to have slain the fighting-men, or to have offered them a direct and stubborn opposition. The fate of the army would have been sure, and its destruction inevitable had such a course been pursued; but there had been no patriotic or fanatic spirit raised, and the marauders, being hounded on solely by the love of plunder, sought rather to carry off a few camels than, by leisurely crippling, ultimately to annihilate the force. The Atchukzyes of the Khojuk reaped as rich a harvest as the Kakurs, Belooch, and other tribes of the Bolan.

The Bengal division had lain eleven days at Quetta, within fifty miles of the Khojuk range, yet no reconnaissance was during that time made of the three passes by which the line of mountains could be traversed; and the army, selecting that reported to have most water, found it a far more serious obstacle than had been anticipated. Whether either of the other passes would have offered less difficulty was never ascertained, for it was held better, notwithstanding abundance of time and capable officers, to blunder blindly into a defile, ignorant of its real character, than to employ leisure-time and officers in exploring the several passes. The army, including the park of artillery, was occupied from the 11th to the 21st in overcoming this obstacle, and lost—besides much baggage, tents, many camels, and a proportion of supplies—27,400 rounds of musket ammunition, and a portion of its spare powder. The time so unprofitably spent at Quetta would have been better employed in effecting the passage of the Khojuk; but, a general of foresight, though forced to halt in obedience to the mandates of his superior, would have made use of the time in ascertaining the practicability of the passes within fifty miles of his position.

Whilst Keane with the Bengal column was surmounting the Khojuk, Willshire at the head of the Bombay column was effecting the passage of the Bolan; yet not unmolested, for he lost grain, camels, and baggage, though Daly, of the 4th Dragoons, and others, ably seized opportunities of inflicting bloody chastisement on the marauders.

Halting on the 19th and 20th a march beyond the foot of the pass, Keane waited until the certainty that his park of artillery was disengaged from the defile should enable him to advance. A body of cavalry was said to threaten an attack on his camp, and Shah Shooja, mindful of former reverses, was in a state of perpetual alarm; but foes never showed themselves, and but for the loss of two elephants belonging to the envoy and minister, and the cowardly slaughter of some followers, the proximity of any of the Afghan horse would never have been credited. Two of the Candahar chiefs, at the head of about 2,000 horse, had, however, advanced to within twenty-five miles of the Khojuk; but when their vedettes, which were in observation of the passes, fell back before the British advance, the main body prepared to retrograde towards Candahar, and did so with impunity, the captured elephants being carried off as trophies.

Haji Khan, a Kakur chief, infamous even among Afghans for faithlessness and insincerity, rightly judged, upon the retreat of the Candahar chiefs, and the reports of the strength by which Shah Shooja was supported, that his masters could not cope with their formidable adversaries. He therefore hastened to desert them, and to secure the merit of being the first to pay homage to Shah Shooja and submit to his authority. That one so notoriously untrue should be the first to offer his submission was an unpropitious omen, though indicative of the weakness of the Candahar chiefs.

Keane, continuing his advance on the 21st, reached Candahar on April 26, 1839; he arrived before the place, a very weak one, with only two days' supply of half-rations for his force, and with his cavalry wholly inefficient, both from actual loss and from the emaciated state of the horses which survived. Starvation, want of water, and fatigue had so reduced them that the cavalry brigade lost in one march (on the 22nd) no less than fifty-eight horses; and when at length the river bank was reached the rush was uncontrollable, and some of the animals fell, utterly exhausted, and perished in the water.

The infantry was in good heart, though half-rations had affected the physical strength of the men, more particularly of the Sepoys, who could not bring themselves to eat of flesh freely. The labour and fatigue at the Khojuk Pass, followed by exposure to a great and sudden increase of heat, and by the use of brackish water, had shaken the health both of Europeans and natives, and a severe bowel complaint was prevalent amongst the troops. The condition of the camp-followers was pitiable; their rations, insufficient for strength, had barely maintained life, and they hailed with joy the sight of the Dooranee capital, confident that their want and misery would there be alleviated. Many of their number had, however, already fallen victims to hunger and to the knives of pitiless plunderers.

Shah Shooja, who after crossing the Khojuk had been haunted by reminiscences of his former expedition against Candahar, and had evinced a painful state of apprehension, even rising to listen to every noise in camp, and neither concealing nor controlling his vain alarm, shook off this extreme timidity when reassured by the defection of Haji Khan Kakur; and having heard on the 23rd that the Candahar chiefs were in the act of flight, he outmarched the troops on the following day and entered the city. His reception was not flattering. The influential chiefs kept aloof until affairs should assume a determinate form, and the conduct of the Shah and his foreign supporters should be developed. The people were indifferent, for although the popularity of their late rulers was at a low ebb, a king established by British bayonets could not be acceptable to a nation in whom the love of independence and the hate of a foreign yoke are alike strong. They saw at once that Shah Shooja, who had formerly fled disgracefully from Candahar, now returned to it equally dishonoured, a mere puppet in our hands. Moreover, discontent was soon excited by the high price to which grain at once rose on the arrival of the Shah and the British army. Although the fields waved with a goodly crop of ripening corn, it was evident, from the great demand caused by the force and its followers, that the distress into which the poor had been thrown would be but little relieved by the approaching harvest, a large portion of which would be consumed by the invaders.

Shah Shooja pressed for the immediate pursuit of the chiefs who fled to the Helmund and occupied Girishk; but Keane's force was not in a condition to despatch a detachment upon such a mission; men and cattle needed rest; the cavalry was in part to be remounted, and there was the imperative duty of taking immediate measures for the supply of the army. Recourse was had, therefore, to negotiation, and overtures were made to the ex-chiefs inviting them to surrender on condition of banishment to India with moderate stipends for a sustenance. They rejected the proffered terms, preferring to keep the one thing now left them—their liberty, and hoping that the future might yet have a happier lot in store for them than an Indian exile, which, from the days of Baber, has ever been the dread of Afghan nobles, even when the victorious and favoured followers of their conquering emperors.

On the last day of April the park of artillery marched into camp, and four days after, Willshire, with the Bombay column, also reached Candahar. Keane now had the main body of his force together, the only corps in the rear being those left to keep open his communications and the two regiments of native infantry escorting the Shah's artillery, which was struggling in the defiles of the Bolan at the time that the Bombay troops effected their junction with the Bengal force under the walls of Candahar.

Having obtained quiet possession of the Dooranee capital and placed Shah Shooja upon his throne on May 8, Keane had accomplished the first object of the expedition, and had gained a new base from whence to start in completion of the operations entrusted to him. These, as the Persians had relinquished their designs on Herat, were now limited to the pursuit of the ex-chiefs of Candahar, the overthrow of the ruler of Cabul, and the capture of his fortresses. The army was not in a state at once to undertake the additional effort of a march upon Ghuznee and Cabul. Its camels needed grazing and rest, and that their loss of numbers should be made good; to remount a portion of its cavalry and to restore this arm to efficiency demanded rest, food, and time; and the provisioning of the army still remained an object of solicitude, for in Candahar the price of grain was exorbitant, and the supply far smaller than had been anticipated. A convoy which, when it quitted Shikarpore, was said to consist of 2,000 camels with 8,000 maunds of grain, reached camp it is true, but delivered only about 1,500 maunds. Another convoy, consisting of Lohanee merchants entrusted with 20,000 maunds of grain, was on its way, but from the line by which it was to travel it was open to attack or diversion by Dost Mahomed, or by independent tribes of plundering Afghans, and could not, therefore, be calculated upon with certainty. The crops, indeed, were good, but they had to be cut and collected, and some time must elapse before this supply could operate towards the relief of the necessities of the army. Keane was, therefore, compelled to continue the issue of half-rations, and had the further mortification to find that as fruit became abundant, and naturally was consumed with avidity by fighting men and followers, the activity of the disorder prevalent in his camp was thereby stimulated ; and the heat being excessive, and the excitement inseparable from a daily march temporarily at an end, the hospitals were full and the deaths, particularly amongst the European soldiery, numerous. So unequal at this time was the force to a great effort, that when an expedition to Girishk was finally resolved upon in order to dislodge the ex-chiefs from their place of refuge, the detachment sent proceeded on half-rations, and the small body of regular cavalry which accompanied it, consisting of about the strength of one squadron, was made up by details of men and horses from two regiments.

Sale was placed in command of this detachment, which, after a fatiguing march to the River Helmund, found the fort of Girishk deserted by the ex-chiefs, who were said to have fled towards Seistan. The Helmund was at the time (May 19) of very swift flow, and Sale, with a hundred European infantry, had with difficulty crossed over upon small rafts floated on empty rum-casks, when he received intimation that the fort was evacuated and that he was to halt on the left bank of the river. A regiment of the Shah's contingent having subsequently crossed over to occupy Girishk, Sale retraced his steps and reached Candahar on May 29. He brought back the political officer it had been thought necessary to send with the detachment, and who was to have proceeded from Girishk to explore Seistan ; the supposed flight of the ex-chiefs in that direction rendered his journey thither for the time inexpedient. The native information collected respecting Seistan was meagre and unsatisfactory; but the person selected to remove this state of ignorance was singularly disqualified for the duty; he knew nothing of Persian, and was so unacquainted with instruments that a portable gnomon, the use of which he did not comprehend, formed the only means by aid of which he had contemplated mapping an unknown country. Macnaghten's ostensible object in deputing this political mission to Seistan was the establishment of British influence and the purchase of grain for the provisioning of Herat; but his choice of an individual to carry such views into effect betrayed that no real importance could have been attached to these objects.

The ruler of Herat, after the angry altercations with Pottinger in January, had been further alarmed by the news he received of the advance of the British army; and though he and his people were living on the generosity of the British Government, yet, suspicious of our ultimate intentions, his Wazeer made overtures in March both to the Persian court and to the Candahar chiefs for a coalition against Shah Shooja and his British allies. The Persians were too much alarmed to respond to these advances, which they mistrusted, and the Candahar chiefs were in May fugitives beyond the the Helmund. Kamran therefore deemed it advisable to despatch his Topshee Bashee to Candahar to congratulate Shah Shooja and the British envoy. He was furnished with instructions to refuse the aid of guns or troops if proffered, and to confine his demand to the one article, money.

Pottinger's expenditure had been lavish and unwise,

and had habituated Kamran and his officers to do nothing, however clearly to the advantage of their power, without being exorbitantly paid for the exertion. Kamran possessed a truly Afghan appetite for gold, and the Topshee Bashee's avowed object was to obtain more. Macnaghten, attaching great importance to Herat, was bent on deputing scientific officers to examine the fortress, and to report upon its capabilities of defence, and to effect such repairs or additions as could be executed; he was also desirous of replacing Pottinger by some other political officer; he therefore succeeded in inducing the Herat envoy to concur in the deputation of Major Todd, accompanied by officers of engineers and artillery, and carrying with him two lacs of rupees. All apprehensions for the immediate safety of the place had subsided; but Macnaghten, under an infatuate dread of Russian machinations, was dissatisfied with the capricious spirit which Kamran exhibited in regard to a closer connection with the British power; and, nothing assured against the sudden apparition of a Russo-Persian force before Herat, the British envoy was eager to bring its ruler to a more cordial and less reserved, if not suspicious, line of policy.

Meanwhile contradictory reports and vague information was received from the direction of Cabul; but Macnaghten, who had discovered, in the Shah's reception at Candahar, popular enthusiasm, and had failed to correct this creation of his own imagination by the marked absence of the people from the pomp and ceremony of the Shah's entertainments, concluded in a like spirit, from the news with which he was furnished, that the march of the army to Cabul would be unopposed; and persuaded Keane, wholly dependent on the envoy for political information, to attach weight to this favourable view of affairs.

Money was scarce, for although there had been more than thirty lacs of rupees expended in Candahar in a short space of time, yet the attempt to negotiate a loan entirely failed. The treasure which was to have started from Shikarpore on May 23 had not been heard of as approaching, neither had the Lohanee convoy with grain; but Macnaghten, impatient of the prolonged halt, and himself convinced of what he desired, sought to diminish the difficulties of the advance by proposing to leave the Bombay troops at Candahar, assuring Keane that this could be done without risk, as he, Macnaghten, would stake his credit that not a shot would be fired in opposition to Shah Shooja's march to Cabul.

Keane had permitted himself to be persuaded and had assented to the proposal; but reflection brought doubts, and having spoken to his engineer, Thomson, the latter reminded him 'that England would look to the general as responsible for the success of the expedition, and that it would be no excuse in the eyes of Europe for the failure and disgrace of a British army that Keane had acted on the advice and assurances of Macnaghten.' Thomson concluded by referring to the Commander-in-Chief's own experience, and begged him 'to consider whether he had found the information hitherto given by the political department in any single instance correct.' Keane perceived his error, and immediately intimated to Macnaghten his more mature decision to carry on with him all the European troops. The resolution was in its result fortunate for his own reputation and for the honour of the British name, which might otherwise have been early tarnished in Afghanistan.

The impunity with which our camels were repeatedly carried off evinced a want of alertness and military precaution not creditable to the army; but the fact also betrayed no very amicable feeling on the part of the villages in the neighbourhood of the Shah's newly acquired capital, who, when not accomplices, must have been cognisant of the haunts and track of the marauders. This, however, might have been viewed as nothing more than an uncontrollable love of plunder excited by gross mismanagement and neglect; but the case was more significant and serious when Macnaghten felt himself under the necessity of warning Keane that the Ghilzye chiefs, although they had taken the money sent to purchase their goodwill, had abstained from submission to Shah Shooja, and contemplated intercepting the convoy which the Lohanee chief was bringing towards Candahar. Keane, alarmed for his convoy, on account of which he had prolonged his halt, trusting to be enabled to restore his army to full rations upon its arrival, despatched a strong detachment of cavalry, infantry, and guns, to discover and escort it. The detachment returned unsuccessful, and a second of similar strength was sent out on a like errand. Fortunately, some time previous to the threatened movement of the Ghilzyes, Keane, as a precautionary measure, had instructed a rissalah of irregular cavalry, under the command of its officer, Uzeem Khan, to proceed from Candahar, and, joining the convoy, to accompany it into camp. Uzeem Khan succeeded in finding his charge; and by great firmness, and a vigilance which kept his men night and day armed and on the alert, he defeated the endeavours of Dost Mahomed's emissaries to induce the Lohanee chief and his followers to divert the convoy from its destination. The chief was himself a person of courage and resolution, and his men were of like temper and numerous; but the evident determination of Uzeem Khan and his troopers to resist treachery with their lives, and the manner in which they always marched and bivouacked, precluded all hope of diverting the convoy from its proper route except at the expense of a sanguinary combat. On June 23 Uzeem Khan convoyed his charge safely into camp, and Keane, alive to the soldierly qualities displayed, warmly lauded him for the important service he had rendered to the army.

Great, however, was the disappointment of Keane and the whole army when this long-expected convoy proved of little further use than as a depôt of grain at Candahar, which lightened the pressure on the harvests of the season and the food of the people. The Lohanee and his followers were unwilling to proceed further, and even had the cash in the military chest admitted of the purchase of their camels, which they were willing to sell, yet without drivers, whom money could not then obtain, the animals would have been useless. Keane, under these circumstances, counting upon the later harvest of the highlands about Cabul, and expecting to obtain partial supplies from the country to be traversed, determined, without endeavouring to effect any arrangement for the better provisioning of his force, to march on Cabul with barely a sufficiency of food to carry his army thither on half-rations. The decision was in itself a hazardous one, but the risk was much increased by the resolve to leave the battering-guns at Candahar. This measure was due to reports of the weakness of Ghuznee, which it was said could be breached by field-guns; to the assurances, as positive as ever, that no resistance would occur, and to a representation from the officer commanding the artillery that the bullocks were unequal to the duty of dragging the four eighteen-pounders. These guns had with great labour been brought to Candahar, and far more serious obstacles had been surmounted than any which would have presented themselves between Candahar and Cabul; the cattle had, it was true, suffered in the march to Candahar, but the long stay at that place had restored them, and there was no assignable reason why the guns should not have continued to accompany the army, instead of a Bombay field-battery of twenty-four-pounder howitzers, a piece utterly useless as a battering-gun, which was preferred. The same motives which led Keane to march with all the available European infantry should have determined him in carrying on his train, whatever the exertion necessary; and he yielded too easily to the wishes of the brigadiers of artillery. Strictly speaking, Keane in this matter committed a grievous military error; but, as if in mockery of human prudence and foresight, war occasionally affords instances in which a mistake becomes, under the inscrutable will of Providence, the immediate cause of brilliant and startling success: and such this error ultimately proved.

As a garrison for the Dooranee capital, about to become the base of a new line of operations, Keane assigned two battalions of native infantry, two troops of horse artillery, a body of the Shah's cavalry, and the battering-guns, with a company of foot artillery. Notwithstanding the alleged popularity of Shah Shooja, the covert hostility of the people was already more than suspected; but as more troops were advancing on Candahar with convoys and with the Shah's artillery, the garrison would be reinforced by the time that the distance of the main army rendered reinforcement desirable; and as the force left in position was well provisioned, Keane could regard Candahar—to him a most important military post—as for the present safe.

Keane was entirely ignorant of what awaited him in advancing against Dost Mahomed, whose amount of force was as variously estimated as the probability of his opposing the march of the British army; he was reported to be strengthening Ghuznee and Cabul, and to be exciting the Ghilzye tribes, through whose country the army must advance, to co-operate in harassing the march of the British force. Keane had little apprehension for the result of an action in the field; his force, consisting of three troops of horse and two batteries of foot artillery, a regiment and a half of European cavalry, two and a half of native cavalry with one and a half of irregular horse, four battalions of European and three of native infantry, was ample to insure victory over undisciplined levies. The fear was that the enemy, avoiding the risk of defeat in a general action, would confine himself to an active guerilla warfare, and to the defence of fortified posts, a system which would have been well calculated to embarrass Keane, with whom, in consequence of his small supply of food, delay and destruction were synonymous.

During the advance upon and occupation of Candahar, Dost Mahomed's attention had been occupied by the direct advance which was to be apprehended from the side of Peshawur, where Wade, playing at royalty with Shahzada Timour in his camp, had since the end of March been assembling a motley levy, and endeavouring to attract partisans to the Shah's cause. The Cabul ruler detached his son, Akbar Khan, to the Khybur to watch the advance of Wade and his Sikh allies, and to excite the Khybur tribes to oppose operations which were doubtless expected to be more rapid and energetic than they proved. Suspicious of these tribes, whose good faith can never be relied upon, he apparently instructed Akbar Khan not to compromise himself and his force by the occupation and defence of the pass, but only to countenance and encourage the Khyburees, keeping Dost Mahomed's detachment of Afghans in reserve. On the Candahar side the advance of Keane might be retarded by the exertions of the Candahar chiefs, aided by the tribes of the Bolan and Khojuk. Considering Dost Mahomed's limited means, both in men and money, for the defence of his country, he evidently selected the most judicious course in resolving thus to await the nearer approach of his foes; judging rightly that it would be difficult to combine accurately the movements of two bodies of troops, acting on different and very distant lines of operations, the intercommunication between which was at his own mercy; and that he would be able, by keeping a central position with his Afghan levies, to afford them the opportunity, if well-inclined to his cause, of attacking the one army before the other could be in a position to influence the issue. Having sent one of his sons to the Khybur, he entrusted to another the defence of Ghuznee, ordering him to build up the gateways, cover them with screen walls, strengthen the works, and provision the place for the 3,000 men thrown into it. Accurately informed, after the army reached Candahar, of its strength, condition, and movements, Dost Mahomed calculated on Ghuznee detaining Keane for a sufficient time to enable him, aided by the Ghilzye tribes, to beset and attack the besieging force with superior numbers and under favourable circumstances; and he knew that if success attended his endeavours against Keane's advance, and fortune again favoured him at the expense of Shah Shooja, Wade, with his heterogeneous levy and Sikh contingent, would be easily thrust back by an appeal to the fanatic spirit of the Afghans against their hated foes of the Punjab. He could also reasonably entertain hopes that the approaching end of Runjeet Singh might lead to a disturbed state of affairs; and that the Sikh contingent of 6,000 men, dreading the Khybur, would, nothing loath, hasten to engage in the political contests more interesting to their passions and nearer to their homes.

CHAPTER X.

JUNE–AUGUST 1839.

THE VALLEY OF THE TURNUK—STORM OF GHUZNEE—FLIGHT OF DOST MAHOMED—ARRIVAL OF THE BRITISH FORCE AT CABUL.

On June 27 Keane quitted Candahar and commenced his march towards Cabul, followed on the 28th by Shah Shooja and the centre column, and on the 29th by Willshire, who with the Bombay division formed the rearward.

The valley of the Turnuk varies much in breadth, and where under culture its soil proves fertile; forage both for camels and horses abounds; and the road, which lies along the right bank of the river, is not bad when compared with the generality of routes in Afghanistan. The lowlands of the valley are confined, like those of the Helmund, by cliff-like banks of calcareous conglomerate, from the edge of which, to the bases of the mountain chains drained by the Turnuk, long glacis-slopes of stony unfertile plain extend. The valley may therefore be characterised as generally consisting of two plateaus, one of low culturable land bordering the river-bed, and a higher one as unproductive as the bluff mountain-ridges by which it is terminated. The road usually lies along the edge of the lowlands, skirting their junction with the cliff-banks in order to avoid the watercourses, small channels, and other minor obstacles which occur in the lowlands ; occasionally, however, the road mounts above the latter, or dips down into the actual channel of the stream, when the river, impinging against the cliff-banks, necessitates the adoption of one or other alternative; on such occasions there are partial difficulties for guns and wheeled carriages, but none meriting serious mention. The volume of water in the Turnuk at the season of harvest is not great, and appears wholly incommensurate with the breadth of the valley and the cliff-like eminences hemming in the lowlands, which would harmonise with a far more gigantic stream. The river in itself forms a trifling military obstacle, and can be crossed with facility throughout its course. The ascent from Candahar to Kelat-i-Ghilzye, upwards of two thousand feet, is effected gradually; as also that to Ghuznee from Kelat-i-Ghilzye, upwards of two thousand feet more; being spread through a number of marches, the acclivity is scarcely perceived, and the route is, therefore, not unfavourable for the march of an army.

As the force advanced towards Ghuznee the climate became cooler and the harvest later; a circumstance favourable not only in respect to partial supplies, but also to a less harassed advance than would have been the case had the crops been all cut and carried, and the Ghilzyes, free from dread for their harvest, at leisure to assemble in greater numbers. Accordingly, although two bodies of their horse were said to move parallel to the march of the army, and to hover on either flank, their strength was not such as to lead them to operate with confidence; and their activity was limited to paltry marauding rather than to systematic attacks upon the scattered length of columns and baggage which strewed for miles the valley of the Turnuk, and offered, in conjunction with the features of the country, great scope for a harassing partisan warfare. Only one serious skirmish took place, and in that the hardy Goorkhas, diminutive in size but of fiery energy, beat off and pursued the Ghilzyes with some loss to the latter.

Thus, little molested in the course of his advance, Keane found himself, on July 18, within a couple of marches of Ghuznee, without having had occasion to alter his order of march or to close up his columns. Now, however, it became essential to instruct the centre and rearward columns to close up by a forced march, information being received that opposition was intended at or near to Ghuznee, where the enemy was said to be collected in force. On the 19th and 20th, Keane, making easy marches, was joined by Shah Shooja and the centre column, and at midnight of the 20th by Willshire with his superb corps of European infantry; having thus his troops together, Keane, on the 21st, marched upon Ghuznee.

The envoy was to the last doubtful whether opposition would be offered; and Burnes, just as Ghuznee came into sight, being informed by an Afghan that the place had been evacuated, reported the statement to Keane, who, uncertain whether the fortress were occupied or not, continued riding onwards ahead of his troops until shots from a garden showed him that the enemy held the suburbs and seemed inclined to dispute them. The force was advancing in columns of march suited to the nature of the ground: the artillery on the road; the cavalry, to the right, advancing over the plain; and the infantry, on the left, over undulating stony ground. Keane, saluted with occasional shots from the Afghan skirmishers, had not to wait long before the heads of the columns came into sight, and the leading brigade of infantry was immediately ordered to push back into the place the skirmishers occupying the gardens; this was rapidly effected, the ground being yielded without contest, excepting at a garden in front of a small outwork. Keane, who had come rather suddenly within half gunshot range of the place, having driven in without difficulty the Afghan outposts, was then able to move his columns into such positions as he pleased, with no other disturbance from the enemy than a few round shot.

The small outwork above-mentioned was on the right bank of the river, the channel of which, swept by the fire of the work, separated the latter from the body of the place. The Afghans, jealous of keeping a hold of the right bank, were loth to quit the garden in front of the work, knowing that it would afford tolerable cover close to their post; but they were driven out by the light companies of the 16th and 48th N.I. These companies maintained themselves in the garden for some time, exchanging a sharp fire with the outwork, under cover of which the engineers carefully examined both the work itself and the southern angle of the place. Meanwhile, the horse artillery drew up on an exposed plateau and opened fire with effect, their shrapnel bursting with accuracy over the battlements; but no advantage was derived from the waste of then very valuable ammunition, and after the fire had lasted some time, both the horse artillery and the light infantry in front of the outwork were withdrawn into safer positions; though not before the officers commanding the companies had been both wounded.

Afghan vineyards consist of a series of parallel excavations, like gigantic furrows, at the bottom of which the vines are planted and trailed up their slopes; the vine obtains in this manner perfect shelter from cutting winds and driving storms, and enjoys the full power of the sun's rays. It may be easily imagined that a vineyard, thus in fact consisting of parallel trenches, affords good cover; and that, aided by such favourable ground on the eastern fronts of the place, the engineers, in spite of a hot and well-directed fire whenever they were seen, could not be prevented effecting a careful examination of the line of the works on that side of the town; but the enemy evinced much jealousy of their scrutiny, and finally pushed back the reconnoitring party by throwing men into the vineyards, before whom the engineers had to fall back on their escort.

On examination the works were found stronger than had been represented, and as the army was without battering-guns a regular attack was out of the question, whilst the great height of the parapet above the plain—60 or 70 feet—with a wet ditch in its front, were insurmountable obstacles to an attack by mining or escalading. The only tangible point appeared to be the Cabul gate, the road up to which was clear, the masonry bridge over the ditch being unbroken; and the ground within 400 yards of the walls offering good positions for the artillery on both sides of the road.

Abdool Rusheed, a nephew of Dost Mahomed, had been led by disaffection to desert his uncle's cause, and to join the Shah; and having been at Ghuznee shortly prior to his transfer of allegiance, he had, together with his attendant, been sent to the chief engineer to give information regarding the place. Their statements had been clear, and left no doubt that up to a late date the Cabul gate had not been built up; for the attendant, a well-scarred Afghan soldier, had been permitted to pass in and out by this gate, and spoke with certainty as to its then condition; all the other gateways were reported to be built up with masonry. In the course of the reconnaissance a horseman was seen to enter the Cabul gate, a fact which rendered improbable any alteration in its state; it had doubtless been kept open for the sake of easy communication with the Cabul road. There was, therefore, in the absence of a less hazardous mode of assaulting the place, a fair chance of success in an attempt to blow open the gate and so to carry the fortress by a *coup de main.*

Such an operation was full of risk, and even success could only be anticipated at the cost of a heavy loss of men. The chief engineer, therefore, when reporting the result of his reconnaissance and the only practicable mode of assault, observed that the operation was necessarily one of great hazard, and would probably be accompanied by severe loss; that to mask the place by a small corps of observation and to attack Dost Mahomed, represented as only five or six marches from Ghuznee, appeared the surer course, as the place was certain to fall, without being stormed, so soon as Dost Mahomed should be beaten in the field. Keane replied that it was not in his power, however desirable, to adopt the safer alternative, as the army had only two, or at the utmost three days' provisions, and could not therefore, from want of supplies, march against Dost Mahomed. This reply settled the question, and Keane approved of the projected assault at the Cabul gate.

The army, which had been drawn off out of gunshot, was now ordered to march from the southern side of the place in two columns by its right and left, and, circling round Ghuznee, to encamp to the north on the Cabul road. The movement was completed late on July 21.

In order that Macnaghten should be prepared for events, whether favourable or the reverse, Keane had communicated to the envoy the decision to storm the place and the mode in which it was to be attempted, never anticipating that Macnaghten would divulge the scheme of attack, success in which mainly depended on secrecy and surprise. Nevertheless, the envoy, ignorant or heedless of the possible consequences, permitted the matter to become generally known in the Shah's camp,[1] from whence it spread to the place, and caused the

[1] Nicolson, then of the Shah's horse, when the army was circling round the fortress, questioned an engineer officer as to the practicability of the contemplated mode of assault, and informed the engineer, much to the astonishment of the latter, that the intended operation was the subject of common discussion in the Shah's camp.

garrison to be all night on the alert and to maintain a dropping fire from the ramparts until daylight.

The morning of the 22nd was passed in a close examination of the Cabul gateway, in the selection of positions for the artillery, and in preparations for the assault. Keane, from the heights which command a view of the northern face of the fortress, having deliberately surveyed the works and the road by which the column must move to their attack, selected, as the spot on which the veteran Sale with his troops was to await the signal for advancing, a space in front of the ancient pillars of Mahmoud of Ghuznee.

During the night of the 21st, blue lights on the citadel were answered by blue lights on the mountain-tops which bound the valley to the eastward, but the purpose of these signals did not become apparent until near noon of the 22nd, when five or six thousand men, suddenly crowning the heights which looked down on the eastward flank of the camp, began to descend their slopes, and to advance towards the Shah's encampment, which lay nearest to the base of the hills. The trumpets sounding, the cavalry, supported by artillery, quickly moved out to meet the Ghilzye horse and foot. Had the Ghilzyes been permitted to descend well into the plain a severe example might have been made; but a few rounds from the guns checked the confidence of their advance, and a charge of horse discomfited the disorderly multitude, who fled rapidly, and disappeared over the heights, leaving a banner and some prisoners in the hands of their pursuers. They effected their retreat with small loss, the ground being unfavourable for the action of the cavalry. The only man of consequence slain among the enemy was a father-in-law of Dost Mahomed.

The night of the 22nd was dark, and a few heavy drops at one time threatened rain, but none fell. At midnight the batteries of artillery moved from camp, and were gradually put into position at about four hundred yards' distance from the ramparts. The enemy, so alert on the previous night when they expected the attack, took no notice of the rumble of the artillery, and suffered it to occupy its ground without molestation.

Whilst the above was being effected, the advance under Dennie, consisting of four companies of Europeans, one from each regiment in camp, and the main column under Sale, consisting of all Keane's European infantry, moved to their point of assembly near Mahmoud's pillars. A wing of native infantry under Hay was at the same time quietly making its way through the gardens to the eastern side of the place, there to await the first fire at the Cabul gate as their signal for commencing a false attack.

In order distinctly to show upon what contingencies the fate of Keane's force, and of the expedition, depended, and how far the errors of the enemy, combined with circumstances unforeseen by the assailants, favoured Keane's daring blow, the detail of events must be more minutely entered into than history would otherwise demand.

The morning star was high in the heavens, and the first red streak of approaching morning was on the horizon, when the explosion party stepped forward to its duty. In perfect silence, led by the engineer Durand, they advanced to within 150 yards of the works, when a challenge from the walls, a shot, and a shout, told that the party was discovered. Instantly the garrison were on the alert; their musketry rang free and quick from the ramparts, and blue lights suddenly glared on the top of the battlements, brilliantly illuminating the approach to the gate. A raking fire from the low outer works, which swept the bridge at half pistol-shot, would have annihilated the engineers and their men, but, strange to say, though the ramparts flashed fire from every loophole, the bridge was passed without a shot from the lower works, at the sally-port of which the engineer Peat took post, prepared, with a small party of the 13th, to repel any sally of swordsmen. Without a blow from a sword or a shot from the lower works, and without the loss of a man from the heavy fire of the battlements, Durand reached the gate, and having laid the first bag of powder containing the end of the hose, man after man stepped up, deposited his powder, and retired as they had advanced, in single file, edging the foot of the wall, and under the eye and charge of the engineer Macleod.

The covering party, outside the ditch, had not been slack in replying to the fire of the works, and the false attack had opened a vigorous and noisy fusillade, when the roar of the artillery, reverberated by the mound of the citadel and the neighbouring hills, told far and wide that Ghuznee was attacked.

The sappers, having deposited the last of the

powder and retired, Durand, aided by Sergeant Robertson, uncoiled the hose, laying it close to the foot of scarp; whilst the defenders, impatient at the restraint of their loopholes, jumped up on the top of their parapets, and poured their fire at the foot of the wall, hurling down also lumps of earth, stones, and bricks, but omitting fortunately blue lights. The officer and his sergeant were hit by the missiles; their force had, however, been broken by striking on the scarped bank on which the wall is built, and this also caused them to bound clear of the train, which was thus laid without injury or accident. The end of the train reaching the sally-port on the right of the gateway, the officer and his sergeant stepped into it and were thus partly sheltered from the fire of battlements; this was fortunate, for on igniting the quick-match the portfire did not light, and the engineer was some time blowing at his slow-match and portfire together before the latter caught and blazed. Even then, however, when laid down on the ground it went out. The engineer, surprised at this, drew his pistol to flash the hose; but finding the piece of portfire in its place he gave it another trial, and once more blew at the slow-match and portfire together until the latter again blazed, when, having watched it burn steadily for some moments the sergeant and himself retired to cover, out of reach of the explosion.[1]

[1] The sally-port could not be seen from the country, and was not known to exist until the charge was laid. The length of the hose, a cloth tube filled with powder, had been determined with the view of affording the officer a chance of escape if, pressed by the enemy, he found himself forced to flash the train with a pistol to avoid the risk of its being cut off whilst

These events produced a short delay, and Peat, fearing that Durand and his sergeant had been slain before they could lay and fire the hose, quitted the lower sally-port, and, ascending towards the gate, came within the sphere of the explosion. He was violently thrown to the ground, and for the time, stunned; but being a calm brave soldier he no sooner recovered his senses than he went up and into the gate to ascertain whether there was a clear passage for the assaulting column. Failing to see the sky through the back of the doomed entrance, and swordsmen showing themselves, he was forced to retire. In the meantime the engineer who had fired the train had lain down in a position from whence he saw its flame in a few moments run up the roadway; a column of flame and smoke rising above the gateway, and followed by a dull heavy report, proved that the charge was sprung; and knowing that there was no second gate, from Abdool Rusheed's minute description of the entrance, he was sure that the gate through which he had seen a light and heard voices must be swept away by the explosion of three hundred pounds of powder. He waited, therefore, two or three minutes anxiously expecting the advance to be sounded; but Peat's bugler had been shot through the head; and Durand, concluding by the delay that some casualty had occurred to Peat and his small party,[1] sought to obtain a bugler from the

an inch of portfire was burning. That the hose reached to the sally-port was no effect of foresight, and had it been but half the length, as was at first intended, in all human probability both officer and sergeant would have been shot down before the second re-lighting could have been executed.

[1] Durand, in passing down the gateway after having lit the portfire,

nearest party of infantry. The fire from the battlements was at the moment heavy; and to repeated demands for a bugler he met with the reply not to draw down fire on the men by speaking; while the officer with the party, instead of furnishing the bugler required, with misplaced punctilio referred the engineer to the field officer, without being able to say where the field officer was to be found. Foiled in his endeavours to have the advance sounded, the signal which Dennie and Sale awaited, Durand was forced to hasten back towards the column. He was met by an officer[1] sent on by the chief engineer to ascertain the cause of delay; and reported, in answer to the question whether the attack was a failure, that all was right, but that the advance must be sounded without loss of time. This being at length done, on went Dennie with his four companies, and after him Sale with the main column.

Peat, much shaken by the explosion, had on retiring

repeatedly called to Peat; but it is strongly characteristic of the difficulties attending night attacks of this description that Durand was neither heard nor seen by Peat. Both officers were very anxious to meet again after the train was lit; but the roar of the guns and of the musketry fire from the battlements, and the glare of the blue lights, making the darkness darker still by contrast, combined to baffle them.

[1] Broadfoot, the youngest of three gallant brothers, and a promising engineer officer. As if petty accidents were to combine in causing delay, Durand, hastening back to expedite the advance, had fallen over a low Mussulman grave of masonry; and, being weak from illness, rose so much hurt and shaken that he had only strength to walk slowly towards the column. Broadfoot, being sound in wind and limb, when given his message, was able to run and deliver it rapidly, otherwise the delay would have been still greater than occurred before the advance was sounded. Every moment was important, as an active enemy might have occupied the gateway in such manner as to render the forcing a passage a matter of great difficulty.

from the gate been unable to reach the head of the column, and had been forced to lie down at the roadside, where he was observed by the chief engineer as the column was advancing. To an inquiry from Thomson, Peat replied that he had not been able to see through the gateway, though he had been into it. Sale overheard the hasty dialogue, and his bugler sounded the retreat before the chief engineer could prevent the mistake; the bugles of his column in rapid succession repeated the fatal sound; and Keane, who was watching from the heights in rear of his artillery the progress of the assault, anxiously despatched his aide-de-camp to learn what had happened. Before he could descend the hill and reach the position of the guns the mistake had been rectified; for the chief engineer had ascertained that Dennie with his four companies was effecting his passage through the gateway; and the bugles of Sale's column were eagerly pealing the advance, whilst Dennie's men, already in part in the town, were cheering loudly, and firing heavily.

Dennie had been enjoined to occupy the ramparts right and left of the gateway in order to secure the command of this all-important point; but, with intermingled rolls of musketry and bursts of cheering, his party pushed on into the town, and neglected the precaution enjoined.

The head of the main column under Sale, led by the chief engineer, was slowly making way in close support of Dennie,[1] through the dark débris-encum-

[1] So close, if not commingled, were the head of Sale's and the rear of Dennie's column, that Lieutenant Marriott, an engineer, finding himself with

bered gateway, when a few Afghan swordsmen, dashing boldly down from the ramparts, fell sword in hand upon the leading section, bore down Sale and the chief engineer, and for a moment checked and pressed back the head of the column. But it was already we jammed into the narrow passage, and the rear, answering the cheers of Dennie's men, and ignorant of what was taking place in the jaws of the gateway, pushed eagerly onwards, and thus the few swordsmen were overborne by weight of numbers, and finally thrust back into the place. This hand-to-hand combat was for a moment critical, and the sword seemed on the point of sweeping back the bayonet; but the effort being only that of a few brave men unsupported, and the column passing through the gate, the loud hurrahs of our men and the storm of musketry told Keane that Ghuznee had been won.

Keane's loss, considering the nature of the operation, was small, amounting only to about 200 men killed and wounded. Any defence of the citadel would have much increased this number, but the enemy, panic-stricken, fled from it, and by sunrise the British colours were floating from its battlements. The loss suffered by the enemy was very great, as, during the desultory fighting after the troops had forced an entrance into the place, one half the garrison was killed or wounded; the

the rear of the latter instead of with the chief engineer at the head of the former, which had been the post assigned to him, had to push his way through the swordsmen in order to rejoin. In doing so he received a long flesh-wound across his breast, an honorable badge won in bold and soldierly attention to orders.

remainder with their Governor, Hyder Khan, were taken prisoners.

To render the success still more complete, the place was found well provisioned, and the pressing wants of the British force were relieved.

Imperative necessity could alone excuse the adoption of a mode of attack extremely hazardous, and liable to failure from numerous causes. The assault was one of simple daring, not founded on the supposed ignorance or negligence of the enemy, but with a full anticipation that success, if obtained, must be bought with much blood. Keane, however, could thus alone retrieve the errors of a position in which a want of battering-guns and provisions had placed him; and he acted with a decision and resolution suited to the emergency. A grateful country may on such an occasion pour forth its titles and its honours, not making men's merits the measure of its bounty; but it will nevertheless act wisely in remembering that war has its principles, and that to hazard, heedless of military prudence, soldiers' lives and a country's fame upon a gamester's throw is to court a stern rebuke.

Dost Mahomed is said to have received intimation of the fall of Ghuznee late on the 23rd. Orders were immediately despatched to his son, Akbar Khan, to fall back rapidly on Cabul, evacuating Jellalabad, and bringing with him all the force that he could muster. Wade's operations at the mouth of the Khybur had begun on July 22, and continued with no very marked results until the 27th, when the fort of Ali Musjid was found evacuated by the Khyburees. Having thus obtained command of the eastern gorge, Wade advanced through the defile, and found his march unopposed; the retreat of Akbar Khan and the news of the fall of Ghuznee having paralysed the exertions of the Khyburees, and smoothed the path of Shahzada Timour towards Cabul.

Keane passed a week at Ghuznee before he again put his army into motion; leaving as a garrison a regiment of native infantry, some artillery, the sick, and the wounded, he quitted the place on the 30th. In the meantime, Dost Mahomed, being joined by his son Akbar Khan, had concentrated his force, and was at the head of 13,000 men and thirty guns; but the fall of Ghuznee, rapid and unexpected, had shaken the confidence of his followers, and a council of war showed him that no reliance could be placed on the constancy or courage of the chiefs. Nevertheless, he moved out of Cabul, and took up a position at Urgundeh, a point on the road to Ghuznee about twenty-five miles from Cabul, which placed at his command the shortest route to Bamian in case his supporters shrank from a trial of strength with the British force.

Keane halted at Sheikabad on the 3rd to close up his columns, purposing, as soon as this was effected, to attack Dost Mahomed; but whilst thus awaiting the arrival of Willshire, he received information that the enemy had disbanded, and that Dost Mahomed, leaving his artillery in position, had fled to Bamian; Akbar Khan, with a chosen body of resolute men, covering the retreat of his father's family. Bodies of horse presenting themselves at the pickets of Keane's camp for permission to proceed to do homage to Shah Shooja, corroborated the news; and after some delay pursuit was determined upon.

During the advance of the British army upon Ghuznee, Hadji Khan Kakur had excited no little suspicion by a conduct indicative of the intention of passing over to whichever side should prove victorious. When Ghuznee had fallen, he presented himself with sudden alacrity, claiming merit for the care he had taken of a quantity of mails and despatches, long looked for, which he had kept. The pursuit of Dost Mahomed now seemed a favourable opportunity for testing the sincerity of the Kakur's loyalty to Shah Shooja, and for effectually compromising him with the fugitive chief. Hadji Khan, accompanied by several European officers, a small detachment of native cavalry, and a body of Afghan horse, was therefore entrusted with the duty of hotly pursuing Dost Mahomed. The Kakur had no stomach for the duty, and, in spite of Outram's fiery energy, he took care to defeat an eagerness which seemed to the wily mountaineer to lack discretion. Perhaps he was not much mistaken; for Akbar Khan, with a party of picked men, kept the top of the pass for twenty-four hours after the departure of Dost Mahomed and his family; and had Outram, with a few struggling troopers, whose horses were worn out with the fatigue of surmounting lofty mountain-passes, reached the summit before Akbar Khan had moved off, the latter could not have failed roughly to handle his pursuers. As it was, after deliberately waiting to check any endeavour to press closely upon his fugitive parents,

Akbar Khan, finding no keenness of pursuit, leisurely descended the western slopes of the Hindu Koosh, having secured the safe retreat of a father whose loss of power and dominion he was destined fearfully to avenge.

Keane, satisfied, by the flight of Dost Mahomed, that no further opposition was contemplated, sent on a small body of cavalry under Cureton, with the view of taking the deserted artillery of the enemy, and of pushing on to Cabul to secure the possession of such guns and military stores as might there have been left. Cureton found no impediment to the accomplishment of the task. Meanwhile the army marched toward Cabul, and by August 6, it was encamped near the city. On the 7th, Shah Shooja made his public entry, and was received in his capital without a show of welcome or enthusiasm. On that day he found himself again upon the throne and in the palace of his ancestors, but placed there by British bayonets; a puppet king, an insult to his people and their chiefs.

In imitation of the customs of Western monarchs, Shah Shooja was persuaded, as a first exercise of his regal power, to institute a Dooranee order; thus gratifying the vanity of British envoys and commanders, and commemorating the subjugation of his country and the recovery of his lost throne in a manner discreditable to himself and dishonouring to his people. Auckland, Keane, Macnaghten, Cotton, Burnes, and Wade, were invested with the highest insignia of this order; and the secondary insignia were liberally distributed to the lower officers of the army and attachés of the political department.

There was less of absurdity in the award to the whole army of a medal commemorative of the storming and capture of Ghuznee, the first military exploit which had broken upon the hitherto peaceful reign of Queen Victoria.

CHAPTER XI.

AUGUST–OCTOBER 1839.

MACNAGHTEN'S POSITION AT CABUL—RESOLVES TO CONTINUE THE MILITARY OCCUPATION OF AFGHANISTAN—PROPOSED EXPEDITION TO BOKHARA—DESPATCH OF A DETACHMENT TO BAMIAN—PROCEEDINGS OF DR. LORD—PREPARATIONS FOR THE LODGING OF THE TROOPS AT CABUL—ABANDONMENT OF THE BALA HISSAR—LEVY OF AFGHAN TROOPS—DISCONTENT OF THE CHIEFS—DANGEROUS NATURE OF MACNAGHTEN'S MEASURES.

THE Shah having thus been speedily replaced on his throne—though not, as the Governor-General had prognosticated, by his own subjects and adherents—a grave question now presented itself for the consideration and decision of Macnaghten. The objects of the British Government had been attained, for, in the words of Lord Auckland's successor, 'the Government of India had directed its army to pass the Indus in order to expel from Afghanistan a chief believed to be hostile to British interests, and to replace upon his throne a sovereign represented to be friendly to those interests, and popular with his former subjects.' Both had been effected, and the question now to be decided was whether the moment contemplated by the Governor-General had arrived; for Lord Auckland's manifesto had promised that 'when once he (Shah Shooja) shall be secured in power, and the independence and integrity of Afghanistan established, the British army will be withdrawn.' The promise, thus vaguely worded and qualified, admitted of fulfilment by the adoption of one of two very different courses. Macnaghten had the option either to take advantage of the favourable juncture when the British army could be withdrawn with the honour and the fame of entire success; and to trust that Shah Shooja, holding with the contingent (upon whose fidelity he could rely) the main points of Cabul, Ghuznee, and Candahar, would not only maintain military hold of the country, but, unshackled by the unpopular tutelage of a British envoy and having in his own hands the civil administration, would also be able gradually to establish his authority throughout the less accessible districts, and reconcile by adroit management their chiefs to his sway:—or, it was open to Macnaghten, mistrusting the Shah's ability thus to maintain himself, to continue the military occupation of Afghanistan by the British troops, and to govern in Shah Shooja's name on the plea that the engagement was not alone to place him on the throne, but also to secure his power, and to establish the independence and integrity of Afghanistan.

Had our policy been truthful and honest, everything combined to favour the first proposition. Macnaghten avowed himself convinced of the popularity of the Shah, whose reception he had represented as being on the part of the Afghans 'with feelings nearly amounting to adoration.' The Shah was known to be by no means deficient in ability; Macnaghten himself described him to Rawlinson as a shrewd, cool, sensible, calculating character. His courage was of a doubtful hue; but this natural timidity could not fail of receiving assurance from the presence of a disciplined body of foreign mercenaries—the contingent—well armed and well officered; whilst the occupation of the key-points of his country would at small cost have enabled the Shah to maintain such a grip of Cabul, Ghuznee, and Candahar, that nothing but an army well provided with battering-guns could have shaken his hold upon these important points. Shah Shooja might possibly, with such a bit in the mouths of the people, and with conciliatory conduct towards the chiefs, for whose restless but petty ambition he could have found scope in the civil and military service of the State, soon have been in a position to brave the return of Dost Mahomed. Freed from the dictation of a British envoy, and from the domineering presence of a British army, provided that his financial measures had proved judicious, his popularity would have increased, and with it his real strength.

He would have had the winter, which from its severity imposes rest and peace, as a season in which to consolidate his administration; it would have given him leisure to work on the characters and wishes of the chiefs, and to raise an influential party favourable to his reign. A person sincere in his conviction of the Shah's popularity, and having a clear perception of our position in Afghanistan, would have seen that it was a critical moment in the Shah's career. But the envoy's representations of the Shah's popularity were the creations of his own imagination; and there is grave reason to doubt whether the Shah, given the opportunity above contemplated, would have had either the tact or the firmness essential to success in his position. It is certain that his failure would have proved the hollowness, if not the falsehood, of our policy, and would have given a denial to the bold assertions advanced in his behalf, and in behalf of the course pursued by the British authorities. It may be, therefore, that the envoy was rather the dupe of his own wishes and of those which he knew to be entertained by the Governor-General, than of any real misapprehension as to the exact degree of the Shah's popularity and influence. Certain it is that, inconsistently with his avowed and often-repeated persuasion of the Shah's favour in the hearts of his chiefs and people, the envoy permitted himself to be influenced by Shah Shooja's fears, whose timidity had no rest so long as Dost Mahomed roamed at large, and who therefore deprecated the immediate withdrawal of the British troops. Macnaghten also was infected, only in a less degree than Burnes, with a dread of the march of Russian battalions and the progress of the Czar's influence in Central Asia. Instead of keeping clearly in sight the primal interests of his Government, and in lieu of seizing the favourable moment for honourably and at once disembarrassing it from a position which everyone saw to be faulty, Macnaghten allowed minor motives, present importunities, and phantasms of a remote danger to warp his judgment from a perception of his country's real honour and advantage; and, by adopting the second proposition, tarnished the one, compromised the other, and wrapped the close of Lord Auckland's Indian career in gloom and consternation.

The objections to the course adopted were many and incontrovertible. The number of troops requisite for the efficient military occupation of such a country as Afghanistan was far greater than India, threatened with disturbances in the Punjab, could spare; the cost of their maintenance was excessive; the difficulty of communicating with an army so far removed from the British frontier was great; all convoys of provisions and munitions of war must traverse the interposed States of doubtful allies, thread long and dangerous mountain defiles beset with wild and lawless, plundering tribes, and be exposed to a multiplicity of risks before they could reach the isolated army; the civil administration, leaning from the first upon the strong arm of a British force, and influenced by a British envoy, acting through a puppet king, could not be expected to mould itself to the habits and feelings of the people, and must therefore be disliked by them. Worst of all, there was no prospect that such a system could possibly end in a period when the Shah, dispensing with his leading-strings and British bayonets, could be left to rule alone, for under such a system nothing native to the soil and people could arise upon which to base his power and authority. A mock king; a civil administration hated because under foreign dictation and dissonant from the feelings of the Afghans; an envoy, the real king, ruling by gleam of British bayonets, and thus enabled to impose his measures, however crude or unpalatable; a large army, raising by its consumption the price of provisions, and preying on the resources of a very poor country: these were the inevitable concomitants of having shrunk from at once, in good faith and in good policy, withdrawing the British army while the moral impression made by its entire success was fresh and deep upon the Afghan mind, and would for some time have been an element of strength to the Shah, had he been left to establish his own throne.

Before entering upon a consideration of the events which followed the occupation of Cabul it is here necessary to notice, and to trace to its source, a system which might otherwise be unintelligible to the common sense of the general reader, and which exercised a fatal influence on the course of affairs hereafter to be narrated.

The civil administration of India forms the rich patrimony of the Directors of the East India Company, and affords affluent provision for their sons, immediate relatives, and the few having most interest with that body. The name, civil service, was well chosen; for though Bentham styles the epithet 'civil' one of the most unmeaning protean terms in all jurisprudence, it is so consonant with English constitutional ideas to strengthen to the uttermost the civil power and jealously to weaken and subordinate the military, that although in reality there was little or no analogy between a free and a conquered country, yet, provided the patrimonial branch bore the honoured designation of 'civil,' the Court of Directors ran no risk of having the tendency of the rules and orders by which all offices of power and emolument in India are restricted to that line called in question.

Governors-General free from paternal solicitude for the interest of the civil service, and actuated by a desire to insure success and the efficient performance of duty, have often been constrained by accidental circumstances to employ military officers in posts of power and influence; and accordingly some of the most distinguished servants of the Company have been officers of their army; but it is always in spite of the injunctions and precautions of the Court of Directors for their exclusion that such men have risen to eminence and fame. As a general rule, the civilian stands no risk from the competition of the military man; power and emolument are his by virtue of his favoured service; whilst the military competitor, if he rise at all, must do so in contravention of the rules and orders of the Court of Directors. In the purely civil administration of the Company's provinces in India no objection could reasonably be raised to this arrangement, provided that the wants of the people were fully met at no overwhelming cost. But the civil service has never been content with such restriction to its pre-eminence. It is so accustomed to regard the monopoly of power and emolument as its right, that where a Governor-General is weak enough to permit it, and makes no stand against the class interest which immediately surrounds him, its members will be thrust into places where common sense and the experience of all ages show that their employment must be productive of confusion, ridicule, or disaster.

If Leadenhall Street and its influences were in part responsible for such a system, the Home Government and the Horse Guards could by no means be exempted from each bearing their own share as part originators, or at least promoters, of a baneful source of error—and error is defeat in military affairs. A Governor-General of India is seldom invested with the authority of Commander-in-Chief. The constitutional jealousy of uniting in one hand the highest civil and political with the highest military authority of a great empire, and the unwillingness of ministers to forego the patronage of two such prizes as the several offices of Governor-General and Commander-in-Chief, have constantly operated against their being conferred upon one person. In peaceful times there is advantage from the arrangement, as a Governor-General's attention can be concentrated on measures for the general improvement of the countries under his rule; but in times of war there has frequently resulted much inconvenience. Although virtually the Governor-General plans and determines all great military operations, yet, when not Commander-in-Chief, the voice of the latter must necessarily have weight in the selection of the officers to whom important commands are to be entrusted; and as such selection more frequently under these circumstances depends upon the accidental rank of individuals than on their general skill and ability, a Governor-General is often tempted to aim at securing the complete execution of his political and strategical measures by the employment of a man of his own choice, to whom, under the title of 'envoy' or some other civil or political designation, controlling authority is in fact given. The attempt, indeed, to separate the conduct of political affairs in a military expedition from that of the army is futile; the two are essentially conjoined, and do not admit of severance, because one man is styled envoy and the other commander-in-chief or general.

The distinction between strategical and tactical operations is well known to every tyro in the military profession. The distinction, however, is one of the *science* of war, where classification is as necessary for a distinct apprehension of the subject-matter as in any other branch of science ; there is in the *practice* of war no such positive, absolute separation. The strategical measures are the preliminary steps by which a certain amount of force is best brought into tactical operation against an enemy—in other words, thrown into immediate conflict in the best order and under the most favourable circumstances. If the connection between the strategical and the tactical be close, that between the political and the strategical is, in the East, fully more so. Where a single military mishap may entail consequences very difficult to estimate or foresee it is imperatively necessary that the commander be thoroughly conversant with every piece and every move upon his chessboard ; no sane person can expect him to take up the game, and to play it well, at a moment's notice and without a pause from the hands of one who has thoroughly embroiled it. In support of this separation of the political and strategical from the merely tactical came the additional fact that the officers in command of armies and divisions, belonging most frequently to the Royal army, were held debarred from the exercise of political functions by their unacquaintance with the general policy of the Government, and their ignorance of the language, feelings, and habits of the people of India and its neighbouring countries. Various, therefore, were the influences, besides the ambition of the individual, which placed a Macnaghten at Cabul; and it must be allowed that, however objectionable might be the system above adverted to, a Cotton and an Elphinstone were not calculated, either by their mental or their physical capacities, to be entrusted with the conduct of affairs in Afghanistan. Men of a higher order of intellect were essential for such a command; and, along with intellect, physical energy was indispensable. Men of this stamp were not wanting, had there been either the will or the ability to select them; and such reasons and motives as have been alleged must be considered a very insufficient apology for shackling a military commander in Afghanistan with a civil commander-in-chief influenced by similar motives to those which lead Governors-General to employ envoys and agents. Macnaghten, in order systematically to keep the thread of events under his own cognisance, and to maintain the exercise of general supervision and control, was forced to have a large staff of subordinate political functionaries, to whom, as his lieutenants, the guidance of such operations as he could not himself superintend were to be entrusted. These deputies were for the most part young men, zealous, indeed, but ignorant of the country and the people, and having yet to purchase that experience of men and practical wisdom in affairs which, moderating the thirst for personal distinction and giving comprehensiveness of view, can alone mature into safe instruments the political servants of a government. They have been much blamed; but the system, rather than the agents, was at fault; and some of them were not only very able men, but did important service in the line prescribed for their exertions.

Shortly after the first occupation of Cabul, Macnaghten heard from Pottinger, at Herat, that a Russian force, destined for Khiva, was assembling at Orenberg, and that Stoddart was still a prisoner at Bokhara, and anticipated being kept there, unless rescued by an English army. This information was coupled with the recommendation that the army, or at least one brigade, should immediately move on Balkh; the recommendation was coupled with the assurance that a single brigade would be quite sufficient, there being no posts on the route to cause delay or give trouble, and no troops that could oppose the march of the brigade. Outram's return from his unsuccessful pursuit of Dost Mahomed, and the escape of the latter to the regions of the Oxus, combined with Pottinger's report, immediately filled the envoy's breast with apprehensions of Russian enterprise upon that famed river, and strengthened him in his resolution not to part with the British army, but to retain as large a portion of it as he could induce Keane to leave or Lord Auckland to sanction; and with this view he at once wrote to Keane in a tone of alarm at the march of Russian battalions upon Khiva, and their occupation of the banks of the Oxus. Keane, who had seen enough in Afghanistan to satisfy him that the Russian expedition from Orenberg might with equal safety and propriety be left to exhaust itself in overcoming the difficulties of its route, replied with good-humoured pleasantry that 'the only banks he now thought of were the banks of the Thames,' and he discountenanced indulgence in such a dread of Russian battalions as invested them with a spectral facility for traversing long tracts of difficult and ill-explored countries. Macnaghten's apprehensions were not, however, to be thus allayed; and he sent for Keane's perusal a letter addressed to Lord Auckland, the tenor of which was to acquaint the Governor-General that the Bombay troops were to return by Kelat; that one brigade was to occupy Cabul; and that a force had moved against Bokhara without awaiting the Governor-General's approval to such an extension of the objects of the expedition, inasmuch as the lateness of the season precluded the delay of a reference to India. This proposal to push a small force across the Hindu Koosh into the heart of countries of which little was known, against a State with which we had no ground for war, with the vague intention of liberating Stoddart, pursuing Dost Mahomed, and forestalling on the Oxus Russian battalions, surprised Keane, who, not trusting himself to write upon a project so quixotic, sent back Macnaghten's letter by the hands of one of his aides-de-camp, with the verbal message that he could not in any way join Macnaghten in forwarding such a letter to Lord Auckland. For the present, therefore, Keane's good sense caused this dreamy enterprise to be abandoned; but Macnaghten, urged by the fears of Shah Shooja, and loath altogether to forego an expedition which had flattered his imagination, resolved on making a demonstration to the westward. For this purpose a regiment of Goorkha infantry and a troop of horse artillery were despatched from Cabul, with instructions to march to Bamian by the Kulloo and Irak passes, which Burnes declared to be perfectly practicable for artillery. In the event of Dr. Lord failing to cross over by the more northerly passes of the Hindu Koosh he was to join the detachment at Bamian, and it was to act under his orders.

To form a conception of this *coup d'essai* by the envoy in military movements, the stupendous character of the passes to be surmounted must be borne in mind. The most practicable are upwards of 12,000 feet above the level of the sea, and present such difficulties that the chief engineer, having examined them, stated as his opinion that the Kulloo Pass alone would retard an army with a respectable battering train at least ten days. The winter was fast approaching, when these lofty mountains ranges are covered with snow; yet the detachment was to winter at Bamian, depending upon Cabul for its supplies—Macnaghten being of opinion that the passes were open for the transport of provisions during the whole winter season. An officer venturing to suggest that it might be as well to delay the march of the troops for two days, within which time the chief engineer would have returned and be able to give accurate information as to the character of the route, met with the rebuff that the envoy did not like difficulties being made. The detachment accordingly marched; and, as might have been anticipated, took a month in surmounting the difficulties of the route, in order, after much toil and labour to the infantry, to lodge an excellent battery of horse artillery in a position where it could not be of any use.

In the meantime Dr. Lord started upon his journey to the Hindu Koosh; but he did not go further than thirty-six miles from Cabul, when, to the astonishment of Macnaghten, he suddenly returned, reporting that the country within forty miles of Cabul was in open rebellion; that Dost Mahomed, established at Koondooz, was drawing the whole country west of the Hindu Koosh together; and that all Toorkistan was pouring forward to join the ex-chief in expelling Shah Shooja and recovering Cabul.

Macnaghten hereupon immediately made a requisition that the whole of the first division of the Bengal army should remain in Afghanistan; a request with which Keane, though very sceptical as to Lord's alarming report, complied.

It soon became known that Lord's sudden retreat to Cabul was the subject of merriment amongst the Afghans, who said 'that it was in no way surprising for Shah Shooja to run away, that being his custom; but that it was not expected that an Englishman would either run so soon or so easily.' Snow had fallen on the mountains; and the sight of their white-capped heads disinclined the Afghans who formed Lord's escort to attempt the passage of the Hindu Koosh at a season when inclement weather and an early winter seemed setting in. They, therefore, caused various reports of the occupation of Koondooz by Dost Mahomed to be brought, in order to try and deter Lord from prosecuting a disagreeable journey. Finding him hesitate, upon these rumours, whether or not to proceed, they were encouraged to dupe him still further by intelligence that a rebellion was around him; upon which in hot haste he rode back to Cabul. Macnaghten, after a few days, finding that the rebellion was a fiction, was not altogether pleased with his own participation in needless alarm, though well satisfied that the occasion had been afforded him of making the requisition with which Keane had complied. Dost Mahomed was meanwhile a fugitive, unable to maintain the few dependents who had followed him, and viewed with suspicion and distrust wherever he went. No better opportunity could, therefore, have presented itself for the entire withdrawal of the British army; but unfortunately Lord Auckland had left the decision, as to the retention of troops from the army of the Indus in the Afghan territories, entirely to the local knowledge and experience of Lord Keane and Sir W. Macnaghten, with the injunction only that he would much rather have them keep too many, than too few, troops for some time after the close of the campaign. Macnaghten, who in the same breath was calling for troops and avowing the Shah's great popularity, was only too well inclined to follow up the line of policy marked out by the Governor-General; and the alleged menacing attitude of Dost Mahomed Khan on the Kooloom and Koondooz frontier, and the ghost of a rebellion of Lord's incantation, opportunely enabled the envoy to demand, and Lord Auckland to accede to, the remaining of a large body of troops under the command of Sir W. Cotton.

The detention of the army being thus determined

upon, there was now leisure to take vengeance on the disaffected, or those whom mismanagement had placed in that category. Accordingly, on September 18, the Bombay column, under Willshire, marched for Kelat by the direct route, with instructions to punish Mehrab Khan for his disloyalty and treachery.

Hadji Khan Kakur had, on his return from the unsuccessful pursuit of Dost Mahomed, been placed in close confinement in consequence of the representations of Outram. To recompense the latter for his disappointment he was subsequently sent with a party of horse to punish the murderers of Colonel Herring. This officer, with his regiment, was escorting treasure from Candahar, and was barbarously butchered when strolling unarmed to a small distance from his camp. Outram effected a junction with a detachment from the garrison of Ghuznee, and captured some plunderers; but the main object of the expedition was not attained. Occupied with the reception of Shahzada Timour, who arrived at Cabul on September 3, with the foregoing expeditions and detachments, and with the establishment of the Shah's court and of his civil administration, Macnaghten for some time neglected to consider how the troops which he kept at Cabul were to be lodged. The question was one demanding instant decision, as the winter of 1839 was rapidly approaching, and there was no suitable cover for troops. Though pressed upon the subject as soon as it was decided that a portion of the British army was to remain, it was not until the end of August that the envoy took any steps in this important matter; and then they consisted in sending the engineer, Durand, accompanied by Mohun Lal, to examine three small forts which Burnes had reported as affording a suitable position for the troops. These diminutive forts were several miles from Cabul; and having neither cover, space, water, nor, in fact, any other requisite for the convenience of the troops, and being, in a military point of view, ill-placed as a position for the force, they were at once rejected by the engineer. This officer had from the first deemed it essential to have military possession of the Bala Hissar, which secured the command of the capital; and admitted, as he represented, of having its upper works or citadel easily placed in such a state of defence as, with a garrison of a thousand men and a few guns, would have been able to defy all that Afghanistan could bring to attack the post. The Shah, upon various pretences, opposed this measure of precaution, and Macnaghten weakly yielded to objections which he felt and acknowledged to be ridiculous. Sale was to be left in command at Cabul; and he had, therefore, a voice in the selection of the locality for the cantonment of his force Accordingly the engineer took him over the different positions outside the city and over the Bala Hissar, but clearly informed both the envoy and Sale that it was impossible before the winter set in to build barracks, hospitals, sheds, and stables for a brigade and its attached cavalry and guns outside the Bala Hissar, building material having as yet to be collected and made; whereas, inside the Bala Hissar, by taking advantage of what already existed, it was possible to obtain good and sufficient cover. The Shah, informed that not only the engineer but also Sale had selected the Bala Hissar, gave a reluctant assent; and the engineer, thinking his reasons and fixed purpose were triumphant, immediately set the pioneers of the force to work, with the view of rendering the citadel a strong work, with cover for its garrison, stores, and ammunition. The Shah, however, no sooner learnt that the work was seriously commenced than he renewed strenuously his objections, urging that the citadel overlooked his own palace and the city; that its occupation would make him unpopular, as the feelings of the inhabitants would be hurt; and that he had already received strong remonstrances against the measure. Macnaghten, with fatal weakness, again yielded, and peremptory orders were issued for the discontinuance of the work. Thus foiled, but still resolved to keep such hold of the Bala Hissar that its citadel could be occupied at any moment, the engineer proposed that Macnaghten, who occupied the houses of Dost Mahomed, one at each end of a spacious garden surrounded by a high wall, the whole at the foot of the citadel, should give up the tenements for the use of the troops; pointing out that the houses at each end of the garden would make fair quarters for the officers, and that the high, thick garden-wall was one-half of the labour accomplished for building cover for the men. The native troops were to be lodged in the Shah's large squares of stables, also within the Bala Hissar, and close to the citadel. As the envoy and the Shah were about to winter at Jellalabad, the engineer thought that he exacted no great sacrifice of private convenience to an important public object. This proposal was, however, by no means well received, and Macnaghten rejected it.

The next proposal was that the Shah's stables should be occupied by the native troops, and that the 13th Regiment, which was then weak in numbers, should be put under temporary cover, on ground close to the stables and in proximity to the citadel. This was acceded to, and the engineer at length appeared to have attained his object; for it seemed that, the troops once in military possession of the Bala Hissar, the evacuation of that stronghold in future was an event as improbable as it would be impolitic, and that the proper occupation of the citadel, and the repair of its works, would in time inevitably follow. Macnaghten could not but coincide with the engineer, and those who succeeded him held similar views; and as the cost would have been trifling in comparison with the sums thrown away in Afghanistan upon objects to which political importance was attached, the envoy for some time contemplated following up the project. But the Shah and the Kuzzilbash party, as well as the Afghans, were averse to a measure which, so long as the British troops remained in Afghanistan, would keep Cabul subject to their efficient control; and Macnaghten, being in the false position of having to reconcile the declared intention of the Government to withdraw the army from Afghanistan with its present actual military occupation in force, wavered on the adoption of necessary measures of precaution, which might countenance the suspicion of a purpose on the part of the British Government permanently to hold the country.

Ultimately, in an evil hour for himself and his country's arms, not only did he entirely neglect such salutary precaution, but gave up the barracks constructed in the Bala Hissar to the Shah as accommodation for his harem, evacuated the fort, and thought no more, until too late, of strengthening himself therein.

At the very time that Macnaghten, endeavouring to unite irreconcilable objects, was thus led to a wavering course in respect to precautionary measures of graver moment than he at that juncture apprehended, he launched boldly upon a revolutionary experiment which was absolutely incompatible with the merely temporary occupation of the country, being in direct antagonism to the feelings of the people, the influence and pride of the chiefs, and the form of government to which for ages both had been accustomed. Rulers in Afghanistan have ever maintained their sway by a politic management of the chiefs, and through them of their tribes. The feuds and rivalries of the chiefs offered great facility for balancing their almost independent powers; and by tact and judgment the preponderance of the ruler was secured and his measures carried out through the support and aid of the Afghan nobles. In fact, therefore, the Government approached more nearly to an aristocratic than an autocratic form, and feelings of independence and pride were strong in the breasts of the nobles. Dost Mahomed had maintained himself at Cabul as the head of this aristocracy with some difficulty; but by a mixture of adroitness and well-timed daring he had succeeded in keeping his position. It was evident that the Shah, who replaced him, could only rule in one of two ways: either by courting, conciliating, and managing the chiefs, as his predecessors had done; or by destroying their power and influence. To attempt the latter demanded the permanent occupation of the country in great strength by the British troops, and held out the prospect of a long struggle, from the difficulties of a strong mountain-country and a bold people attached to their chiefs. Yet, Macnaghten, professing merely the temporary occupation of Afghanistan, entered upon this hazardous experiment, and as a first and an important step towards the accomplishment of his object, began to raise levies of Khyburees, Juzailchees, Kohistanees, and Janbaz corps, who, looking to the royal treasury for payment and being under the supervision of British officers, it was supposed would prove devoted to the Shah's cause and curb the power and pride of the chiefs. The nobles were quick to perceive the blow thus struck at their influence, and feelings of resentment, ill-suppressed through present dread of the British force, broke forth in remarks which betokened that the step taken was fatal to the Shah's popularity amongst his nobles. The measure alienated the chiefs without having the effect of attaching the very men who enrolled themselves and received the Shah's pay; for the Afghans are fickle, impatient of control, naturally averse to the restraints of discipline, and however they might admire the gallant bearing of the British officer when the hour of danger called him to their front, yet he was an infidel in their eyes, connected with them by no ties of clan, religion, or common country; ignorant of their feelings, language, and habits, and, with the strict notions of a British soldier, quite unable to soften their rigour by that community of sentiment and tongue which goes far to alleviate the pressure and irksomeness of military rule. The experiment was, in short, thoroughly anti-national; and the chiefs were active from the first in doing all in their power to render the service unpopular—no difficult task, as it was palpable that the Shah's standing army must be paid, and that the burden of payment must fall on the people.

If Macnaghten's course in military affairs was at starting dubious and inconsistent, that which he pursued in the administration of the government of the country was of the same character. The envoy deemed it possible to reconcile the assumption by himself of the main powers of sovereignty with the treatment of Shah Shooja as an independent monarch, and sought to effect this by leaving the administration of civil and criminal justice, the settlement and collection of the revenue and its irresponsible appropriation, entirely in the hands of Shah Shooja, precluding him, however, from any control in measures concerning the external relations of his Government, or those having reference to independent or to revolting tribes. Although allowed to make grants to his favourites, and to authorise aggressions and usurpations when these could be effected without troops, the Shah had no voice in deciding on the employment of force in support of his own or the envoy's measures. The Shah had thus much power for evil, and could commit the Government to measures the odium of supporting which must fall on Macnaghten, who alone ordered expeditions, settled the strength of detachments, gave instructions to their commanders, and pointed out the objects to be attained and the mode of accomplishment. It was a vain hope, by thus incurring the opprobrium of all harsh and violent measures, and by leaving to the misrule of the Shah's greedy favourites the credit of evoking them, to dream of blinding the nobles and the people to the really servile condition of their king. The farce was too broad, and too cuttingly insulting. From the first it was pregnant with danger, and Keane, immediately before his departure, remarked to an officer who was to accompany him : 'I wished you to remain in Afghanistan for the good of the public service, but since circumstances have rendered that impossible, I cannot but congratulate you on quitting the country, for, mark my words, it will not be long before there is here some signal catastrophe.'

No such foreboding found place in the minds of the envoy or the Shah. The former sent for Lady Macnaghten ; and the Shah, without compunction, gave away to British officers and others the houses of chiefs who had withdrawn from Cabul, as if their property was confiscated and no door open to conciliation. The first mission to Cabul had established for the British moral character an ill reputation, and as the conduct of some individuals, whom it is needless to particularise, was not calculated to remove this unfavourable impression, the consequence was, that, even before Keane marched from Cabul, officers searching for residences in the city, with the desire of purchasing them from the owners, heard their guides execrated by the neighbourhood for bringing licentious infidels into the vicinity.

CHAPTER XII.

OCTOBER—NOVEMBER 1839.

RISING OF THE KHYBUREES—ATTACK ON ALI MUSJID—PASSAGE OF KEANE THROUGH THE KHYBUR.

Among the first results of the anomalous government now established at Cabul was the rising of the Khybur tribes. The circumstances which had facilitated Wade's advance through the Khybur Pass with Shahzada Timour have been already related; and to them might have been added that the establishment of Shah Shooja on the throne of his ancestors was viewed with favour by the wild Khyburees, who hoped for a grateful return from the monarch whom they had received, concealed, and faithfully protected when formerly driven from his throne and deserted by his dependents. These hopes had been countenanced by Wade, who, while skirmishing with the Khyburees, was also treating with their chiefs, and assuring them of the confirmation by Shah Shooja of their ancient privileges. Shah Shooja had not forgotten their generous conduct, of which he never spoke without warmth and emotion; and sensible of the extreme value to the British troops in Afghanistan of a free passage of the defile for their convoys, he had not hesitated, as one of his first acts, to gratify his own inclinations, and to evince goodwill to the staunch friends of his adversity, by promising to the Khyburees, unknown to Macnaghten, the annual subsidy which in former times they had been accustomed to receive. During the troubled sway of Dost Mahomed, this black mail had dwindled down to 12,000 rupees, but was again raised by him to 20,000, a sum far less, however, than the amounts paid in former days by the kings of Cabul; and it was to these higher scales that Shah Shooja was held to have referred.

Wade, on his return from Cabul, on October 5, was entrusted by Macnaghten with no powers to treat with the Khyburees; and being met by their chiefs at the western entrance of the defile, he desired them to proceed to Jumrood, the eastern mouth of the pass, informing them that there their affairs should be settled. He thus effected his passage without obstruction, and when the chiefs arrived they were further informed that an officer bearing letters from the Shah might be expected in the course of a few days, and that then the question as to the annual subsidy would be finally arranged. To the Khyburees, who had seen Wade in a position of dignity and importance, and at the head of a considerable force invading their defile, this reference to an officer of minor rank, who was to follow at a future day, had the appearance of finesse, and excited their suspicions, whilst at the same time their cupidity was inflamed by the intelligence that treasure to the amount of thirteen lacs of rupees was about to quit Peshawur and be escorted through the pass. A rising of the tribes was the consequence, and a resolution to attack, and, if possible, to recover, Ali Musjid, a post to which the Khyburees attach great value as the key of their defile. Its garrison consisted originally of two companies of Sepoys, but sickness had destroyed many, and the remainder were in hospital at Peshawur; five only were able to stand to their arms. The officer in command had also, however, a few irregular horse, and a body of irregular infantry, or Nujeebs; with these he held the fort, and various outposts; the main body of the Nujeebs being placed in a very ill-chosen position, far too distant from the fort to receive support from its weak garrison, and in itself so disadvantageously situated that it was exposed to the fire of surrounding heights, from whence, with impunity to the assailants, severe loss could be inflicted on the defenders.

The Khyburees made a show of attacking Ali Musjid, insulting the fort with a smart fire of juzails; but their serious attack was upon the main body of the Nujeebs, who, in spite of their unfavourable position and exposure to a galling fire, maintained their post until nightfall, when, having expended their ammunition, and upwards of three hundred of them having fallen killed or severely wounded, the survivors quitted the post, leaving their wounded, their arms, ammunition, and treasure. The Khyburees then entered the breastwork, slew the wounded, and possessing themselves of the arms and money which had been left, made known their success far and wide, which encouraged numbers to flock in to aid in the recapture of the key of the Khybur.

Ali Musjid is a military post of great antiquity; and the remains of old walls of a peculiar construction, enclosing a considerable area, and not unskilfully carried down the abrupt face of the rocky hill to the water at its foot, attest that the Kafirs, a convenient term which the Afghans, who are no antiquarians, apply to all early inhabitants of the country, knew the value of this stronghold. Both at Ali Musjid and at Lundee Khana, a halting-place within the pass, these ancient remains betoken a careful selection of posts for securing the pass, but under circumstances when ignorance of firearms amongst men caused military posts and their defences to be of a construction unsuitable to the missiles and weapons now employed. The modern fort of Ali Musjid was of a very circumscribed area, and, except in position, extremely weak and insignificant; its reputation was, however, great amongst the Khyburees, and under this false impression of its strength its works were more respected than they deserved; they might have been easily surmounted and carried by a *coup de main*, and the feeble garrison must have succumbed to numbers. Fortunately, however, although the Khyburees advanced in great strength of numbers, they were disheartened by an unexpected volley from a breastwork, which killing and wounding many, checked their advance, and was followed by a retreat. The near approach of the troops returning to India under Keane, now becoming known, the Khyburees desisted from renewing their attacks, and deemed it advisable temporarily to withdraw from infesting the pass.

Mackeson, the political officer to whom Macnaghten had entrusted the Khybur negotiations, arrived in time to find affairs thoroughly embroiled, and the chiefs in no humour to be quickly or easily appeased. Nevertheless, the presence of Keane with a force which the Khyburees thought stronger than it was, caused a momentary lull in their operations and enabled Mackeson to open negotiations in the name of the Shah.

Keane's force consisted chiefly of cavalry, for he brought back with him the 16th Lancers, the 3rd Light Cavalry, the 4th Irregular Horse, and a battery of horse artillery; his infantry consisted of a couple of companies of sappers and miners, four of Sepoys, some invalids of Her Majesty's 13th, a draft of eighty-two men to join a new corps of Europeans, and a few drafts and invalids from the Sepoy regiments in Afghanistan. The quantity of baggage, notwithstanding the losses of the campaign, was very great; much of it was on bullock-carts, which made slow progress through the pass; the larger portion was on camels, but these animals were worn-out with fatigue. The defile presented, therefore, a long straggling line of carts, camels, and camp-followers, entirely at the mercy of the tribes, had they known the inability of the infantry, from paucity of numbers, to defend and protect so unmanageable a train. Keane, having passed through to Ali Musjid, halted on November 3 and 4 to disengage this cumbrous mass of baggage, which took that time in getting through the defile and coming into camp, but fortunately without any other obstruction or opposition than the nature of the pass.

Mackeson's negotiations were not prospering, for Macnaghten's terms were less liberal than the chiefs had been led to expect by Shah Shooja's unsanctioned communication; and, instead of satisfaction, disappointment was the result, and diminished confidence. Not only was the amount of subsidy less than the chiefs had in the first instance been led to expect, but its payment was shackled with conditions novel to the Khyburees, and entirely superseding their authority and influence in the defile; the proffered terms were consequently very unpalatable, and as Keane was through, and his force of infantry was now known to be insignificant, the tribes re-assembled to infest Ali Musjid and to close the pass. It became requisite, therefore, to throw into the fort a supply of provision and ammunition; in order to effect which, Keane despatched a detachment on November 10 from Peshawur. It consisted of the half of his Sepoys and fifty sappers, supported by a body of about 800 Sikh infantry which the Governor, Avitabile, ordered to co-operate.

The detachment reached Ali Musjid without difficulty on the 11th, and delivered the munitions into the fort, the only opposition having been some distant skirmishing with the Khyburees, who yielded ground freely, but remained hovering round the post. The next morning the camels of the detachment, which had gone out to graze, were driven in again in order to preserve them from the Khyburees, to repel whom the detachment turned out, and drove the enemy back from the immediate vicinity of their ground. The commanding officer then determined to halt that day, as it was past noon; upon which Mackeson, supported by the fifty sappers under Macleod, went out against the Khyburees, and proceeded skirmishing to some distance from the camp before it was observed that the detachment had marched; this sudden change of plan jeopardised Macleod and his small party, who fell back rapidly to regain the road on which the detachment was now in full march. The Khyburees pressed sharply on the party, whose ammunition was nearly exhausted; but could not prevent their gaining the track and effecting a junction with part of the detachment, also engaged in a sharp skirmish and making good its way towards the body of 700 Sikhs, who were in position and were intended to act as a support. The Sikhs, however, no sooner saw the small party of sappers and Sepoys fighting their way bravely towards them than they took flight. Their panic was such that they swept everything before them, and threw the whole convoy of camels into confusion; for, finding that on the narrow road the animals impeded their retreat, the Sikhs cut and stabbed without hesitation in order to drive the camels on or off the roadway, and in their frenzy of fear fired right and left, sometimes at their own friends, more often into the bare hills, or at nothing; blind with terror they never halted until they felt that a secure distance from the Khyburees and the convoy had been attained. Thus deserted, the sappers and their officer were nearly cut off, and with difficulty disengaged themselves from the Khyburees. The convoy lost between four and five hundred camels in this ill-conducted affair, and the Khyburees could now boast, not only of having cut off a battalion of Nujeebs, but of having worsted a strong detachment of regular troops, British and Sikh, and of having taken their convoy.

The Khyburees, thus emboldened, were expected to lose no time in following up their success by a serious attack on Ali Musjid. Keane therefore ordered the whole of the infantry in his camp, only retaining a company of sappers, to march to the relief of the fort, and to hold it until Wheeler, with two regiments of Sepoys from Jellalabad, should reach the fort. The detachment marched on November 14 from Peshawur; but the officer in command having resigned the conduct of the expedition to the political agent, the latter did not advance from Jumrood until the 18th. The troops made good their way, driving the Khyburees from their positions without difficulty, and reached Ali Musjid before Wheeler.

The latter officer had been despatched by Macnaghten with two regiments of Sepoys and two guns, with orders to march upon Ali Musjid by Choora, the point of rendezvous of the tribes, and the road to which was represented as practicable for artillery. Without guides, and ignorant whether he were to act on the offensive or not, Wheeler attempted to obey his instructions, but finding the route impracticable for guns, he was forced to double back into the Khybur and take the usual route to Ali Musjid, which he reached after some sharp but petty affairs between his rearguard and the Khyburees. When arrived, he found Mackeson carrying on negotiations with the Khyburees, assembled in numbers, beleaguering the post, firing occasional shots into the camp, and maintaining a hostile and threatening behaviour. Wheeler immediately took command of the troops and notified to Mackeson that their honour was in his charge, and that he could not without disgrace allow the Khyburees to take the post in a manner alike threatening and insulting. He, however, allowed Mackeson, who remonstrated against an immediate attack as an interruption of pending negotiations, until noon the next day, when, if the negotiations were not brought to a close, and the enemy had not retired to more respectful distance, Wheeler was resolved to attack them. He was saved the trouble, for during the night the treaty was concluded, and Mackeson announced in the morning that the pass was open. He had agreed to the payment of an annual subsidy of 8,000*l.*, and had given a small sum as earnest-money to the chiefs on the spot.

Affairs being thus pronounced settled, and Ali Musjid secure, the detachment marched on November 22, to return to Keane's camp, accompanied by 2,000 camels, and supported by Wheeler's two regiments of native infantry. The troops were soon taught the value of the treaty; so large a convoy of camels was an irresistible temptation to our new allies; and they accordingly made a bold and sudden dash down two branch defiles and swept up them a considerable number of camels. But Wheeler's men were quick and resolute; and having punished the Khyburees severely for their audacity, they recovered the camels, excepting such as, being hamstrung, had to be left.

With this rough farewell to Keane's returning detachments of infantry, the Khyburees celebrated the conclusion of Mackeson's treaty.

CHAPTER XIII.

NOVEMBER 1839.

STORMING OF KELAT—DEATH OF MEHRAB KHAN—ELEVATION OF SHAH NAWAZ KHAN.

WHILST Keane was thus delayed at Peshawur, in consequence of the rising of the Khybur tribes, Macnaghten's alarm on account of Russian battalions had received a fresh spur from the information which reached him of their advance from Orenberg, and the alleged capture of Khiva; he wrote, therefore, expressing his wish that the Bombay column marching on Kelat should be detained in Afghanistan. Keane ridiculed such fears; and even Lord Auckland's patience and credulity were wearied by these repeated requisitions for additional troops, evidently and avowedly founded on an uncalculating dread of a far distant and scarce rival power.

Willshire, having marched from Cabul to Ghuznee, struck off thence to his left, and leaving to his right the line of the Turnuk, by which Keane had advanced, he took a new and untried route, passing close to a salt-water lake called the Ab-istadat; he thus moved in a more direct line upon Quetta, and, besides shortening by eighty-five miles the distance to be traversed, he avoided the Khojuk range and pass. Notwithstanding that ninety-two miles of the road before reaching the Pisheen valley were through a hilly and difficult country, he effected the whole distance to Quetta, three hundred and eighty miles, in forty-three days; and immediately placed himself in communication with Bean, the political agent, regarding the duty imposed upon the Bombay column, the deposition of Mehrab Khan of Kelat, on the alleged grounds of the hostility that chief had displayed on the first advance of the army under Cotton. Bean, who knew that Mehrab Khan had not called out the Brahuee tribes, nor made any preparations, anticipated no resistance, and expected that the Khan would submit without opposition to the degradation dictated by Macnaghten. The route from Quetta to Kelat was represented as deficient in forage, and the march of the troops upon the wretched capital of Beloochistan being supposed to have no other object than to receive charge of Mehrab Khan's person, and to forward him to Hindustan, Willshire sent his cavalry and the greater part of his artillery down the Bolan Pass to Cutch Gundava; he took with him, however, those fine regiments the 2nd and the 17th, as also a regiment of Bengal Sepoys, the 31st, which he found at Quetta, six field-pieces, and the Bombay sappers.

Upon the receipt of the proffered terms, Mehrab Khan rejected them with indignation, and declared his intention, however hopeless the contest, of resisting the British troops if they approached Kelat; but, having long earnestly sought to negotiate and to appease the Shah's and the envoy's displeasure, Mehrab Khan had delayed till too late making an appeal to the Belooch tribes, and Willshire was in front of Kelat before measures of defence could be adopted. The Khan seemed well aware that his town was of no strength as a fortification, and therefore he occupied, with the few men he could collect from the town and neighbour villages, some high ground about two hundred and fifty or three hundred yards from the north-west angle of the wall. These heights encircled the northern extremity of the western suburbs, and commanded the approach to the northern gate by the road from Quetta; they were under the fire of the citadel and the wall of the town, which flanked and strongly supported the Khan's position, but the place being ill manned and worse armed, it was a rash measure of the Khan to draw out its weak and hastily assembled garrison in battle array beyond the walls of the town, leaving the latter almost bare of defenders. The Belooch force may have been 2,000 strong, with five guns; Willshire had about 950 bayonets and six guns, a force, considering the quality of the troops, far more than a match for its opponents.

Willshire halted his troops within half gunshot range of the enemy, and made preparations for the attack of the heights; during which time the engineer Peat made a rapid reconnaissance of the northern front; and ascertaining that there was nothing to screen the gate, which could be seen from the country, and the approach to which was free from obstacles, he reported what he had observed, and that the gate was left open, apparently with the view of receiving the garrison, should it retreat from the position on the heights. Willshire formed his plan of attack accordingly, determining to drive the enemy from the hills, and to endeavour to storm the town by pushing in with the fugitives. To secure this object he threw forward to some gardens on his left front, about three hundred yards from the gate, the ultimate point of assault, two companies of the 2nd, supporting them by two companies of the 17th, so placed on the plain as to connect them with the main body. Keeping a small reserve in hand, Willshire then ordered the three regiments to advance in column, each pointing at one of the three eminences occupied by the enemy; but the latter did not await their approach, for the field pieces opening fire, their well-sent spherical case-shot shook the courage of the Belooch, who retreated hastily into the town, trying to withdraw their guns with them; this they were not permitted to effect, the columns advancing rapidly enough to force the enemy either to leave their guns or to have a close contest for them. They shunned the latter alternative by a hasty flight into the town, which being observed by the companies thrown forward by Willshire, these rushed forward, and one company of the 2nd made a daring dash to accomplish Willshire's object; but the moment had passed, and with the loss of an officer and a good many men, this gallant band had to fall back from the gate. Fortunately the four companies, though foiled in their attempt, found good cover close to the wall, and to right and left of the gate; and there, with the calm courage of resolute, though for the moment baffled Englishmen, awaited their general's orders. Meantime the guns had moved forward with the columns; two were firing on the defences of the gate, whilst Cooper with the remainder was leisurely battering at the gate within 300 yards from the wall. His men behaved admirably, and his round shot soon knocked in one half of the gate; upon which Willshire descending from the hill and pointing to the opening, the troops near to the wall rose from their cover, and gallantly again rushed at the gate. A company of the 17th was nearest, and Pennycuick at its head was the first in, but he was closely followed by the remainder of the troops, who were all soon engaged in sharp firing inside the place. The fighting was desultory; no systematic defence was attempted, and the citadel was carried without difficulty, the ill-starred Mehrab Khan being slain in a struggle which he knew to be hopeless, and from exposure to which he had sent away his son, with the farewell warning not hastily after his father's fall to surrender himself to the British authorities.

Although as a fortified post the place was weak, and the fire through loopholes, from a *banquette* made of boughs stuck into the wall and covered with mud, could not be heavy, yet, to carry a walled place by a *coup de main* in broad daylight is always a dangerous affair, and Willshire deserved credit for the decision and judgment he displayed; as also his troops, for their cool courage. The success was not obtained without cost, for the 2nd Regiment came out of the assault with a loss in killed and wounded of one-fourth of its numbers, and the other two corps also suffered, though not so severely, having been less compromised in the first gallant rush at the gate.

Willshire having thus effected the objects of his

mission, left the Sepoy regiment with Cooper's guns to garrison Kelat; and determined, in lieu of retracing his steps to Quetta and descending the Bolan, to try the Moola or Gundava Pass, from which Keane after a hasty reconnaissance had turned away. It was found extremely rough and stony, the road lying along the course of the river for the whole distance, and crossing it many times every march; a slight increase to the size of the stream would have rendered it nearly impassable, and it proved even in descending extremely fatiguing. The hills were higher and bolder than those of the Bolan, and the pass more continuously narrow, never opening out as does occasionally the Bolan, but contracting in several places to a mere defile hemmed in by high and precipitous rocks. Abundance of water, fuel, and camel forage, the tamarisk being plentiful throughout, appeared the only advantages of this pass. Whilst thus himself testing with guns and troops the character of our route to the highlands of Beloochistan, Willshire found employment for Outram's energy by sending him to explore the direct route to Sommeanee.

For former hospitality, and for protection from sanguinary pursuers, the gratitude of Shah Shooja, under British influence, awarded to Mehrab Khan the loss of his poor capital and a soldier's death. After his honourable fall documents were found which proved the manner in which the Khan had been betrayed and his endeavours to negotiate frustrated; nevertheless it was thought advisable to consummate the threat formerly made, and to place Shah Nawaz Khan, to the exclusion of the son of the fallen chief, upon the masnad of Kelat. He was the descendant of one who a hundred years before had ruled in Kelat, and it was thought that he would not fail of being a pliable instrument in the hands of the British authorities, to whom he owed his elevation. He had the sense to perceive that his hold of power must be insecure so long as the son of Mehrab Khan was at liberty to roam amongst the Brahuees, and to excite their sympathies by the sight of his destitution and the remembrance of the fate of his father; Shah Nawaz Khan, therefore, urged an active pursuit of the unfortunate and innocent youth. Loveday, to whom Bean entrusted the political affairs of Kelat, twice attempted by rapid marches to capture the fugitive, who, receiving timely warning, effected his escape. A third attempt was prevented by Macnaghten, who, although he had not scrupled to take vengeance on the father and to set aside the son, objected to Loveday taking an active part in the rigorous pursuit of the ejected heir to the masnad. The unpopularity of the intruded Khan did not permit him, unaided by Loveday's escort, to continue the pursuit, and Mehrab Khan's son, therefore, remained at large unmolested.

Shah Nawaz Khan did not receive the Kelat territory unshorne, for the opportunity was taken to transfer the northern province, with Quetta and its dependencies, as also Cutch Gundava, to Shah Shooja; whilst the provinces of Harund and Dajil on the Indus were made over to the rulers of the Punjab. Entire control of the Bolan Pass, to which at the moment the Governor-General attached great importance, was intended to be secured, for Macnaghten's requisition for the detention of Willshire's column in Afghanistan, based on the progress of the Russian army in Central Asia, had so far operated with Lord Auckland, that although he would not comply with the envoy's request, yet he contemplated concentrating the bulk of the British force on the Indus in Upper Scinde, holding it in readiness to proceed on emergency above the Bolan Pass at the proper season. The neighbourhood of Sukkur or Shikarpore was by him held to be the best position for such a force, which thus placed was expected to control both Upper and Lower Scinde, maintain communications with Afghanistan, and receive aid and support from Ferozepore. The Bombay column was therefore to be halted in Upper Scinde, with the exception of the 2nd Regiment, now reduced to 200 men, a wing of the 4th Dragoons and the 5th N.I., which were to be embarked for Bombay.

CHAPTER XIV.

WINTER OF 1839-40.

DR. LORD'S PROCEEDINGS AT BAMIAN—DOST MAHOMED'S IMPRISONMENT IN BOKHARA—ALARM CAUSED BY DR. LORD'S AGGRESSIVE MEASURES —RELEASE OF DOST MAHOMED.

WHILST the Khybur and Kelat, the northern and the southern lines of access to Afghanistan from India, were the scene of the foregoing events, Dr. Lord, having arrived at Bamian, lost no time in making the north-eastern or Usbeg frontier of Afghanistan the scene of petty aggressive operations, calculated in his opinion to prove alike the necessity of his mission and his ability to fulfil its objects.

The approach, or rather the setting in, of winter rendered it imperative at once to procure shelter for the troops, and there was no other course for adoption than to turn out the occupants of three small forts, and to assign these to the detachment, whose tents had already been silvered with flakes of snow. To the Goorkhas were allotted two of the forts, whilst the third, being the largest and most commodious, was reserved for the horse artillery. The want of forage, and the great reluctance with which the inhabitants parted with that which it is always their custom to store for the winter food of their cattle and ponies, quickly showed the necessity of sending back to Cabul the details of irregular cavalry and the body of Afghan horse which had accompanied the detachment to Bamian. Dr. Lord, always rapid in apprehending danger, had on his arrival discovered that the Afghan horse were in active correspondence with Dost Mahomed, and thus, when ridding himself of useless mouths, found occasion to keep alive alarm and to invest with fictitious importance his advanced position.

The attainment of these objects seemed to him also facilitated by the circumstances under which he found the Syghan valley, which lay between himself and Kooloom, to which place Dost Mahomed had in the first instance fled. The valley of Syghan had been tributary both to the rulers of Cabul and to those of Koondooz, according as the strength of either enabled them temporarily to assert and enforce their supremacy. Latterly, in consequence of the ruler of Koondooz being weakened by the revolt of Kooloom and its adjacent districts, Dost Mahomed's son, Meer Akram Khan, had taken Syghan and Kamurd, and marched as far as Kooloom. Syghan was in fact debateable territory, and exposed not only to the antagonistic claims and raids of Cabul and Koondooz, but also to a subordinate struggle between two petty chiefs for the possession of local rule and authority. The weaker of these contending chiefs applied to Kooloom for aid, and as the ruler of that petty place was desirous of extending his authority and of strengthening himself in his newly acquired independence, he so far complied with the request as to send a detachment of Usbegs, who beleaguered the hitherto successful rival in the chief fort of the valley, Sar-i-Sung, purposing to subject Syghan to Kooloom.

The connection of this purely Usbeg attempt on Sar-i-Sung with the influence of Dost Mahomed, and the assumption that it had been made at his instigation, were matters of no difficulty to Dr. Lord, who determined to march to the aid of the beleaguered chief and to drive back the Usbegs. The valley of Syghan, drained by a stream which falls into the Koondooz river, is nearly parallel to that of Bamian, which lies at the head of that stream; the two valleys are, however, separated by lofty mountains, and intercommunication in winter is difficult. In engaging to secure the ascendency of an insignificant chief, supposed to have usurped power by the murder of his rivals, father and uncle; and in making a hostile attack upon a race with whom neither the British nor the Shah's authorities could pretend a cause of quarrel, Dr. Lord had not even the excuse that the security of the troops was threatened. The aggression, purely arbitrary, was wholly indefensible both in point of principle and of expediency. Nevertheless it was energetically executed, for Broadfoot, in command of the Goorkhas, and Mackenzie, in command of his horse artillerymen, acting as cavalry, were good and resolute officers, and the expedition relieved the tedium of a Hindu Koosh winter.

Dr. Lord, as a preliminary, despatched a message to the Usbeg leader, Gholam Beg, warning the latter to quit Syghan before sunset of the 30th. On the evening of that day one hundred and twenty Goorkhas, mounted on ponies, and sixty-five horse artillerymen, started from Bamian, and marching all night surprised the Usbeg camp in the morning. No opposition was offered, the Usbegs and their leader mounting and galloping off as soon as the British detachment was seen; the pursuit was short, Mackenzie's horses being fatigued by their night's march over the mountains and the ground being unfavourable, so that as the Usbegs were fresh, and had a good start, they effected their retreat with small loss of killed and wounded, and thus, fortunately, Dr. Lord's needless exploit was spared the ignominy of much bloodshed. None of Dost Mahomed's family or dependents were with Gholam Beg, and there was nothing to confirm the assertion that the ex-ruler of Cabul had instigated the Usbeg advance; in reality Dost Mahomed, though granted an asylum in spite of the large sums offered for his capture, which were nobly spurned, was viewed with distrust; and, unable to obtain the means for maintaining his family and dependents, was hesitating as to the method of providing for the security of these and for his own safe flight to Persia.

Dr. Lord having established his *protégé* in the Syghan valley, the detachment returned to Bamian, and prepared in earnest for the severity of winter. Its rest was soon disturbed, for Dr. Lord, ingenious in alarm, discovered a conspiracy amongst the petty heads of villages in the valley, and took credit for frustrating the plans of an embryo insurrection. This was followed, early in December, by his receipt of intelligence that

Dost Mahomed was at Bokhara, the ruler of which place had resolved on despatching an army to destroy the troops at Bamian and to aid the ex-chief of Cabul in the recovery of power. Without heed to the season, a reinforcement of four companies of infantry from Cabul was immediately applied for, and the Bamian detachment, already occupying these very defensible forts, set to work on the construction of intrenchments, in order to be prepared for the possibility of an attack in force by Dost Mahomed, at the time treacherously thrown into confinement by the Bokhara chief. Having called for reinforcements and begun intrenchments, Dr. Lord, dissatisfied with the position of the detachment at Bamian, which he considered insecure, resolved on seeking a more favourable post in advance and in the valley of Syghan. Partly with this view, and also on account of the moral influence which he expected a forward movement would create, he therefore marched to Sar-i-Sung, the fortalice of his *protégé*, with two companies of infantry, twenty-five troopers, two mortars, and a three-pounder gun, leaving the remainder of the detachment to labour at the intrenchments. These singular proceedings, for the purpose of strengthening the position of the troops to the west of the Hindu Koosh, by their dispersion, were rendered the more remarkable by the fact that Sar-i-Sung, the fort in which Dr. Lord placed the two companies of Goorkhas, was effectually commanded by a hill within musket shot, which looked well into the interior of the fort and took in reverse its northern face. Having in this manner weakened the detachment at

Bamian, in order to place two good companies in an untenable post cut off from all support, Dr. Lord returned to Bamian.

Well might Lord Auckland bemoan the inattention to his wishes, and Keane ridicule Dr. Lord's despatches, when the report of such fatuous vagaries reached them. Dr. Lord's proceedings, however, merited the most marked disapproval, for they bore out Dost Mahomed's assertions, and imparted to them a weight of which they would have been deprived by a wiser and less aggressive conduct on the part of the political agent.

The ex-ruler of Cabul, whilst at Kooloom, had entered into communications with the ruler of Bokhara, and sought to make a partisan of the latter by magnifying the danger which threatened the countries on the Oxus from the advance of the Anglo-Indian power to the sources of that river and from the British occupation of Afghanistan. The Khan of Bokhara was not so easily alarmed or duped; for he felt that distance was in itself a security, that the representations of a discomfited ruler are always highly coloured, and that if danger were indeed to be apprehended, the possession of Dost Mahomed's person would, notwithstanding the imprisonment of Stoddart, be the certain means of purchasing immunity for Bokhara and of establishing a cordial understanding with Shah Shooja and the British envoy. Influenced by such considerations, the Khan pretended to be blinded by Dost Mahomed's communications, and to partake of religious zeal for the expulsion of an infidel power from a Moslem country. In order to entrap the fugitive, and to divert him from seeking an asylum in Persia, warm assurances of sympathy, of relief, and of assistance were sent to Dost Mahomed, accompanied by the recommendation that he should himself proceed to Bokhara to receive the money and take command of the troops which would be placed at his disposal. The Ameer's fortunes were desperate, and he determined therefore to risk a visit to Bokhara; but, himself an adept in deceit and deeply versed in the faithlessness of all professions from Eastern rulers, he resolved to place no hostages in the Khan's power, and left his family under the charge of his astute brother, Jubbar Khan, at Kooloom. Jubbar Khan was a man of greater foresight, depth, caution, and moderation than any other on the troubled theatre of Afghan affairs, and in extremity was the person to whose judgment the more active and ambitious spirit of Dost Mahomed ever had recourse; the family of the latter was therefore in safe hands when entrusted to the care of this prudent and vigilant chief.

The Khan of Bokhara, disappointed at Dost Mahomed's precaution, sought to ensnare him with the proposal of strengthening their alliance by intermarriages, and pressed the Ameer to write for his family to join him in order that these espousals might be consummated. Dost Mahomed had a clear perception of the plot, and while complying by penning an overt despatch which instructed Jubbar Khan to forward his family to Bokhara, he took care by a secret mandate to warn his wary brother rather to put the family to death than to obey a letter dictated by fear and the necessity for temporising. Foiled again in his designs, which he now knew to have been fathomed, the Bokhara ruler avenged himself by casting Dost Mahomed into confinement, accompanied by threats of a speedy termination to its continuance by a violent death; but Dr. Lord's measures to the west of the Hindu Koosh procured his liberation. Those measures had created alarm throughout the neighbouring countries, the rulers of which naturally began to entertain apprehensions of the ulterior designs of the Anglo-Indian power, and to regard with favour the victim, for such to them he appeared, of British aggression. Hence the Khan of Kokan not only remonstrated with the Bokhara chief against the line of policy he was pursuing, but also moved a force from the banks of the Jaxartes to compel attention to demands in behalf of a Moslem ruler expelled by unbelievers from his territory, and oppressed by the person from whom he had sought an asylum, protection, and support. The irritating aggressions of Dr. Lord thus raised up a friend for Dost Mahomed where he otherwise would have found none, and extricated him from a position in which he might have remained, powerless to disturb our occupation of Afghanistan, until released by British interference and diplomacy.

CHAPTER XV.

JUNE 1839–FEBRUARY 1840.

TODD'S MISSION TO HERAT—INTRIGUES OF YAR MAHOMED—ABBOTT'S MISSION TO KHIVA.

THE condition of the north-western frontier of Afghanistan having been described, it is necessary to note the march of events at Herat.

Macnaghten had accustomed himself and his subordinates to regard that place as of vital importance to our dominion in India and our sway in Afghanistan. Jealous of a fortress to which he attached such value, and not concealing his dissatisfaction with Pottinger's proceedings, the envoy had, when Keane's army was at Candahar, despatched Todd to Herat upon a special mission, the main objects of which were to draw Shah Kamran into closer and more cordial alliance with the British, and to examine and place in a state of defence the works of the fortress. This avowed object was to be secured by the negotiation of a treaty of friendship and alliance between the British Government and Shah Kamran, guaranteeing the independence of the Herat State, and stipulating that the slave-dealing which had justified the advance of Persia should be abolished, and that the Herat Government would abstain from correspondence with foreign powers without the knowledge and consent of the British authorities. Todd found some difficulty in concluding a treaty upon these terms; but by pledging the British Government to the payment of a fixed monthly stipend, equal to the original revenues of the country. for the maintenance of Kamran's Government, and the exemption of the people from all taxation until after the harvest of 1840, and by making large advances, to enable the cultivators to resume their long interrupted labours and trade to reopen its channels and activity, he succeeded in winning, from the avarice of Kamran and his minister an unwilling assent to the articles of the proposed treaty.

Macnaghten, bent on counteracting Russian influence, had determined to spread the web of his ever-radiating diplomacy to the shores of the Aral and the Caspian. Todd, therefore, shortly after his arrival at Herat, sent a letter to the Khan of Khiva with the tender of British friendship and alliance. The Khan was at the time under the dread of Russian invasion, and he consequently received with favour the advances of the British authorities, and deputed an ambassador to Todd with a reply, and propositions to which he desired the assent of the British Government; but they were of a nature which Todd could not countenance, and he therefore alleged his inability to entertain them without a reference to Macnaghten and the orders of his Government.

Kamran, and his unscrupulous minister, Yar Mahomed, with the example of the military occupation of Afghanistan before their eyes, had viewed with keen suspicion the eager interest displayed to acquire a thorough knowledge of the strength of the place and the resources of the Herat territory. Their apprehensions were not allayed by the diplomatic activity which sought to form alliances with the States on the Oxus, and thus threatened to envelope Herat in a mesh inimical to its independence and importance. The British agent was liberal of money, and Kamran's necessities and love of lucre, combined with the fear of incurring the hostility of the British power, did not permit him to break with Todd; nevertheless, he knew that such profusion was not disinterested, and he apprehended that the wide expansion of diplomatic relations was only the forerunner of a proportionate extension of military activity, as soon as the state of Afghanistan admitted of the diversion of a part of the troops to the regions about Herat. Such an advance had been the subject of repeated discussion; and the desire of Macnaghten was well known to Yar Mahomed and his master. The fear of Persia now became secondary to that of a foreign and infidel yoke; communications were consequently reopened with the Shah of Persia; and the expulsion of the British power from the countries to the west of the Indus became the topic of correspondence. Yar Mahomed never seriously anticipated such a result; but he sought to counterbalance the preponderating influence of the British power about to ally itself with the countries on the Oxus, by initiating a friendly understanding with Persia, and rousing her jealousy against the sweeping ramifications of British negotiation and intrigue.

Yar Mahomed did not confine his communications

to Persia. When he drove Stoddart from Herat he had done his utmost to excite the apprehensions of the Bokhara ruler, who was so far acted upon that he cast Stoddart into confinement. As the measures of Macnaghten became more developed, Yar Mahomed, pointing to the activity of the British agents at the heads and near the mouth of the Oxus, sought to kindle the jealousy of the Khan, who, although not deeming the danger to himself imminent, could not but view with distrust the march of the envoy's exertions. In a similar manner, Yar Mahomed endeavoured to counteract the negotiations which Todd had opened with Khiva, and sought, by intrigue, by misrepresentation, and by palpable and undeniable truths, to instil into the Khiva Khan the same spirit of wakeful suspicion and hostility to British influence which animated his own breast. To the Khan, however, the Russian advance from Orenberg had been a positive and a pressing danger, and the alleged ambitious machinations of the British power were a less definite and more remote source of alarm; their scope was evidently and avowedly antagonistic to those of his older and nearer foes, the Russians; and their tendency was therefore rather advantageous than the reverse to Khiva, which, separated by 600 miles of barren wastes from Herat, and by about the same extent of difficult country from Kooloom, felt that British desire for territorial aggrandisement had to appropriate vast and unproductive regions before it could think of absorbing the Khiva State. Its ruler was accordingly not unwilling to derive any benefit which might accrue from the countenance of the Anglo-Indian Government, and still less averse to share in that lavish distribution of money for which the British political agents were famed throughout Central Asia. The Khan of Khiva therefore received Abbott, whom Todd sent from Herat in the end of December 1839, if not very cordially, still with more of consideration and attention than the malevolent representations of the Herat minister, and the exaggerated rumours of British aggression on Kooloom and of ulterior designs on the line of the Oxus, were likely, but for the Russian operations on the Yembah, to have secured for Todd's deputy.

Fortunately, also, Abbott was a man of temper; and though not qualified for his mission by acquaintance with the languages of the country, and therefore labouring under sore disadvantage, he made himself respected by a conduct alike creditable to him as a Christian gentleman and a resolute officer. He had been sent on the spur of the moment, without even credentials from his Government, and found that the seeds of distrust and suspicion had been sown by Yar Mahomed, in order to frustrate the objects of his mission. These, indeed, were not very clearly defined; for, with proffers of friendship and alliance in his mouth, Abbott was powerless to incur engagements, or to accept and encourage any of the demands which the Khan of Khiva, with practical notions of international compacts, naturally made. The Khan remarked, almost in the same words which Dost Mahomed had once addressed to Burnes, 'What, then, *have* you come hither for? If you will grant none of our demands, of what use is it to call yourselves our allies?' But Abbott and Burnes were two very different men; and though nothing could well seem more hopeless or chimerical than Abbott's extemporised mission, at a time when the regions of the Oxus and Jaxartes were rife with alarm, and the Moslem rulers seemed menaced with conquest either by the Russians from the Caspian or the Anglo-Indian army from the Hindoo Koosh, yet the patient, truthful, and pious lieutenant of artillery won the confidence of the Khan, and ultimately became his ambassador, on a message of peace and restitution of captive slaves, to the Czar of Russia.

Todd had discovered Yar Mahomed's correspondence with the Persian Assuf-ud-Dowlah at Meshed in October, and had acquainted his Government with the fact. But Lord Auckland, perceiving that it was attributable to the jealousy and apprehension caused by the diplomatic measures of Macnaghten and his subordinates, and that it was neither practicable nor expedient to take serious notice of this early infraction of the treaty, forgave the minister of Herat; and foreseeing that such breach of faith would probably not be the only one brought to light, and that the political agents on the spot, angered and excited by the irritating conduct of Kamran and his minister, might attach undue importance to such events, and seriously compromise the British Government by a breach which would still further embroil and embarrass the Trans-Indus affairs, he extended his pardon to every such offence which might have occurred previous to the receipt of his letter. Being received in February 1840, this pardon embraced the communications made to Persia in the preceding January, on which occasion Kamran addressed his late besieger to the effect, 'that he (Kamran) merely tolerated the presence of the English envoy from motives of expediency, and from the necessity in which he and his people stood of the money liberally provided by the English envoy; but that his hopes centred in the aid and favour of the Shah of Persia.' The advances to the people and Government of Herat at this time amounted to 100,000*l.*; a sum, in respect to the country, about equivalent to the subsidy of a million to a petty German State. It had saved ruler, chiefs, and people from starvation, and had moreover replenished the ruler's coffers; but the instinct of power, dreading British encroachment, was too sensitive to allow such munificence to outweigh the fear which our political measures and the military occupation of Afghanistan had called into being.

CHAPTER XVI.

NOVEMBER 1839–APRIL 1840.

SHAH SHOOJA'S REMOVAL TO JELLALABAD—DISTRIBUTION OF THE FORCES IN AFGHANISTAN DURING THE WINTER OF 1839—ORCHARD'S REPULSE AT PUSHOOT—RETURN OF THE SHAH TO CABUL.

THE Shah, accompanied by Macnaghten, quitted Cabul early in November, and marched to Jellalabad, there to pass the winter. The capital and its fort had disappointed his expectations. He often sat at a window of the palace, whiling away time, his eye wandering over the different objects which the city and its plain offered. On one of these occasions, after a long silent pause, Shah Shooja made the remark 'that everything appeared to him shrunk, small, and miserable, and that the Cabul of his old age in no respect corresponded with the recollections of the Cabul of his youth.' He was glad therefore to escape from the severity of the winter of a place the ideal charms of which age, and experience of the reality, had banished. Jellalabad, though a still more wretched town, enjoys, from its lower altitude above the sea level, a warmer climate, and the winter is far less severe.

After the fall of Kelat and the conclusion of negotiations with the Khyburees, the setting in of the winter season caused a lull in Afghanistan ; and Macnaghten and the Shah for a time flattered themselves with the hope that affairs would settle into order and quiet. There was boundless activity over the whole field of diplomacy, which, extending from the shores of the Caspian to the banks of the Indus, effectually alarmed and unsettled the minds of rulers and people; but, for the moment, the British soldier had rest, and it may be well, before entering upon the events which so quickly followed to disturb this quiescent state, to note the distribution of the forces by which Macnaghten held Afghanistan, and also that of the troops in Scinde; for though not under Macnaghten, yet the Scinde army bore a most important relation to that above the passes.

Afghanistan may henceforth be considered as divided into two military commands. Cotton had the northern one, which comprised the military occupation of Cabul, Ghuznee, Bamian, Jellalabad, and the Khybur Pass. Nott had the southern, which comprised Candahar, Girishk on the Helmund, Kelat, and Quetta; he thus commanded the heads of two passes to the plains of India, the Bolan, and the Moola or Gundava, by which he could effect communication with the army in Scinde. The latter country was one military command, having in Upper Scinde the maintenance of the positions of Bukkur on the Indus, Shikarpore, Bagh, and Dadur; and in Lower Scinde that of Tatta and Kurrachee, which secured the communications with the sea-board. Nott was in a position, if all remained quiet in Scinde, to receive support from the army below the passes; but Cotton had the Punjab between the eastern *débouché* of the Khybur and Ferozepore; and, as the continuance of friendly relations with the Sikhs was very precarious, he could not be regarded as holding safe communication with his own base. Even his connection with Candahar was indifferently secured, for Kelat-i-Ghilzie, an intermediate post between Ghuznee and Candahar, was not for some time established, and, moreover, the severity of winter on the highlands of Ghuznee and the neighbouring districts was for some months an effectual bar to the interchange of military support between Cabul and Candahar. Cotton's command was therefore the most difficult and important, the troops under him being isolated in a country known to be turbulent and hostilely inclined; and every precaution ought to have been taken to render the hold of the military posts secure, and to place the stores of food and of munitions of war in such strongholds as would enable a few resolute defenders to defy insurgents in whatever numbers; but such necessary precautions, in spite of the urgent representations of the engineers were ultimately wholly neglected.

The distribution of the troops was as follows:

CABUL.

H.M.'s 13th Light Infantry. 35th Native Infantry.
Three guns No. 6 battery.

GHUZNEE.

16th Native Infantry. 1 Rissalah Skinner's Horse.

BAMIAN.

Shah's Goorkha regiment Infantry. 1 troop of Horse Artillery.

JELLALABAD.

48th Native Infantry.
1st European Regiment.
37th Native Infantry.
Detachment Sappers and Miners.
2nd Native Cavalry.
1 Rissalah Skinner's Horse.
Three guns No. 6 battery.

CANDAHAR.

42nd Native Infantry.
43rd Native Infantry.
1 company Foot Artillery.
1 Rissalah 4th Local Horse.
1 battalion Shah's Infantry.
2 troops Shah's Horse Artillery.
4 eighteen-pounders.

GIRISHK.

1 battalion Shah's Infantry.

KELAT.

31st Native Infantry.
Shah's Artillery (detachment).

QUETTA.

1 battalion Shah's Infantry.
2 guns.

In addition to the above force, Afghan levies of different denominations were in course of formation at Quetta, Killa-Abdoolah, Candahar, Cabul, and the Khybur; but they were not yet in a state to admit of their being classed as an effective portion of the army.

The presence of a considerable body of troops at Jellalabad encouraged Macnaghten to assert the authority of Shah Shooja over the surrounding districts, the petty chiefs of which, awed by the British force, gave in their adherence and submitted to the Shah's supremacy. The chief of Kooner was an exception, and the envoy was under the necessity of sending a detachment, under the command of Colonel Orchard, with the view of making the contumacy of this refractory chieftain an example, and of replacing him by one more subservient to the Shah's interests.

The valley called Kama, or Kooner, is drained by one of the tributaries which falls into the Cabul river a little below Jellalabad. The length of the valley is considerable, but its territorial value is trifling, and the petty chieftain might have been with advantage left to the enjoyment of his poverty and independence had not the punishment of disaffection to the Royal cause been deemed expedient. Matters having been first well embroiled by the attempt, under pretence of conciliation, to reduce the Kooner chieftain to subjection, Colonel Orchard marched with three nine-pounder guns, twenty sappers, eighty Europeans, a battalion and a half of Native Infantry, and Christie's Horse, to try the effect of force in supercession of a futile ill-conducted petty diplomacy. After a march of fifty miles he reached the neighbourhood of Pushoot, a fortlet in which the refractory chieftain had resolved to make a stand. At daybreak of January 18, Abbott opened a fire from his three guns, battering the sides of the gate and so loosening its connection with the masonry that the engineer Pigou, with a party of fifteen Europeans and twenty-five Sepoys, having advanced to the gate, pushed it down, but found further progress checked by an inner gate, which was intact. Pigou returned to the main body, and, having obtained powder, again advanced to the gate, lodged the charge, and fired it. Heavy rain had, however, fallen during the whole of the attack, and the powder, besides being injured, could not be placed close to the gate, the enemy, in anticipation of such a mode of attack, having taken the precaution of partly protecting it by earth and rubbish. Under these circumstances the explosion failed to produce effect. The ground was such that it was held impracticable to have recourse to the expedient, frequently successful in India, of running up a gun close to the gate and so destroying it; another attempt was therefore made to lodge a charge of powder and blow down the obstacle; but, though this third endeavour was gallantly made by Pigou, it was unsuccessful. Thus baffled, having expended nearly the whole of his gun-ammunition, and lost sixty-five men killed and wounded, Orchard drew off from the attack. The *coup de main* had failed. But the enemy, disheartened by the attack, weak in numbers, and aware that Orchard had only withdrawn from before the walls until better weather and a supply of gun-ammunition should enable him to deliver another assault, resolved not to await it, and retired, leaving to the British commander the fortlet from which he had been repulsed, and another on the opposite side of the river. The escape of the Kooner chieftain and his weak garrison in the face of such numbers was more discreditable to the vigilance of the troops than the repulse which they had sustained in their bold endeavour to storm the petty stronghold had been to their skill, for the cavalry was numerous and ought to have prevented the escape of anyone from the garrison.

The event was so far unfortunate that it gave the Afghans an early lesson that British troops could be opposed with success, and subsequently, in the neighbouring district of Bajore, it was shown that the lesson had not been thrown away. For the moment the occurrence was only a trifling break to the lull of winter. More stirring events were, however, at hand, and the Shah, accompanied by the main body of the British troops from Jellalabad, had no sooner returned to Cabul in April than it became evident that the repose of Afghanistan was to be of short continuance, and with the spring came rebellion.

CHAPTER XVII.

MAY 1840.

RISE OF THE GHILZYES—ANDERSON'S ACTION AT TAZEE—OCCUPATION OF KELAT-I-GHILZYE.

From the one general name applied to designate a large tract of country, Afghanistan, there is some danger of investing its inhabitants with a correlative national unity. Such an idea would be extremely erroneous, and in order to guard against its reception it is essential here to observe, that although Dost Mahomed ruled Cabul, Ghuznee, and Jellalabad, with their neighbour districts, and his brothers held Candahar with a certain circle of country round that place, yet, nearly the whole line of the Turnuk, by which Keane advanced from Candahar, and much of the country between Cabul and Jellalabad, acknowledged no authority but that of its own Ghilzye chiefs.

The Ghilzyes may, rather for the sake of convenience than from the existence of any real distinction, be divided into the eastern and western Ghilzyes.

The eastern Ghilzyes probably derive their name of the 'Suliman Khel' from the Suliman range of mountains; they occupy the tracts to the east of Ghuznee, and their ramifications extend to the vicinity of Cabul, and the country lying between Cabul and Jellalabad. The western Ghilzyes occupy the line of the Turnuk from the neighbourhood of Candahar to Ghuznee, and also extend to the north and west of the line of the Turnuk, being found even between Furruk and Herat.

They are both an agricultural and a pastoral people, the degree to which either mode of life predominates amongst the tribes being dependent upon the local circumstances of the territories they severally occupy. Where these are favourable to agricultural pursuits, villages and fortlets are found; where the country is better adapted to the pastoral life, villages and fortlets are scarce, and the tribes, more nomadic, live in tents, wandering for pasture within certain generally recognised limits. Except a few articles prepared from the wool of their flocks and the camel-hair, they have scarcely any manufactures, and they depend for articles of better attire, and for their arms, upon the industry and skill of foreign merchants and the more civilised inhabitants of the Afghan cities.

From time immemorial they have been the dread of the latter class, for a great part of the revenue of the chiefs has always depended on the transit-fees exacted from the Kafilas of merchandise which traversed or came near to the Ghilzye territory.

The Ghilzyes are a fine muscular race, characterised by an untamed ferocity of disposition, the result of ages of habitual rapine and of constant petty warfare. Ever jealous of their wild independence, and once for a short time supreme in Afghanistan, they have never failed to prove the most obstinate opponents to invaders, whether from the east or the west; and have, when themselves the aggressors, recorded their prowess on the plains of India by many a sanguinary contest. Hardy, confident, and expert in the use of musket, sword, and knife, they are to a man at the beck of their chiefs for any expedition which affords a prospect of booty. The chiefs had never submitted to the authority of the Cabul and Candahar rulers; for, although Dost Mahomed had made tributary a portion of the Suliman Khel Ghilzyes holding districts to the east of Ghuznee, and though the Andari Ghilzyes were his subjects, yet these formed but an inconsiderable part of the tribes, who in a mass disowned all submission or obedience to the Ameer or his brothers, and, despising their retainers and followers of other Afghan tribes, continued with perfect impunity the long-established system of Ghilzye transit-fees and plunder.

The advance of Keane from Candahar by the line of the Turnuk had excited the hostility of the Ghilzyes, who, jealous of independence and mistrustful of the Shah and the formidable power which had seated him on the throne, rejected Macnaghten's advances and proposals. The ill-timed attack by the Suliman Khel Ghilzyes on the British camp the day before Ghuznee was taken, the fall of this stronghold, Outram's subsequent raid through a part of their country, and the setting-in of the winter, curbed for a while any overt acts of habitual resistance to the Cabul and Candahar authorities. But it was impossible for the Ghilzyes to view with patience the apparent consolidation of a power which threatened entirely to annihilate their authority on the highways between Candahar, Cabul, and Jellalabad, and therefore to strip them of the fees and plunder which both chiefs and people regarded as a right. Every detachment that marched, every convoy that traversed their country, was a source of irritation, exciting the avidity and hurting the pride of the Ghilzyes and their leaders. As spring set in, and the weather became more favourable, the Ghilzye discontent took new life, and disturbances arose which showed that the tribes were afoot, and that measures must be taken to crush rebellion before it had time to become formidable.

Accordingly, from the side of Candahar, a detachment of 800 infantry, 360 cavalry, and a battery of horse artillery marched, under the command of Captain Anderson, and in the neighbourhood of Tazee, on the right bank of the Turnuk, were offered battle by a body of about 2,000 or 2,500 horse and foot. Anderson, hearing of the vicinity of the enemy, but not knowing his exact position, had divided his cavalry and sent the detachments by routes to his right and left, to feel for the Ghilzyes, himself advancing with the guns and infantry by the direct road. This lay parallel to the course of the Turnuk, and at the foot of the heights on its right bank; but at one place, in order to cross a ravine which drained into the river, the road on reaching the ravine took a sudden turn, and, edging it for some distance, crossed it at a higher point, less deep and difficult, and then skirted a height, leaving the latter between the river and itself. This height, and the low ground which separated it from the river, was the position chosen by the Ghilzyes for opposing Anderson's advance; their main body and horse were on the height; their musketry occupied the low land up to and even beyond the ravine; they were thus well placed to receive and resist an attack. Anderson's cavalry were not in sight, and his infantry being a Shah's corps, new, untried, and with but two or three European officers attached to it, he was not tempted to risk an attack upon cavalry and superior numbers in a well-chosen position, but drew up his infantry with the ravine in its front, its left flank resting on a height upon which the guns took post, its right towards the low ground bordering the river. To support the guns, a company under Spence, a gallant soldier, was placed on the height; and another was thrown into the low ground near the river to clear the right from the musketeers of the enemy. Anderson's guns told heavily across the hollow amongst the Ghilzye horse, who, finding, contrary to their expectation, that no attempt was made to dislodge them from their position, became impatient of the galling fire of the guns, and, sweeping boldly round the head of the ravine which separated the combatants, made a dash intending to fall upon the left flank of the guns and infantry. Spence checked them, and the close fire of the guns shook their resolution; twice they charged gallantly enough up to Spence's bayonets, but his men were firm, and the grape shot was deadly; the Ghilzye horse wheeled round and withdrew, accompanied by their foot, but leaving 200 men killed in front of Anderson's guns and infantry. Part of Anderson's cavalry, hearing the guns, made towards the sound of their firing; but the affair was settled before they could co-operate. The combat was a sharp one, and very creditable to the courage of the Ghilzyes, who, though superior in numbers, were without artillery. The result somewhat disheartened them; and Nott, having sent forward Wallace with a detachment to occupy Kelat-i-Ghilzye and to destroy the fortlets *en route*, the communication between Candahar and Ghuznee was rendered more secure, and the Ghilzyes for the time held in check along the line of the Turnuk. Subsequently measures were taken by Macnaghten to conciliate the chiefs, who consented to abstain from infesting the highways on the condition of being paid by the Shah an annual stipend of 3,000*l.* Upon these easy, though perhaps not very honourable terms, the communications lying along the Cabul and Turnuk rivers were exempted from a guerrilla interruption, always harassing, and not unaccompanied by loss of men, cattle, and munitions. It was a moderate price to pay for the pacific conduct of chiefs swaying tribes which, when combined, could bring 40,000 combatants into the field; and which, but for the difficulty of uniting them in co-operating for a common purpose, were the most powerful and formidable in Afghanistan.

CHAPTER XVIII.

MAY—NOVEMBER 1840.

COURSE OF EVENTS IN BELOOCHISTAN—OCCUPATION OF KAHUN—DESTRUCTION OF CLERK'S DETACHMENT BY THE MURREES AT THE NUFFOOSK PASS—RISE OF THE KAKURS—ATTACK ON QUETTA—FALL OF KELAT—LOVEDAY MADE PRISONER BY NUSSEER KHAN—CLIBBORN'S DEFEAT IN THE NUFFOOSK PASS—NUSSEER KHAN'S DEFEAT BY MARSHALL, NEAR KOTRAH.

THE communications between Candahar and Cabul having been thus temporarily freed from Ghilzye interruption, those between Candahar and Shikarpore became suddenly endangered by the occurrence of unforeseen events at Kelat, Quetta, and in Upper Scinde.

At Quetta, Bean, the political agent, deeming his own position and that of Shah Nawaz Khan secure, had despatched the 31st Native Infantry to the plains of India, and held his post with 230 bayonets of a Shah's battalion and two guns. At the time that he parted with the corps of regular infantry Upper Scinde was quiet, and his understanding with the Kakurs, who infest the Bolan Pass, was on a favourable footing. The Murrees, another tribe of Beloochees, occupying a tract of hill country to the north of the road from Shikarpore to the mouth of the Bolan, had, however, never entirely ceased, as opportunities offered, to plunder upon this line of route; the political authorities therefore determined, by the occupation of Kahun, a fort which was the residence of the chief of the Murrees and his dependents, to curb the predatory habits of the tribe, and thus to obtain greater security for the line of communications between the army in Upper Scinde and that above the passes. To effect this object Captain Brown, with 300 bayonets, fifty sabres, and one twelve-pounder howitzer, marched, on May 2, from the advanced post of Poolajee; and after a very fatiguing march from the difficulties of the Nuffoosk route and the intense heat of the season, reached and occupied Kahun on the 11th. The fort was found deserted, the gates removed, and the place was in a dilapidated condition. It was an irregular hexagon of 900 yards in circumference, with walls about twenty-five feet high, and tapering to so thin a section as they rose that the defence of the enclosure depended mainly on the six towers at the angles, and not on their connecting walls. Brown immediately set his small garrison to work in cleaning out wells, preparing a tower near the gateway for his single gun, and otherwise strengthening his post. He had brought with him four months' supplies, and having lodged these, the camels were to return in order to bring up an additional four months' supply of provisions. With this view, on May 16 the 700 camels, under an escort of 160 bayonets and fifty horse, commanded by Lieutenant Clerk, started from Kahun, and returned by the Nuffoosk Pass, where, finding no opposition, and knowing the weakness of the Kahun garrison, Clerk ordered back half his infantry. The native officer in command of this party having seen the rear of the convoy clear of the top of the pass, commenced his descent towards Kahun, but, when half-way down, suddenly found himself surrounded by superior numbers. After a severe combat the whole party were slain by the Beloochees, a single camp follower being the only soul that escaped to bear the disheartening news to Kahun.

Clerk and his convoy met a similar fate. The Murrees, emboldened by their success in cutting off the party returning to Kahun, took up a position on the top of a hill over which the convoy must pass. Clerk was a daring soldier, and boldly attacked with his sepoys the overwhelming numbers opposed to him ; but the combat was too unequal, and Clerk being slain fighting hand to hand with the enemy, his men were repulsed, and seventy of his eighty sepoys killed. The horsemen fled to Poolajee. Thus the Murrees cut off two detachments of regular infantry and carried off 700 camels.

The news of their success spread rapidly, and was hailed with pleasure by all the Belooch tribes, who resented the restraint which the British arms had imposed on their predatory habits, and whose chiefs were besides discontented with the measures carried into effect against the estates in Cutchee of those supposed to be disaffected. The adherents of Mehrab Khan's son rejoiced at the intelligence, and began seriously to devise measures for the deposition of Shah Nawaz Khan, who, without influence amongst the Brahuees, and leaning on the unpopular political agent, Loveday, was powerless, and disliked by his subjects. The Kakurs, too, heard of the triumph of their old antagonists, the Murrees, with satisfaction; for the hatred of British supremacy exceeded even the bitterness of a blood feud of long standing and a rivalry of ages in acts of rapine. They knew that Bean calculated upon the strength of these feelings as a sure bond of union between the Kakurs and the British interests, and by encouraging this idea they trusted to lull Bean's vigilance, and to be enabled to compass his destruction and that of the small force at Quetta.

Bean was so far from fathoming the intentions of the Kakurs, and the hollowness of their pretended devotion to the British or Shah's cause, that he communicated to the political authorities in Upper Scinde the remarkable fact that the Kakurs, at his instigation, were about to attack the Murrees. He also wrote to Brown, then closely beleaguered in Kahun, that he might expect aid from Kakur allies. Fortunately Brown placed no reliance on receiving aid from any quarter; but, like a good soldier, strengthened himself to the uttermost of his means, and with his weak garrison of 140 bayonets and one gun trusted to unwearied vigilance for the safety of his dangerous post.

Bean was soon undeceived, and found that the Kakurs assembled with a far different object than the one he had planned for them. He had ordered Loveday to send twenty-five of the sixty sepoys he had at Kelat to Moostung, a place between Kelat and Quetta, an order with which Loveday complied. The order was unfortunate, for such a detachment was too weak to hazard amidst an excited, wild people, only awaiting an opportune moment to break out into open revolt. It afforded them the occasion. Accordingly, emulating the Murrees, the insurgents made the destruction of this small party the signal of rebellion; the sepoys at Moostung were cut to pieces, and the tribes of the Kelatee province of Saharawan were at onc ein full rebellion. Their councils were divided between the policy of an attack upon Quetta and the recovery of Kelat. The former was the more difficult and the more important operation; the latter was deemed of comparatively easy execution. However, before consultation had resolved itself into action, the Kakurs, apprised of the deed done at Moostung, and satisfied that it irremediably embroiled the tribes of Saharawan with the British, determined to forestall the intentions of the insurgents against Quetta, and to appropriate both the honour and the booty which must accrue from the capture of the place and the slaughter of the detachment.

By June 21 the Kakurs had assembled in some force not far from Quetta, and two days after they made a night attack upon Bean's post. The assault was languidly made, and the enemy, repulsed by a few rounds from the two guns, drew off with some loss into the hills. Quetta was thus relieved from immediate danger, but Bean, now aware of the error committed by denuding this important post of troops, pressed earnestly for reinforcements from Candahar.

Both Nott, and Leech, then political agent at Candahar, were alive to the importance of maintaining the integrity of their communications with Scinde by the Bolan and to the urgent necessity of reinforcing Bean, and of placing Quetta out of all danger. The nearest post, Killa Abdoollah, was ordered to furnish by forced marches all the support possible, and a considerable sum of money was given by Leech to the Atchukzye chief, Salu Khan, with the view of his marching as many horsemen as could without too great delay be mustered for the relief of the threatened place. From Killa Abdoollah the reinforcement arrived in time, and Bean's numbers were so considerably increased before July 9 that he could assemble 600 muskets for the defence of the walls within which he had then taken post.

The Kakurs, having failed in their first attempt, had renewed their communications with the Brahuee insurgents, who, with Mehrab Khan's son, had assembled at Moostung. A combined attack on Quetta was determined upon in consequence of these resumed negotiations ; scaling ladders were prepared, and on July 9 the Beloochee forces encamped before the place. For a week the garrison was kept on the alert, expecting daily and nightly to be assaulted, and on the 16th the enemy advanced in earnest to the attack. But the sudden arrival of a body of 150 horse, despatched by Leech, disconcerted them, and, deceived as to the number of the reinforcement, or regarding it only as the advanced guard of a larger force, they desisted from the threatened assault and returned to their camp. During the ensuing night a consultation was held respecting a renewal of the attack, but disputes arose regarding the points to be assigned to the several tribes, and an influential chief withdrawing in disgust, the camp, suspicious of treachery, broke up, and Mehrab Khan's son fell back upon Moostung, leaving Quetta on the 17th free from any beleaguering force.

Bean was now strong enough to have pursued the insurgent chiefs, and to have re-opened his communications with Loveday; but he neglected doing so, and the insurgents, finding themselves unmolested, proceeded to reorganise their forces and to mature their plans for the recovery of Kelat.

Shah Nawaz Khan had for some time been in expectation of such an expedition, and he depended upon the tribes of Jhalawan, between whom and those of Saharawan, who had sided with his rival, jealousy had always existed. He called upon those well affected towards him to throw themselves into Kelat, and his summons was responded to by the assemblage of between six hundred and seven hundred men. These, strengthened as they were by the presence of the party of sepoys with Loveday, and having his abundant supply of powder and lead in store, were quite equal if well managed to have made good the defence of Kelat against Mehrab Khan's son, Nusseer Khan. He could not bring more than 1,200 men against the place, and was ill-provided with fire-arms or ammunition; moreover, he had not a single piece of artillery, whereas the fort contained several, which, though old and bad, were dreaded by the ignorant Brahuees. Loveday, who had shown when first sent to Kelat remarkable activity in the pursuit of Nusseer Khan, now displayed but little ability to meet the crisis; the traveller Masson, however, who happened to be there, proved active and resolute, and organised the defence to the best of his means and influence. At first the besieged showed some spirit, and forced the enemy to desist from a partial attack; but on a subsequent occasion, when an attempt was made at night to carry the place by escalade, the ladders of the assailants being too short, the garrison aided the storming party at the point assaulted, and about fifty men thus gained footing on the wall. Their success was, however, short-lived, for a party of ten or twelve sepoys, detached by Loveday, at once attacked them, slew fifteen, and drove the remainder from the wall to seek shelter in the town. The enemy, disheartened by the resolute conduct of these few men, withdrew discomfited, leaving their ladders and their killed and wounded at the foot of the wall to attest the spirited conduct of the sepoys. Although the assault had failed, yet it had brought to light the undoubted existence of treachery, and proved that part of the garrison was tainted; nevertheless no measures were taken to expel the disaffected, and thus the repulse which the enemy had received, in lieu of encouraging the defenders, dispirited them. Masson and Loveday were fired upon by a portion of the garrison, and Shah Nawaz Khan found himself no longer able to depend on the fidelity of the Jhalawan men by whom he was surrounded. Thus circumstanced he permitted negotiations to be opened, and the result was that the heads of the Jhalawan and Saharawan tribes concluded an engagement restoring Kelat to Nusseer Khan, assigning to Shah Nawaz Khan, who after three days was to evacuate Kelat, Bhagwana Zodi and Kozdar, and undertaking to ensure the safety of Loveday and his party of sepoys, who were to be escorted whither they would. Loveday was given a copy of the engagement, but instead of preparing to leave Kelat, and either to accompany Shah Nawaz Khan or boldly to march to Quetta, claiming the fulfilment of the terms, he with singular fatuity opened negotiations with Nusseer Khan, and was induced by specious promises, belied by every act of the Brahuees, to remain. He thus fell into the hands of the insurgents, and was treated with the utmost contumely, shackled as a prisoner, and made to attend the new Khan in his advance from Kelat to Moostung.

Whilst these events were taking place amongst the Beloochees above the Bolan Pass, those below obtained a signal triumph. It has been seen that the grave error of occupying in the month of May the isolated post of Kahun had already cost the entire loss of two detachments of infantry and of a large convoy of camels, and had kindled a flame which spread throughout Beloochistan. These disasters were to be followed by still graver errors and more heavy and dishonourable losses, and the Pass of Nuffoosk was again to witness Murree success and British discomfiture.

Having committed the mistake of placing Brown with 140 men in a position where he was useless, and could receive no support, it was resolved to maintain him there, and to throw into Kahun a quantity of supplies, of which Brown was in want, his provisions then fast failing him. A convoy of 1,200 camels and 600 bullocks, under the charge of 464 bayonets and three twelve-pounder howitzers, the whole commanded by Major Clibborn, marched from Sukkur on August

12, and by moving at night reached Poolajee with less distress to the troops and cattle than could at that dreadful season have been expected. At this advanced post the force was increased by 200 sabres, and then resumed its march, which, as difficulties in an enemy's country had to be surmounted, was thenceforth necessarily conducted by day, the troops being thus exposed to great heat and fatigue. The Surtoff mountain, the scene of Clerk's disaster, was surmounted without opposition, and at ten A.M. of August 31, after a march of eight hours in accomplishing six or seven miles, the foot of the ascent of the Nuffoosk Pass was reached. The heat was intense, and both men and cattle were already suffering from the want of water. Unfortunately, instead of search being made, the word of the guides that there was no water was taken, and, ignorant that an abundant supply was within two miles of his position, Clibborn determined as soon as his rear guard came up to force the Nuffoosk Pass, looking to obtain water upon the Kahun side. By half-past one the rear guard came up, and by two o'clock, his dispositions being made, two companies and fifty dismounted troopers, under cover of the fire from the howitzers, and supported by reserves, gallantly ascended the pass. The road had been destroyed, breast-works thrown across it, and other minor obstacles prepared by the enemy. All these were surmounted, but not without fatigue, some loss from the enemy's fire, and the disorder inevitable to scrambling up and over such ground, so that when the crest of the ridge was attained the men arrived out of breath, exhausted with heat, thirst, and the fatigue of the ascent. The Beloochees saw their advantage; with a wild yell they rushed sword in hand upon the sepoys, dashed them down the side of the mountain, and covered its slope with their slain and wounded. The supports, seeing the fate of the storming party, retreated to the colours and guns on the plain, and could with difficulty be formed before the Beloochees boldly advanced and sought by a second gallant onset to complete their success; but Stamford's guns were well served and swept their front with deadly effect, whilst the sepoys likewise maintained a heavy musketry fire and stood firmly in support of the artillery. In this onset the Beloochees sustained a great slaughter, and, leaving several of their leaders amongst the fallen, were compelled to retreat upon the pass, of which they kept possession. Clibborn did not feel himself in a condition to follow up the enemy; his loss was severe, and his men were worn out; he therefore permitted the Beloochees to retire unmolested.

The cries of the wounded for water excited the frenzy and despair of their comrades, who, weary and exhausted, clamoured for drink. That which prior to the action ought to have been done was now thought of: parties were sent in search of water, and one of the guides returned, having found it about a mile or a mile and a half from Clibborn's position. Thither the water-carriers and the camel puckauls of the force, with the gun horses, and an escort of irregular horse, were sent; but they had no infantry, and being attacked were easily dispersed and all the gun horses taken.

This additional misfortune was reported about sunset, but instead of immediately marching to the water, Clibborn waited until ten at night, when he resolved on retreating to the Surtoff mountain, sacrificing guns, convoy, and stores to the enemy, and uncertain whether he might not with his worn-out men have to force that position from fresh foes before he could ultimately reach water.

At eleven at night the sepoys, frantic from thirst, commenced their retreat; the guns were spiked, the wounded were carried on the few camels that could be taken, and, the enemy not discovering the march of the detachment for some time, Clibborn surmounted the Surtoff without opposition. The Beloochees had, however, pressed after him; many of the camp followers were there slaughtered; his rear guard was sharply engaged; and as soon as the sepoys could be got from the water they were reformed, and the morning was awaited with anxiety. When day broke they found themselves without provisions, and nothing was open to this unfortunate detachment but a forced march upon Poolajee, distant fifty miles. Many died on that march, and when Clibborn reached Poolajee numerous casualties had been added to the 271 men killed and wounded in the Nuffoosk combat. The calamity was a serious one, and a military commission condemned Major Clibborn and all the superior officers who had ordered and provided for his expedition. Errors of detail there were on the part of Clibborn, and of those who organised the expedition; but by far the most blameworthy were they who had led to its being deemed necessary by thrusting Brown's small detachment into a dangerous and useless position.

At Kahun, Brown soon learnt that the hopes of being relieved had passed away. On the 31st he had watched the Beloochees, assembled and in motion, at the Nuffoosk Pass; had seen the shrapnell shells bursting over the crest of the ridge; and had been disappointed by not seeing the mountain top capped with victorious British troops. Subsequently the fate of Clibborn's detachment was ascertained but too clearly, for through his telescope Brown saw the three howitzers. The tents could be easily recognised with the naked eye, as also the Beloochee want of skill in pitching them; and the enemy, by careering around the place mounted upon the gun horses, was bent upon informing the weak garrison that they must look for no external aid. The Beloochees, however, abstained from making any serious assault, and with his single gun Erskine occasionally punished any attempt at impudent bravado and exacted respect from the beleaguering force. The latter, though successful in their opposition to the march of the convoy, had suffered very severely, and were loath again to encounter the fire of artillery and musketry; of the spiked howitzers which they had taken they could make no use, and they were unskilled in the attack of walled places. Their chief therefore sent a message that 'he should be happy to make any terms with the British commandant provided he would leave his fort.' The proffer was made on September 23, nearly a month after Clibborn's defeat, of which Brown had in the meantime received official intimation, accompanied by the warning that no measures could be taken for his relief. Having no prospect of succour, and being only able to hold out on quarter rations until October 15, Brown did not rebut these advances, but wrote to the chief, promising to give back the fort in three days' time on condition of the unmolested withdrawal of the troops. The Murree leader having submitted the proposal to an assembly of chiefs, the terms were accepted, an oath taken on the Koran to fulfil them, and Brown invited to a conference with the nephew of the Murree chief. Rather as a test of the intentions of the enemy than from any advantage which could be anticipated to arise from the meeting, Brown, accompanied by Erskine, left the fort, and had an amicable conference with the Murree deputy. The Beloochees were gratified by this mark of confidence, and Brown returned from the conference satisfied that no treachery was intended to his small detachment, and that he could make preparations for the surrender of his post. He determined to take the gun, and chose thirty of the best bullocks to drag it; the waggon and forge cart were burnt. No less than forty sick had to be carried in such way as Brown and his companions could devise for placing them on the miserable camels at their disposal. Half the ammunition, the tents, and all the private baggage was destroyed; and thus lightened to the uttermost, on the morning of the 28th Brown marched his small band out of Kahun, and by two P.M. had, with great labour and fatigue to his weak and exhausted men, dragged his single cannon to the top of the Nuffoosk Pass. At four P.M. the descent on the opposite side was commenced, and the gun was lowered inch by inch down the steep declivity. In the course of this operation the body of Raitt, who had led Clibborn's attack on the pass, was first seen, then those of his men; but Brown's party could stay to perform no offices to the dead. With great toil the march continued until seven P.M., when at length they bivouacked on the bank of a deep water-course where water was abundant, and where, after being nineteen hours under arms, labouring a portion of that time without food or water under a burning sun, his weary men found rest and refreshment. On the 31st this small party reached Poolajee in safety, and its commander had the gratification of finding that the conduct of himself, his officers, and men, was the theme of general and well-founded admiration.

The news of Clibborn's defeat, and of the capture of his guns and convoy, was an additional spur to the Brahuee insurgents; but their means were poor, and the co-operation of the tribes liable to frequent disruption; while Bean held Quetta with a force sufficient of itself to have driven them from Moostung, and Nott was shortly expected with a large force from Candahar. Under these circumstances Nusseer Khan and his party were very desirous of bringing affairs to a settlement by negotiation, and their prisoner Loveday was accordingly permitted to address Bean. His communications were accompanied by letters from the leader of Nusseer Khan's party, which, though high in tone, evidently sought an opening for a friendly renewal of negotiations. Bean met these advances by a reply to the Khan demanding the surrender of Kelat; that the young Khan should proceed to Candahar and do obeisance to the Shah; and that the Khan should further engage to submit to act in subordination to the Shah's authority. To such terms the Khan, under existing circumstances, could not, had he wished, have assented; his chiefs were willing to treat with the British Government, but Shah Shooja's conduct to their fallen ruler had excited a burning hate, and the idea of the abject submission of the son of Mehrab Khan to the man whose base ingratitude was a theme of horror and detestation among them was indignantly rejected by Nusseer Khan's council. Loveday then moved that Masson should be despatched to Bean with letters in order to urge more moderate and less unpalatable demands, and the suggestion, though at first disapproved, was finally acted upon, Masson engaging to return with Bean's reply. Masson started upon his mission, and having arrived at Quetta delivered his despatches to Bean, who, with a ludicrous infelicity of judgment, rewarded the traveller's exertions by placing him under arrest, apparently suspecting Masson of being a Russian agent or spy. There were prisoners at Bukkur for whom the Brahuee insurgents might have been induced to exchange Loveday, but neither this nor any other effectual step was taken to obtain his liberation; and the emissaries who accompanied Masson returned to the Brahuee camp with the astounding intelligence that Masson was detained a prisoner, and the less surprising information that the recovery of Kelat was a matter resolved upon, and that Nott with a strong force would soon advance against the place. Disappointed at the result of the attempt to open negotiations through the agency of Masson, and feeling too weak to oppose Nott's proposed advance, the insurgents threw a garrison into Kelat, and determined to descend into Cutchee, and, co-operating with the successful Murrees in attacks on small British posts and detachments, to make head against the British army by acting on its line of communications with a greater combination of Beloochee strength. With this object in view, and taking with them the unfortunate Loveday, Nusseer Khan and his supporters broke up their encampment at Moostung, and, striking into the Bolan, descended into the plains of Cutchee.

The political authorities in Upper Scinde had, after the destruction of Clerk's detachments and the blaze of Belooch insurrection, pressed earnestly for reinforcements from Kurrachee, and a wing of Her Majesty's 40th, under Boscawen, had by August 10 quitted that place. They no sooner reached Sukkur than the events which had taken place at the Nuffoosk Pass, and the movements of Nusseer Khan, rendered it essential to push forward this small body of European infantry in support of the advanced posts, now not only seriously threatened, but obstinately attacked by the enemy. At the same time requisitions for additional reinforcements were made on Kurrachee, and the remaining wing of Her Majesty's 40th was accordingly marched from that place on October 18, being replaced by Her Majesty's 41st, which arrived on the same day.

Before reinforcements could reach the advanced posts in the plains of Cutchee they had been attacked. On October 28 Nusseer Khan emerged from the Bolan and encamped close to Dadur; on the 29th he attacked the post but was repulsed, his men being checked in their onset by a charge of 120 of Skinner's Horse. This handful of men dashed boldly at the enemy, and, regardless of numbers, went headlong into the mass. Macpherson, their leader, was wounded; so, too, were all the native officers and fifteen of the troopers, but the mass gave, and leaving only a risaldar and two troopers dead on the field, Skinner's Horse returned victors from their brilliant feat. On the two subsequent days the Beloochees renewed their desultory attacks, but without success, and reinforcements being near, the enemy discontinued them. Boscawen, with the troops under his command, no sooner reached Dadur than he moved against Nusseer Khan. The latter, well apprised of the movements of the British detachments, withdrew before Boscawen could come up with him, and left on the ground of the Belooch encampment the warm, still bleeding body of the murdered Loveday—the first victim sacrificed from amongst its members to the rapidly growing hate towards the political department.

Nott had on November 3 occupied Kelat, the garrison having evacuated the place before the British general reached it. Nusseer Khan, unable to retire upon his capital, remained in the strong hill country between the plains of Cutchee and the highlands of Beloochistan, and being reinforced by the fighting men whom Nott's advance had driven from Kelat, he drew to the southward, and occupied a strong hill position about eight miles from Kotrah. He had been disappointed in his expectations of Murree co-operation for the surrender of Kahun, and the experience bought in front of Clibborn's guns had for a time cooled their ardour, the Murrees having learnt that even success was costly. The Murrees, too, could not act cordially with the Brahuees, allied as these were with the Kakurs, their rivals; and the latter tribes, dispirited by the turn of affairs at Quetta and Kelat, and seeing but little prospect of plunder, left the young Khan and his supporters to their own resources. Nusseer Khan was not ill-placed to take advantage of circumstances, and the insurgents probably calculated on being able to conceal their movements from the British commanders and to surprise the force at Kotrah. If such were their intentions they were forestalled by the decision of the general in Upper Scinde, Brookes, who, receiving intimation of the encampment of the young Khan within so short a distance from one of his military posts, ordered Colonel Marshall immediately to attack him. Marshall was at the head of 850 bayonets, sixty sabres, and two guns; and having received the order on November 30, by daybreak of the next day he surprised and boldly attacked the enemy. Their resistance was stubborn, and their loss great before the commander, Meer Bohur, with seven chiefs and 130 followers, surrendered. Many fled, amongst whom was Nusseer Khan, who, being separately encamped in rear of his forces, escaped as soon as the action commenced. The blow, struck with comparatively small loss to the British sepoys engaged, was a severe one to the Beloochees; their leaders were killed or taken; and their young Khan, a fugitive in the wild country around Kelat, dreaded the wrath of the British authorities, and feared to cast himself upon the generosity of a Government whose representative had been cruelly butchered by his Brahuee supporters.

Nott's communications with the line of the Indus were again secure, and the fresh troops called into Upper Scinde, and about to be pushed up the Bolan Pass to Quetta and Candahar, rendered the southern military division of Afghanistan free from serious danger. To the progress of events in the northern division we must now revert.

CHAPTER XIX.

MARCH—NOVEMBER, 1840.

OCCUPATION OF BAJGAH—SURRENDER OF DOST MAHOMED'S FAMILY—DOST MAHOMED'S ARRIVAL ON THE FRONTIER—HIS DEFEAT BY DENNIE—HIS APPEARANCE IN THE KOHISTAN—ACTION OF PURWANDURRAH—SURRENDER OF DOST MAHOMED.

THE aggressive measures of Dr. Lord had, as has been shown, already excited alarm along the lines of the Jaxartes and Oxus, and had pervaded the countries westward of Afghanistan with a general spirit of apprehension. Wisdom and prudence would have allayed such a feeling by forbearance and a studied abstinence from further acts of violence; but the unhealthy activity nurtured by the desire of personal distinction, was uncontrollable in Dr. Lord, and spring had no sooner smiled upon the wintry summits of the Hindu Koosh than the troops under his orders were found occupation. They had indeed been employed even before the winter was well ended, for the month of March had been signalised by the capture of an Hazarah fortlet and the destruction of its defenders under circumstances of a most painful nature. This event, which spread a feeling of hatred amongst an innocent and, at our hands, a well-deserving race, was the consequence of Macnaghten's sending a troop of horse artillery to Bamian, without inquiry or preparation, and therefore without advertence to the difficulty of procuring forage during the winter months for a large number of horses. Once in its mountain position, it became essential to procure sustenance for the horses of the troop, and the only available resource was the small quantities of dried lucerne and straw which the Hazarahs habitually store for the support of their live stock during the severities of a protracted winter. To obtain this partial supply of forage from owners to whom it was most valuable the influence and exertions of the political agent, backed by a free expenditure of cash, were necessary. Practically, notwithstanding the price paid, this was an oppressive exaction, although for a time unaccompanied by any overt disaffection. Considering the locality, the demand was too great, and the exaction, though well remunerated, and therefore at first borne without murmur, became vexatious and injurious in proportion as it was unavoidably extended. The Hazarah impatience broke out on the occasion of a quarrel with some Afghans of Dr. Lord's detachment; supplies of forage were refused; and the political agent, having failed in his attempts at pacific negotiation, marched with a force against the contumacious Hazarah fortlet. The troops forced an entrance into it, and made prisoners of a part of the garrison; but, a portion having taken post in a tower, refused to surrender, and fired upon the troops; the latter fired the fodder-straw on the ground floor of the tower, and its ill-fated defenders were all killed either by shot or flame. Such success was of course bought at the expense of the good-will of the neighbourhood, and the

Hazarahs and other tribes only awaited a favourable moment to evince their hostile feelings. After the spring fairly set in, Dr. Lord's measures soon produced one.

Jabbar Khan, in charge of Dost Mahomed's family, was some time at Kooloom, where he maintained himself and his charge by levying the transit duties of the place, a supply which the Kooloom chief, partly through fear and partly through better motives, assigned for the provision of a party still too numerous and well armed to be treated with disrespect. Macnaghten, anxious to have hostages as a check on Dost Mahomed's designs, endeavoured to induce Jabbar Khan to submit himself and his charge to British protection and generosity. The subtle chief was doubtful of the intentions of the Khan of Bokhara and of the ultimate fate of Dost Mahomed, and felt also the insecurity of his own position on sufferance at Kooloom. He was not disinclined therefore to the only course which held out a certainty of security and liberal provision. Dr. Lord, on the other hand, was anxious to be doing, and to hint to Jabbar Khan that his residence at Kooloom was within reach of the British troops. Accordingly a reconnaissance to the northward was determined, and the officers, weary of their winter's confinement, were eager for so amusing and interesting an expedition. In the course of its progress an offer was made of the fortlet of Bajgah, which is situated at the mouth of the defile beyond Kamurd, and is considered by the natives of the country a stronghold of some importance. The offer of the chief, if not suggested, was the result of apprehension, and not of good-will or policy; nevertheless, it was without hesitation accepted, and a small party of infantry was lodged in the post. Dr. Lord, if he had not planned the offer, evinced as great readiness as his reconnoitring officers to take advantage of it, and wrote to Macnaghten and Cotton, urging the expediency of garrisoning Bajgah, and making it a frontier post. The envoy acceded; and Dr. Lord, having his force increased by 300 men of Hopkins's Afghan corps, pushed forward five companies of Goorkhas to Bajgah, occupying Syghan with two companies, and retaining one at Bamian.

The rumour of these forward movements had hastened Jabbar Khan's decision, and on July 3 he reached Bamian with his brother's family, and proceeded onwards to place himself and them under British protection.

This advantage was more than counterbalanced by the effect which the occupation of Bajgah produced upon the surrounding countries. It was regarded as the first step towards ulterior operations, and a strong feeling of hostility was at once engendered amongst those who anticipated that a struggle with the British power was imminent. The Wallee of Kooloom, in particular, as most threatened, was most alarmed; and Dr. Lord thus prepared a cordial ally for Dost Mahomed where hitherto he had usually encountered jealous enmity.

Bajgah was an ill-chosen post, and the engineer, Sturt, at once condemned it; but both Dr. Lord's political consistency and military genius would have been compromised by a withdrawal from a position which he had pronounced excellent and imposing, and he therefore disregarded the engineer's objections. Hay was in command of the post, but, being disabled by sickness, he was desirous, when he found bodies of armed men assembling and hovering around the place, to secure the presence of another European officer with the detachment; he therefore ordered Golding to move from Syghan with one company, and to hasten to Bajgah. Golding was, however, no longer in command, and the officer who was so, in lieu of acting upon Hay's request, deferred to the political agent, who gave a qualified assent conditional on his assistant deeming the movement essential. Meanwhile, Hay, ignorant of the reference, and nothing doubtful but that Golding would march to his support, detached two companies under Sergeant Douglas, with orders to proceed to Kamurd, and, effecting a junction with Golding and his company, to facilitate the progress of the latter, in the event of opposition being offered, along the difficult track which the detachment must traverse between Kamurd and Bajgah.

The political agent's assistant had decided that the movement of Golding was unnecessary. Douglas, therefore, when he arrived at Kamurd, which he did without interruption, found no detachment from the opposite quarter. Concluding that Golding had been accidentally delayed, and suspecting no treachery, he bivouacked for the night, with the permission of the chief, under the walls of one of the forts. Sula Beg partook of the general apprehension which Lord's aggressive movements had excited, and was a party to the rising which was then taking place; he therefore immediately summoned Baba Beg, the chief of the Ajuree tribe, to assemble his men and aid in destroying the Goorkha companies. The latter were undisturbed during the night, and in the morning, Golding and his detachment failing to appear, Douglas prepared to return to Bajgah. The road lies along a narrow, tortuous defile, flanked by stupendous rocks, and drained by a narrow deep stream with steep banks. At Kamurd, the vicinity of the two forts, one on each side of the stream, was occupied by orchards enclosed with walls; as the road cleared the neighbourhood of Kamurd, the orchards were changed for fields, but the aspect and character of the defile were not altered; it continued narrow and hemmed in by precipitous heights as far as Bajgah. Douglas and his men were preparing to start when a sharp fire from the forts and from the orchard walls around spoke in unmistakable language that the return of the party to Bajgah must be won, if at all, with loss and hard, unequal fighting. The Goorkhas sprung to their arms. Though surprised, and well aware that they were caught in an evil position, their courage was good, and their leader, Douglas, equal to the moment. He had barely formed his men when the Usbeg Horse, calculating on an easy victory, charged; but the Goorkha fire made the horsemen draw bridle, and they fell back without charging home. The Ajuree foot, however, lining the orchard walls, maintained a galling fire, to which Douglas's party could seldom reply, but from which they suffered much and fell fast. This unequal contest was kept up for some miles, Douglas making his way steadily and in good order, leaving no wounded, and flinging the arms and ammunition of his slain into the deep river which edged the road. Much distance remained to be accomplished, many were wounded, ammunition was nearly expended, and the destruction of the gallant Goorkhas seemed at hand, when two companies, marching rapidly towards the combat under the engineer, Sturt, broke suddenly into view of Douglas and his enemies, and hastening to their comrades saved Douglas and his men from their impending fate. Checked by the unexpected appearance of the reinforcement, the ardour of the Usbegs and Ajurees cooled, and they no longer pressed upon the Goorkhas, who without further serious loss or opposition reached Bajgah.

This event occurred in the beginning of August, and though the success obtained by treachery was partial, redounding rather to the credit of Douglas and his Goorkhas than to Sula Beg and Baba Beg, yet the Usbegs and the neighbouring hill tribes were much encouraged by what they considered the defeat of a body of British troops, so that Dost Mahomed, who was now on the field to reap the full advantage of the spirit which Dr. Lord's proceedings had evoked, not only found the Wallee of Kooloom a staunch ally, but the Wallee's subjects and the tribes of the hill countries eager to make his cause their own.

By the end of August the Usbegs appeared around Bajgah and threatened to attack the post. The Goorkhas, with their usual gallantry, drove the foot from the heights, whilst the Afghan Horse, under Rattray, cleared the defile of Usbeg Horse; the assailants were thus speedily forced to retire, but did so with small loss, and nothing shaken in confidence or resolution. Their arrangements were scarcely mature, and the affair had rather the air of a demonstration or a reconnaissance in force than the semblance of a real attack.

Dost Mahomed, supported by the Wallee of Kooloom, was now actively engaged in raising followers, and there could be no doubt that the moment he fancied himself in sufficient strength he would advance. Dr. Lord therefore resolved upon withdrawing his detachment from Bajgah before that measure should be rendered difficult, if not impossible, by the nearer approach of the Ameer. Hay, with his Goorkhas, fell back upon Syghan, where Hopkins's Afghans and Hart's Janbaz, with two six-pounders, were in position. Thus reinforced, the occupation of Kamurd was again contemplated, and a forward movement even made; but the news of Dost Mahomed's advance and the spread of disaffection amongst the Shah's Afghans, altered the political agent's plans, and he ordered the troops to fall back to Bamian.

Macnaghten, apprised of disturbances on the Bamian frontier, had at first considered them unimportant, rightly ascribing to them a local origin; but finding that time did not allay them; that Dost Mahomed, escaped from Bokhara, was on the frontier profiting by the spirit which pervaded all tribes and classes; that Bajgah had been threatened; that the Afghan levies had been tampered with, and could not be trusted; and that the troops had fallen back on Bamian, he reinforced them with a regiment of native infantry, sending up Dennie to command.

The recovery of Kelat by the son of Mehrab Khan; the uncertain state of Nott's communications with Upper Scinde; the Murree successes; the insurrection in Bajore, accompanied by the loss of a gun and the discomfiture of a party of the Shah's troops; the near approach of Dost Mahomed, which not only operated to disturb the Bamian frontier but likewise kindled the hopes and the activity of the disaffected in the Kohistan and in Cabul, foreboded little peace to the Shah's rule in Afghanistan. Fortunately the Khyburees, as also the Ghilzyes, who had shortly before been granted an annual subsidy of 30,000 rupees, seemed to prefer British tribute to British grape shot and musketry. Provided the Punjab remained friendly, Macnaghten's communications with Ferozepore might be considered for the time secure. But rapid changes were taking place; the Government of Lahore and the Sikh feudatories at Peshawur were in active correspondence with Dost Mahomed, and were sedulously fomenting disaffection to the Shah and fear and hatred towards the British power. Dost Mahomed's two sons, who had escaped from Ghuznee, were at large in Zurmut and the neighbouring districts, seeking the means and the opportunity of furthering their father's cause. The general aspect of affairs was, therefore, extremely sombre.

When the troops fell back upon Bamian, Hopkins's

Afghans displayed their spirit by plundering their commander's baggage and by deserting to Dost Mahomed's standard in considerable numbers with their arms, ammunition, and booty. Matters were in this state when Dennie reached Bamian on September 14; his first care was to disarm the remainder of Hopkins's Afghans, who laid down their arms in the presence of the resolute Goorkhas, drawn out to enforce obedience should the Afghans hesitate in complying with the unwelcome injunction.

Information of Dost Mahomed's movements and of his strength was contradictory and uncertain, and it was not until the 17th that Dennie, learning that parties of horse were in the valley, and that a friendly village had been burnt, resolved to push back the advanced parties of the enemy. With this object in view the British commander moved out with only a third of his force, consisting of two guns, 500 bayonets, and 300 sabres. Having driven back the enemy's outposts, Dennie suddenly found himself before Dost Mahomed's whole force, an irregular mass of Usbeg horse and foot. Mackenzies' guns instantly opened, and by their effect shook the courage of the undisciplined horde, whilst the Goorkhas and the 35th Native Infantry marched boldly on to close with their adversaries. The latter made small show of resistance, and were soon in a panic flight, followed up and sabred by Anderson's Horse and Hart's Janbaz. During the pursuit many of Hopkins's deserters were cut down, and Dost Mahomed lost his kettle drums, a small gun, his standard, and camp equipage, but escaped with a few followers from his pursuers. He had been led to advance upon Bamian in consequence of the violent feeling which Dr. Lord's aggressive movements had excited in the Wallee of Kooloom and the Usbegs, who were eager to thrust back the British to the eastern side of the Hindu Koosh. Also, having knowledge of the disposition of the Afghans and Janbaz corps to join his standard as soon as a favourable opportunity presented itself, Dost Mahomed entertained hopes that, by taking advantage of the anxiety of the Usbegs and the disaffection of the Shah's Afghan levies, he might be able to force the pass, and that then the Kohistanees, in whom his confidence had been shaken by forged letters from Macnaghten, would flock to his aid. The defeat of September 18 destroyed these hopes, and the fugitive Ameer, fearful of treachery from the Wallee of Kooloom, who now lost no time in treating with Dr. Lord and tendering submission to the Shah, resolved at all hazards to throw himself into the Kohistan.

Macnaghten's difficulties were but partially relieved by Dennie's action, which in fact only restored matters to the same footing on which Dr. Lord had found them, and therefore contented the Wallee of Kooloom, whose sole anxiety was on account of British encroachment, and who, in reality cared little for Dost Mahomed's cause, provided the British troops were withdrawn from the advanced posts into which Dr. Lord had so unwisely thrust them. The events at Bamian had rather added to Macnaghten's perplexities, for it was no longer doubtful whether reliance should be placed on the Afghan levies; and the envoy, now convinced of the futility of the measure by which he had alienated the good-will of the chiefs, pointed out to the Governor-General that the hope of raising a loyal Afghan army must be relinquished, and that, unless the Bengal troops were instantly strengthened, the country could not be held. Alarmed by Sikh intrigues, the envoy also at this time became alive to the capital error of Lord Auckland's operations beyond the Indus, with the unsubdued power of the Punjab between the army engaged in Afghanistan and its reserves in Northern India; and, irritated by the machinations of the Sikh agents to excite revolt, and to feed it with supplies of money, he pressed the Governor-General to break with the ruler of the Punjab. Lord Auckland, however, felt that the crisis which Macnaghten depicted in Afghanistan was not the moment to select for opening serious hostilities with a formidable State; and that to maintain a hold of Afghanistan and furnish the reinforcements so urgently demanded, a temporising policy with the Court of Lahore and a prolongation of peaceable relations were essential.

Meanwhile Macnaghten, in order to strengthen himself at Cabul, recalled Dennie, with the battery of horse artillery and the 35th Native Infantry, from Bamian. Dost Mahomed's intrigues were actively carried on, not only in the Kohistan, but in the city of Cabul itself; his two sons were busy in Zoormut; the Sikh feudatories were doing all in their power to raise the country between Peshawur and Cabul, and to make it pronounce in favour of Dost Mahomed against the Shah; look where he would, Macnaghten found no stay for the support of the Shah's authority but the British guns and bayonets at his disposal.

The Kohistan chiefs, when summoned to the capital, had obeyed the call, made obeisance to the Shah, and sworn allegiance. Their simulated submission was intended the better to cover deep treachery and a fixed resolve to overthrow Shah Shooja's hated rule; they returned to their forts banded together by solemn engagements, and encouraged by the knowledge they had acquired of the smallness of the force at Cabul. Neither the envoy nor the Shah were blinded by the readiness with which allegiance had been tendered; for, the letters of the chiefs being intercepted, their schemes and temper were disclosed; and Macnaghten, uncertain of Dost Mahomed's movements, sent Sir A. Burnes with a force under Sale's orders to punish the hostile chiefs of Kohistan, and to oppose the entrance of the Ameer into districts ripe for insurrection. Dennie's action at Bamian, followed by the escape of Dost Mahomed, by no means diminished the necessity of this measure, and on September 29 Burnes and Sale, at the head of Her Majesty's 13th, two companies of the 27th, and two of the 37th Native Infantry, with five guns and two squadrons of the 2nd Bengal Light Cavalry, marched from Charikar to Tootundurrah, a small fort, which fell into their hands without opposition, and which with neighbouring towers was levelled to the ground. Sale next attacked Julgah, a fortlet which, though garrisoned by no more than about fifty men, offered a stout resistance; and the storming party, notwithstanding that four gallant officers, Kershaw, Wood, King, and Wade, for some time held the crest of the wall, failed to make good their entrance. At night the fortlet was evacuated by the small garrison, who, by the treachery of the Janbaz, were permitted to escape through the lines of that portion of the investing force. Julgah was levelled with the ground, and on the 8th Sale was again in movement, expecting to meet Dost Mahomed at Charikar; but he was disappointed, and marched to Karabagh, the Ameer being reported at Nijrow. On the 13th a body of horse under Dowson attempted to surprise the Ameer at Tootundurrah; but the latter, having accurate and timely information of all Sale's movements, retired from thence the same morning. In the meantime Dost Mahomed's intrigues were successfully operating upon the minds of all classes, and the corps of Kohistanees participating in the general feeling, a whole company deserted, and there was every probability of the greater part of the corps following the example. On the 17th Sale took and destroyed Baboo Khoosh Ghur, which he obtained without resistance. On the 18th a desultory night attack was made upon his camp, which, beyond keeping the troops under arms, had little effect. On the 19th Sale was reinforced by six companies of the 37th Native Infantry and two 9-pounder guns; and on the 21st he marched to attack the enemy, who had taken up a strong position at Kardurrah, but did not attempt to defend it. Kardurrah was treated as Tootundurrah and Baboo Koosh Ghur had been. After these fatiguing but not brilliant marches, and the destruction of obnoxious fortlets and villages, the troops, baffled in their attempts to meet the Ameer, had rest until October 29, when the defection of part of the corps of Kohistanees caused Sale to move; and then, learning that Dost Mahomed had quitted the Nijrow valley and crossed over into the Kohistan, strong reconnoitring parties were sent out on the 30th and 31st, and on November 2 a march was made upon Purwan Durrah, to which place it had been ascertained that the Ameer had gone. Sale's advanced guard was under Colonel Salter, and consisted of two guns, seven companies of infantry, two squadrons of the 2nd Cavalry, and 200 of Anderson's Horse. The ground to be traversed was difficult from ravines, irrigation watercourses, and the passage of the Ghorbund river, but as the troops drew near to Purwan the enemy was seen in motion, evacuating the forts and villages and gaining the hills. Salter, upon Dr. Lord's suggestion, now sent forward Anderson's Horse to his left to cut off the enemy from the Ghorbund direction, whilst the two squadrons of the 2nd Cavalry were ordered to skirt the hills to the right, and to prevent escape in that direction; the infantry, with the guns, retarded by the difficulties of the road, was a mile or more in the rear when the horse advanced to right and left upon its mission. The two squadrons having neared the base of the hills, found themselves heading a small body of Afghan horse, who, not equal to the cavalry in strength, and finding their retreat compromised, turned and descended leisurely towards the two squadrons. Fraser, who commanded the latter, formed up his men, whilst the Afghans closing slowly occasionally fired, a few cavaliers dismounting to do so. At this juncture orders arrived recalling the cavalry;

but Fraser, finding the enemy few and near him, felt that he could neither with honour nor safety obey, and, in lieu of retiring, he gave the word to charge. Vain was the example and the leading of the officers; the troopers wavered, fell back, and ultimately fled in dismay, leaving their officers engaged hand-to-hand amidst the enemy. Dr. Lord, Broadfoot of the engineers, and Crispin of the cavalry fell; Ponsonby, severely wounded, and with his reins cut, was carried off the field by his charger. Fraser, covered with blood, severely wounded, and with his sword-arm disabled, broke through his assailants, and, riding up to Sale, calmly reported the defeat of his squadrons. Sale with his infantry and guns drove the enemy from the hills and recovered the bodies of the slain officers; but Dost Mahomed, who had commanded in person at the attack on the two squadrons, escaped from the field without pursuit or difficulty. The result of the day was a deep disappointment to all engaged. The conduct of the two squadrons was wholly inexplicable. They were attacked by inferior numbers, very ill mounted; and had the troopers but charged they would have ridden over their antagonists, who advanced at a walk and in disorder; and Dost Mahomed must either have fallen or been taken.

Prior to this discreditable affair, Macnaghten, alarmed by the feeling which he knew to pervade the country and the inhabitants of Cabul, wrote to the Governor-General gloomily anticipating the probability of having to 'submit to the disgrace of being shut up in Cabul for a time,' and prepared the Bala Hissar for such a contingency, mounting guns so as to command the city, and strengthening the guards of the citadel gates. The envoy's apprehensions were not allayed when he received from Burnes an account of the action at Purwan Durrah, accompanied by the suggestion that Sale should be recalled and all the troops concentrated at Cabul for its defence. Macnaghten had received this letter on November 3, and was returning from his evening ride, pondering on its contents, when a horseman rode up to him, and having ascertained that he was the envoy, announced the presence of Dost Mahomed. This voluntary surrender at once altered the whole state of affairs. Macnaghten and the Shah, in possession of Dost Mahomed and the greater part of his family, were now at liberty to indulge in the hope that their difficulties were at an end, and that the Shah's authority could be established. The step thus taken by the Ameer must be regarded as evincing a strange pusillanimity, and was dissonant from the expectations formed of his character. The hasty resolution was probably the result of a moment of weariness at the life which for months he had been leading, and of the fear that the Kohistanees, who only hated him a degree less than the British, might find it more convenient to betray him, and thus obtain peace and the large reward set upon his head, than to maintain hostilities which cost them forts, villages, and vineyards, and threatened to render their country hopelessly desolate.

Macnaghten had written to the Governor-General: 'No mercy should be shown to the man who is the author of all the evils that are now distracting the country; but, should we be so fortunate as to secure the person of Dost Mahomed, I shall request his Majesty not to execute him till I can ascertain his Lordship's sentiments.' Shortly after the voluntary surrender of the Ameer the envoy wrote: 'I trust that the Dost will be treated with liberality. His case has been compared to that of Shah Shooja; and I have seen it argued that he should not be treated more handsomely than his Majesty was; but surely the cases are not parallel. The Shah had no claim on us. We had no hand in depriving him of his kingdom; whereas we ejected the Dost, who never offended us, in support of our policy, of which he was the victim.' As the latter view, ingenuously truthful and correct, ill corresponded with the sanguinary tone of the former, the Governor-General, probably acquainted with Vattel's chapter 'of the sovereign who wages an unjust war,' abstained from expressing his sentiments on a question admitting such contrariety of personal application as that of the execution of 'the author of all the evils' then distracting the country; and Macnaghten, overjoyed at the unexpected issue of events, not only frankly urged the truth in favour of his prisoner, but treated him from the first with the attention and consideration which the English gentleman has ever shown to those whom the chances of war may throw into his power.

On November 12 Dost Mahomed marched with Sir W. Cotton towards Jellalabad, and was ultimately escorted across the Punjab to Loodianah.

CHAPTER XX.

1840.

COURSE OF EVENTS AT HERAT—YAR MAHOMED'S INTRIGUES WITH THE PERSIANS.

THE expedient leniency of Lord Auckland to Kamran and his minister, Yar Mahomed, did not, as may have been surmised, produce a permanently favourable effect upon the counsels and acts of the Herat authorities. At first, indeed, Yar Mahomed seemed earnestly desirous of giving proof that his gratitude was sincere, and his attachment to the British Government not confined to mere profession. Accordingly he proposed the expulsion of the Persians from the fortress of Ghorian, possession of which they still retained. The bait took. Todd, aware that Macnaghten and the Indian Government were anxious that the Persians should retire to a greater distance from Herat, credulously put faith in Yar Mahomed's avowed intention of capturing Ghorian, and advanced, on the strength of his promises, upwards of two lacs of rupees to aid in equipping the force with which this stroke of policy was to be accomplished.

Pretended penitence for perfidy having secured so liberal a largess, Yar Mahomed, surprised at his own success, wrote to the Governor of Ghorian to allay the fears which the vaunt of contemplated operations against that fortress might have excited; and to assure the Persian that the machinations of the British agent might be despised, and reliance be placed on the friendly disposition of the Herat authorities. Todd, at length convinced that he had been grossly duped, discontinued all further advances for the alleged preparations against Ghorian, and, about August 1840, reduced the monthly subsidy paid to Kamran and his minister to 25,000 rupees. The measure was a source of disappointment to the ruler of Herat; but his minister, nothing abashed, determined to change his game, and to play after another fashion upon the credulity of the British agent. Communications with the Persian Minister for Foreign Affairs were actively renewed, and finally arrangements made for a conference at Ghorian between accredited envoys from the Persian Court and from Herat. The Persian minister quitted Meshed, and, with the view of attending the conference, marched towards Ghorian; but Yar Mahomed, having brought affairs to this pass, thought he had at disposal a political secret sure to command a good price. Accordingly, making great merit of revealing his own device, he claimed from Todd a reward corresponding in magnitude to the importance of the secret. Upwards of 200,000*l.* had, however, been by this time thrown away at Herat, and the patient credulity of the British authorities had been taxed beyond further endurance. Yar Mahomed's scheme for adding to the hoards won by his duplicity therefore failed.

Baffled in what he had considered very skilful finesse,

the minister's ingenuity was nevertheless but a short time at fault. Avarice has no shame. When, therefore, in October 1840, the state of affairs in Afghanistan became known at Herat, Yar Mahomed, thinking the moment favourable for intimidating Todd into compliance, again urgently demanded money. The successes of the Murrees in Upper Scinde, the attacks on Quetta, the capture of Kelat by the son of Mehrab Khan, and the advance of Dost Mahomed upon Cabul, formed a combination of circumstances sufficiently unfavourable to Shah Shooja's authority. By receiving communications from disaffected persons in Afghanistan, and by threatening to march on Candahar, Yar Mahomed thought that the dread of such additional countenance and support of the insurgents would compel Todd to purchase the forbearance of Herat by a further heavy subsidy. These hopes were not without real foundation; but they were suddenly blasted by the surrender of Dost Mahomed, and the complete re-establishment of security on the line of communications between Shikarpore and Quetta. Todd, reassured in his position at Herat by the favourable turn of affairs towards the close of the year 1840, refused these demands, and continued to limit the expenditure to the monthly stipend before mentioned. In the course of one year an outlay of upwards of 150,000*l.* had been incurred by Todd at Herat; and the expenditure initiated by Pottinger, instead of being diminished, had been carried to an extravagant excess without any resulting advantage. Indeed, so far from British influence being thereby strengthened, Macnaghten, alarmed by the reports received from Todd, had repeatedly urged the necessity of moving British troops to Herat; and the Governor-General, though averse to such an operation, had so far yielded as to have been led to contemplate the movement as a possible event; and a battering train, sent from Bombay, was in preparation at Sukkur, and under orders to be held in readiness for a march to Candahar in case of being wanted for the forementioned distant expedition. The events of November allayed the apprehensions of the British authorities in Afghanistan; and, producing temporarily an effect at Herat, the advance of a force to that fortress was for the time not pressed.

The lull in Yar Mahomed's intrigues was not of long continuance; for the events which have now to be narrated no sooner began than Kamran's minister engaged with great activity in correspondence and intrigue with the Dooranee insurgents of Zemindawar.

CHAPTER XXI.

DECEMBER 1840–AUGUST 1841.

MOOLLA SHOOKOOR—DISCONTENT OF THE DOORANEE CHIEFS—RISING OF UKTAR KHAN—NOTT AND RAWLINSON AT CANDAHAR—RISING OF THE GHILZYES—THEIR DEFEAT BY WYMER—WOODBURN'S EXPEDITION TO GIRISHK—DEFEAT OF UKTUR KHAN BY GRIFFIN—DEFEAT OF THE GHILZYES BY CHAMBERS.

THE Dooranee chiefs, whatever their hopes when Shah Shooja was first placed upon the throne, were rapidly undeceived in their expectations of attaining power and influence under the sway of their Dooranee master. All real power was in the hands of the British functionaries, who, ignorant of the country, the people, and the chiefs, and naturally jealous of the influence of the latter, were peculiarly liable to err in the selection of subordinates where the nomination of these was entrusted to them. The political agents were also frequently compromised by the necessity of acting in official connection with persons deriving their dignities and charges from the appointment of the Shah. Moolla Shookoor, his first minister, had been a faithful follower of his exile, but possessed no other qualification for so important a post, and was alike ignorant of the spirit which pervaded the people and the chiefs, with whom he was therefore unpopular. His influence was great;

and the Shah, placing confidence in his minister's judgment and intentions, overlooked the fact that in choosing the men to be placed around Prince Timour at Candahar the fitness of the individuals for the duties to be devolved upon them was made an entirely minor consideration to the qualification of old companionship. Accordingly Timour's counsellors were the minister's old Loodianah fellow-exiles. These men and their satellites were eager to seize the golden opportunity for enriching themselves at the expense of the province; and, knowing that they could safely calculate upon the weakness and connivance of the minister, they had no hesitation in committing acts of oppressive injustice in the collection of revenue from the people and in the interception of royal bounty from the Dooranee chiefs. The latter haughtily resented the bearing of greedy upstarts, whose only merit was long exile from the country they now plundered; and the chiefs soon found that they could rely on the sympathy of the common people, who were equally disgusted, and animated by a deep feeling of hostility towards the instruments of misrule and the power which supported them.

It has been noted that the intrigues of Kamran's minister were busy in exciting and encouraging the disaffected; and there came in aid of the projects of the discontented chiefs a rumour which, whether well or ill founded, was widely circulated, that Shah Shooja, jealous of British supremacy, and impatient of the subjection in which he was kept, desired to free himself and the Afghans from a galling yoke, and only awaited a favourable result to any revolt which might shake the British power, in order to declare himself openly, and cordially to aid in the expulsion of allies whose presence overshadowed the authority of the throne.

Foremost amongst the discontented chiefs was Uktur Khan, a bold, designing man, disappointed by not obtaining charge of Zemindawar, and otherwise angered by the Shah's Candahar authorities. He raised the standard of rebellion, and on December 29 routed Mahomed Allum Khan, took his guns, and drove the royalist followers from the field. Nott had despatched a regiment of native infantry, with cavalry and guns, to disperse the insurgents; but Mahomed Allum Khan was beaten before Farrington and his detachment could arrive. Farrington, however, followed up the successful enemy, crossed the Helmund at Girishk, and on the morning of January 3 came up with them at Lundee Nowah, where, to the number of 1,500 horse and foot, Uktur Khan had drawn up his force, ensconced amongst sand-hills, to screen it from the dreaded fire of the British artillery. Farrington attacked them, and drove Uktur Khan from his position, capturing a standard, and pursuing the fugitives for some distance. This smart affair, in which the enemy left sixty killed upon the field, was a partial check to the spirit of revolt, and somewhat disheartened the insurgents. The weather being severe, they dispersed, and the detachment was withdrawn from Zemindawar.

Two men were now at Candahar who had a clear perception of the real state of affairs in Afghanistan—General Nott and Captain Rawlinson—both men of talent, and both good soldiers; the one an able, high-minded commander, whose strong feelings and military pride had been most undeservedly wounded by repeated and unjustifiable supercession; the other, a man who added to the qualities of a good officer those of an accomplished Eastern scholar, and was in the political department an active and intelligent agent. The general, compelled by accident to remain in Afghanistan, now began to anticipate that, although others had reaped laurels at Ghuznee and Kelat, a sterner struggle was at hand, and that he might have to strike a blow for his country's honour and the fame of her arms. By careful attention to the *morale* and the discipline of his troops, and by considerate conduct towards the Afghans, he sought to allay the passions and prejudices of the latter, and to gain their respect and good-will, coupled with a well-founded dread of the formidable, but orderly, force under his control. The civil being separate from the military authority, and in other hands, Nott could only watch the progress of misrule and embroilment, and prepare, as best he could, for the storm which he saw approaching, and which he knew, though not raised by him, must of necessity burst upon himself and his men. Rawlinson, entrusted with examining the revenue accounts of the province, and reporting upon the expenditure of six lacs of rupees at a place where there was no expense of a court to keep up, and also with inquiring into and ascertaining the origin of the late disturbances, quickly perceived the false position of the British in Afghanistan, and early and repeatedly endeavoured to impress Macnaghten with a sense of the danger attending that position. These warnings were accompanied by expressions which implicated Shah Shooja as having countenanced the revolt of Uktur Khan, and intimated the existence of intrigues of a dangerous and little suspected character. Macnaghten entirely discredited such machinations, and acquainted the Shah with all he heard from Rawlinson. The monarch either was, or pretended to be, 'well-nigh frantic;' and, ascribing such rumours to the creatures of his lately deposed minister, Moolla Shookoor, threatened to send for the officials the latter had placed around Timour at Candahar, and, 'having ripped up their bellies, to hang them up as food for the crows.' The Shah had reasonable ground of anger against these functionaries, as one of them had directly charged him with having made a communication by letter hostile in tone to his British allies. Macnaghten would not doubt the Shah's sincerity, and wrote to Rawlinson: 'I think you should sift these atrocious rumours to their head as diligently as possible. You have had a troublesome task lately, and have been doubtless without leisure to weigh probabilities; but it may make the consideration of all questions more simple if you will hereafter take for granted that as regards us "the king can do no wrong." He is not so disposed, and if he were this is not the time' (January 23, 1841). Rawlinson, however, was neither so assured of the Shah's sincerity nor so sanguine as was Macnaghten of the probable facility of effectually tranquillising the provinces, except resort were had to what he naïvely termed 'the correct and forcible removal to India of at least fifty or sixty of the most powerful and turbulent of the Dooranee Khans;' a project which Macnaghten could not entertain, observing that 'Government would never tolerate for a moment the notion of such wholesale expatriation.' Having deposed the minister, Moolla Shookoor, the envoy and the Shah founded their hopes of restoring to order the province of Candahar by the removal, and despatch to Cabul, of the minister's creatures, who had abetted Timour in acts of violence, profited by exactions which had discontented the people, and had succeeded in rendering the British power, themselves, and the Shah, obnoxious to the chiefs and their numerous followers. This measure, and a contemplated visit to his Dooranee capital in the autumn by the Shah, when he hoped to conciliate the chiefs, who were invited in the meantime to lay their grievances before him by petition, were the means through which the envoy trusted to restore confidence and good-will.

The removal of the culpable functionaries produced a very transient effect. The evil lay deeper; and the spirit of disaffection to the Shah and hatred to the British power from day to day acquired strength, and began more and more to move the hearts of the people. The universal venality of the public officers and the authorised exactions of former Governments may have been occasionally what Macnaghten, when contrasting them with existing circumstances, represented them, hardily credible. But they were so only when there was the power to coerce, and that, owing to the disordered state of the country, was not often. Amidst the struggles for dominant authority, official rapacity was effectually kept in check by the independent spirit of the people, by the readiness with which they flew to arms in order to resent oppression or oppose exaction, and by the dread of thus strengthening political adversaries. Under the twofold Government of the Shah and the envoy the misdeeds of the native collectors had no compensating reaction to fear. The political agents were, however well-intentioned, unable to cope with the interested duplicity of their subordinates; and the latter knew that the strong arm of the British force was ever at hand to strike down rebellion and enforce the payments of revenue. Amid much that was anarchical in consequence of the oscillations of superior power, the people had for years enjoyed a wild freedom and an immunity from heavy taxation which made them impatient of a condition such as that which was suddenly imposed upon them. The system was the more severe from the practice of paying the Shah's levies by assignments on the revenues of particular districts. These levies were larger and of a more permanent character than those heretofore entertained; and the collectors quartered themselves on the assigned districts, living at the cost of the inhabitants until the latter liquidated the prescribed contribution. Macnaghten, aware that such a custom must alienate the people and render them as hostile to the Shah as to his British allies, instructed the new minister, Usman Khan, to abolish the system of assignments, and to replace it by one less oppressive and unpopular. But the wants of the Shah were urgent; the Indian Government, meeting the enormous outlay in Afghanistan with reluctance, was unwilling to increase it; and the minister, surrounded with difficulties, could not in the midst of disorder and rebellion introduce ameliorations in the fiscal system of the country. Matters therefore necessarily continued much upon their old footing; and the prospect was remote of radical improvement.

Macnaghten, no longer able to shut his eyes to a fact against which he had long contended, the Shah's unpopularity, was nevertheless resolved to view affairs in a favourable light; and he combated the opinion that the position of the British power in Afghanistan was a false one, and that either it should take the government of the country into its own hands or relinquish all military occupation of it. 'If either McNeill or Sir J. Hobhouse should entertain a similar opinion, I have little doubt that it has originated in the atrociously false reports that have been circulated regarding his Majesty's personal character. In common honesty we can neither take the country nor withdraw our troops so long as his Majesty is sincere in his alliance. If we are to take countries on account of the misgovernment of their rulers, why should we not begin with Lucknow, Hyderabad, &c.? Surely, our unfortunate Shah ought not to be the only victim, and condemned without trial. He has incurred the odium that attaches to him from his alliance with us; and it would be an act of downright dishonesty to desert him before he has found the means of taking root in the soil to which we have transplanted him.' After denouncing either alternative as impolitic and impracticable, and urging that 'we should require ten times the number of troops that we now have to support our position, were we ostensibly to appear as rulers of the country,' he expressed his opinion in allusion to the Dooranee and Ghilzye disaffection, which he deemed transient: 'All things considered, the present tranquillity of this country is to my mind perfectly miraculous. Already our presence has been infinitely beneficial in allaying animosities and pointing out abuses; but our proceedings must be guided by extreme caution—Rome was not built in a day—but I look forward to the time when his Majesty will have an honest and efficient administration of his own, though the time must be far distant, if ever it should arrive (certainly it cannot arrive during the present generation, to whom anarchy is second nature) when we can dispense with the presence of our Hindustanee contingent. Here we are gradually ferreting out abuses and placing matters on a firm and satisfactory basis.—February 27, 1841. Jellalabad.'

Written at a time when the punishment of the Sungo Khel in the Nazian Valley was only delayed until the necessary disposition could be effected, and Shelton with a strong force could be detached upon the duty, Macnaghten's view of affairs was little in accordance with reality. Truth is seldom insulted with impunity. The *miraculous tranquillity* existed nowhere except in Macnaghten's wishes and imagination, for whilst he was engaged in checking, through the operations of Shelton on February 24, the rising spirit of revolt amongst the tribes bordering the Khybur, the Ghilzyes in the vicinity of Candahar, and between that place and Ghuznee, were evincing an implacable hostility, which determined the British authorities to occupy Kelat-i-Ghilzye, and thus, by establishing a garrison in the heart of the disturbed districts, to curb insurrectionary movements, and to ensure greater security of communication along the line of the Turnuk. The expedition upon which Shelton was sent into the Nazian Valley had a colourable pretext in justification of the measures enforced; but the Ghilzye rising on the line of the Turnuk was preceded by the capture of a small fort under circumstances in which the gallantry of Sanders, Macan, and others was no excuse for the original error which led to its attack, and the destruction of its chief with fifteen of his men. The occurrence embittered the Ghilzye hatred of their invaders, and they were resolved to contest the permanent occupation of their country. With great jealousy they watched the preparations for rendering the old post of Kelat-i-Ghilzye tenable, and began to assemble, in order if possible to interrupt and prevent the completion of the design. Nott, hearing of this, and having to despatch stores of various descriptions to the post, sent them under the escort of 700 bayonets, a detachment of horse, and two guns, the whole commanded by Colonel Wymer. When the convoy neared its destination the Ghilzyes broke up from the loose beleaguer of Kelat-i-Ghilzye and marched to oppose Wymer. Macan followed them; but, apprehensive of a *ruse*, and that the enemy, having lured him from his post, might double back and carry it in his absence, he halted. The Ghilzyes were, however, intent upon Wymer, and at five P.M. on May 9 they boldly attacked him. Having a large convoy to protect, he was forced to stand on the defensive. In spite of Hawkins's guns, which threw their shot with effect amongst the Ghilzye masses, the latter advanced with good courage, and sought to assail one of Wymer's flanks and thus discomfit him. Whilst making a partial change of position to meet fairly this movement, the Ghilzyes, thinking the sepoys shaken, rushed sword in hand to the charge; but the 38th were quick and steady in forming, and their close, well-delivered fire, aided by the grape of the guns, made the swordsmen reel and recoil from before the bayonets. The combat nevertheless lasted until ten P.M., when the Ghilzyes, despairing of success, having lost many killed, and having to carry off many wounded, withdrew from their purpose, and left Wymer to accomplish his march.

Meantime Uktur Khan had been actively engaged in recovering from the check Farrington had given him, and a number of fresh followers had gathered around him. Macnaghten, warned that the state of the country was becoming 'worse and worse every day,' chafed at the truth, and received it ungraciously. 'These idle statements,' he wrote, 'may cause much mischief, and, often repeated as they are, they neutralise my protestations to the contrary. I know them to be utterly false as regards this part of the country (Cabul), and I have no reason to believe them true as regards your portion of the kingdom (Candahar), merely because the Tukkees are indulging in their accustomed habits of rebellion, or because Uktur Khan has a parcel of ragamuffins at his heels.' The seizure of Uktur Khan by a night march of the Janbaz, whom he knew to be untrustworthy; the offer of a large pecuniary reward for the capture of the rebel leader; and the notice that when caught he should be hung 'as high as Haman,' were Macnaghten's instructions for the tranquillisation of the districts to the west of Candahar; whilst he hoped, by transferring to another Ghilzye chief, on condition of his seizing the Goroo, who had beleaguered Kelat-i-Ghilzye and attacked Wymer, the Gooroo's portion of the stipulated allowances, or black mail, to sow dissension amongst the Ghilzye leaders, and to obtain by treachery possession of an inveterate enemy of the British power.

Uktur Khan, who was to be thus summarily dealt with, had assembled about 6,000 men, and had taken up a safe position before Girishk, on the right bank of the Helmund, which rapid river effectually secured him from surprise. Nott sent Woodburn at the head of his regiment of sepoys, the Janbaz Horse, and a detail of guns under Cooper, to search for and attack the insurgents. Woodburn, learning their position, marched to the left bank of the Helmund, and on July 3 found the fords opposite Girishk in possession of the enemy, and reported at the time to be impracticable. Lower down a ford was said to be fit for infantry, whilst three miles above Girishk, at Sumboolee, another was practicable for cavalry. Hart's Janbaz were accordingly ordered to cross the river at the upper ford, and to move down the right bank towards the enemy, whilst Woodburn with the infantry should effect the passage at the lower ford. Hart crossed and advanced towards the enemy; but, observing that Woodburn had failed to make good his passage, Hart fell back again upon the ford at Sumboolee, followed, but not pressed, by the enemy; Woodburn in the meantime making a parallel movement up the left bank, until at eight A.M. the infantry, exhausted with heat and fatigue, effected a junction with Hart, who recrossed the river without being harassed. At half-past four P.M. the enemy were in motion; and Woodburn, surmising that they intended to attack him, despatched Hart with the Janbaz to oppose the enemy's passage of the river; but the latter had effected their purpose before Hart's Janbaz, who were not eager for a skirmish, reached the ford chosen by Uktur Khan. Hart had therefore to retire upon Woodburn, who prepared to receive his opponent's attack by placing the guns in the centre of the line of infantry and the Janbaz horse on both flanks. Two attempts against the infantry and guns were repulsed, but the enemy, sweeping round Woodburn's right, pushed back a Janbaz corps in confusion, and threatened to break in upon the infantry; the rear rank of the sepoys, to the left of the guns, faced about and with their fire checked the partial success of Uktur Khan. Woodburn's position was now critical, for the Janbaz endangered the infantry by their panic and disorder; he therefore moved a gun, supported by his Grenadiers, to disembarrass his rear, which with a few rounds of grape and musketry he fortunately accomplished. Uktur Khan, having failed to follow up the partial advantage which the disorder of the Janbaz presented, then drew off, with a loss of about 300 killed and many wounded. Hart and Golding pursued; but these gallant men, followed by few of their Janbaz, could effect little; and Woodburn, unable with his exhausted sepoys and guns to move in support, and not confident of the mass of the Janbaz, threw his infantry and guns into an enclosure which afforded cover, and could if assailed be stoutly defended. Uktur Khan, having reformed his men, again advanced, and repeated attacks were made on Woodburn's post, but were repulsed by the fire of the guns and infantry, and proved less daring than at the beginning of the fight. Desultory firing continued until about eleven o'clock at night, after which it ceased. The enemy finding themselves unmolested, were occupied throughout the night in carrying off their dead and wounded, in re-fording the river, and retreating towards Zemindawar. Woodburn the next morning crossed the river and encamped at Girishk. He could show three standards taken from the enemy as trophies of the combat; but he wrote to Nott that the conduct of the Janbaz, his only cavalry, the notoriously disaffected state of the country, and the numbers of the enemy, did not seem to warrant the pursuit of Uktur Khan unless a reinforcement of cavalry and infantry joined him.

Nott determined to strike both at the Ghilzyes and at Uktur Khan. Two detachments, therefore, one under Colonel Chambers, against the Ghilzyes, and another under Captain Griffin, against Uktur Khan, marched from Candahar, both strong in cavalry. Chambers on August 5 was slightly engaged; the enemy, however, made no stand, but fled from the charges of the troops of horse before the infantry and guns came into action. Griffin had more decided fortune; for on August 17, at the head of four guns, 800 sabres, and 350 bayonets, he drove Uktur Khan from a position at Khawind. The rebel leader had chosen ground on which walls and gardens afforded cover for his men, about 5,000 in number, and promised to nullify the fire of the artillery and the compact discipline of the handful of infantry; but Griffin boldly attacked him, drove the rebels from their cover, and forced them out of their position. They were in the act of forming beyond the broken ground they had yielded, when Hart, seeing that the moment was favourable, charged with his Janbaz; Suftur Jung, a son of Shah Shooja, shared in the honour of this charge; and the Janbaz displayed no slackness, but, following their leaders, broke the enemy, and hotly pursued them.

The victory was decisive; and thus both the Dooranee and the Ghilzye outbreaks received severe, disheartening blows from Nott's detachments. Whilst the result of the military operations was still uncertain, Macnaghten had rebutted the existence of any difficulty in overcoming the national feeling against British supremacy. 'From Mookoor to the Khybur Pass all is content and tranquillity, and wherever we Europeans go we are received with respect, and attention, and welcome.' Persisting in regarding the insurrections in the vicinity of Candahar as transient manifestations of an habitual spirit of independence, from which nothing unfavourable to the popularity of the British rule was to be inferred, he unhesitatingly denied the difficulty of its position in Afghanistan. 'On the contrary, I think our prospects are most cheering; and, with the materials we have, there ought to be little or no difficulty in the management of the country. It is true the population is exclusively Mahomedan; but it is split into rival sects, and we all know that of all antipathies the sectarian is the most virulent. We have Hazarahs, Ghilzyes, Dooranees, and Kuzzilbash all at daggers drawn with each other; and in every family there are rivals and enemies. Some faults of management must necessarily be committed on the first assumption of the administration of a new country, and the Dooranee outbreak may be partially attributable to such faults; but what, after all, do such outbreaks signify?' Supporting his opinion of the evanescent character of such insurrections by examples drawn from the history of India, Macnaghten, in allusion to Uktur Khan and his followers, thus summed up his views:—'But these people are perfect children, and they should be treated as such. If we put our naughty boy in the corner the rest will be terrified. We have taken their plaything, Power, out of the hands of the Dooranee chiefs, and they are pouting a good deal in consequence. They did not know how to use it. In their hands it was useless and even hurtful to their master, and we were obliged to transfer it to scholars of our own. They instigate the Moollahs, and the Moollahs preach to the people; but this will be very temporary. The evil of it is, we must have force; we have abandoned all hope of forming a national army.' Thus thought and wrote the envoy. Nott, to the full as bold a man, in spite of the successes of his troops, took a wholly different view of affairs from Macnaghten. 'The conduct of the thousand and one politicals has ruined our cause, and bared the throat of every European in this country to the sword and knife of the revengeful Afghan and bloody Belooch; and unless several regiments be quickly sent not a man will be left to note the fate of his comrades. Nothing but force will ever make them submit to the hated Shah Shooja, who is most certainly as great a scoundrel as ever lived.' Nothing could thus be more opposed than were the views of the envoy and the general, who only concurred on the single point of ascribing blame to the subordinate political functionaries. Their errors, admitted by Macnaghten and prominently adduced by Nott, were, however, as has been seen, but secondary causes, rather affording occasion for the exhibition of than originating that deep hate which now pulsed in the hearts of the Afghans. The whole policy of the Anglo-Indian Government was a grievous wrong to this people; and the instruments who strove to work out a faulty system with a devotion and zeal worthy of a better cause, cannot justly be made responsible for its failure. If some were vain, shallow, and immoral, others were able, good, and valorous men. The usual proportion of ability and merit was there; but these qualities had to struggle against adverse circumstances and false positions, and were expected to reconcile incompatibilities.

CHAPTER XXII.

DECEMBER 1840–AUGUST 1841.

TODD'S WITHDRAWAL FROM HERAT—DISAVOWAL OF HIS MEASURES BY LORD AUCKLAND.

CONTEMPORANEOUSLY with the Dooranee insurrection in Zemindawar, events took place at Herat which must now be noted.

Yar Mahomed, in constant communication with Uktur Khan and the rebels, sought to encourage the outbreak, and, by embarrassing the British Government, and finding full occupation for its troops in the suppression of revolts in Afghanistan, to oppose an insurmountable obstacle to the military occupation of Herat. He knew that so long as the Dooranees and Ghilzyes were in arms Nott could not spare men and cattle for a march on Herat. Secure on this point, the object next in importance was to devise means for reopening the sluices of British prodigality. The minister was well aware that from the side of Persia there was now nothing to dread. A confidential agent was therefore despatched to Meshed, inviting Persian co-operation; pointing out the distracted state of Zemindawar and the Ghilzye country; and urging the opportunity as favourable for an armed demonstration in support of the kindling spirit of insurrection,—the northern division of the British army of occupation having its communications with the southern interrupted by the snow on the highlands of Ghuznee. Yar Mahomed was well apprised of the inability and unwillingness of Persia to act on his suggestions. His purpose was, to operate upon the apprehensions of the British agent, and thus again to effect a renewal of the now staunched donations. Todd, however, at the same time that he ascertained the nature of Yar Mahomed's letters to Meshed, learnt that strong reinforcements were in Upper Scinde, and that there was a probability of Nott's hands being early strengthened. He therefore deemed the occasion favourable for marking his sense of the conduct of Kamran, by enforcing a measure which would be a severe blow to that avaricious ruler and his minister. On February 1, 1841, he informed the Herat authorities that even the monthly stipend would be discontinued until the pleasure of the British Government was known. Yar Mahomed sought to parry this blow by artfully offering to accede to the admission of a British force into Herat—a measure which Macnaghten had much at heart, and which had been the real object of the mission. Hitherto Yar Mahomed had carefully thwarted its fulfilment, nor had he any intention of altering his policy in this respect; but he rightly judged that it would at once induce Todd to reopen negotiations; that it might not improbably lead to a grant of money; and that it was entirely free from danger, as no troops were disposable, nor for months could be, to despatch to Herat. The immediate payment of two lacs of rupees was the condition coupled with the professed concession. Todd, without adverting to the fact whether troops were available or not for Herat, eagerly caught at the hope of realising the object of his mission; but he required as a guarantee, before payment of the demand to which he otherwise made no objection, that Yar Mahomed's son should proceed to Girishk to meet and conduct the force to Herat, should the arrangement meet with the approval of the Anglo-Indian Government. The security demanded was in accordance with the envoy's views; but Yar Mahomed, who never dreamt of admitting willingly a contingent of British troops, finding that Todd was no longer to be duped into actual payment without an equivalent, declined to furnish the desired guarantee, and, as a last resource for compelling Todd to submit to exaction, demanded either the payment of the stipulated allowance or the withdrawal of the mission. Kamran's minister in adopting this course thought that the state of Zemindawar and the Ghilzye country would render Todd averse to taking a step which involved open rupture with Herat; but Todd, having failed in his ill-timed endeavour to accomplish the grand object of his mission, refused to meet the requisition, and, to the alarm of Yar Mahomed, withdrew the mission from Herat.

The news of this rupture reached the Governor-General, accompanied by the envoy's strenuous advocacy of a military expedition to re-establish British influence by the occupation of Herat, at a time which rendered the event, and Macnaghten's suggestions thereon, extremely unpalatable. By the cession of Ghorian the differences with Persia had been brought to a conclusion;

and there appeared, therefore, no real basis for the stringent measures pursued by Todd, founded on a jealousy of Heratee intrigues with Persia. Not only, however, did the grounds for the sudden break with Herat appear insufficient, but the latter event had the effect of casting ridicule on the whole of the operations in Afghanistan—clearly announcing to the world that British interference and protection were more dreaded by Herat than Persian thirst for conquest.

The Dooranee and Ghilzye outbreaks were a source of alarm to the Government of India, which was further irritated by the fact that the Secret Committee, startled by the cost of the war, which, after exhausting the accumulated treasure, had plunged India into debt, had addressed the Government of India in terms which in reality called in question the whole policy of the war.

The weak Government in England, conscious that the then approaching elections would prove the downfall of the existing Ministry, would, when too late, have gladly withdrawn from a conquest the evils of which were forcing themselves upon the convictions of their originators, and could not stand scrutiny should power pass into other hands. Lord Auckland, vexed at the aspect of affairs, resolved at once to disavow Todd's measures. Conciliatory letters were immediately written to the Herat authorities, and regret expressed at the occurrences which had partially interrupted mutual good understanding.

Todd had certainly acted imprudently in pressing a measure which Macnaghten, at the time, from the want of available troops and the state of the country around Candahar, was clearly unable to carry into effect; but the envoy was as eager as his deputy, and, having led him into the mis-timed attempt, deserved as much blame. It fell, however, wholly on Todd, who was removed from political employment; whilst Macnaghten was simply advised that 'we should first learn to quiet and to control the positions we occupied before we plunged onwards.'

Yar Mahomed's fears were completely allayed by the letters of the Governor-General. Both Kamran and his minister regretted the cessation of the large sums which at one time were lavishly granted them; but, as the patience and credulity of the British Government had on this point been exhausted, the Herat authorities were glad to find themselves independent of its tutelage and domination. The envoy was, indeed, amused by a friendly correspondence, particularly as such still held out the prospect of a continuance of the stipend of three lacs of rupees per annum, which Yar Mahomed did not despair of obtaining upon very easy terms; but it was only on such that he entertained any intention of favouring the British Government by the acceptance of its subsidy. Macnaghten, as late as August 1841, still hoped to effect a reconciliation, and to bring round Yar Mahomed to a more cordial understanding. The Government was advised to stipulate that Yar Mahomed must agree to follow the advice of the British authorities in all matters; that no demand beyond the three lacs per annum should be made; and that one of Yar

Mahomed's sons was to reside at Calcutta or Bombay as a hostage for his father's sincerity. But events soon followed which threw into utter insignificance Yar Mahomed, his petty intrigues, and the credulity of our overreached agent's proceedings at Herat.

CHAPTER XXIII.

SEPTEMBER–OCTOBER 1841.

ALARM IN ENGLAND AT THE FRUITS OF LORD AUCKLAND'S POLICY—HE RESOLVES TO MAINTAIN THE OCCUPATION OF AFGHANISTAN—REDUCTION OF THE SUBSIDIES TO CHIEFS—RISE OF THE GHILZYES—MARCH OF SALE'S BRIGADE FOR HINDUSTAN—GENERAL ELPHINSTONE—SALE FORCES THE KHOORD CABUL PASS—MONTEITH ATTACKED BY THE ENEMY—HIS RELIEF BY SALE—TREATY WITH THE GHILZYES—SALE MARCHES TO GUNDAMUK.

THE observation has already been made, that the Secret Committee had taken alarm at the aspect of affairs to the westward of the Indus; and as the altered tone in which they suddenly expressed themselves upon the operations in Afghanistan had a marked and an unfortunate effect upon the envoy's measures, it here becomes essential to note the manner in which the opinions of the Secret Committee influenced the current of events.

Most readers are aware that the control of the Governments of India is a power entrusted to the President of the Board of Control, a member of the Ministry, and empowered by Act of Parliament to dictate instructions to the Secret Committee of the Court of Directors. The influence of the latter body is, therefore, in all matters of real importance of a purely subordinate character, and is entirely dependent upon the ability and energy of the President, and the interest which the Ministry for the time being may take in the welfare and good government of the vast empire under the sway of the British Crown. The name of the Secret Committee, the channel for the injunctions of the President of the Board of Control, must not, therefore, when subsequently used, be misunderstood as attaching undue importance to that small section of the Court of Directors which has always a qualified, and often a nominal, rather than a real, participation in the conduct of affairs of weight.

The insurrection which recovered Kelat for the son of Mehrab Khan; the reverses sustained in Upper Sinde; the attacks on Quetta; the alarm produced by the return of Dost Mahomed, and his movements and intrigues in the Kohistan; the great cost of the occupation of Afghanistan; and the state of anarchy into which the Punjab seemed fast falling, and by which the position of the army to the west of the Indus threatened to be still further compromised,—had excited the vivid apprehensions of the Home Government, who, under the impulse of anxiety, addressed the Governor-General in a tone of complaint and reprehension, inconsistent with the spirit of full approbation which had encouraged the opening of the war. The series of reverses were attributed to the error of having, at the close of 1839, withdrawn too many troops from Afghanistan; whilst the spirit of hostility to the Shah's Government was charged to an absence of sufficient vigour in amending the defects of the civil administration of the country. The difficulty of meeting the extraordinary disbursements consequent on the war and the continued occupation of the conquered territories, and the financial embarrassment which the deficiency of revenue as compared with expenditure could not fail to entail on India, were with reason mooted; it being evident that, unless a change of policy took place, for many years to come the restored monarchy would have need of a British force, and that not a small one, in order to maintain peace in its own territory, and prevent aggression from without. The Indian Government was, therefore, called upon to consider with the utmost seriousness the question of its future policy with respect to Afghanistan; the British position in that country being one which must be either abandoned or fully maintained, at whatever sacrifice, and with all the consequences which a movement so far beyond our frontiers must entail.

These instructions, penned under a sense of alarm at a threatening crisis, reached the Governor-General when the surrender of Dost Mahomed, the re-occupation of Kelat and flight of Mehrab Khan's son, and the successes of Nott's detachments against the Dooranee and Ghilzye insurgents, had not only improved the aspect of affairs in Afghanistan, but also brought about an opportunity most favourable for withdrawing with credit from an erroneous and dangerous policy. The unexpected surrender of Dost Mahomed was a second test of the honesty and sincerity of the Indian Government in its trans-Indus operations. No more striking event could be conceived for an honourable termination to the armed occupation of Afghanistan, and for the triumphant return of the Anglo-Indian army to its own frontier. By furnishing so unhoped an occasion Providence removed all reasonable ground of excuse or hesitation, and afforded the Indian Government the very moment which it professed to await. But man, in his shortsighted elation, clung to ill-gotten conquests, and, rejecting the proffered opportunity, was overtaken by a fearful and terrible retribution.

The Governor-General, vexed at the altered tone of the Secret Committee, and at the blame imputed to the course pursued, was gratified that circumstances were such as enabled him in reply to adduce plausible reasons for continuing the policy which had been called in question, and to speak, with a show of confidence in its ultimate success, of the necessity for maintaining the military occupation of Afghanistan, and supporting Shah Shooja until his authority should be securely established. Lord Auckland admitted that the British power was unpopular in Afghanistan, and that it rendered Shah Shooja so; that the latter, leaning entirely on his British allies, had no military means of his own worthy of the least reliance; that the actual condition of feeling in the country, whatever the degree of discontent with the established order of things, was owing rather to our presence and pervading ascendency, than to any general sentiment of personal dissatisfaction toward Shah Shooja, whom the Governor-General believed to be intelligent, just, lenient, and zealously attentive to the duties of his station; that the cost of the British force in Afghanistan was a heavy burthen upon the Indian finances—so much so, indeed, that it caused a yearly deficiency of a million and a quarter, which could only be provided for by loan, and was, therefore, rapidly plunging the Indian Government into a heavy public debt; that it was clear the Indian Government could not go on for many years providing for a deficit so considerable; that the restored monarchy, if we remained on the scene, would, for many years to come, need the maintenance, at an overwhelming cost, of a strong British force; that Russia had receded from her advance towards the Oxus; and that invasion from the westward by a large force over an immense extent of barren country, occupied by tribes destitute of union and strength, could only be made with much time and preparation. Yet, notwithstanding these plain and forcible admissions of the difficulties and embarrassments attending our position in Afghanistan, and of the withdrawal of Russia from the attempt to establish her influence on the Oxus, the Governor-General was averse to seizing the opportunity of retiring with honour from a false position; and found a countervailing advantage in the repose of the public mind in India, from our command of the avenues by which the approach of invasion was alleged to have been apprehended, and in the facility which the tenure of Afghanistan was asserted to afford for watching and counteracting the first movements of hostile intrigue. On such visionary grounds, dignified with the name of advantages of vital importance, he, with the greatest earnestness, deprecated a retrograde movement from Afghanistan, unless under the control of an imperious necessity.

To palliate this decision in favour of the alternative of continuing to occupy Afghanistan, necessarily in great force and at the cost of the financial prosperity of India, hopes were held out that the embarrassments of the latter country might be ameliorated by its growing resources—from the falling in of large pensions, the escheat of lands, and reductions in the cost of the civil establishments—all remote, and some of them but insignificant contingencies.

The alleged neglect of the civil administration of Afghanistan was rebutted, and the impolicy and impracticability of the sweeping reforms, contemplated and recommended by the Secret Committee, in the system of collecting the revenue and of paying the Afghan troops, were characterised as admirably calculated to throw everything into confusion. Nevertheless, anxious to reduce the expenditure as much as possible, and to evince a spirit of economy in consonance with the objects of the Secret Committee, Lord Auckland pressed Macnaghten to effect reductions of outlay, and to diminish the amount of the various subsidies paid to the different chiefs in Afghanistan. The envoy had objected to this measure, foreseeing some of its possible consequences; he had urged that the payments to the chiefs were nothing more nor less than a compensation for the privileges given up of plundering the high roads through their respective jurisdictions, and that 'we should be found in the end to have made a cheap bargain;' but finding himself alone in his opinion, and pressed to reduce these stipends by Burnes, the Governor-General, and the Secret Committee, he resolved—as the outward aspect of affairs was improved, and his position strengthened by the presence of the troops sent to relieve the corps which were to return to India—to satisfy the wishes of the home authorities and of the Government of India before resigning control and authority to his successor. The envoy therefore summoned the Ghilzye chiefs to Cabul, and communicated to them that the necessities of the State rendered the reduction of their stipends necessary. The chiefs received the announcement without any apparent discontent or remonstrance; but they were no sooner clear of Cabul, and amongst their own dependents and followers, than they issued orders to infest the passes between Cabul and Jellalabad, and to interrupt the line of communication with India.

Such was the discretion which, after selecting on the question of the main policy to be pursued in the worst of two alternatives, injudiciously and perniciously sought at once to enforce a petty economy incompatible with the course adopted. The heedless profusion which could waste upwards of two hundred thousand pounds upon Kamran and his minister, in the course of little more than a twelvemonth, suddenly turned with a nice parsimony to pare down the stipends of the Ghilzye chiefs, in order to boast of a saving of three thousand pounds per annum!

Macnaghten, warned throughout 1841, both by Rawlinson at Candahar and by Pottinger in Kohistan, of the real state of feeling pervading the country, but blinded by his own wishes, reasonings, and fancied strength, was obstinate in depicting the Ghilzye rising as a partial and easily quelled revolt. Yet he knew that Uktur Khan was on the Bamian frontier, and that intrigue and disaffection were rife in Cabul, Zoormut, and the Kohistan; and he soon learnt that the Ghilzyes were assembling in earnest on the line of the Cabul river. Nevertheless Sale's brigade was permitted to march upon its return towards Hindustan as if the passes were clear, the Ghilzyes contented, and no opposition to be anticipated. Monteith, with the 35th Native Infantry, marched in advance on October 9, and halted at Bootkak, about nine miles from Cabul; Sale, with the rest of the brigade, remaining at Cabul to complete his wants in baggage cattle. The fact is the more inexplicable, as it was known at Cabul on the 2nd that the passes were blocked up, and Burnes on the 3rd wrote to an officer, Captain Gray, returning with a small escort to India, to join a chief who with a party of 400 men was marching to Lughman. Gray did so, and on October 4 the chief, Mahomed Uzeen Khan, attempted to march first by the Khoord Cabul Pass, then by the Chinaree; but finding both occupied in great force, he, after consultation, struck into a very difficult, little frequented mountain path, and evading the Ghilzyes, who were intent on watching the more practicable routes, reached without skirmish a point between Sa Baba and Tazeen. His march had not, however, escaped the observation of the Ghilzyes, who, having surrounded the party, demanded the delivery of Gray and another officer, his companion, offering 3,000 rupees for each. The reply of Uzeen Khan and his men was noble: 'The officers were under their protection, and protect them they would to the very last.' The words had scarcely been uttered when a heavy fire, poured from the surrounding heights upon the party, told that chivalrous speech must be maintained by chivalrous deed. The enemy had waited until the moon, between eight and nine at night, lit up the ravine in which the small party was encamped, and showed where they lay. On receiving the Ghilzye fire they sprung to their arms, and, gallantly ascending the heights which overhung them, after a combat which lasted until four o'clock in the morning, drove the Ghilzyes from their commanding position. For the moment the valour of the party had saved it; but with daylight came the question whether to proceed on their journey or to retire to Cabul. The small band had expended its ammunition; the Ghilzyes were in great force in front and rear, one chief alone having 5,000 men in the passes ahead; and Gray, who was of the council of war, advised 'returning to Cabul.' But a son of Naib Shereef's, a mere youth, rose and said: 'I am directed to escort these officers as far as Gundamuk; we have sustained the attack of last night, and why should we fly? No! forward is the word with me.' The youth's lion counsel kindled the heroism of his hearers: 'Forward, forward!' was the unanimous cry; and, after causing the two officers to disguise themselves, onwards marched the party, until, reaching the mouth of the Purree Durrah, or Fairy's Vale, they found it swarming with the foe. The jagged junctures of a skull are not more tortuous than this chasm, which, reft across a mountain chain, is a narrow defile hemmed in by perpendicular rocks. To force this formidable passage, held by superior numbers, was hopeless.

Mahomed Uzeen Khan therefore turned off to his left, and, by a barely practicable path, boldly struck into the mountains; his advance eluded the Ghilzyes and reached the Lughman Valley in safety; but he was hotly pursued, and the enemy cut up the followers who, being ill mounted or on foot, formed the rear of the party. Fellowship in danger makes hearty friends: Mahomed Uzeen Khan, interested in the fate of Gray and his companion, to save whom he had perilled himself and his followers, now frankly told Gray that 'all Afghanistan were determined to make one cause, and to murder or drive out every Feringhee in the country; that the whole country, and Cabul itself, was ready to break out; that no confidence could be placed in the escort; and that the safety of Gray and his companion was matter of alarm and anxiety to him.' Gray wrote to Burnes on the morning of the 7th, and reported officially all that had occurred, and the plot revealed by his gallant protector. The letter reached Burnes, for he wrote to the chief acknowledging its receipt; yet Monteith marched on the 9th exactly as if all between Bootkak and Jellalabad were as quiet as the envoy, about to proceed to take up the government of Bombay, wished to be the case; and Sale, the firearms of whose corps were worn-out by constant service, failed to obtain permission to replace the bad weapons with new, though four thousand lay idle in store at Cabul.

Elphinstone, the general who had relieved Cotton, was a brave gentleman, but inexperienced in command, a tyro in Eastern warfare, ignorant of Afghanistan and its people, and so shaken by severe attacks of gout and illness before he quitted Hindustan, that he accepted the command in Afghanistan because repeatedly desired by the Government, and from the honourable feeling that it is a soldier's duty to go wherever his services may be required, but from no personal wish; for he felt that, although partial recovery forbade him to decline the service, it left him in reality physically unequal to much exertion. Had he been experienced in men and affairs, and gifted with mental energy and ability, the vigour of a commanding intellect might in some degree have counterbalanced the disadvantages of physical debility, and have prevented his infirmities from rendering him a mere cypher. The proper man to have succeeded to command in Afghanistan was Nott; but it was felt, from his known character, that if he were appointed it must be to real, and not to nominal, command; and this was not what either Burnes or Macnaghten desired. He had, therefore, again the mortification of being thrown into the background and a secondary position, in order that the highest military authority might rest in the hands of a more manageable man.

Monteith's intimation of the state of the country was a rough one. On the night of October 9 his camp was attacked at Bootkak; the assailants were repulsed; and, as the firing might have been heard at Cabul, and a report of the event was quickly communicated, Sale, with the 13th, was suddenly ordered on October 10 to move out to Bootkak, and to clear the passes. Having joined Monteith, Sale was at the head of two regiments of infantry, Dawes' guns, Oldfield's squadron of the 5th

Cavalry, a rissalah of Irregular Horse, and Broadfoot's Sappers; besides two hundred Juzailchees under Jan Fishan Khan. Sale, with this very respectable force, resolved to force the Khoord Cabul Pass, and to encamp the 35th Native Infantry in the Khoord Cabul Valley, the 13th returning to Bootkak after this should have been accomplished. Accordingly, on the morning of the 12th, he attacked and forced the Khoord Cabul Pass, with small loss, considering its length, strength, and the numbers of the enemy. The 35th was encamped as intended; and the 13th, again traversing the Khoord Cabul Pass, returned to Bootkak. Sale, wounded on first entering the pass, was thenceforward carried in a doolee throughout the subsequent operations of his force.

The isolation of the 35th Native Infantry in an unfavourable position encouraged the Ghilzyes again to attempt a night attack, and with greater chance of success than at Bootkak, where an open plain offered no special advantage to Ghilzye tactics. From the 12th to the 17th full leisure was enjoyed to observe Monteith's encampment; and Macgregor, as political agent, being with him, it was no difficult matter, through the political functionary, to obtain permission for a body of friendly Afghans to pitch their camp close to Macgregor, and therefore virtually in the British camp. Suspicious of no treachey within, Monteith's pickets were on the alert without; and on the night of the 17th they reported the advance of a strong column of the enemy on the rear of the camp. Thither the Grenadier company was sent; and it had passed the place where the camels were parked together, when, from behind the baggage cattle, a body of armed men sprang up, fired, and brought to the ground Captain Jenkins and thirty of his men. The 'friendly' Afghans having given this signal to the advancing column of the enemy, the latter pushed on to take advantage of the confusion which unexpected treachery was likely to create, and in a short time the 35th was warmly engaged. Monteith, a cool soldier, though partially surprised, was not to be easily beaten; on the contrary, he repulsed his assailants, friends and foes, and made them pay for their audacity by some loss, but could not prevent eighty camels being taken off—at the moment a serious loss.

Sale now saw the error he had committed; that the Ghilzyes, flushed with partial success, would not fail to be encouraged, and that the 35th Native Infantry left for days isolated and useless in the Khoord Cabul Valley, was likely to suffer. Having received reinforcements from Cabul, he therefore marched on the 20th to effect a junction with Monteith; and, having accomplished this without loss or difficulty, and on the 21st obtained additional camels from Cabul, he on the 22nd marched towards Tazeen.

He had with him three corps of infantry, Abbott's battery of 9-pounders, Backhouse's Mountain Train, Broadfoot's Sappers, Oldfield's squadron, a rissalah of Irregular Horse, and the Juzailchees. The Ghilzyes offered no opposition on the Huft Kotul; and the column was permitted to thread the deep defile which opens upon the Valley of Tazeen without contest; but the enemy were in force around the *débouché* into the valley, and seemed to contemplate there making a stand. A few rounds from the guns made them give ground; and the force took post in the plain without difficulty. An ill-managed, unnecessary skirmish, for which Sale, who was lying wounded in his doolee, was not responsible, cost him a gallant young officer killed, two wounded, and, worst of all, a run before a pursuing enemy, which was a baneful occurrence amongst young soldiers.

Sale, with a stout force, was now in a position to strike a blow from which important effects might have resulted; for the fort and possessions of one of the leaders in the revolt were within his grasp. The chief had kept his men together in the valley, rather than on the Huft Kotul and Tazeen defile, in order to defend his property and the winter stock of food for his cattle and followers; but the skirmish of the 22nd had, though very ill-managed on the part of the British, shown him that to save his fort he must have recourse to artifice rather than to the valour of the Ghilzyes. Afghan chiefs were avowedly of the opinion of an old French author: 'Et sans point de doute (comme j'ay dit ailleurs) les anglois ne sont pas si subtils en traietés et appointemens comme sont les François; et quelque chose que l'on en die, ils vont assez grossement en besogne; mais il faut avoir un peu de patience, et ne débattre point colériquement avec eux.' The chief, therefore, determined to open negotiations, and again to overreach Macgregor. Sale had given orders for an attack on the fort in question, and Dennie, with half the infantry and most of the artillery, was about to proceed upon the execution of the enterprise, known to be an easy one by the acting engineer, Broadfoot, when a messenger from the chief presented himself before the political agent, tendered the submission of his master and the chiefs leagued with him, and deprecated the impending attack on his castle. Macgregor, whose eyes were nothing opened by the conduct of the 'friendly' Afghans and the attack on the 35th before described, was immediately satisfied of the sincerity of these advances, and prevailed upon Sale to countermand the attack, whilst an agreement to prescribe conditions should be concluded and the chief furnish hostages. This was a fatal error. Hostages were known to be perfectly safe in a British camp, and the British authorities equally known to be ignorant of the personal appearance of the individuals demanded. To furnish ten miserable-looking men and to subscribe the treaty of submission was, therefore, an easy mode of staving off a punishment and loss which could not fail of proving most disheartening to the Ghilzyes; and the chief had consequently no hesitation in accepting terms of such present advantage to himself. How they were to be kept was soon shown; but in the meantime it was an object in any way to be rid of Sale and his troops, and to effect their complete separation from the force at Cabul; that is, without the permanent establishment of a strong detachment in the valley of Tazeen, a measure which the Ghilzyes dreaded, as sure to consume their resources, cramp their activity, and curb their confidence of action in the passes.

Macnaghten, who felt the importance of the duty

entrusted to Sale, expected sterner and more vigorous measures; and, in evident disappointment at the delays which had even then occurred, he thus wrote on October 21:—'Our troops have halted to-day at Khoord Cabul from want of camels! I had hoped ere evening to have announced to you the capture or dispersion of the Tazeen rebels; but of this there is no hope till to-morrow. Our people in this quarter have a happy knack of "bitching" matters. However, let that pass. "All's well that ends well." In the meantime it is very satisfactory to think that, notwithstanding we had rebellion at our very doors, not a single tribe has joined the rebels. The interruption of our communications is very provoking; but the road will soon be opened.' Sale, however, on Macgregor's advice, let slip the opportunity of giving an effective blow to the Ghilzye revolt, and wasted three days in nonsensical negotiations. It was a time for action—for striking, and not for talking; but Sale failed to comprehend his position and the importance to Macnaghten of the blow aimed, the moment for which had arrived. Macnaghten had given Sale a strong force, and the following part of the letter of October 21, already quoted, shows the expectations of, and the view of affairs taken by, the unfortunate envoy: 'I do not think I can possibly get away from this before the 1st prox. The storm will speedily subside; but there will be a heaving of the billows for some time, and I should like to see everything right and tight before I quit the helm. Burnes is naturally in an agony of suspense about the succession to me. I think and hope he will get it. I know no one so fit for the office. "Quieta non movere" is his motto; and now that tranquillity is restored (or will be in a day or two) all that is required will be to preserve it.' Wilfully blind, and seeking to blind others, as to the real state of the country, Macnaghten had yet acted on a perception of the necessity for instantly crushing, if possible, the Ghilzye rising, the danger of which he felt far more than he could bring himself to confess. Bitter, therefore, must have been his disappointment to learn that Sale's arm, when uplifted to strike the desired blow, had been paralysed by the credulity which, after the events in forcing the Khoord Cabul Pass, and the treacherous attacks on the 35th Native Infantry, could conclude a treaty betraying the utmost weakness, and calculated to breed rebellion, had it not already existed. The original cause of the revolt, the reduction of the stipendiary allowance, was retracted; 10,000 rupees were granted to the Ghilzyes to enable them to raise the tribes, in order to keep clear the passes; and they in return promised to restore the property plundered by their followers, who were courteously assumed to be acting in violation of the wishes and authority of their chiefs. Had the purpose been to stamp with crass imbecility the conduct of affairs, to excite the scorn of embittered foes, and to debase the British character as wanting alike in courage and common sense, no surer course could have been pursued. Its fruits were such as might have been anticipated.

Sale, not satisfied with the quantity of baggage cattle at his disposal, now resolved to part with the 37th Native Infantry, three of the Mountain Train guns under Green, and three companies of Broadfoot's Sappers —appropriating to the use of the troops he took with him the disposable cattle of the detachments with whose services, after the conclusion of the treaty, he dispensed. In so doing he left the 37th Native Infantry, the guns, and sappers in a more perilous situation than that into which he had first thrust the 35th Native Infantry, and then been compelled to extricate it. With the Tazeen defile, the Huft Kotul, and the Khoord Cabul Pass in their rear, no means of movement, and no hold of the valley in which they were placed, the 37th Native Infantry was to be left in a truly unenviable position. Sale's measures at this period may have been affected to some extent by his inability to move, and therefore to see things with his own eyes. Be this as it may, they were very unfortunate.

Whilst the enemy was thus amusing Sale and Macgregor with a show of submission, a stout resistance was in preparation at the Purree Durrah and the Jugdulluk Pass. Sale marched on the 26th, and reached his first encamping ground with no other opposition than some sharp skirmishing between his baggage and rear guards and the enemy. There was no intention, however, of allowing him to effect the next march so easily. But Sale's eyes had been opened, in spite of Macgregor's assurances, to the real value of the treaty; and, mistrusting the good faith of his allies, he wisely avoided the Pass of the Fairy, and, taking the road to the south, baulked the enemy who were massed on the edge of the defile, and thus reached the valley of Jugdulluk with small loss or opposition. He had the opportunity in the course of this march of avenging on the Ghilzyes their late treacherous attacks. Their plans had been laid on the supposition that Sale, placing the same confidence as Magregor in their professions, would move by the usual route along the Pass of the Fairy; and their bands were accordingly collected, chiefly along its southern margin, prepared to overwhelm the column when once fairly locked in amid the windings of the chasm. Sale, instead of playing into their hands, moved along the chord of the irregular arch a segment of which was occupied by the enemy; and had he turned when opposite to the defile sharp to his left, he would have caught the Ghilzyes in this hopeless position, and forced them to give battle on the edge of the chasm, with that obstacle in their rear. It was the moment for striking the most terrible blow ever delivered in Afghanistan, for the enemy was snared in his own net; but Sale's was not the eye or mind to seize the opportunity, and the Ghilzyes took good care not to draw on a fight which must have proved their ruin. They therefore let him pass quietly on, and deferred their hopes of a successful contest for the Jugdulluk Pass, the last serious military obstacle to Sale's safe withdrawal to Gundamuk. It is both possible and probable that, notwithstanding the time that Afghanistan had been occupied by our army, no one in Sale's camp knew how completely, from the singular conformation of the country, the Ghilzyes were on the foregoing occasion at the mercy of the British bayonets; or that, notwithstanding the attacks on his baggage and rear guards, Sale still thought himself bound by the Tazeen compact, and was loath to jeopardise, whatever the amount of provocation, a peaceful termination to so dangerous a revolt. Whatever the reason, certain it is that Sale again lost the occasion for striking terror into his foes, and the moment for crushing Ghilzye insurrection.

Between Sale and Gundamuk now lay that spur from the Suffeid Koh range of mountains which constitutes a great step in the face of the country. All to the west of it are highlands, for the Tazeen Valley is at the same elevation above the sea as that of Cabul, upwards of six thousand feet, and the Jugdulluk Valley itself is between five and six thousand feet. To the eastward of the spur the descent is rapid to the lowlands; Gundamuk is between four and five thousand feet; Futtehabad three thousand feet; Sultanpore two thousand three hundred feet; and Jellalabad only one thousand nine hundred and sixty-four feet above the sea-level. Travelling from the westward, or Cabul side, the ascent from the encamping ground at Jugdulluk is along three miles of road, very trying for laden camels and gun horses, and following the bends of a ravine, which receives the drainage of part of the western side of the spur. The road is, therefore, commanded by the heights on both sides of the ravine until the summit is reached, when the snow-capped range called the Suffeid Koh, or White Mountains, bursts in all its magnificence upon the view, and forms the gigantic southern boundary of the prospect. As far as the eye can range east the lower mountain ridges, which form the northerly offshoots from the main axis, cast their snow-derived streams into the Cabul river.

Up the three miles of ascent, under every disadvantage of ground, Sale's baggage-encumbered column advanced; and so timorously conducted were the efforts of the enemy, that the crest of the spur was reached and won with small loss, and complete command of the pass and of the descent towards Gundamuk obtained. Due advantage was not taken of this success; but the long trail of slow-moving baggage, with its harassed rear guard, was left to disengage itself, apparently on the presumption that, as the enemy had yielded the most difficult gorges without a severe struggle with the main body, they would be disinclined to renew a conflict from which they had shrunk. Ghilzye tactics are, however, of a different character. As soon as they found that the main body of the fighting men had left the baggage and rear guard to make good their own way, the Ghilzyes boldly attacked, threw the rear guard into disorder, and spread confusion and dismay amongst the baggage cattle and their drivers. Matters were going very ill in the rear when three brave and excellent officers, Broadfoot, Backhouse, and Fenwick, reformed the fight, and checked the pursuers; but not before upwards of 120 men were killed and wounded,—so costly is retreat and confusion. The only officer killed, Wyndham, a captain of the 35th Native Infantry, fell nobly. Lame from a hurt, he had dismounted at that moment of peril to save the life of a wounded soldier by bearing him from the combat on his charger. When the rear guard broke before the onset of the Ghilzyes, Wyndham, unable to keep pace with the pursued, turned, fought, and, overpowered by numbers, fell beneath the swords and knives of an unsparing foe.

On the 30th Sale encamped at Gundamuk, where Burns's Juzailchees were cantoned. The troops there, had concert and forethought existed, were admirably placed for co-operating with Sale and facilitating his march over the Jugdulluk Pass. But they were permitted to remain without orders, and in ignorance of his movements. Their sudden march, and occupation of the crest of the Jugdulluk spur, would have baffled the Ghilzyes, and saved Sale his loss in men and officers, and a very serious check to the confidence of his young European soldiers. When too late to be of any other use than to join the insurgents, Bukhtar Khan, the chief in charge of the district, sent five hundred of his tribe to Jugdulluk; and strong bodies of Juzailchees were to be pushed still further westward, to keep open the road as far as Seh Baba.

CHAPTER XXIV

OCTOBER–NOVEMBER 1841.

DISAFFECTION OF THE KOHISTANEES—PREPARATIONS FOR A REVOLT AT CABUL—POSITION OF THE BRITISH FORCE ON NOVEMBER 2, 1841—OUTBREAK OF THE INSURRECTION—MURDER OF BURNES—LOSS OF THE TREASURY—INACTION OF ELPHINSTONE—LOSS OF THE COMMISSARIAT FORT—SALE'S RETREAT TO JELLALABAD.

THE impunity with which the Ghilzyes had raised the standard of rebellion, had repeatedly and not altogether unsuccessfully attacked the 35th Native Infantry, and finally freed themselves from Sale, not only without any serious check or loss to themselves, but with considerable booty in camels, baggage, treasure, arms, and ammunition, to attest their pretensions to victory, proved a spur to the spirit of revolt which pervaded Cabul and the Kohistan. Macnaghten's attempt to crush the insurgent Ghilzyes had undeniably failed. Macgregor's treaty and concessions evoked a feeling of contempt, and countenanced the general belief, which moollahs and chiefs not only spread but actually entertained, that Sale, too weak to perform his hostile mission, had thus purchased permission to retreat at the expense of the honour of his troops and the credit and character of the British power. Supreme authority was about to be transferred to Burnes, a man hated as the treacherous cause of the invasion and occupation of the country. Macnaghten, accompanied by Elphinstone, whose sufferings and infirmities forced him to quit his unsought command, was about to leave Cabul. Nott, an able soldier, had, indeed, been summoned to assume command; but winter was close, and it was as improbable that Nott would be able when the order reached him to march for Cabul as that Sale with his weary force could, or would, return to the capital. There, Macnaghten, anxious to impose upon the world the false notion that he quitted Afghanistan in a peaceful and prosperous condition under her puppet king, had not only obstinately shut his own eyes to danger, but also had systematically sought to blind others; and, afraid to betray any want of confidence and to be charged with inconsistency, had allowed the most obviously necessary military precautions to be neglected. Shelton and his troops were new to the place and to the people, and not fully aware of the ill-suppressed spirit which animated the latter. Now, therefore, time and circumstances combined to favour an attempt to throw off a yoke which, it had long been rumoured throughout the length and breadth of the land, was as hateful to Shah Shooja as to his subjects, and which evidently the Indian Government had no purpose of voluntarily removing. The Kohistanees, thoroughly disaffected, as Pottinger had early in the summer reported, had long nursed a deep resolve to avenge themselves for the demolished forts and desolated villages by which Burnes and Sale had rendered their names peculiarly obnoxious to these sanguinary mountainers. The news of the

Ghilzye successess against Sale roused their passions; and, still further excited by the emissaries of Akbar Khan and the preaching of the moollahs, they now felt that the moment had arrived for wreaking vengeance on Burnes and on the British power. The tidings of the Ghilzye attacks and Macgregor's treaty, followed by still more marked successes on the part of the Ghilzyes —for thus ran the news—spread with great rapidity. On the night of November 1 a considerable number of Kohistanees introduced themselves into the city of Cabul; and being met by parties from the Ghilzye insurgents, and by the disaffected, at the head of whom was Ameenoollah of Logur, a chief in the confidence of Macnaghten and the Shah, all was found ripe for revolt,—the foreigner sleeping the while in fancied security.

It has been already noted that the engineer Durand had induced Macnaghten and the reluctant Shah to sanction the precaution of constructing barracks and occupying with troops the Bala Hissar; also it has been mentioned that the envoy subsequently gave up these barracks to the Shah for the use of the 860 ladies and women of the Harem, and threw up all real military hold of this important post. Sturt, Durand's successor, was in nowise a participant in this grievous error; for he also pertinaciously advocated placing the troops in the Bala Hissar, clearing it of all private houses, and rendering it a good stronghold. It is bitter to think that had the repair of the works, and their improvement, been commenced in 1839, when urged by the first engineer, or even later, when again pressed by the second engineer, a tithe of the sums thrown away at Herat would have rendered the Bala Hissar by November 1841 a fortress impregnable, when held by a British garrison, against all that the disaffected Afghans could have brought before its walls.

The error of neglecting so vital a post was not alleviated by the selection made by Sir. W. Cotton of the site for the cantonment. Had it been clearly understood that the cantonment was not to be regarded as a defensible post, in which the troops could shut themselves up to stand a siege; had the surrounding forts been occupied or demolished; had easy and secure communication with the Bala Hissar by good bridges over the river and a small canal been ensured; had, in short, occupation of the cantonment been held as entirely conditional on our undoubted supremacy in the field and on the loyalty of the city of Cabul, no great objection could have been advanced to this site. But when Cotton threw up a weak breastwork round a space of 1,000 by 600 yards, commanded and swept by forts in every direction, which he neither occupied nor demolished, he induced the blunder of attempting to defend these wretched works rather than the Bala Hissar. This was still further induced by lodging the commissariat stores, on which the efficiency and existence of the force depended, in a small ill-placed fort, access to which from the cantonments was at the mercy of an unoccupied fort and the walled Shah Bagh, or King's Garden, on the opposite side of the road. The commissariat and all other stores and magazines might, and ought from the first to, have been lodged in security in the Bala Hissar. These grave errors had been committed, it must be remembered in justice to the memory of the gallant but luckless Elphinstone, before his arrival at Cabul. He at once observed them, and sought to have them remedied; but, holding a secondary place, the safety of his troops and their magazines was made likewise of secondary consideration, and sacrificed to a false show of security.

On the morning of November 2 Shelton was encamped on the Seah Sung hills, about a mile and a half from the cantonments, from which he was separated by the Cabul River. He was about the same distance from the Bala Hissar, and had with him H.M. 44th Foot, a wing of the 54th Native Infantry, the 6th Shah's Infantry, the 5th Cavalry, and a battery of European horse artillery. In cantonments were the 5th Native Infantry, a wing of the 54th Native Infantry, Warburton's battery of five 6-pounders, three companies of Broadfoot's Sappers, and two rissalahs of Irregular Horse. Elphinstone had, therefore, on that eventful morning four regiments of infantry, two batteries of field artillery, three companies of sappers, a regiment of cavalry, and two rissalahs of Irregular Horse,—a strong, well-equipped force.

The Shah was in the Bala Hissar, and had as a guard what was called Campbell's Hindustanee regiment, some Afghans, 400 Jazailchees, 500 Hindustanees, and several guns.

The Bala Hissar, particularly the citadel, completely commands the city; but the streets are so narrow and winding that from the summit of the fort an expanse of flat-roofed houses is alone seen, and the thoroughfares of the city are seldom to be traced. The houses, of unburnt brick walls and mud roofs, have as little timber as possible in their construction, this material being costly at Cabul; it follows, therefore, that they are not easily set on fire. From their irregularity of height and structure, and from the jealousy which guards each flat roof from the gaze of the curious by surrounding walls, communication from housetop to housetop would be very difficult, except in a few portions of the more regular parts of the city. The line of hills, between which and the river the city lies, is steep and difficult, but accessible; and its domineering aspect formerly led to its being included within the defences of Cabul, for a stone wall with a crenelated parapet runs along its summit, and dips down to the gorge by which the Cabul River, breaking through the chain, enters the city. The ends of some of the streets which cross the main thoroughfares abut upon the foot of the hill, which thus looks into them; but as the minor streets are still more tortuous than the main ones such views along them are very partial.

In utter disregard of every sane precaution, the Treasury, containing at the time a lac and 70,000 rupees, besides other sums not public property, was in a house close to that of Burnes, distant from the Bala Hissar about 900 yards, and only approachable through narrow streets, unless the base of the hill were followed.

The juxtaposition of Burnes and the Treasury, far from support, and in houses presenting no particular advantages for defence, was a circumstance well known to the Kohistanees and other insurgents. To kill Burnes and sack the Treasury was to open the revolt in a manner that would silence the timid or wavering, feed the thirst for gold, and compromise all irrecoverably. It was to open the insurrection in the city of Cabul with imposing success. Accordingly on November 2 the rebels, having occupied the surrounding houses, opened fire upon the Treasury and Burnes's house. Burnes hastily informed Macnaghten of the excited state of the populace ; but, mistaking the attack for a desultory riot, he endeavoured to harangue the insurgents, and to induce them to disperse. The sepoy guards in both houses were with this view at first restrained from returning their assailants' fire and from defending their posts ; but they were soon compelled to maintain a gallant struggle ; and a fierce combat raged, until both Burnes and his brother and the intrepid William Broadfoot being slain, the houses were taken, and the Treasury rewarded the victors.

Shah Shooja, hearing that Burnes was attacked and the city in revolt, ordered Campbell's regiment and a couple of guns to march to Burnes's assistance. Macnaghten, as soon as he received notice of the state of affairs, called upon Elphinstone to act, and the latter immediately sent orders to Shelton to proceed to the Bala Hissar, taking with him a company of the 44th, a regiment and a half of sepoys, and four horse artillery guns. The remainder of the troops encamped at Seah Sung were ordered into cantonments ; and instructions were despatched to the 37th Native Infantry to march with all haste from the position in which Sale had left them to Cabul.

Shelton, who received final orders to advance to the Bala Hissar about midday, was upon arriving there to act upon his own judgment, in communication with the Shah. The latter, when he ordered the march of Campbell's corps into the city, left the movement to the discretion of the commandant, who thoughtlessly plunged his men and guns into the narrow main thoroughfare opposite to the north-western end of the fort, and nearest to the city gate by which he quitted the Bala Hissar. Had he moved without the embarrassment of guns along the hill base he could have reached without difficulty or danger the end of the short street in which Burnes and the Treasury were, and could easily have forced his way to them; but by endeavouring to make good his passage through the heart of the city, struggling in vain to drag his guns through its winding, obstructed streets, he courted defeat. Accordingly he was resolutely attacked and repulsed, with a heavy loss of men, without being able to reach the scene of plunder and butchery.

Shelton, on reaching the Bala Hissar, kept his detachment under arms, but took no steps against the insurgents. After losing an hour in inactivity the sound of the fight drew nearer, and he then sent an officer to ascertain how matters were proceeding. The officer quickly returned, and reported that Campbell's corps was beaten and retreating. Shelton then ordered a company of sepoys to move out and cover the retreat of the fugitives. They fell back, bringing their guns with them up to the ditch of the fort; but here the pieces were left both by Campbell's corps and the company of Native Infantry, though the latter had only lost one man killed and four wounded in the skirmish, and the guns were so close under the walls that the Afghans never could succeed in removing them until the troops were withdrawn from the Bala Hissar. The Shah was thus the only person who made any endeavour to quell the rising revolt. Had Campbell's corps, without guns, been sent either all by the base of the hill, or part by the main thoroughfare and part by the hill foot, Shah Shooja would have saved Burnes and the Treasury. Although he failed he yet deserves the credit of having displayed more resolution and energy than either Shelton or Elphinstone. The former did nothing; the latter, upon whose conduct and decision all now depended, broken down by ill-health, proved unequal to the emergency.

Long misled as to the state of feeling in the city and country, Elphinstone, at the mercy of Macnaghten for all his political information, may be excused for having failed to observe the coming storm. When it burst upon the gallant but health-shattered veteran he may be pardoned for having been taken by surprise, and for having failed, deceived by both Macnaghten and Burnes as to the real character of the revolt on the very morning in question, vigorously to crush it. But, that he should have limited his exertions to a recall of the 37th Native Infantry and to the mounting of artillery for the defence of cantonments, admits of no apology, except that pain and severe suffering had not only worn the frame but weakened the judgment and mental energy of as brave a gentleman as ever fought under his country's colours.

After the death of Burnes, the loss of the Treasury, and the defeat of Campbell's corps became known, much was to be done—even though it had been resolved not to hazard regular troops by exposing them to a murderous contest amid narrow streets. Trevor and Mackenzie[1] should have been immediately supported, and the Shah's commissariat stores either brought off or destroyed. Self-preservation pointed out the vital importance of the commissariat fort near to cantonments, and neither skill nor military genius was requisite, by a prompt occupation of the King's Garden, Mahmoud Khan's and Mahomed Shereef's forts, to secure the communication with this all-important post. There was no want of cattle; and the transport of the commissariat stores from the crazy fort in which they had been carelessly lodged to the Bala Hissar should have occupied day and night until completed. With ordinary exertion every woman and child, all stores, whether commissariat or ordnance, every gun, and every fighting man, might have been within the Bala Hissar before daybreak of November 4. The force thus concentrated, with its magazines secure from insult or capture, would have been at liberty to act either on the offensive or defensive, according as circumstances required. All this was safe, obvious, and practicable. But ordinary military prudence, let alone ability or

[1] Mackenzie was in charge of the commissariat fort, in which the supplies for Shah Shooja's force were stored, and Trevor occupied a neighbouring fort.

decision, were on this occasion wanting; and Elphinstone preferred paralysing his whole force by giving it two separate *enceintes* to defend instead of one; the larger of the two being in reality indefensible, and but little strengthened by the precaution that mounted guns for which there were not gunners. Trevor and Mackenzie he left to their fate.

In contrast with all this, right soldierly was the conduct of Major Griffiths, who, on receiving the order to return to Cabul, made good his way through the passes in spite of the Ghilzye attacks, and, on the morning of the 3rd, brought in his regiment, the 37th Native Infantry, without even the loss of any baggage to comfort the enemy for the men they threw away in vain endeavours to disorder the march of this gallant corps. Griffiths was pressed hotly and boldly by the Ghilzyes, 3,000 of whom continued the pursuit of his column almost within range of Elphinstone's guns; but the enemy gained no advantage, and suffered severely from Green's three mountain guns, which were throughout this difficult movement skilfully and boldly worked.

Thus reinforced, Elphinstone now strengthened Shelton in the Bala Hissar, sending him the remainder of the 54th Native Infantry, four guns of different calibres, and two small mortars, with the gallant but ill-fated young soldier Green. Shelton then made dispositions for the security of the Bala Hissar, occupying the Lahore and city gates and the citadel with detachments, and the palace square with his reserve.

Unfortunately, Sturt, the only engineer present, had been severely wounded by an assassin when entering the Shah's palace on the morning of the 2nd. He was a good and a resolute officer; and as soon as partial recovery from his wounds enabled him to speak or write, he urged the occupation of the Bala Hissar and the abandonment of the cantonments. But petty difficulties are the bugbears of petty minds; and unhappily around the general, himself weak and undecided in judgment, were men with whom the minor consideration of the value of the public and private property to be sacrificed weighed more than the young soldier's counsel and the crisis which evoked it. Small objections and poor cavils swayed the general to delay.

Meanwhile the enemy, successful beyond their expectations, were encouraged to act with energy. They occupied those parts of the city which looked upon the plain between the Bala Hissar and the cantonments; they occupied the Shah's Garden, Mahmoud Khan's and Mahomed Shereef's forts, and thus, with good cover to protect them, threatened the commissariat fort, and closely beset the south-western end of the cantonments. The officer defending the commissariat fort with a party of sepoys, entertaining apprehensions of the firmness of his men, repeatedly throughout the 5th applied for reinforcements. Elphinstone, in lieu of reinforcing him, endeavoured to withdraw the garrison, sending out three several detachments to effect this suicidal measure. The enemy, never dreaming of such imbecility, and regarding the detachments as reinforcements, fired heavily from Mahomed Shereef's fort and the Shah's Garden, and forced them back into cantonments with severe loss.

The execution of the order to evacuate the fort

being thus prevented, Elphinstone, now aware of the criminal folly of the step, in consequence of the entreaties of the staff officers, contemplated reinforcing the garrison during the night, which might easily have been accomplished. But the time of action was spent in discussion; and when the morning of the 5th broke the parties destined to attack Mahomed Shereef's fort, and to reinforce the commissariat one, were only assembling when the fatal announcement was made that Lieutenant Warren, despairing of maintaining his post, had evacuated it, having cut a passage through the wall of his fort on the cantonment side. Thus, without a struggle for its defence, was this vital post abandoned and given up to the enemy, who as easily became masters of the means of existence of the force as if the 5,000 British troops in whose face it was done had been spellbound to the Bala Hissar and cantonments. Well might the Shah, as he gazed upon the melancholy spectacle from the Bala Hissar, exclaim, 'The English are mad!'

Very different had been Mackenzie's defence of Anquetil's fort, the Shah's commissariat depôt. Nevertheless, being unsupported, he too had been forced to evacuate his post, and escaped to cantonments with great difficulty. Thus by the 5th the insurgents were in possession of the Treasury and of the provisions of the force, without having endured other than a trifling loss of men. The capture of the Treasury had been a sufficiently disagreeable event; for there can be no doubt that had Shelton moved early to the support of Campbell's regiment, and Elphinstone, from the side of Anquetil's fort and the Kuzzilbash quarter, pushed detachments to Burnes's house, the insurgents, attacked along the line of the main bazaar, from the hill side, and from the Kuzzilbash and Deh Afghan quarters, could not have had permanent success, but would have been dispersed, and probably with heavy retribution for the onslaught on the Treasury. The ignorance or the apathy of the military leaders was sufficiently inexcusable on that first occasion. Yet it must be remembered that the political chiefs had misled everyone up to the very moment when they suddenly called upon the military chief to act; and that Elphinstone, into whose hands the game was thus flung at a most critical moment, from his ignorance of the train of political events, was not in a fair position to judge the nature of the crisis and to cope with it in the manner which full acquaintance with the thread of affairs might have ensured. After matters have been embroiled to the uttermost and rebellion is rampant, a broken, pain-worn man may be pardoned if he fails at once to apprehend distinctly the difficulties of a position into which two years of continuous error and mismanagement, on the part of others, unexpectedly plunge him. But, although such considerations may account for some indecision on the first flash of revolt, they form no excuse for the palsied patience with which the commissariat fort was, not lost in fight, but ignominiously relinquished to the enemy. Many were the gallant officers around Elphinstone who urged a more manly resolution; and had Eyre's advice been taken, the commissariat fort would have been immediately attacked in force, and must have been recaptured; but his counsel was too wise and soldierly for the vacillating weakness of the general; and though the storm of Mahomed Shereef's fort was ultimately decided upon, and Eyre, with his guns, acted his part gallantly, the storming party never stirred from a wall under which they found cover, and the general, though the 37th Native Infantry were burning with desire to be permitted to do that from which others shrank, could not be induced to allow them. The evacuation and loss of the commissariat fort and the abortive show of assailing Mahomed Shereef's fort were equally disgraceful.

Orders were now sent to Sale and to Nott directing an advance upon Cabul. From the season at which he received them it was impracticable for Nott to obey his instructions; but Sale was differently circumstanced, for he received the order at Gundamuk, the messenger bearing the despatches having been so fortunate as to effect the journey with speed and in safety. It has already been seen that Griffiths, with a single regiment of sepoys and three mountain guns, had, in obedience to a similar mandate, made good his march to Cabul from the dangerous position in which Sale had left him; and, in spite of Ghilzye attacks, had, after forcing the Khoord Cabul Pass, reached cantonments with small loss in men and much gain of honour. It is true that Elphinstone by thus suddenly withdrawing Griffiths from his isolated position on the road between Gundamuk and Cabul had apparently somewhat diminished the facility of Sale's advance; but, on the other hand, Griffiths's departure had drawn after him a strong body of Ghilzyes, who not only pursued him to Cabul, but remained there to strengthen the insurgents and to partake in their successes. Sale would, therefore, have found the enemy weak on the line of road had he, on receipt of his despatches, made immediate arrangements for the security of his sick, wounded, and baggage in one of the defensible forts in his neighbourhood, and then, unincumbered, made a rapid march upon Cabul. No doubt can be entertained that his unexpected appearance on the scene of conflict would have given a severe blow to the insurrection and new life to the British cause.

But Sale, instead of acting upon his instructions, called a council of war, wherein compliance with the mandate from Cabul was pronounced unadvisable. He thereupon prepared to march in a contrary direction, and, throwing up connection with Cabul, to occupy Jellalabad. This decision was regretted by some of the ablest officers in his force, foremost amongst whom was Broadfoot. Humanly speaking, Sale thus denied himself the honour and the satisfaction of retrieving the state of affairs at the capital.

The relief, or reinforcement, of Elphinstone was, however, a wholly distinct question from a hasty retrograde movement from Gundamuk, in order to throw his brigade, which was perfectly well able to keep the field, into Jellalabad, a place of no military strength or importance, without magazines, in utter disrepair, and so situated that to coop up the brigade within its dilapidated walls served no conceivable purpose except to betray weakness and still further encourage revolt. At Gundamuk, Sale's brigade threatened the passes between that place and Cabul, necessarily paralysed a portion of the Ghilzye strength, and checked Ghilzye co-operation with the insurgents at the capital; whilst at the same time ensuring to Elphinstone the comparatively safe and easy withdrawal of the force from Cabul should circumstances compel the adoption of so extreme a measure. Had Sale maintained his position at, or near to, Gundamuk, he might have influenced the fate of Elphinstone's army; and one of the most disastrous retreats on record would have been spared to the British arms by the co-operation of his movable column. The severest comment upon the inutility of the occupation of Jellalabad was afforded by Sale himself, when, after having long suffered himself to be blockaded and bearded by a foe flushed with the successful destruction of Elphinstone's force, he overthrew without difficulty Mahomed Akbar in the open field, driving the Afghans in confusion from the plain, with no other troops than that very brigade which, when the issue of the rebellion was as yet uncertain, and energy might have quelled it, he withdrew from the struggle and shut up within distant walls, there to court and abide investment, at the leisure of an unembarrassed and triumphant enemy.

CHAPTER XXV.

NOVEMBER 1841–JANUARY 1842.

MACNAGHTEN'S NEGOTIATIONS WITH THE CHIEFS—HIS MURDER—DESTRUCTION OF THE FORCE.

If Macnaghten be culpable for the effrontery with which he sought to blind and mislead others, as well as himself, as to the feelings of the Afghan people and the state of their country, he proved free from that imbecile weakness which henceforward characterised the military leaders and their measures. His spirit chafed at the despondency evinced, at the errors committed, and at the resulting disasters. Himself a man of courage, the gloom of others did not unnerve him; and had he insisted energetically upon the adoption of his counsel, the occupation of the Bala Hissar, Elphinstone must have yielded, and affairs might have been retrieved. But the puerile arguments brought forward by Shelton and others against this necessary step not only influenced Elphinstone but also led Macnaghten to waive his own and adopt analogous opinions, and, in an evil hour, to coincide in rejecting the only wise and safe course. However brightened by traits of individual heroism, it would be needless to trace in detail the gallant defence by the Goorkha battalion of Chareekar, the destruction of these brave soldiers and their excellent officers, of whom Pottinger and Haughton alone miraculously escaped; the wretchedly conducted actions at the village of Beymaroo, ending in discomfiture and indelible disgrace; the shameful loss of Mahomed Shereef's fort, the relaxation of discipline, and the prostration of energy and courage which ensued upon a long series of dishonouring reverses. The normal errors from which flowed such fatal consequences have been already noted, and the harrowing details of incompetency, written in the blood of brave officers and valiant men—for there were many such who fell—only form a heartrending commentary upon the grievous truth that the lives and, worse still, the honour of soldiers, is the price paid for the gross political and military blunders of those in authority.

By the time that Mahomed Akbar arrived at Cabul (November 22) the military leaders had lost all confidence in themselves and their men; and Macnaghten was pressed to save the force by negotiating for its safe retreat upon the humiliating condition of evacuating the whole of Afghanistan. The envoy was loth to entertain a proposal so derogatory to the fame of the British name, and so subversive of the policy and plans which he had strenuously advocated and proved mainly instrumental in furthering. Moreover, he nursed hopes of accomplishing by secret intrigue and the distribution of large sums of money that which the British arms failed to effect. To create discord among the rebels, and thus break up the league against Shah Shooja and his allies, was Macnaghten's dream. It must not be supposed that upon the outbreak of November 2 the envoy limited his exertions to the request that Elphinstone should act; at the same time that Macnaghten called upon the military authorities to quell the revolt by the employment of force, he secretly, with the same object in view, adopted measures of a different character, which, failing of issue, subsequently exercised a most unfortunate influence not alone upon his own individual fate but upon that of the whole force at Cabul.

Mohun Lal, who was in the suite of Burnes, escaping massacre when his chief and all with him were killed, ultimately found an asylum in the house of the Kuzzilbash chief, Khan Sheereen Khan, in the Kuzzilbash or Persian quarter of the city. Mohun Lal, in the opinion of the envoy, was there favourably situated for carrying on negotiations and intrigues with such chiefs as Macnaghten entertained hopes of winning to his cause, and of rendering them willing instruments in the fulfilment of his purposes. Accordingly Mohun Lal was, shortly after the first burst of the rebellion, in daily communication with both Macnaghten and Captain J. B. Conolly, the envoy's political assistant. He was directed to enter into negotiations with the Kuzzilbash chiefs; to promise high rewards for their co-operation against the rebels; to excite dissension between the Sunnis and the Shiahs by working on the fears of the latter; and in every way to sow disunion and distrust among the enemies of the British. Mohun Lal entered upon his task as soon as he could do so with safety to himself, and was not altogether unsuccessful. But such intrigues could hardly be carried on without some rumour of them coming to the ears of the rebel chiefs; and the latter were soon on their guard against the machinations of the Moonshee.

Unhappily those machinations were not confined to the objects above stated. At the same time that Mohun Lal was set to work to spread disunion in the rebel ranks he received other instructions which led him to suppose that the British envoy required him to compass by means of secret murder the death of the rebel leaders. It has been disputed whether Macnaghten ever in reality entertained the design imputed to him by his agent. At a later period he denied that it was his object to encourage assassination. Certain it is, however, that Mohun Lal believed himself to be acting in accordance with the envoy's wishes when he set about the deed; equally certain that the terms of the instructions given to him by Captain Conolly were such as to justify the belief, and that the tenor of subsequent communications from the envoy was not calculated to remove it.

Mohun Lal, therefore, did not hesitate to advance at once 9,000 rupees, and to promise that a balance of 12,000 rupees would be paid as soon as the heads of Meer Musjidi and Abdullah Khan were brought in —selecting these chiefs as the first victims, because he believed them to have been actively concerned in the attack upon the Treasury and Burnes's house, and in the slaughter of his patron, and knew them to be the boldest and most influential leaders of the insurgents. Two men, Abdul Azeez and Mahomed Oolah, were bribed to effect Mohun Lal's purpose.

Meer Musjidi and Abdullah Khan were soon numbered amongst the dead. The former died very suddenly; how, Mohun Lal could not with certainty learn, but Mahomed Oolah assured him that in fulfilment of the engagement the wretched man had been suffocated when asleep by the hands of Mahomed Oolah himself. Abdullah Khan fell severely wounded by a shot whilst standing amongst his countrymen engaged in fight with the British troops; but whether struck down by a ball from the piece of Abdul Azeez, who claimed the merit of having shot his victim from behind a wall, or by the fire of the troops, Mohun Lal was not confident. Abdul Azeez, however, assured him that Abdullah Khan would soon die, as poison would complete what the shot had not done. He lingered for a week, and then fulfilled the prediction; and Abdul Azeez as well as Mahomed Oolah then demanded, through their suborners, Hazee Allee and Agha Mahomed, the balance of the reward due to them. Mohun Lal, with a Shylock nicety, refused to pay the balance, alleging that the heads had not, according to agreement, been brought in, and that Abdullah Khan might probably have been wounded by the musketry of our troops.

The two ablest and most resolute leaders of the rebels in field and council being thus, either by fair or foul means, struck down, Macnaghten was unwilling to comply with the urgent but, as he thought, premature request of the military authorities to treat; for he laid much stress on the effect which might result from the fall of these two obnoxious chiefs, and anticipated deriving advantage from an event which must leave the insurgents a prey to the factious emulation of the less influential leaders. Subsequently to the fall of Abdullah Khan, severely wounded in the last action at Beymaroo, circumstances seemed to favour the indulgence of such a hope, as not only did the enemy fail to follow up their success when our troops fled in disorder to cantonments, but for a while there was a lull in the activity with which hostilities were prosecuted, and the enemy seemed unaccountably paralysed. Mohun Lal had not, however, been sufficiently cautious in the overtures made to accomplish the destruction of the principal rebels. Too many persons had been entrusted with the secret, and some of them men upon whom it is wonderful that reliance should have been placed. When, therefore, in addition to such a dangerous diffusion of the secret, Mohun Lal refused to fulfil the promises made and withheld the rewards claimed, not only was it impossible for him to find instruments willing to strike down more of the obnoxious chiefs, but the latter became aware of the price set upon their heads, as they believed, by the British envoy, and were exasperated at the discovery of a tampering with the cupidity of their Afghan followers and a base endeavour to effect by the knife or shot of the assassin that which the courage of the troops was unequal to secure. Their minds were, therefore, well disposed to support any leader who could control their minor jealousies and advance undeniable claims to their allegiance. At this juncture Akbar Khan appeared upon the scene, and immediately became the rallying centre of hostile feeling and action. Naturally embittered against the British power, the intimation he received of the secret machinations against the lives of the chiefs enabled him to keep alive their suspicions, destroy all confidence in British good faith, and fan into flame the spirit of implacable hostility.

Macnaghten, constantly pressed by the general, and himself aware that the supplies of the force were nearly exhausted, the troops spiritless and disorganised, and with few (but those noble) exceptions to be depended upon for the exercise of either discipline or courage, at length, in spite of his own aversion to a task beset with so much dishonour and difficulty, began in apparent earnest to negotiate for the safe withdrawal of the army and the evacuation of Afghanistan. Never was courage more conspicuous than in the case of the ill-fated envoy, who sought, by the display of a truly daring confidence towards the chiefs, to inspire them with trust in the sincerity of his intentions. On December 11, accompanied by Lawrence, Mackenzie, and Trevor, Macnaghten met the assembled leaders of the rebellion on the plain near the Seah Sung Hill, and there discussed the conditions of a draft treaty which he had sketched. The unmolested withdrawal not only of the force at Cabul, but also of all the British troops in Afghanistan; their supply with food, fodder, and means of transport; the return from India of Dost Mahomed and every Afghan in exile; that Shah Shooja was to be given the option of remaining at Cabul or accompanying the British army to India; an amnesty for all political opponents and the partisans of the Shah; and that no

British force should again be sent into Afghanistan, unless called for by the Afghan government, were the main features of the treaty. Mahomed Akbar, distrustful of Macnaghten, would not accede to an engagement which bound the rebel party to furnish provisions for the force without any stipulation for the immediate evacuation of the Bala Hissar and the cantonments, and he forced the British envoy to specify three days as the period after which the troops were bound to quit the cantonments. Upon this compact the terms of the treaty were accepted; but, as there was a thorough want of confidence in the envoy's sincerity, Captain Trevor had to accompany the chiefs as hostage for the good faith of Macnaghten.

Cold weather had now set in, but snow had not fallen; and as it was sure to fall in the course of a few days it was of the greatest importance, after once retreat had been decided on, that all further delay should be avoided. Thus, not only did the obligations of good faith impose a necessity for the rapid withdrawal of the troops, but every consideration for their safety and existence imperatively urged the most prompt fulfilment of this condition. Four thousand five hundred fighting men, and from 12,000 to 15,000 followers, by an immediate march might surmount the lofty passes between them and Gundamuk, whilst still free from snow; and thus, with comparatively little hardship and suffering, make good their way over a country which when once enveloped in snow could only be passed with extreme difficulty and the severest misery and loss. The loose manner in which the treaty was worded and the insertion of conditions in terms so general as to render, if not their import, their fulfilment matter of easy cavil, afforded Macnaghten specious grounds for delay; he still clung to the hope of receiving aid from Nott, who had despatched Maclaren with a brigade; and he was not sorry at being able to allege the irresolution of the Shah, and the non-fulfilment on the part of the enemy of their agreement to furnish provisions and baggage cattle, as reasons for procrastinating and prolonging his stay at Cabul. In despair at the disgrace with which so ignoble a treaty overwhelmed himself and the British name, he clung to the faintest hope of retrieving events.

The Shah, perplexed at the position in which the treaty placed him, was still further embarrassed by the conduct of the rebel chiefs, who on the 12th invited him to remain as king, only stipulating the intermarriage of his daughters with the leaders of the revolt, and discontinuance of some of the ceremonials of royalty to which Shah Shooja was attached, but which were distasteful to the Afghan nobles. Whether this proposal was made as a test of the sincerity of the Shah's generally alleged aversion to British domination, or to confirm the impression by inducing him at this juncture to make common cause with the rebels; or, as is most probable, to ascertain, by the mode in which such a decided separation from British connection was received, the ultimate real purposes of the envoy, is uncertain. Shah Shooja, after deliberation, consented to hold his throne upon the proffered conditions, and signified his assent to the chiefs accordingly.

On the 13th and 14th the Bala Hissar was evacuated, but in a manner so ill-conducted that the greater part of 1,600 maunds of wheat and flour, which Captain Kirby had had the foresight to collect for transport to the cantonments, where provisions were very scarce, instead of being taken with the garrison were left in the fort for the enemy's advantage. Ten days' supply for the whole force was thus madly deserted at a time when the utmost dearth prevailed in the cantonments, when the camp followers were feeding upon the flesh of the animals dying from starvation, and when there was barely two days' supply of flour on half-rations for the fighting men.

Shah Shooja, always timid and irresolute, now refused to accept the throne which the rebel chiefs had on easy conditions permitted him to retain. As the moment for the departure of the British troops appeared to draw near his heart failed him, and he shrank from the dangerous allegiance of such men as Mahomed Akbar and the banded chiefs. His change of purpose increased their suspicions, and they declined to furnish provisions to the force unless, in fulfilment of the compact, the cantonments were evacuated.

On the 18th snow fell; but Macnaghten still procrastinated. The distrust of the chiefs waxing greater in proportion as the specified time was exceeded, their demands also increased, and on the 20th the delivery of guns and ammunition, and of Brigadier Shelton as a hostage, was required. The engineer, Sturt, perceiving that every day's delay was fraught with peril, now urged that the treaty, which had been broken by both sides, should be no longer considered binding; and that, making every possible arrangement for the conveyance of the sick, the wounded, ammunition and stores, the army should march to Jellalabad. The envoy's hopes of aid from Nott had now vanished, as Maclaren had countermarched with his brigade, finding snow upon the highlands as he drew towards Ghuznee, and despairing at that season of effecting his march to Cabul. Macnaghten, therefore, had now no motive for putting off the march of the force, the destruction of which from starvation was imminent, and could only be avoided by a movement of decision such as the engineer recommended. Elphinstone and his advisers thought otherwise. There was an unearthly faintness upon their hearts; and it was as though some great crime had caused the wrath of God to settle down upon the host, withering the hearts of its leaders, unnerving the right arms of England's soldiery, and leaving them no power to stand before their enemies.

On December 20 the envoy again met Mahomed Akbar and other chiefs. Two hostages, Conolly and Airey, were at once given over, and two more were to follow. The dilatory conduct of the envoy and of the military leaders had now so confirmed the suspicions of Mahomed Akbar and the principal rebels that they determined to test the intentions of Macnaghten, whose supposed secret schemes for the destruction of the most influential chiefs had never been forgotten, and whose present conduct, ignorant as the enemy were of the utter prostration of energy and courage among the military authorities, seemed inexplicable, except on the supposition of the existence of some deep design against the lives and power of the chiefs.

Captain Skinner, an officer to whom Mahomed Akbar had given protection, was sent by the latter with secret proposals to Macnaghten to the following effect: that Mahomed Akbar undertook to seize Ameer Oollah, one of the most obnoxious and powerful of the rebel leaders, and deliver him up to the envoy; that Shah Shooja, remaining king, was to reward Mahomed Akbar for this important service and for supporting his throne by making him Wazeer; that the Bala Hissar and Mahomed Khan's fort were to be immediately reoccupied by the British troops, who were to remain in their then position until the spring, upon the arrival of which they were with honour to evacuate the country, Mahomed Akbar receiving from the British Government for these services a donation of thirty lacs of rupees, and an annual pension of four lacs. Skinner did not himself deliver the message, but he was accompanied by one, Mahomed Sudeek, and other Afghans in the confidence of Mahomed Akbar, who were entrusted with sounding the envoy, and to whom Skinner, ignorant of any hidden design, referred Macnaghten for the particulars of his mission. Mahomed Sudeek, in the course of stating the foregoing propositions, made one which should have put the envoy upon his guard: the head of Ameer Oollah was to be presented to the envoy for a certain sum of money. Macnaghten's eyes were, however, not opened by this remarkable offer of Ameer Oollah's head, coupled with the promise of Mahomed Akbar's co-operation in subduing the other Khans; and he eagerly caught at the general proposal, disclaiming, however, any willingness to give a price for blood, and therefore rejecting the specific offer of Ameer Oollah's head, though not of his capture by treachery, in which the envoy and the British troops were to play a conspicuous part.

The distinction was too nice to weigh with men who believed the envoy to have compassed the secret murder of Abdullah Khan and Meer Musjidi, and who judged of his sincerity by the eager readiness with which he was captivated by an offer too specious to have imposed upon any man of sound thought and principle, and which involved the perfidious sacrifice of one of their own members. Hitherto, however shaken by what was known of Mohun Lal's proceedings, the British character for integrity and good faith stood high enough to command some respect for the representative of the Anglo-Indian Government. But the deliberate faithlessness which led the envoy to accept Mahomed Akbar's proposal sealed his doom. The worst suspicions of the confederate chiefs and their exasperated leader were confirmed; and they resolved, as no dependence could after such proof be placed on the most solemn and formal engagements, to ensnare Macnaghten in the net he was spreading for another, and to take vengeance upon him and the starving disorganised force for the insults and injuries which an injudicious, selfish, and ambitious policy had heaped upon Afghanistan.

On December 23, Macnaghten, with a courage undiminished by the sense that, like a desperate gamester, he was risking all upon a hazard cast, went out to hold conference with Mahomed Akbar and to carry into effect the projected measures. The envoy, accompanied by his three brave companions, Mackenzie, Trevor, and Lawrence, heedless of the warning which the first-mentioned officer gave him, boldly met the assembled chiefs, among whom was a brother of Ameer Oollah. No suitable preparations had been made in the cantonments on the part of the military ; and even the envoy's escort were so backward in assembling and following him, that he had ridden on and confidently entrusted himself to the mercy of his enemies without his body-guard being at hand to protect him.

When warned of the danger of the meeting and the perfidious character of Mahomed Akbar, the envoy had replied, 'Dangerous it is, but if it succeeds, it is worth all risks ; the rebels have not fulfilled even one article of the treaty, and I have no confidence in them ; and if by it we can only save our honour, all will be well ; at any rate, I would rather suffer a hundred deaths than live the last six weeks over again.'

Thus felt Macnaghten as he rode forth to meet his murderer. The violation of the treaty had been mutual, the first infraction being on the part of the Afghans under Mahomed Akbar, who attacked the troops when they evacuated the Bala Hissar ; but instead of immediately breaking with them, on this plea, Macnaghten had continued to treat and negotiate as if the compact were valid, although, by prolonging the stay of the troops at Cabul, he himself violated its most essential specification.

After having made the customary salutations and presented a handsome Arab horse to Mahomed Akbar, both parties dismounted, and Macnaghten with his three companions seated themselves beside Mahomed Akbar, surrounded by Afghans, upon a small hillock which partly concealed them from the cantonments. Lawrence, eyeing with suspicion the number of armed attendants which encircled them, remarked to the envoy that if the conference were of a secret nature they had better be removed. Macnaghten spoke to Mahomed Akbar, who replied, 'No, they are all in the secret.' In an instant the three officers were seized, overpowered, disarmed, and carried off, whilst Macnaghten, struggling on the ground with Mahomed Akbar, was shot by the latter, and then cut to pieces by his followers. The escort, instead of charging to the rescue, fled to the cantonments, and left the envoy and his brave companions to their fate.

In the cantonments all was apathy, and indecision. Although within sight of the scene, no attempt was made to avenge the slaughtered envoy and to recover his body from a cowardly mob who bore off in triumph his mangled remains, to parade them in the city of Cabul.

Energy might still have saved the wretched force; and Pottinger, now called upon by Elphinstone to renew negotiations with the enemy upon the basis of the treaty violated by Macnaghten, made a last effort to rekindle the military spirit of the council of war convened by the general. Declaring his own conviction that no confidence could be placed in any treaty with the Afghan chiefs, he disapproved of all humiliating negotiations; and, instead of binding the hands of Government by ignoble promises to evacuate the country, to subsidise the rebel chiefs, and to restore Dost Mahomed, he counselled either to hold out to the last at Cabul or to march to Jellalabad. His own high courage and undaunted spirit met with no sympathy in that gloomy, depressed council, which overruled his opinion and instructed him to negotiate at all cost alike of money and of honour.

The deplorable weakness which could adopt a resolution unexampled in British military history was productive of the results which might have been anticipated. It is unnecessary to examine in detail the transactions which occupied the political and military leaders from December 26 to January 13. Macnaghten might well prefer death to such protracted humiliation and ignominy. Would that oblivion could swallow up all record, all memory of that dire destruction of a well-equipped army, sufficient, in the hands of a Nott or a Napier, to have swept its discomfited foes in haughty triumph before the colours of England; but these, alas, were doomed to droop beneath a withering spell of fatuous imbecility; to see their host, delivered into the hands of the enemy, confounded and utterly destroyed; to witness the fiat of supreme vengeance which had given over 20,000 souls as a prey to famine, cold, and the edge of the sword.

On January 13, Dr. Brydon, sorely wounded, and barely able from exhaustion to sit upon the emaciated beast that bore him, reached Jellalabad, and told that

Elphinstone's army, guns, standards, honour, all being lost, was itself completely annihilated.

Such was the consummation of a line of policy which from first to last held truth in derision, trod right under foot, and, acting on a remote scene, was enabled for a time unscrupulously to mislead the public mind. But time brings truth to light; and gradually the collection of facts from indubitable sources, and the perusal of private and public memoranda, have enabled us to form a more correct idea of the envoy's policy and conduct. Its victims were many; for insulted Truth amply avenged herself, recording a terrible lesson for the contemplation of man's ignorant, short-sighted ambition.

Amongst these victims many a man fell whose heart burned with a soldier's indignation at the ignominy brought upon his country's arms. Foremost in this feeling, in justice to his memory be it said, was the ill-fated Macnaghten. His high courage almost atones for his moral and political errors. The victim of his own truthless and unscrupulous policy, he shrank from no personal risk, and fell in the vain hope and endeavour to accomplish by subtilty a blow which might prove, if successful, the saving of the force and, in his opinion, of its honour. On this he daringly staked his own life and fame. Mere courage, however, cannot palliate moral delinquency; nor should the melancholy end of a talented and erudite gentleman's career blind us to the lesson and example it affords of the falsity of Macchiavelli's advice: 'Non può pertanto un Signore prudente, nè debbe, osservare la fede, quando tale osservanza gli torni contro, e che sono spente le cagioni che la fecero promettere. E se gli uomini fussero tutti buoni, questo precetto non sarebbe buono; ma perchè sono tristi, e non l' osserverebbero a te, tu ancora non l' hai da osservare a loro.' (A prudent lord cannot, however, neither ought he to, keep faith when such keeping turns against himself, and the reasons which induced him to promise exist no longer. And if men were all good, this precept would not be good; but because they are bad, and will not keep faith with you, you also need not keep it with them.)

Macnaghten was not single in his high courage. The bones of many a chivalrous soldier long bleached upon the barren mountains and deep defiles between Cabul and Jellalabad. But if any called for the avenging swords of their countrymen with peculiar emphasis it was those of the European horse artillery, who, calm and stern to the last in their discipline and daring valour, fought and fell heroically, the admiration of all who witnessed their conduct and survived to tell the tale.

CHAPTER XXVI.

NOVEMBER 1841–FEBRUARY 1842.

SIEGE OF JELLALABAD—WILD'S BRIGADE AT PESHAWUR—EVACUATION OF ALI MUSJID—THE COUNCIL OF WAR—PROPOSED EVACUATION OF JELLALABAD—CONDUCT OF BROADFOOT—THE GARRISON RESOLVES TO HOLD OUT.

SALE'S withdrawal from Gundamuk had not been without molestation. Dennie, in command of the rear guard, had gone through some sharp skirmishing, skilfully conducted, and in the course of which he enabled Oldfield, always a ready officer, to make a successful charge with his squadron. The enemy, roughly handled by the horsemen, were more cautious afterwards, and the pursuit was less eager. On November 12 the force reached Jellalabad, and immediately occupied the place. After some discussion it was determined to hold not only the citadel, but also the city, the walls of which were in utter disrepair, the towers partly in ruins, the parapets incomplete, various breaches practicable, and the ditch a nominal rather than a real obstacle.

The retreat to Jellalabad was, however, the cause of the whole country rising from Gundamuk to the mouth of the Khybur; the movement was held confirmatory of the exaggerated reports which spread with strange rapidity upon the first outburst of revolt at Cabul; and Burn, a gallant officer, left by Sale to hold Gundamuk, found himself not only deserted but attacked by the Afreedees and Janbaz under his command, and was forced with the Juzailchees who remained true to him to follow Sale, leaving two guns in the hands of the enemy. Ferris's post at Pesh Bolak being attacked, that officer drew in his outposts, which occupied points in the Khybur, in order to strengthen himself; whilst the Afreedees, flushed with the success at Gundamuk, spread the flame of revolt throughout the Khybur tribes, and a fierce attack was made on Ali Musjid in order to recover the only post commanding the defile now in the hands of the British. Mr. Mackeson, a volunteer, had been left in charge of this important fort, with a weak garrison of 150 Eusufzyes. He was closely invested and resolutely assailed, and offers were repeatedly made to himself and his men to induce the immediate surrender of the post; but these were rejected, and the garrison made so stout a defence that they gave Captain Mackeson, the political agent, time to tamper with the Khyburee leaders, who, finding that the Eusufzyes would not yield, and hearing that affairs were not so desperately against the British troops at Cabul and at Jellalabad as at first imagined, permitted themselves to be bribed, and discontinued the attack on Ali Musjid.

The fact was that at Jellalabad, Sale being closely invested, it had become essential as soon as the permanent occupation of the works was determined on, to make the Afghans show greater respect to the force, and to drive them from the immediate vicinity of the walls and defences, about to be repaired. The duty had been well executed, on November 14, by Monteith, who, at the head of 1,100 men of all arms, sallied forth and unhesitatingly swept the Afghans from the neighbourhood of the place. This affair, though followed by the loss of Pesh Bolak and 38,000 rupees of treasure, with much baggage, on the 16th, damped the ardour of the Khyburees when they found that, after the fall of many men before Ali Musjid during the attacks of the 16th, 17th, 18th, and 19th, no impression had been made upon that small stronghold. Sale, from the side of Jellalabad, *might* act, and Captain Mackeson *might* be able to induce the Sikhs at Peshawur to co-operate. For the present, therefore, until affairs took a more decided turn, to accept British gold, and to cease partially from hostilities, was agreeable and not disadvantageous.

The collection of provisions from the neighbourhood, and the execution of repairs to the line of wall, gave occupation to Sale from November 14 to 28, during which time the Jellalabad garrison was undisturbed, except by the fluctuating, uncertain tidings from Cabul, Ghuznee, and Candahar, and the more accurate information of the course of events at Pesh Bolak and in the Khybur. It has been already stated that Ferris, in command at Pesh Bolak, drew in his outposts; but unfortunately he had been left with an inadequate supply of ammunition, and finding, after a stout defence, that he ran short of this essential, he cut his way through the beleaguering force, and made good his retreat to Lalpoora. Ultimately, through the friendly aid and guidance of Tora Baz Khan, he eluded the Khyburees by following a mountain track of great difficulty, and reached the plain of Peshawur in safety. Sale thus lost the intermediate posts which connected Jellalabad with Ali Musjid, but not all intercommunication; for, through the resolution of Mr. Mackeson and the Eusufzyes, the key of the Khybur from the eastward was kept to the British; and Captain Mackeson, an active and intelligent officer, not only succeeded in conveying letters to Sale, but also treasure.

The Afghans, apparently bent on threatening Jellalabad, began on November 28 again to collect around the place, and to push up their skirmishers with some boldness, interrupting the progress of Broadfoot's exertions and the labour of his sappers at the works. Sale permitted the enemy to continue their renewal of a close investment until December 1, when he again ordered a sally to be made; and this time Dennie, in the like effective manner with Monteith, thoroughly worsted the enemy, and drove them from their ground.

Between December 1 and 17 ominous reports reached the garrison, but it was not until the latter day that Sale received a despatch from Macnaghten acquainting him with the disgraceful treaty of the 11th, by which the envoy, in compliance with the urgent representations of the military leaders, sought to secure the safety of the troops on the condition of the evacuation of Afghanistan. A long interval elapsed without any further accurate information; at length, on January 2, Sale received a letter from Pottinger announcing the murder of Macnaghten; whilst an intercepted despatch from Akbar Khan himself to a chief in the neighbourhood of Jellalabad called upon the Faithful, in the name of the Prophet, to assemble and fight against the infidels. In this despatch Akbar Khan boasted of having slain with his own hand the British envoy. From the side of Candahar it was known that Maclaren had failed to march to Cabul; and from the side of Peshawur, though report spoke of assembling reinforcements, nothing decisive or very encouraging was ascertained, except the safety of Ali Musjid. Anxiously, therefore, was further news awaited. On the 9th the long-expected tidings came. Sale received messengers bearing a letter from Elphinstone officially announcing the convention with the chiefs, and ordering the garrison to evacuate Jellalabad, and, with its arms, stores, and ammunition, to march to Peshawur; the movement of the army from Cabul being delayed until Sale's brigade should have commenced its march in obedience to the injunction. Imbecility was fearfully stamped upon every syllable of this despatch, which spoke, after the murder of Macnaghten, to the following effect: 'Everything has been done in good faith; you will not be molested on your way; and to the safe conduct which Akbar Khan has given I trust for the passage of the troops under my immediate orders through the passes.' [1] Sale and the council of war he assembled, bearing in

[1] I cannot find the letter from which this passage is quoted. Kaye gives the text of a joint letter from Pottinger and Elphinstone to Macgregor announcing the convention and ordering the return of the Jellalabad force to India. The same joint letter is also given in the published papers of 1843. But it does not contain the passage quoted. Probably a letter from Elphinstone to Sale accompanied the joint letter to Macgregor.—Ed.

mind Macgregor's ill-fortune-breeding Tazeen treaty, and the manner it had been observed; the date of Elphinstone's order, subsequent to the treacherous murder of the envoy and the delivery to the enemy of stores and munitions of war; the intercepted despatch of Akbar Khan ordering a fanatic war and the extermination of the British troops; and the glaring folly of obedience to an order, under such circumstances, which would deprive the Cabul army of all support from Sale's brigade,—wisely came to the resolution 'that it would not be prudent to act upon such a document; and that the garrison would, therefore, abide where it was till further orders.'

It has been seen that whilst the slaughter of Elphinstone's army was being deliberately effected the Jellalabad garrison remained quietly occupied in strengthening their works; and it was not until January 12, when Dr. Brydon rode in, that the miserable fate of the Cabul force became a certainty—a doom which must have been averted had Sale, instead of a hasty retreat to Jellalabad, held his ground at Gundamuk, and been in a position to co-operate with the retiring army. But all men had failed Macnaghten in his hour of need. From the moment when Macgregor's Tazeen treaty, inducing Sale to forego the purpose of his mission, and to abstain from striking a decisive blow at the rising Ghilzyes, gave life and strength to the rebellion, every staff the ill-fated envoy leant on proved a broken reed. Both Elphinstone and Shelton failed him utterly; Nott, indeed, by detaching Maclaren, made an ineffectual effort to send aid; but Sale made none, and instead of responding to the envoy's call, and to that of Elphinstone, he threw himself into a position from whence he could not even lend support to that general's retreat. What Sale's brigade might have done if at Gundamuk, and thus within the sphere of operations, was satisfactorily proved on every occasion that it sallied forth from behind the walls of Jellalabad against the enemy.

Early in November Mr. George Clerk, agent on the North-West Frontier, a man of ability, energy, and great influence with the Lahore Durbar, having received reports of the insurrection at Cabul, of Sale's retreat to Jellalabad, of the investment of that place by the enemy, of the rise of the Khyburees, the loss of Pesh Bolak and the subordinate outposts in the defile of the Khybur, accompanied by repeated attacks on Ali Musjid, took immediate measures to expedite the march of reinforcements to Peshawur. In consequence of his representations to Sir Jasper Nicolls, the commander-in-chief, four regiments of Native infantry, a small detail of irregular horse, a company of sappers, and one of Golundauze, with guns, were pushed forward. A corps of European infantry and one of Native infantry, a rissalah of irregular horse, and half a light field battery of artillery were held in readiness to follow, should events so require. The 64th and 60th Native Infantry crossed the Sutlej at Ferozepore on November 18 and 20, and took with them eight lacs of treasure. They were followed by the 30th and 53rd Native Infantry on November 27. The whole, under the command of Wild, formed a force of 4,145 bayonets, 100 sabres, 137 sappers and miners, and 164 Golundauze.

Clerk at the same time pressed the Government of Lahore to strengthen their troops at Peshawur, and to render all possible aid in men and guns to Captain Mackeson, the political agent.

Wild reached Peshawur on December 27, and on the 30th his rear detachment came up to him. He immediately placed himself in communication with Mackeson and Sale, and turned his attention to the fulfilment of his instructions. These were that, guided by his own judgment, he was to act independently of Sale until he could effect a junction with him, a measure which Nicolls held to be highly desirable, but which he did not authorise Wild to execute unless he should feel confident of his ability to advance with three corps to Jellalabad, and to maintain by aid of the fourth the integrity of his communications with Peshawur. He was not unnecessarily to run any very great risk.

Wild soon found that no reliance could be placed on the Sikh troops, who were not only in a state of insubordination, but also very ill-disposed to co-operate with their British allies anywhere, and least of all in the Khybur, of which defile the Sikh soldiery had a dread. Wild in vain asked for the promised field artillery; the Sikh soldiery were clearly averse to its transfer; and for long Avitabile, the governor of the province, could not induce his mutinous troops to sanction the loan—one to which Wild attached undue importance.

As the progress of the rebellion in Afghanistan became more fully known in India the despatch of the second brigade, under General McCaskill, was determined; and Wild was informed that it would cross the

Sutlej on January 1. It effected the passage of the river on January 4; and Wild, who had arrived at Peshawur after the news of Macnaghten's death and Akbar Khan's inflammatory missives had excited the fanatic spirit of the whole country in which he was to act, decided at first on awaiting its junction. Though urgently pressed by Sale to force the Khybur and relieve Jellalabad, Wild felt that, as Sale represented himself secure and in no apprehension for the safety of the place he held, it would be unwise to run the risk of enhancing existing difficulties by exposing the brigade to the contingency of a severe check, Sale himself being of opinion that 6,000 men were essential for the operation he so strongly urged. By awaiting McCaskill's arrival a fine force of upwards of 7,000 fighting men of all arms would be available for freeing the Khybur and disengaging Sale.

Wild's reasoning was sound, and in conformity to the soldierly and sensible instructions of Nicolls, who, himself an experienced man in hill warfare, knew its difficulties, and that against a resolute enemy well acquainted with the ground upon which he is acting new troops and a new commander, ignorant of the country, need caution, skill, and numbers to secure success. The annihilation of Elphinstone's force; the blaze into which that event threw the whole country, giving heart and courage to the few tribes who had held somewhat aloof from open revolt; the immediate attempt to recover Ali Musjid; and the earnest call of Sale, had, however, the effect of swaying Wild from his own deliberately formed decision, and of precipitating his endeavour to force the Khybur and relieve Jellalabad. Ali Musjid was sternly assailed, and Mr. Mackeson, still holding and gallantly defending the post of danger with a weak garrison of the Eusufzye tribe of Afghans, was so sharply pressed that he announced to Captain Mackeson that though the fierce attack had been beaten off he could not count on the valour of his men holding out for twelve hours longer against the overwhelming numbers by which the fort was beset. Ali Musjid was not in reality of that extreme importance which the Khyburees attach to it; but the value with which a post is invested, though often exaggerated, is very infectious, and both Captain Mackeson and Brigadier Wild were under an analogous impression of the worth of the key of the defile and the necessity for relieving and reinforcing Captain Mackeson. Captain Mackeson was a bold officer, and knew every inch of the ground; he proposed, therefore, to Wild to relieve the garrison by a night march, offering to lead the column. Wild resolved to make the attempt, being loth that Ali Musjid should fall into the hands of the enemy, and that Sale should feel that the line of communications between himself and Peshawur was entirely under the control of the Afghans. The enterprise was successful, and Captain Mackeson had the satisfaction of saving Ali Musjid and its brave garrison by the skill with which he conducted the two regiments of Native infantry sent upon this hazardous duty; but on the morning of the 16th (that on which this daring plan was executed) he learnt that, instead of 350 bullock-loads of provisions, between fifty and sixty only had reached, the remainder, through negligence or mismanagement, having been permitted to stray and be lost. After remaining eight days, on half-rations, in possession of Ali Musjid it became necessary to evacuate it, as neither the Eusufzyes nor a garrison of volunteers from the sepoys could be obtained to remain any longer in a post which must be left to its own resources, with a very remote prospect of aid or relief. On the 25th, therefore, the place was deserted, and the two corps, accompanied by the Eusufzyes, fought their way back to the mouth of the pass, with heavy loss. The remainder of Wild's brigade was in position to cover and aid in their withdrawal; but Wild himself, who had endeavoured on the 20th, with his two remaining corps and some guns borrowed from the Sikhs, to force his way to Ali Musjid, was lying severely wounded, having been struck as the fight of the 20th commenced, and borne disabled from a combat in which, to his deep and bitter mortification, the two corps signally failed of success.

Wild's failure did not surprise the defenders of Jellalabad, for early in January Captain Mackeson had announced his purpose of dividing Wild's brigade; and success was so far from being anticipated that, on the 13th, when Dr. Brydon came in, bringing the news of the destruction of the Cabul army, and that all its guns, stores, and ammunition had fallen into the hands of the enemy, Broadfoot, the acting engineer, laid the condition of the place clearly before Sale, telling him that if he found himself unequal to a defence to extremity he should retreat that night, while retreat was still possible, for that the moment had arrived when a definitive decision must be taken, either to defend Jellalabad to the last or at once to march to Peshawur.

Sale decided on standing his ground, and that day announced to the commander-in-chief that, relying on his Excellency's promise to relieve the garrison as soon as possible, he had resolved on the most determined defence of the place.

The defeat of Wild's brigade and the fall of Ali Musjid soon became known at Jellalabad; and no sooner did the prospect of immediate relief vanish than it was quickly found that the resolve to defend the place to extremity was one of short life.

A council of war being called, it assembled at Sale's quarters, who opened the deliberations by informing the members that he had called them together to consult on a matter on which Macgregor and himself were agreed, and which the latter would explain.

Having laid before the council the papers bearing on the question, Macgregor then proceeded to detail the circumstances of danger and difficulty in which the garrison was placed. He concluded by announcing that though he reserved the right to do as he pleased, yet he was willing to hear the opinion of the council as to offers he had received from Akbar Khan, then in Lughman, to treat for the evacuation of the country and the restoration of Dost Mahomed; that both Sale and himself had resolved to yield, and negotiate for a safe retreat; and that they had drawn up a Persian letter addressed to Shah Shooja, to which they wished the assent of the council. The tenor of this letter was as follows :—

'That his Majesty's letter had been received, and that the garrison held Jellalabad and the country around only for him ; that of course, as he wished it, the British troops were now ready to march back to India ; but that after what had happened it was thought necessary to propose the following terms :—

'That the British troops would forthwith evacuate Jellalabad and Afghanistan.

'That the British authorities would give up four hostages in proof of their sincerity.

'That the Shah should send a force to escort Sale's brigade in safety and honour to Peshawur—that is, with its arms, colours, guns, &c.—and that the escort should be commanded by one of the princes, his sons.

'That Akbar Khan should be withdrawn from Ningrahar before the garrison quitted Jellalabad.

'That the Shah should deliver hostages, to be retained as far as Peshawur, and then exchanged for the British hostages in the Afghans' hands.

'That these hostages should be Sooltan Jan (a favourite cousin of Akbar Khan), a son of the Nawab Zeman Khan, a son of Ameer Oollah Khan, besides some Shinwaree, Afreedee, and other chiefs.

'That the British force should receive assistance in supplies and carriage.'

This letter purported to be a reply to one from Shah Shooja, addressed to Macgregor, in which, with many professions of friendship, that monarch stated,

'Your people have concluded a treaty with us. You are still in Jellalabad. What are your intentions? Tell us quickly.' He had also intimated that if supplied with money he did not want troops, but would hold the country for the British Government. Macgregor's letter, though pretending to reply to these communications from Shah Shooja, was, however, virtually what it was termed by its author, treating with Akbar Khan, and that in phraseology so submissive and abject that one of the council, Broadfoot, on reading it, flung it from him in indignant disgust, and it fell on the floor.

Here followed a scene of intense excitement. Broadfoot, who had suggested the right moment for deciding on a defence to extremity, or a retreat to Peshawur, rose and vehemently opposed Sale and Macgregor's sudden change of purpose and the resolution to yield. He maintained that, however weak the measures for their relief, the council had no grounds for thinking that the Government had abandoned them; that reinforcements were being pushed forward to Peshawur; and that every consideration, whether of safety or of honour, militated against treating as proposed with Akbar Khan, in order to involve Sale's brigade in a similar fate with Elphinstone's army. Sale, in the heat of dispute, quoted the terms of a letter in French which Macgregor had received. The latter denied that its purport was as strong as Sale's quotation rendered it; whereupon Broadfoot insisted on its being laid before the council, and Macgregor had to produce it. Sale's version proved correct, and the burst of indignation against the Governor-General upon its perusal was so violent that Broadfoot was almost borne down. Yet, determined to fight to the last, he strongly urged that a new Governor-General was on his way out, and perhaps already in India; that the Duke of Wellington was in office; and that a feeble war policy was impossible. He was ridiculed and unable to prevail; but, trusting that the council, when the keen feelings excited by the unhappy letter should be somewhat allayed, might prove more reasonable, he now moved for an adjournment. It was carried; and thus for a while he obstructed the rash timidity which threatened to destroy Sale's brigade.

When the council of war reassembled after the adjournment recourse was again had to ridicule; and Broadfoot's opponents sought to damage his opinions by sneers and hints that his judgment was obscured by the warmth of his temperament. He stood alone in his opinion, for Havelock was only present as Sale's staff officer; and though of the mettle to concur in and occasionally support Broadfoot's views, yet, speaking on sufferance, he did so under disadvantage; nevertheless, being able, resolute, and high-minded, he shrank not from intimating his adhesion to the bolder and more soldierly counsel.

In spite of the endeavour to put him down by ridicule Broadfoot obtained a hearing, and point by point Macgregor's letter was argued, Broadfoot taking notes as the discussion proceeded.

Macgregor, who spoke for Sale and himself, argued that the garrison was abandoned by the Government, who would send nothing but Wild's force; and that this having failed, nothing more was to be looked for; that the garrison could not retreat; that it could not hold out much longer; that the convention now under consideration was safe and honourable. So confidently did he assure the council of his belief in Afghan good faith under his proposed treaty, that few at last seemed to doubt it. He represented that Macnaghten had mismanaged in not getting hostages, and that if this had been done the Cabul force would have been alive; that the securities now demanded were so great he feared they would scarcely be given; that the prisoners and hostages then in the hands of Akbar Khan would infallibly be got back when the garrison reached Peshawur; that, so long as the treaty was pending, time was gained to see if Wild could renew his attempts to force the Khybur and relieve Jellalabad. In order to strengthen his opinions with respect to the desertion of the garrison by Government Macgregor urged his own experience (he had been on Lord Auckland's staff) of men in high place, and that it was folly to look to them on such an emergency.

Broadfoot, on the contrary, urged that even the then Governor-General would not sacrifice them, and that the new one most assuredly would not abandon them; that the letter which had produced so deep an effect on the council was evidently written under the first impulse of a panic, from which the Governor-General and his Council would awake; that the garrison could, in his opinion, hold out for any time it pleased, even till relieved from Candahar by Nott, if no one else appeared; that no value could surely be attached to hostages after the experience Macgregor himself had afforded the council of war by the hostages received from the enemy at Tazeen, when, instead of crushing the Ghilzyes, a treaty had been granted them; that to assert that the brigade held Jellalabad for Shah Shooja was a fallacy; that, after the events which had lately taken place, Sale was not justified in giving up the town upon any such pretext except by order of the British Government; that, so far from gaining time, the enemy, apprised by the offer to negotiate that the hearts of the garrison had failed them, would be encouraged to quicken his preparations, and energetically, with his lately increased means, to renew his attacks; that, finally, whatever the conduct of the Governor-General in failing to support the garrison, that conduct could not cancel the higher obligation of duty to their country, with reference to which Sale had no right to save the troops, except when so doing was more useful to the State than risking their loss; that such was not their case; that prior to the destruction of Elphinstone's army he, Broadfoot, had been of opinion that the occupation of Jellalabad was a source of weakness rather than of strength; that the brigade was less assailable outside, and might, if not shut up, have been better employed; but that now the Cabul army was no more, and Jellalabad the only hold on Northern Afghanistan—to abandon it might produce disastrous impressions in India, and could not fail greatly to augment the difficulty of restoring the credit of the British arms.

The general question of negotiating with Akbar

Khan upon the basis of Macgregor's letter was, however, carried, Broadfoot being left without a single supporting vote, and that too amongst gallant men with the fate of the Cabul army brought home to their feelings by the recital of the horrors of Elphinstone's retreat from the mouth of one escaped as if by a miracle to warn the garrison against running into similar errors and a like doom. Such, however, are councils of war!

The discussion upon points of detail was scarcely more satisfactory. Sale and Macgregor contended earnestly for the propriety of delivering up hostages, and Macgregor volunteered to go as one. Broadfoot opposed the measure, as equally disgraceful and worthless, and carried the majority of the council with him; but it was his only success, except obtaining that certain abject Persian phrases in the letter should be altered. He objected to showing fear of Akbar Khan by asking for his removal, but was overruled. He proposed to demand that all the British prisoners should be given up to the brigade before it moved from the place, and on this point urged every argument calculated to have effect on the minds of high-minded men. The appeal to the more noble feelings of the council was so strong that at first no one ventured to reply; but at length Sale and Macgregor opposed it, arguing that it was useless to make a demand which would not be complied with, and which might only prejudice the proposed convention, which secured the restoration of the prisoners, together with the hostages, at Peshawur.

Broadfoot then moved that if the force was to evacuate the country it was better to do so as a military operation, without first inviting all Afghanistan round; on the contrary, the object should be to deceive the enemy as to the intention entertained until the moment when, boldly and rapidly, fighting if obstructed, the retreat should be effected. Against this was urged the fact, that the baggage cattle had been surrendered a few days before, a measure to which at the time Broadfoot had been vehemently opposed. In reply to this objection he submitted to the council a plan for still effecting the operation. Its details were attentively listened to and no cavil raised until Dennie ironically observed that there was *genius* in the plan, when, after a short discussion, all thoughts of it were given up. Failing to carry the council with him on any really essential points, Broadfoot asked, 'What would they do if attacked?' Sale answered, 'Fight' 'Why, then, call all Afghanistan around you before fighting?' was the retort, to which no answer could be given. Sale, however, added that he 'would execute a hostage if the brigade were attacked.' He was met by the answer, 'Would you do so if the enemy hanged before our faces two ladies for every Afghan hostage we put to death?' This strange debate, in which Broadfoot stood alone in his noble and soldierly views, he closed by stating, 'So long as we are an army I obey all orders; but once we capitulate, the first shot which violates the capitulation sets me free to act as I please.' And well would he have acted on the deep resolve of an heroic mind had matters come to such a point.

The letter went to Cabul, signed by Macgregor.

The spirits of the soldiery of all arms were much depressed by observing the repeated assemblage of councils of war. Though ignorant of what passed, their minds began to be filled with vague apprehensions. But work at the ditch being about this time begun, the men were somewhat reassured by an indication which cheered them in the belief that the councils had not ended in weak and irresolute decisions.

Broadfoot's opinions, although they had failed at the time to produce effect on the minds of the council, gradually began to operate as indignation at the Governor-General subsided and a calmer mood gave his reasons and manly sentiments fairer play. Anticipating that Afghan finesse and treachery would probably delay the answer, or clog it with evasive conditions or reservations, Broadfoot employed the interval in inculcating that any such course on the part of the enemy released the council from propositions to which several of its members already repented having given assent.

In due time the answer came, saying, 'If you are sincere in your offers let all the chief gentlemen put their seals.' It was accompanied by a long, incoherent private letter from Shah Shooja, professing friendship, and attributing, with some justice, the misfortunes of the envoy and Elphinstone to neglect of his advice. The council of war was hereupon again assembled, when Sale and Macgregor urged the members to affix their seals.

Broadfoot immmediately moved 'that the whole matter should be reconsidered; that the reply, conveying a doubt of the sincerity of the council in its offers, set it free; that a letter be sent to the Shah informing him that, as he and the chiefs had not chosen to answer the proposals made by Macgregor even by a "Yes" or a "No," he and the chiefs were now referred to the Governor-General, whose orders alone the garrison would obey.'

A warm debate followed; but the council rejected the proposal as violent; whereupon Backhouse rose and proposed an excellent and most temperate letter to the same effect as Broadfoot's, but met with no better success. Still the tendency to submission had been shaken in the council; and though Sale used strong language respecting the opposition he met with, and high words followed, yet, after an adjournment of an hour, the council again met, and in better humour than at parting. The majority of the council had now been won to the opinion that it was advisable to hold out, and accordingly Monteith prepared a letter which, though not so explicit as either Broadfoot's or Backhouse's, yet was no continuation of the negotiations. It was adopted, Sale and Macgregor alone continuing to think capitulation the best course, but the general resolving to be guided by the majority of the council. Macgregor, however, warned the council that the day might yet come when it would be regretted that such terms as he could have secured had been neglected. The messenger with Monteith's letter was sent back to Cabul; and thus the firmness of one man, and he nearly the junior in the council of war, preserved his country's arms from suffering another deep and disgraceful blow.

Broadfoot's views had gained the ascendency, and most fortunately so for the military reputation of the council, as, the day after the despatch of the messenger to Cabul, a letter reached Jellalabad from Peshawur announcing that every effort would be made to relieve the garrison. The latter were in high health and good spirits, having nearly completed the ditch round the place, and feeling confident that there was no intention on the part of their officers to compromise either their safety or honour.

Nor was their confidence destroyed, or their courage damped, by seeing the labour of months thrown down in a moment by the violence of the earthquake of February 19. With stout hearts and in good spirits the brigade resumed its labours on the 20th, and, under the energetic Broadfoot and his subordinate engineers, aided by Fenwick and others of the 13th, the works were rapidly restored, first to temporary security, and subsequently to a more than pristine strength, though more than a hundred shocks during the month subsequent to the 19th threatened at any moment again to lay bare the defences.

CHAPTER XXVII.

NOVEMBER 1841–FEBRUARY 1842.

EVENTS AT CANDAHAR—MEERZA AHMED—DEFEAT OF THE DOORANEES BY NOTT—POSITION OF NOTT.

WHILST the foregoing events were taking place in the northern military division of Afghanistan, the southern, under Nott, was soon rippled by the rapidly diverging wave of rebellion. Maclaren's brigade, which had marched for India on November 7, was first ordered to stand fast, in consequence of the news that Woodburn, famed for his fight on the Helmund, had, with a small detachment (little more than a personal guard), been cut to pieces between Ghuznee and Cabul. Rawlinson thought the event ominous, and asked Nott to halt the brigade; which the general, himself having long foreseen the now bursting storm, readily consented to do; for he was loath to part with such good troops, who, he felt sure, would soon be needed. Upon November 14 the orders of the envoy and of Elphinstone calling for the march of Maclaren's brigade upon Cabul, in consequence of the insurrection at the capital, were received; and Nott, immediately complying with the requisition, though it left him comparatively weak in his available power for the constraint of a turbulent province, strengthened Maclaren by a troop of horse artillery, and on November 19 started that fine brigade for Cabul, followed by Hart's Janbaz. In order in some degree to replace them, and to be in strength, Nott at the same time called in two of his outposts, bringing in the Shah's corps from Neesh and Dehrawat.

It has been already mentioned that Maclaren turned back before reaching Cabul. The intimation that he had decided on a retrograde movement, in consequence of the inclemency of the weather, reached Nott on December 3; upon which, anticipating that disturbances must follow, Nott determined to concentrate his force, and accordingly called in the regiments and guns from Zemindawar, as also the Janbaz Horse, who were there. Maclaren reached Candahar on December 8, and the Zemindawar detachment on the 9th, so that by the 10th Nott was in formidable strength at the Dooranee capital, from whence he patiently watched the spread of a revolt which he knew must have its course.

Quetta was reinforced by the detachments at Killa-Abdoollah falling back upon the former place, leaving Salu Khan to hold the abandoned post and watch the Khojuk. This Atchukzye chief, whom Rawlinson deputed thither, subsequently did good service in maintaining Nott's communications with Quetta and Sinde.

At Candahar the troops were distributed partly in garrison in the town, and partly in cantonments. The former, under Nott, consisted of the artillery, five regiments of Native infantry, and Skinner's Horse;

the latter, under Maclaren, were held by H.M. 40th, two regiments of Native infantry, and a regiment of Shah's cavalry. In the latter arm, cavalry, Nott's force was deficient; for the Janbaz Horse, whom at first he had in considerable strength, could not be depended upon, and proved the first source of serious trouble.

Rawlinson, finding that the leaders of the Cabul insurrection were principally Dooranee noblemen, became suspicious of the Candahar chiefs of the same tribe, and was embarrassed as to the line he should pursue towards influential men in whose good faith he could place no confidence. Anxious not to precipitate events in the Candahar province, he decided on adopting a temporising course, and tried the hazardous experiment of furnishing the suspected chiefs with money in order to raise and maintain in the field a body of Dooranee troops under the nominal headship of Prince Timour. The Dooranee party thus raised was intended to act in opposition to Uktur Khan, who again appeared in the field, the emissary of the Cabul insurgents, and the partisan of the Barukzye sirdars. The decision was a strange one; but Rawlinson, clever man as he was, and a good soldier, was no match in cunning for a man in whom he placed some confidence, and of whose ability and subtilty he had a just appreciation, Meerza Ahmed. The latter foresaw the coming struggle, and at first, uncertain how the issue of events might turn, wished to be in a position in which according to circumstances he could side with the successful party, and that in a commanding and effective manner. Rawlinson was persuaded to entrust this partisan service to the designing Meerza Ahmed, who, with Prince Timour's son, Sikunder, a lac of rupees, and the more than doubtful chiefs, went forth to prepare for the fast-coming events. Perhaps the skill of the Afghans in imposing upon the political agents was never better illustrated than in this instance; for Rawlinson, doubtful of the good faith of Shah Shooja and his sons, had, as has been shown, early made very clear-sighted, sensible representations to Macnaghten upon the subject of the real feelings of the Dooranee nobles, and the general spirit of hostility which they were sedulously raising against the British power. Yet he permitted himself to be led into a line of policy inconsistent with his own deliberately formed opinions, and ill calculated to meet the crisis which his own sound judgment had foreshadowed. For a time Meerza Ahmed awaited the fuller development of events at Cabul; Uktur Khan and his party were similarly occupied, with the additional motive which the dread of Nott's grim strength imposed for delaying an advance upon Candahar; but the rapid and disastrous march of affairs at Cabul soon determined both, and Rawlinson found himself deceived by the instrument of his own selection and raising.

The news of Macnaghten's murder and of the abject conduct of the military leaders at Cabul passed with electric speed through the country; all hesitation on the part of Meerza Ahmed and the Candahar chiefs vanished; whilst Uktur Khan, strengthened by the Janbaz Horse, who had deserted, part from Salu Khan and part from Candahar, after murdering their officer, Golding, found himself not only supported by these accessions from the ranks of his opponent, but also encouraged by the presence of Suftur Jung, a son of Shah Shooja. This prince, jealous of his brother, and displeased at lacking power and authority, joined the rebels on December 29. Thus reinforced, Uktur Khan first took post at Dehla, about five-and-forty-miles from Nott. Finding, however, that the British general, who wished to avoid needlessly harassing his troops at that inclement season, took no notice of him, Uktur Khan moved down the valley of the Urgandab, and on January 12 encamped between five and six miles westward of the city, keeping the river between himself and Nott. The latter thought that the opportunity for which he had long patiently waited had now arrived, and resolved to strike A brigade of infantry, three batteries of field artillery, and his disposable horse were sent by the usual and more practicable road; whilst, with Maclaren's brigade, Nott, marching by the Babawalee Pass, entered the Urgandab Valley. If he looked to have caught the enemy on the left bank of the river, Nott was disappointed; for he found him on the opposite bank, about four miles distant, safe to draw off or fight as he should please, and only patrolling the left bank in order to keep himself acquainted with the movements of the British general. Nott immediately moved down the left bank, to effect a junction with his artillery and cavalry, and then prepared to force the passage of the river.

The Dooranees no sooner saw Nott in motion than they made a parallel movement on their own bank of the river; and judging correctly that it was Nott's purpose to cross over to attack, they took up a strong position at Killa Shuk, the village in their centre, and the flanks of their line resting on walled orchards; their front was swampy ground, or rather partially flooded from the irrigation watercourses, of which several intersected the ground between the position of the Dooranees and the Urgandab. The enemy, awed by Nott's guns, and not choosing to place the inundated ground in their own rear, made no attempt to contest the passage of the river, which was effected without loss; but the banks of the watercourses, affording some cover, were lined with skirmishers, and from these the advance of the troops threatened to be disputed. Nott, throwing out to his front his own light troops, drove the Afghan skirmishers from the watercourses, whilst the main body of his infantry made good its way, necessarily somewhat slowly, through and over the marshy ground; the artillery meantime playing on the enemy's masses. The unfavourable ground being passed, and the prospect of fairly closing with the foe before the troops, a cheer rose from the glittering line of bayonets as with increased alacrity the brigade sprang forward; but it was to easy victory, for the Dooranees had not the courage to stand, and, having delivered a wild, ineffectual fire, they retired swiftly, leaving Nott undisputed master of the field. The cavalry had, unfortunately, made so long a *détour*, to avoid the swamp, that they were not at hand to take advantage of the disorderly flight of the Dooranees across a plain which would have given fair scope for a sweeping charge of horse, and which was immediately in rear of their position. The enemy, little pressed, rallied, re-formed, and then continued to fall back with all practicable alacrity, never permitting Nott's pursuing infantry to approach near enough to engage. The horse artillery and cavalry at length, however, came up, and, overtaking the flying foot of the Dooranee force, some were cut down by Leeson's sabres, and many slain by the fire of the well-served guns.

Having recalled his troops from pursuing the enemy, Nott now returned towards Candahar, and, crossing unexpectedly at a deep ford lower down the river than that by which he had passed over to his successful attack, he suddenly found his columns headed by a large body of horsemen, whose line of march to join the enemy he had thus accidentally intersected. The ready and clever Meerza Ahmed was, however, with them, and he persuaded Rawlinson that he had brought the body of Dooranee horse to co-operate with Nott. The latter was consequently prevented from attacking them, and thus lost the opportunity of defeating both Uktur Khan and Meerza Ahmed on one and the same day. Nott continued his march to Candahar, whilst Meerza Ahmed forthwith joined the insurgents, to whose cause he not only restored confidence after their late humiliating rout, but by his tact and skill kept the heterogeneous body together, swayed their counsels, and managed, through his acquaintance with the revenue of the country and financial ability, to fill the coffers of the rebels and maintain them in the field, when but for his exertions the assembled bands of disorderly Afghans must have separated, from the need of supplies, and internal disputes. He not only, by drawing to their camp the resources of the surrounding country, kept together the Dooranees, but also materially increased the difficulties against which Nott had to struggle in the collection of provision for the troops and forage for the horses and cattle of his force. The latter suffered severely from want; and the loss sustained proved a serious embarrassment to the general, who soon found the efficiency of his force crippled by the want of camels and other baggage animals.

Nott, however, on the very day which saw the annihilation of Elphinstone's army consummated, proved to Afghanistan that a different spirit pervaded the general and the army at Candahar, and that so long as he and his force were there the country was not lost to the British power.

Nevertheless success did not lull the vigilance of the general, or blind him to the real aspect of affairs and the difficulties of his isolated position in the heart of a hostile country. In spite of Meerza Ahmed's dexterous expedients and constant intrigues, Nott by February 20 had collected five months' supplies for the troops; had partially strengthened the Candahar defences; and patiently awaited the time when milder weather and the growing confidence of the Dooranees should offer him the opportunity for striking a second and a more decisive blow. An order signed by Elphinstone and Pottinger for the evacuation of Candahar met with the like treatment from Nott which had been given to a similar injunction by Sale. As a proof of the utter prostration of energy and resolution amongst the military leaders at Cabul the order was an impressive warning to Nott to prepare for the worst that could befall, and, looking for no external aid, to rely on his own means; improving these to the uttermost by conduct the opposite of that which had brought ruin on the Cabul army. The appalling proof of his superiors' imbecility reached Nott on February 21; and he resolved thenceforth, pending the receipt of instructions from Calcutta, not to enter into negotiations with any of the Afghan leaders, but, by assiduous attention to the *morale* and discipline of his troops, and by a vigilance as untiring as his adversaries were designing and subtile, to maintain his own position in formidable and compact strength. A keen, honour-loving soldier, Nott had felt acutely being cast into the background. Now what had once bitterly grieved his spirit as an unmerited slight appeared fulfilling his deepest wish. He was in a position in which much hung upon the conduct and ability he might display; and the hope of distinction as a commander seemed no longer a mere dream, but a reality within his grasp. The greater the gloom with which the Cabul disasters might envelope Afghanistan, the brighter the lustre of the sword which should dispel it; and the old soldier's heart, instead of quailing before the storm which others had raised, kindled, like Broadfoot's, at the prospect of the hour of trial, of victory, and of fame.

It was fortunate that Jellalabad and Candahar had two such congenial spirits to influence and guide the course of events. The valour and the lofty aspirations of both were not their only points of resemblance.

Patriotism was a living principle in their breasts. In that far banishment the name of England, her power and her honour, were a pride and a joy to these two men irrespective of all personal considerations and ambition. Well would it have been if all our countrymen in Afghanistan had been animated by the same high feelings which filled the breasts of Broadfoot and of Nott.

CHAPTER XXVIII.

NOVEMBER 1841–FEBRUARY 1842.

VIEWS OF SIR JASPER NICOLLS AND SIR GEORGE CLERK—DEJECTION OF LORD AUCKLAND AND HIS COUNCIL—CONTEMPLATED WITHDRAWAL OF NOTT FROM CANDAHAR.

OCCUPIED in Calcutta with the control of warlike operations on a petty scale against the vast empire of China, Lord Auckland had been very desirous that events should proceed smoothly in Afghanistan. He had, therefore, received with pleasure, and willingly accredited, Macnaghten's statements of the improved condition and pacific disposition of the Afghans. Both from the envoy and from his subordinates nothing was written but what was calculated to lull apprehension and flatter the policy adopted with regard to the countries to the west of the Indus. When, therefore, revolt broke forth, belying all that had been favourably prognosticated, the disappointment was crushing in its effects; and as disasters thickened and disgrace deepened the most gloomy despondency replaced baseless hopes.

Nearer to the scene of such unprecedented disasters, and therefore better able to act according to the emergency of affairs, were Sir Jasper Nicolls and Mr.

George Clerk. The former, an able soldier, had been long acquainted with the nature of the British power in India, and was experienced in Eastern warfare. He had never viewed with favour the occupation of Afghanistan—being keenly alive to the various difficulties attending the isolation of a large portion of the Indian army in a position so disadvantageous. Holding opinions so little consonant with those entertained by the originators of the war, his judgment had been decried; and though in official communications customary courtesy was maintained, yet he had enjoyed but little confidence and less good will for his heterodox views. When the rebellion broke forth, fulfilling in some measure his anticipations, the state of feeling towards him was not thereby improved. Upon the outbreak of the insurrection Nicolls, calculating upon a wiser and more efficient conduct on the part of Elphinstone, participated neither in despondency nor in any exaggerated alarm. He had from the first envisaged affairs with a calm deliberation which foresaw the ultimate necessity for withdrawal from the military occupation of the countries to the west of the Indus, not because, if temporarily shaken from our hold, he apprehended any difficulty in again temporarily recovering it, but because he knew that the means for a permanent maintenance of the British army in Afghanistan were wanting. The drain was too great on the resources of India in men, money, and material; the effort, an extraordinary one, could not, compatibly with the sound and healthy condition of our Indian Government, be long maintained; and, sooner or later, collapse was inevitable. When news of the revolt reached the Sutlej, Clerk, acting on the information received from his subordinates, pressed for the immediate despatch of the troops under orders to march in relief of corps in Afghanistan. Nicolls readily concurred, and completing Wild's brigade, sent it forward to Peshawur, furnishing its leader with careful instructions for his guidance. When evil tidings thickened, and Nicolls was urged to hurry forward additional reinforcements, he prepared a strong brigade under McCaskill, but awaited the views of Government before despatching that general. When at length the full measure of our reverses before the final retreat from Cabul became known, and Mackeson, Macgregor, and Sale called for more troops, a train of battering guns, and a copious supply of field artillery, Nicolls, who saw that such demands were made in forgetfulness of India and the position of its magazines, and without regard to the physical considerations of time and distance, demurred at hasty compliance. Under the generals Elphinstone, Sale, and Pollock[1] a force of 14,000 men of all arms, with 28 field-guns, exclusive of the Shah's contingent and guns, might fairly be expected to effect a junction at Jellalabad by January 15, thus forcing the Khybur and reaching Peshawur before the reinforcements called for could be at the latter place. Although qualified by a reservation in flattery of fortune's favours, the Governor-General had repeatedly made the avowal that ulterior operations against Cabul were abandoned, and that the sole object

[1] Pollock was to command the troops at Peshawur.

was to withdraw the troops into a position of safety and strength at Peshawur. Nicolls, calculating, as any other soldier would, that such a force of regular troops ought easily to extricate themselves after effecting a junction at Jellalabad, declined still further to strip the north-western frontier by throwing forward the large and various reinforcements eagerly demanded; but, obeying the instructions of the Government, drew together his troops in positions from whence, if need were, he could with tolerable rapidity assemble an imposing force. No amount of available troops then thrown forward could influence the fate of Elphinstone's army; and Nicolls justly remarked, 'It will be most unlooked for, and probably most disastrous, if our corps should not have effected their passage through the Khybur before March 5.' He, however, made the mistake natural to a good officer, measuring the military ability and efficiency of other commanders in some degree by his own; and thus his calculations were falsified by events, and the contingency which the gallant soldier would scarce contemplate as possible had proved a stern reality. The despatch containing Nicolls' views was scarce fairly out of the hands of the writer and on its way to Calcutta when Clerk reported Dr. Brydon's escape and the annihilation of Elphinstone's army.

Equally fearless with Nicolls, inexperienced in war, but of a resolute, and chivalrous spirit, confident in his influence over the Lahore Durbar, and in his power to direct or restrain its course of policy, Clerk, feeling with all a soldier's indignation the ignominy brought upon the British arms, was urgent for holding ground at Jellalabad, with the view of retrieving our position at Cabul by a simultaneous advance at the fit season from Jellalabad and Candahar. He argued that, having thus gained our position, and the influence which such proof of power must give, not only in Afghanistan but amongst all the neighbouring States, we could then withdraw with dignity and undiminished honour.

Nicolls, admitting the force of Clerk's arguments, yet thought differently as to the course to be pursued. He foresaw the general disaffection which the news of the disaster would foster throughout India, being well aware that emissaries had been long actively engaged amid the native States in exciting turbulence and in forging trouble. Material was in many places collected, and it needed but a spark to kindle into conflagration wide tracts of country. Having regard to this and other important considerations, Nicolls wrote as follows to the Governor-General, in allusion to Clerk's views:—

'Admitting the undeniable force of this argument, I am greatly inclined to doubt that we have, at present, either army or funds sufficient to renew this contest. Money may perhaps be obtainable, but soldiers are not, without leaving India bare.

'Shortly before I left Calcutta there were at least 33,000 men in our pay in Afghanistan and Sinde, including Shah Shooja's troops, but not the rabble attached to his person.

'How insufficient that number has been to awe the barbarous, and at first disunited, tribes of Afghanistan and Sinde, our numerous conflicts, our late reverses, and our heavy losses fully prove. I admit that a blind confidence in persons around the late envoy; a total want of forethought and foresight on his part; unaccountable indecision at first, followed by cessions which, day by day, rendered our force more helpless; inactivity, perhaps, on some occasions, have led to these reverses; but we must not overlook the effects of climate, the difficulty of communication, the distance from our frontier, and the fanatical zeal of our opponents.

'No doubt your Lordship can cause our army to force its way to Cabul, if you think our name and predominance in India cannot otherwise be supported; but our means are utterly insufficient to ensure our dominion over that country. If this be granted, the questions for your Lordship's decision are, whether we shall retake Cabul, to assert our paramount power; and whether, if we subsequently retire, our subjects and neighbours will not attribute our withdrawal, even then, to conscious inability to hold the country.

'Reading your Lordship's instructions literally, especially those of December 3 and January 6, I have not countenanced any preparation for a renewal of the contest. I thought the return of our twenty regiments of cavalry and infantry, a troop and four companies of artillery, and some irregular cavalry, together with the vast reduction of expenditure which would immediately follow the return of this large army, would place the Government in such a position of strength that it might summarily chastise any neighbouring prince, or even two, who might dare to act upon a mistaken view of our weakness.'

Such were the conflicting views of the chief political and military authorities on the North-West Frontier; they were at least clear, strong, and statesmanlike, and formed a remarkable contrast with those of the Governor-General and his council, who, on becoming acquainted with the utter destruction of Elphinstone's army, seemed overwhelmed with gloom, despondency, and indecision. This paralysis of energy was the more surprising, as the occurrence of such a disaster had been viewed as a probable event so early as December 2, when Nott was informed that, in case Cabul were lost—a calamity which must give fresh impulse to the spirit of rebellion in the Candahar provinces—it was not the intention of the Governor-General to direct new and extensive operations for the re-establishment of British supremacy in Afghanistan; and that the commander-in-chief had been directed under such circumstances to instruct the commanding officers 'to make it their first aim to fall back on the nearest support, and so to save their troops from the risk of being isolated; it being, of course, a paramount consideration to provide for the safety of the different detachments as far as possible.' Specially Major-General Nott or the officer commanding at Candahar was to be ordered by Nicolls, in the event of the loss of Cabul, to take the force at Ghuznee under his orders, and to provide Colonel Palmer, to whom the defence had been entrusted, with suitable instructions. Indicative of what these instructions were expected to be, the Governor-General proceeded to add: 'With regard to the regiment at Ghuznee, we shall instruct Mr. Clerk to arrange with the Sikh government for giving every aid in its power, should the retirement of that corps to Dera Ismael Khan or other point on the frontier be determined upon.' Vaguely worded, as if to shun the ignominy of a clear, perspicuous injunction to retreat, these communications admitted of no other interpretation; and in full expectation that Nott would at once act up to their spirit, he was again addressed on February 10, after the fate of Elphinstone's army was known, in a similar strain; being advised to make every effort to relieve and bring off the garrison of Kelat-i-Ghilzye, as also that of Ghuznee, if within the compass of his means; and informed that Brigadier England and Major Outram would apprise him of the means of co-operation available in support of a retrograde movement upon the Quetta side of the Khojuk Pass. As if balancing between their conflicting views, the instructions to the commander-in-chief and to Mr. Clerk, also written on February 10, betrayed the greatest indecision and an utter want of military ability. Pollock, unless any unforeseen contingency should give a decidedly favourable turn to affairs, was to be ordered to confine himself to measures for withdrawing the Jellalabad garrison in safety to Peshawur. If there were any rational hope that they could be of use towards extricating Sale's brigade from Jellalabad; if Pollock's force had suffered in action; if Pollock appeared to require them; finally, if Mr. Clerk should think it advisable on political grounds to apply for their march, the commander-in-chief was to send forward additional reinforcements. Upon Clerk was devolved the onus of deciding what was to become of Pollock's army, and of the reinforcements in march to join it, or which might be put into motion for that purpose. No distinct line of general policy was imparted as that adopted by the Government under the new aspect of affairs, and upon which their agent was to shape his course. He was to announce to the Lahore Durbar, as the resolution of the Government, the withdrawal of the army from Jellalabad to Peshawur, unless events took some unexpected turn which would obviously require or encourage a forward move. With reference to ulterior operations for another advance beyond the Indus, it was held highly desirable that Pollock's army, after the withdrawal of the Jellalabad garrison, should fall back on the Sutlej, there to await the more matured plans of the Governor-General, who indicated the intention of again invading Afghanistan, but by another than the Khybur route, after full preparation, with a complete equipment, and in fresh and well-organised strength. The Sikh Durbar was, therefore, to be required to make arrangements for the protection of its own Peshawur frontier, when the countermarch of Pollock to the Sutlej should lay it bare. Clerk was empowered to call for reinforcements in support of this retrograde movement across the Punjab; and, as if he were better able to take a comprehensive view of the state of the Anglo-Indian Empire and its resources than the Governor-General and his council, he was further authorised, should it be his deliberate opinion that important and vital interests of the British Government in India, and the wellbeing of the British and Sikh States, rendered the retrograde movement from Peshawur, or at least the withdrawal of the troops beyond Rawul Pindee, inadvisable, to suspend such countermarch of Pollock's army, and to halt it in the heart of the Sikh States. Unless included among the unforeseen contingencies which might encourage an advance, the action of Nott and his army was not alluded to; he was about to be furnished with imperative instructions which, had he obeyed them, could not have failed still further to tarnish the honour of the British arms by the destruction of his fine force. It was high time for a Governor-General of another stamp to step upon the field; fortunately he was one capable of forming a more soldierly view of the position of the British armies than to approve of the contemplated directions to Nott—to retire from Candahar, sacrificing guns, stores, and followers, and trusting to what food the fighting men could carry in their havresacks as provision for his force on its suicidal flight. But for the new Governor-General's arrival, however, this crowning piece of panic folly would, if reliance can be placed on the intentions of men whose vacillating weakness excited the pity of all who saw them, have been carried into execution. It would have met from Nott, who at that very time was beating his enemies in the open field, with well-merited scorn and neglect.

CHAPTER XXIX.

FEBRUARY–MARCH 1842.

ARRIVAL OF LORD ELLENBOROUGH AT MADRAS—DISCONTENT AMONG THE MADRAS TROOPS—LORD ELLENBOROUGH AT CALCUTTA—POSITION OF AFFAIRS IN FEBRUARY 1842—THE WAR WITH CHINA—SPIRIT PERVADING THE MADRAS ARMY—POLLOCK AT PESHAWUR—INSTRUCTIONS ISSUED BY LORD ELLENBOROUGH.

When, on February 21, 1842, the frigate bearing the new ruler of India hove in sight of Madras, all were on deck, gazing at the low, burnt, forbidding aspect of the shore, and watching, as the vessel swept up to her position in the open roadstead, the various objects which the town of Madras and the battlements of Fort St. George presented to break the long line of flat coast. Curiosity was, however, quickly changed into excitement when, after the customary signals and compliments had passed, the Madras flagstaff hastened to hoist colours which, as their import was gradually deciphered, spoke of disastrous news from the North-West, and of the destruction of the British army at Cabul. Whatever dreams of a peaceable rule, rendered illustrious by the advancement of the internal prosperity and civilisation of India, Lord Ellenborough might have entertained and eloquently depicted on leaving England, or indulged during a four months' voyage, were thus at once sternly dissipated by the ominous welcome which awaited him. Nor did affairs assume a brighter or a more promising aspect when the brevity of the signal was succeeded by the receipt of ample and detailed communications reporting the murder of Macnaghten; the annihilation of Elphinstone's ill-fated division; the danger that Ghuznee must fall; the failure of Wild to force the Khybur and relieve Jellalabad; the disheartened and enfeebled state of the troops under Pollock, and his inability to hasten to Sale's assistance; the difficulty of communicating with Nott, and the ignorance of the Government as to that general's position, for the safety of which fears were entertained. Whilst in the North of India and in Calcutta all was gloom and misfortune, the state of affairs at Madras was by no means cheering. A native regiment had mutinied at Hyderabad; and Lord Elphinstone, his council, and the chief military authorities, laboured under the most serious apprehensions that the two native regiments then about to embark for service in China would refuse to do so unless satisfaction were granted upon points relating to batta and pensions. On the evening of the day preceding the arrival of Lord Ellenborough a large number of the men, Hindoos as well as Mussulmans, having met to deliberate, had taken an oath to stand by each other, and not to put foot on board a ship until the batta and pension questions should be set at rest; and the Madras authorities, fearful lest the troops might imitate those at Hyderabad and be guilty of like flagrant acts, were inclined to anticipate any remonstrance, or act of open insubordination, by immediately retracting the obnoxious order, and conceding the demands of their discontented soldiery.

Dauntless of mind, and confident in his own great ability, the new Governor-General turned from the bright visions of peace to the rugged realities of war, nothing disheartened by the complication of difficulties and startling misfortunes which the errors of his predecessor had bequeathed to him. The history of India recorded no blow so humiliating to our power and so full of dishonour to our arms as that which had crowned Mahomed Akbar with renown, and raised the hopes of all hostile to British supremacy in the East. Its moral effect in damping the confidence of the native army was out of all proportion to the loss sustained; for though in reality, as compared with masses of troops in British pay, a mere handful of men had been destroyed, yet this had occurred under circumstances of such supreme disgrace that the sepoys drooped beneath the doubt whether the spirit of Lake, Wellesley, and Ochterlony had passed for ever away from the colours emblazoned with the record of their victories. Commanders of a different stamp seemed to sway the destinies of our armies; and the old spirit which inspired daring thoughts and brilliant deeds had been replaced by a mediocrity, or imbecility, which recklessly cast away the pride and fame of the soldier to be trodden under foot by the foe he had conquered.

But, though depressed in confidence, the native troops had shown no want of gallantry or fidelity; and with these qualities unshaken Lord Ellenborough held that every misfortune was repairable; and that the honour of our arms must be established in Afghanistan before it would be safe to contemplate as a practicable course withdrawal from that country. He called for the replacement of H.M. 44th Regiment by two Queen's regiments from England and asked that if the 13th—the fate of which was at the time very doubtful—should be lost, it too might in like manner be replaced by two corps; the object being, in such a crisis, to prove to India that the European force could always be kept up and made adequate to any service demanded from it. Unswayed by the opinions urged upon his consideration that the danger on the North-West Frontier was such as to preclude the Government of India from parting with more of its available force to feed the distant and protracted contest in China, he made known his resolve that nothing which had occurred in Afghanistan would be suffered to affect the plans previously adopted for the campaign of 1842 in the remote quarter of the globe which was the scene of Gough's and Parker's enterprise. That war he was bent upon rapidly bringing to a conclusion, and he would not weakly permit the aspect of a near danger to turn him from the attainment of an object of such paramount importance to his country as the termination of hostilities ruinously costly to the Government, and threatening not only temporarily to disturb a lucrative branch of commerce, but to cast it entirely into the hands of a rival people. Present peril to weak minds assumes a gigantic, all-absorbing importance, but fails to shake a strong one, or to disturb its perceptions of the relative magnitude and value of events.

Lord Ellenborough's arrival at Madras occurred most opportunely, for it checked the growing spirit of discontent among the troops, and prevented its assuming an unmanageable form. At the same time the spirit of feeble concession on the part of the Governor and his council was restrained, and the authority of the Government preserved from self-degradation. The presence for a couple of days of a resolute man arrested the precipitate weakness of the local authorities and the murmurs of their armed servants; the conduct of both parties took a modified direction; and the serious aspect of affairs was improved. The issue was, however, sufficiently uncertain to render the speedy assumption of authority by the new Governor-General at Calcutta the more urgent, and on February 28, 1842, India passed under his rule.

Three grave questions pressed upon his attention —the war with China; the spirit pervading the Madras army on account of the recent and very ill-timed changes in the batta and pensions of the troops; the policy and measures to be pursued in Afghanistan.

It has been already seen that on the first question he justly held that a regard for the character and the interests of England forbade any relaxation of endeavours to bring the war to a successful and early conclusion. Not only, therefore, was he determined to refrain from diminishing the amount of force prepared, but, although India could at the time ill afford to spare men, he resolved to add to the strength of the reinforcements for China. Nothing was permitted to distract his attention from the completion and despatch of all he held essential for the energetic prosecution of that war. He had, upon information derived from Lord Colchester, a naval officer of observation and ability, arrived at a clear conviction that the most accessible and the most vulnerable point on which a combined naval and military force could with advantage operate was the Yang-tse-Kiang, that river affording the means of striking at the very heart of the Chinese empire, by severing the internal communication on which the prosperity and almost the existence of whole provinces depended. The plan of operations was based upon this well-founded opinion; and when he left England the Government was fully resolved upon its execution. Lord Auckland, however, had latterly contemplated acting on the Pei-Ho against Pekin; and the Home Government, in the interval between Lord Ellenborough's departure and his arrival in India, having been won over to entertain the project, instructed him to carry it out. The objections to this scheme were numerous. The lateness of the season at which the attack by the Pei-Ho must have been made; the certainty of great loss by sickness during protracted operations on shore; the separation of the troops from the fleet; the difficulty of landing the force, there being no anchorage within some miles of the shore; the helpless state in which the troops would land, without the means of movement for guns, baggage, and munitions; the insecurity of the open roadway of the Gulf of Peitchelee, in which as soon as winter sets in vessels cannot remain; these, and other circumstances, combined to render the change of plan full of difficulty, danger, and uncertainty. Notwithstanding the weight of the authorities who had been led to adopt this alteration from the original well-arranged expedition, Lord Ellenborough adhered to the latter; and, pointing out the objections to the Pei-Ho as a line of operations for Gough and Parker, made no change in the destination of the reinforcements, and authorised the general to act upon the Yang-tse-Kiang.

Although this subject does not belong to the conduct of the war in Afghanistan, yet, in estimating the man upon whom all now depended it is necessary to keep in view the various difficulties which beset him; the demands upon the resources at his disposal; and the exertions which, while keenly alive to the severity of the blow under which our power in India was staggering, he had to put forth for the successful conduct of a war which few statesmen were sanguine enough to hope would in one season be brought to a close under the walls of Nankin. His own apprehension was that the pressure of the naval and military operations might lead to the overthrow of the Imperial Government, for the people of China evinced no hostility to the British forces. The war was strictly one against the Government, and not against the people, who seemed indifferent as to the issue of the contest, and in the midst of hostilities were actively engaged in commercial transactions with their invaders. A war of so peculiar a character threatened the overthrow of the Chinese government, and an ambitious spirit might have been tempted to engage, under the plea of the exigencies of war, in such a course of policy as won for us our Indian empire; but, with a purer and higher principle than has generally characterised our Eastern transactions, the British commanders were particularly cautioned against affording any countenance to insurrection, and doing anything which could lead to territorial acquisition on the mainland. Having thus done all that human foresight and prudence at so great a distance from the theatre of operations could effect to ensure success and scrupulous moderation in China, Lord Ellenborough turned to meet, and master, the other difficulties of his position.

The ebullition in the Madras army was one of grave importance, and it involved, if mismanaged, most serious consequences. Lord Auckland, after postponing for several years the change in the batta allowance of the sepoys, had most inopportunely selected the crisis in which the Cabul disaster and the Chinese war rendered the goodwill of the native soldiery essential, as the moment for experimenting on their temper and loyalty by carrying into effect a measure which was sure to prove unpopular. The result was that a regiment of cavalry at Hyderabad mutinied, and grossly insulted its officers. The feeling spread, and the troops about to embark for China were, as has been told, in a state of smouldering insubordination, when the arrival of Lord Ellenborough for the time prevented any overt exhibition of disaffection or disobedience. But he had no sooner quitted Madras than the civil and military authorities hastened, if not to absolute concession, to language which raised in the troops about to be embarked the expectation that their demands would be complied with.

The reduction of the pensions to heirs had come with very ill grace at a time when the nature of service beyond the seas had been exemplified by the loss of the 'Golconda' in a hurricane, and the heavy mortality consequent on the sickness which broke out amongst the troops in China. In the 'Golconda' the head-quarters of the 37th Native Infantry, amounting to about 300 fighting men, with their proportion of camp followers, had gone down. Their families, and those of others who had fallen in the distant war, were most of them in Madras; and the reduced sum granted by the newly enforced scale of pensions being represented as really insufficient for their maintenance, the soldier about to proceed on foreign service beyond seas had a practical sermon upon the gratitude and consideration of the Government, and a powerful appeal to his feelings as a husband and father. There was some excuse for the conduct of these swarthy warriors, for soldiers when staking life in the execution of duty cease not to be men.

At Hyderabad matters had assumed a very unpleasant aspect, for, besides the cavalry regiment which had most grossly misconducted itself, other corps had been compromised; and the resident had embarrassed the Madras government by marching off in one body 730 prisoners belonging to the different infected corps, first under charge of some European companies, but afterwards under that of a native regiment. That portion of the force which was most amenable to authority had received their pay without the contested allowance of batta; but even this compromise was only resorted to in expectation that the batta would be restored; an expectation not a little countenanced by the appointment of a committee of officers to inquire how far the complaints of the men were well founded.

However imprudent, the implied concessions, both at Madras and Hyderabad, solved, for the time, the wounded and exasperated feelings of the native soldiery; but it was impossible to foresee how long this superficial calm might last; and it was very unfortunate that, at a moment when the Madras troops might, by disengaging Bengal regiments in the central provinces of India, be of the utmost use in enabling the Governor-General to strengthen himself on the North-West Frontier, a deep feeling of discontent should have been spread in their ranks, and a degree of uncertainty cast upon the extent to which Government might rely on their aid. The additional embarrassment thus created by no means facilitated the amelioration of affairs on the war frontier.

Matters in that quarter wore a most unpromising aspect. Pollock, on reaching Peshawur, found himself at the head of three brigades of infantry, besides cavalry, artillery, and sappers; but Wild's defeat in the Khybur had so dispirited two of these brigades that, on March 14, Pollock wrote: 'You are already aware of the unfortunate panic among the sepoys, those who suffered in the late attacks under Brigadier Wild. I have contrived to smother it, but should be sorry to attempt to advance without the dragoons and horse artillery.' Labouring under this impression, which appears to have been exaggerated, and conscious that the severe sickness which had filled up the measure of the misfortunes of these unlucky brigades, and from which they were slowly recovering, had left them in a state of physical debility, Pollock was awaiting anxiously the arrival of European and native reinforcements, and in the meanwhile was endeavouring to negotiate with the Khyburees for a free passage, being ready to purchase immunity for his columns if the tribes could be induced to grant it. Sale was earnestly pressing for relief; but Pollock, profiting by Wild's error, had determined to act with more caution. Knowing that the leading division of his reinforcements could not reach him before the end of the month, and the second division probably a month after, he on March 12 had informed Sale that though extremely anxious at once to have marched to his relief, the step had proved impracticable; 1,900 sick, and '*no heart*' among the sepoys, having rendered it imperative to await the arrival of the first division of the reinforcements.

On February 27, when put in possession of Lord Auckland's positive instructions of February 15, to direct all his efforts and measures to the withdrawal of Sale's force from Jellalabad to Peshawur with the least possible delay, Pollock had signified his disapprobation of these instructions, and had advanced as arguments in favour of a forward movement from Jellalabad towards Cabul the state of his negotiations for securing the opening of the pass; the friendship of two or three petty chiefs; and the opinions of Torabaz Khan and Syud Adeen that the district of Ningrahar could furnish supplies for a twelvemonth to Pollock's army, if stationed at Gundamuk. He had urged that the success of an advance with the intention of merely withdrawing the garrison of Jellalabad to Peshawur would depend chiefly on concealing that intention, for that every man would rise to molest his retreat, if known or anticipated; that the troops at Peshawur would be sickly, whereas at Gundamuk they would be healthy; that, moreover, they would there be in a position to inflict punishment on the enemy in the open field, and to liberate the British prisoners in the hands of Akbar Khan; and that if the Khybur Pass were open they would have as available for their support the resources of the Punjab and of Peshawur. At a moment when the Sikhs had about 25,000 men in observation at and near to Peshawur—a force hostile in feeling, insolent in behaviour, and under the leading of men upon whom no reliance could be placed; when, too, there was but shadowy hope of obtaining by purchase the opening of the pass, and none of permanently securing it, Pollock's arguments were sufficiently extraordinary. However, discovering that the feeling in Wild's scarce convalescent brigade was strong against a march to Cabul, and that the Khybur tribes were not easily won to become traitors to the national cause, and hearing from Conolly, then in Mahomed Akbar's hands, that Rajah Golab Singh, at the head of the 25,000 men at Peshawur, had written to Mahomed Akbar promising to co-operate against the British, if he took Jellalabad before the end of the month, and engaging in the meantime to deny them Sikh aid and impede their movements, Pollock, withdrew his objections, and, contemplating the fulfilment of his instructions, merely dwelt upon the necessity of blinding the enemy by threatening a forward movement from Jellalabad upon Cabul. The suspicions of the Sikhs had unfortunately been roused by the manner in which the necessity for holding Peshawur in our own possession had been frequently advocated. Provoked at the open expression of opinions so little in unison with the spirit of our alliance with them, they either did not distinguish between the short-sighted avidity of individuals and the professed intentions of the British Government, or they thought the views of the former so consonant with the real spirit of that Government as to be a sure prognostication of its ultimate purpose.

Sale was known to have provisions for his garrison up to the middle of April; and, having parted with his carriage cattle, he was under no difficulty respecting the maintenance of any but a few camels necessarily retained and the horses of his force. For these he scarcely expected to secure fodder sufficient to carry them on to the same period as the fighting men. Pollock must, therefore, have calculated on having to furnish much of the carriage requisite to enable the garrison to move from Jellalabad in retreat to Peshawur; and this he could not hope to do unless the camels with the leading division, then midway in the Punjab, joined him. Hence a further motive for awaiting the arrival of reinforcements.

Since Nott's victory of January 12 no news of the movements or intentions of that commander had been received; and, in so far as the instructions furnished to him by Lord Auckland were calculated to influence his measures, a rapid retreat upon Quetta would have been anticipated as the most probable event, had not the manner in which his movements were crippled from want of cattle thrown doubt on the fact of a retirement being in his power ;—265 camels and 148 bullocks were evidently inadequate for the march in efficiency of nearly 9,000 fighting men. To ameliorate a state of destitution not confined to means of movement, but also comprising want of treasure, medicines, and other stores, England was about to advance through the Bolan Pass, and hoped early in April to be at Quetta, with two squadrons, four battalions, and fourteen guns, and from thence to push on to Candahar with a force of 2,500 men, encumbered with an equal number of camels. Outraged as the Ameers of Sinde had been by the encroaching policy of Lord Auckland's administration, it was not surprising that a doubt of their fidelity should be entertained by Outram, the political agent, and that he should have been apprehensive of a serious exhibition of hostility at a moment when the Ameers must have been aware of the difficult circumstances under which the British commanders and their scattered troops were placed. Outram and England were equally alive to the peril of exposing Nott's communications to any hostile movements which might compromise the safety of his army. In co-operating with Nott from the side of Quetta it was essential not to weaken the available force in Sinde to an extent which might encourage the Ameers to hazard open rupture. England, therefore, both with respect to the state of Sinde and to the available carriage cattle, which after the utmost exertions amounted to a very limited supply for Nott's and his own forces, could not leave Sinde with greater strength under his leading than that above detailed.

Pollock, paralysed by Wild's failure and the sickness in his camp, not daring to move until his reinforcements should arrive, was in a position of secondary importance to that of Nott. Sale, beleaguered, indeed, but not besieged, was safe for a time; and Pollock himself was in no immediate danger. His position if the Sikhs proved treacherous was, it is true, a very critical one, and the contemplation of such a turn of affairs elicited from him the remark, 'What a situation ours would be, with detachments all over *their* country, and I with four rivers in my rear, none fordable, and at the mercy of the Sikhs for boats!' Twenty-five thousand men were at hand to watch him; whilst of his reinforcements the leading division was still in the heart of the Punjab, and the other had not crossed the Sutlej. Nevertheless the fanatic hate of Sikhs against Afghans outweighed the suspicion of British good faith, and the respect for Nicolls and his reserves was operative in maintaining, if not cordial good will, at least a not hostile connection. With Nott circumstances were entirely different. Ghuznee could hope for relief from him alone; yet, even after England's expected junction, the means of movement at Nott's disposal would be so inadequate that the utmost uncertainty prevailed as to his ability to effect even a retreat on Quetta. If he could be furnished with a sufficiency of carriage cattle he was clearly in a position to save Ghuznee; and, should opportunity offer, he might by some signal success redeem the shaken credit of our arms. But, unless his means were ample, Nott laboured under peculiar difficulties. Not the least of these was the growing uncertainty as to the state of Sinde. The Ameers were not likely to be curbed by respect for Nicolls's reserves, already sufficiently occupied with furnishing Pollock reinforcements, and with watching a powerful, well-organised Sikh army, which hung like a thundercloud upon our frontier and Pollock's line of communications; whilst from Bombay the Sinde army could look for no aid. If well placed for striking, Nott was the most exposed to a blow, and that of such severity as, following hard upon the Cabul disaster, would have been almost irreparable; for the Anglo-Indian power could have ill sustained a second defeat of magnitude without suffering a moral humiliation destructive of its haughty supremacy. It was under such circumstances that the new Governor-General wrote, on March 15, a letter to the commander-in-chief which, from the soundness of its military and the justice of its political views, merits insertion. With admirable force of thought and precision of language it swept away the fallacies which had hitherto been permitted to obscure the plans of Government and to pervade its instructions with indecision. Nicolls, Nott, Pollock, and Clerk were addressed as follows:—

'The insurrection which has existed in parts of Afghanistan almost from the time of our obtaining possession of Cabul; which, in the summer of last year, led to more than one serious conflict with considerable bodies of men in the vicinity of Candahar; and, extending itself in October to the vicinity of Cabul, impeded the march of Major-General Sir Robert Sale's brigade to Jellalabad; still more the revolution, rather than insurrection, which commenced at Cabul on November 2, and which, after many disastrous and lamentable events, led to the ultimate destruction of a numerous division of the British army—a calamity wholly without parallel in our history in India; all these circumstances, followed as they have been by the universal hostility of the whole people of Afghanistan, united at the present moment against us in a war which has assumed a religious as well as national character, compel us to adopt the conclusion that the possession of Afghanistan, could we recover it, would be a source of weakness, rather than of strength, in resisting the invasion of any army from the west, and, therefore, that the ground upon which the policy of the advance of our troops to that country mainly rested has already ceased to exist.

'The information received with respect to the conduct of Shah Shooja during the late transactions is necessarily imperfect, and, moreover, of a somewhat contradictory character. It is not probable that the insurrection against our troops should have originated with him. It is most probable, and it is almost proved, that he has adopted it, and, powerless in himself, is prepared to side with either party by which he may hope to be maintained upon his precarious throne.

'Certainly, as we are at present informed, the conduct of Shah Shooja has not been such as to compel the British Government, in blind and solitary observance of the Tripartite Treaty, of which the ground has ceased to exist, to peril its armies, and, with its armies, its Indian empire, in his support.

'Whatever course we may hereafter take must rest solely upon military considerations, and have, in the first instance, regard to the safety of the detached bodies of our troops at Jellalabad, at Ghuznee, at Kelat-i-Ghilzye, and Candahar; to the security of our troops now in the field from all unnecessary risk; and, finally, to the re-establishment of our military reputation by the infliction of some signal and decisive blow upon the Afghans, which may make it appear to them, to our own subjects, and to our allies, that we have the power of inflicting punishment upon those who commit atrocities and violate their faith, and that we withdraw ultimately from Afghanistan, not from any deficiency of means to maintain our position, but because we are satisfied that the king we have set up has not, as we were erroneously led to imagine, the support of the nation over which he has been placed.

'But, while the facts before us justify the withdrawal of our troops from Afghanistan, and the refusal of all further assistance to Shah Shooja, they are yet not such as to make it consistent with our reputation to give our future support, as is suggested by Major Rawlinson, to Shah Kamran, and to make over Candahar to that nominal ruler of Herat, even were it consistent with prudence to engage in a new speculative enterprise beyond the Indus, which might render it necessary for us to retain, at an enormous cost, a large body of troops in the difficult country between that river and Candahar, for the purpose of maintaining in the country so made over to him a sovereign personally incapable, and for many years unknown to its inhabitants otherwise than by the fame of his degrading vices.

'We are of opinion that it would be erroneous to suppose that a forward position in Upper Afghanistan would have the effect of controlling the Sikhs, or that a forward position above the passes of Lower Afghanistan would have the effect of controlling the Beloochees and the Sindians, by the appearance of confidence and of strength. That which will really and will alone control the Sikhs, the Beloochees, and the Sindians, and all the other nations beyond and within the Indus, is the knowledge that we possess an army, perfect in its equipment, possessed of all the means of movement, and so secure in its communications with the country from which its supplies and its reinforcements are drawn, as to be able at any time to act with vigour and effect against any enemy.

'In war reputation is strength; but reputation is lost by the rash exposure of the most gallant troops under circumstances which render defeat more probable than victory; and a succession of reverses will dishearten any soldiers, and most of all those whose courage and devotion have been mainly the result of their confidence that they were always led to certain success. We would, therefore, strongly impress upon the commanders of the forces employed in Afghanistan and Sinde the importance of incurring no unnecessary risk, and of bringing their troops into action under circumstances which may afford full scope to the superiority they derive from their discipline. At the same time we are aware that no great object can be accomplished without incurring some risk; and we should consider that the object of striking a decisive blow at the Afghans, more especially if such blow could be struck in combination with measures for the relief of Ghuznee—a blow which might re-establish our military character beyond the Indus, and leave a deep impression of our power, and of the vigour with which it would be applied to punish an atrocious enemy—would be one for which risk might be justifiably incurred, all due and possible precaution being taken to diminish such necessary risk, and to secure decisive success.

'The commanders of the forces in Upper and Lower Afghanistan will, in all the operations they may design, bear in mind these general views and opinions of the Government of India. They will, in the first instance, endeavour to relieve all the garrisons in Afghanistan which are now surrounded by the enemy. The relief of these garrisons is a point deeply affecting the character of the army, and deeply interesting to the feelings of their country; but to make a rash attempt to effect such relief, in any case, without a reasonable prospect of success, would be to afford no real aid to the brave men who are surrounded, and fruitlessly to sacrifice other good soldiers, whose preservation is equally dear to the Government they serve. To effect the release of the prisoners taken at Cabul is an object likewise deeply interesting in point of feeling and of honour.

That object can, probably, only be accomplished by taking hostages from such part of the country as may be in, or may come into, our possession; and, with reference to this object, and to that of the relief of Ghuznee, it may possibly become a question, in the event of Major-General Pollock's effecting a junction with Sir Robert Sale, whether the united force shall return to the country below the Khybur Pass, or take a forward position near Jellalabad, or even advance to Cabul.

'We are fully sensible of the advantages which would be derived from the reoccupation of Cabul, the scene of our great disaster and of so much crime, even for a week, of the means which it might afford of recovering the prisoners, of the gratification which it would give to the army, and of the effect which it would have upon our enemies. Our withdrawal might then be made to rest upon an official declaration of the grounds upon which we retired as solemn as that which accompanied our advance; and we should retire as a conquering, not as a defeated, power; but we cannot sanction the occupation of an advanced position beyond the Khybur Pass by Major-General Pollock, unless that general should be satisfied that he can, without depending upon the forbearance of the tribes near the pass, which, obtained only by purchase, must, under all circumstances, be precarious, and without depending upon the fidelity of the Sikh chiefs, or upon the power of those chiefs to restrain their troops—upon neither of which can any reliance be safely placed—feel assured that he can, by his own strength, overawe and overcome all who dispute the pass, and keep up at all times his communication with Peshawur and the Indus; and we would caution Major-General Pollock, and all the officers commanding the troops in the field, not to place reliance upon, or to be biassed by, the representations of native chiefs who may have been expelled from their country, in consequence of their adherence to us, and who will naturally be ready to lead us into any danger by operations which may have the possible effect of restoring them to their former possessions.

'We have been informed that Major-General Pollock does not consider himself strong enough to force, and to keep, the Khybur Pass, without the first Reserve Brigade, which was not known to have crossed the Ravee on the 2nd of this month, and which can hardly join him before the second week in April; and being informed likewise that Major-General Sir Robert Sale had, on the 21st of last month, only forage sufficient to last about thirty days, we cannot but expect that those officers will have endeavoured to effect their junction before the arrival of the first Reserve Brigade, and that they will, when that junction shall have been effected, occupy a secure position near the Khybur.

'In such a position they will, under all circumstances, be better enabled to assist any operations of Major-General Nott on the side of Ghuznee, by the moral effect of their concentrated strength, than they would be in a more advanced position of extreme hazard to the troops under their command.

'We look, further, to the effect which the concentration of a large force under your Excellency's command upon the Sutlej would have upon the policy of the Sikhs, and of all Indian States, exhibiting the British Government in an attitude of imposing strength, and giving confidence to its army and to its subjects.

'The operations of the large force under Major-General Nott and Brigadier England—a force numerous enough to overcome all resistance whenever it might march, if its numbers comprised a due proportion of cavalry, and if it possessed the perfect equipment and ample means of movement without which numbers of the bravest and best disciplined men have not the character of an army—are necessarily so crippled by the want of cavalry and of animals of burden and draught, that we cannot safely rely upon those officers being able to effect any object beyond that of withdrawing the garrison of Kelat-i-Ghilzye, and securing their own retreat at the proper season, and their communications in the meantime with the Indus.

'We cannot review all the circumstances of the present crisis without being deeply impressed with a sense of the danger arising from the dissemination of troops in an enemy's country, having difficult communication, and of the further danger of leaving any force intended for operations in the field, and at any time liable to be called into action, so composed in the several arms of infantry, cavalry, and artillery, and so supplied with ammunition, provisions, and the means of movement as to be, in fact, incapable of executing with promptitude and effect, and even of attempting, without peril to itself, any important operations with which it may be entrusted.'

None of those who read could doubt the author of that letter. A just appreciation, in so far as the intelligence received at Calcutta offered means of judging, of the difficulties of the several commanders and of their relative positions with respect to the offensive or defensive operations, pervaded it. Truthful in its estimate of the political as well as of the military aspect of affairs, it bore the stamp of a strong mind, and gave promise of energetic action, should wisdom countenance and Providence favour its display. Nott, when he received it, accompanied or shortly followed by a communication which placed him in command of the army of Sinde in addition to his own, and gave him supreme control over the political agents in those parts, must have felt that the man who thus wrote, weighing accurately the value and the danger of the forward position of the Candahar army, and strengthening to the uttermost the power of its leader, was prepared, unless unforeseen events interfered, or want of means forbade, boldly to carry out the operations which the letter evidently contemplated.

Much time was, however, necessary before a despatch written in Calcutta could reach Candahar. In the meanwhile Nott was not idle, and, so far from acting on Lord Auckland's instructions, was engaging in offensive operations to which we must now advert.[1]

[1] Sir Henry Durand's manuscript ended here.